A Nation of Politicians

History *of* Ireland
and the Irish Diaspora

James S. Donnelly, Jr.
and
Thomas Archdeacon

SERIES EDITORS

A Nation of Politicians

*Gender, Patriotism, and
Political Culture in
Late Eighteenth-Century Ireland*

Padhraig Higgins

THE UNIVERSITY OF WISCONSIN PRESS

This book was published with support from the
ANONYMOUS FUND OF THE COLLEGE of LETTERS AND SCIENCE
at the University of Wisconsin–Madison.

The University of Wisconsin Press
1930 Monroe Street, 3rd Floor
Madison, Wisconsin 53711-2059
uwpress.wisc.edu

3 Henrietta Street
London WCE 8LU, England
eurospanbookstore.com

5   4   3   2   1

Library of Congress Cataloging-in-Publication Data
Higgins, Padhraig.
    A nation of politicians : gender, patriotism, and political culture in late eighteenth-
century Ireland / Padhraig Higgins.
    p.   cm.—(History of Ireland and the Irish diaspora)
    Includes bibliographical references and index.
    ISBN 978-0-299-23334-1 (pbk.: alk. paper)
    ISBN 978-0-299-23333-4 (e-book)
    1. Ireland—History—1760-1820.   2. Ireland—Politics and government—
1760-1820.   3. Irish—Political activity—History—18th century.   4. Political
participation—Ireland—History—18th century.   5. Ireland—Militia—History—
18th century.   I. Title.   II. Series: History of Ireland and the Irish diaspora.
DA948.4.H54   2010
941.507—dc22
2009015029

Contents

Illustrations

Acknowledgments

The rituals of eighteenth-century sociability often led patriots to gather in taverns. At evenings end, numerous toasts were proposed to honor intellectual debts and to embody friendship and fellowship. In a somewhat drier fashion but with as much pleasure, I am happy to acknowledge my many debts and thank many friends. I must first acknowledge the generous financial support from several entities that allowed me time to research and write this book. At Penn State, a Hill Dissertation Fellowship from the Department of History, a Dissertation Fellowship from the Research and Graduate Studies Office, and an Interdisciplinary Dissertation Research and Creative Projects Award from the College of the Liberal Arts funded my dissertation research and writing. Further research was made possible by a fellowship from the Henry E. Huntington Library, San Marino, an American Society for Eighteenth-Century Studies–Lewis Walpole Library Fellowship from the Lewis Walpole Library, Yale University, and a Bernadotte E. Schmitt Grant for Research from the American Historical Association.

Many friends, colleagues, and mentors helped me in the completion of this project. This book began life as a Pennsylvania State University PhD dissertation. My advisor Dan Beaver provided unstinting support and valuable criticism. As a mentor and teacher, he has shaped my thinking as a historian in ways that are greatly appreciated. Joan Landes and Kumkum Chatterjee, as members of my committee and as teachers, provided both guidance and important perspectives from French and Indian history. I have benefited greatly from the comments and insights of Paul Durrenberger and Bill Pencak. Ian McBride's work provided the inspiration for this project, and he has been generous with his encouragement and with invitations to present papers based on the arguments

x   *Acknowledgments*

in this book to audiences at Queen Mary, University of London, and the University of Warwick; he also read two drafts of the entire manuscript, and his comments and suggestions have made this a much better book. Jim Smyth read a draft of the manuscript and challenged me to think more seriously about the theoretical structure of the book. Kevin Whelan, as a reader for the Press, and Thomas Archdeacon and Jim Donnelly as editors of the series provided their expertise on late eighteenth-century Ireland and saved me from many infelicities and errors. The work of Breandán Mac Suibhne also helped my thinking on a number of issues discussed here.

In the archives and libraries I visited in Dublin, London, and Belfast, librarians and archivists were unfailingly generous in their assistance. I am particularly grateful to the staff in the National Library of Ireland, the Royal Irish Academy, and the Ulster Museum. Mary Broderick in the Department of Prints and Drawings at the National Library of Ireland and the staff in the print room at the Lewis Walpole Library went beyond the call of duty in helping me find a number of the prints for this book.

At Penn State, Jana Byars, Jennifer Davis, Mary Faulkner, Jan Logemann, and Mike Smith all read various drafts of this work and provided both judicious critiques and convivial company. In Dublin, my family and friends provided me with great hospitality during my frequent returns. During my initial research, Pat and Patricia Buchanan generously gave me a pleasant place to stay on Estate Avenue. Gavin, Rory, Susan, and Kathy offered welcome respite from the archives. In Philadelphia, Carrie has provided love and support while I have been revising this manuscript and has even tolerated the clutter. My parents remained encouraging and loving throughout my years of study and research; I dedicate this book to my mother and to the memory of my father.

A Nation of Politicians

Introduction

IN AUGUST 1784, as Ireland descended into political turmoil, Charles Francis Sheridan, MP and pamphleteer, wrote to Lord Northington, reflecting on the great changes he had witnessed in recent months. In April, a crowd had invaded the House of Commons and called for the execution of several leading members of the parliament. In the following months, Dublin "mobs" tarred and feathered those suspected of breaking a nonimportation agreement. Violent clashes between crowds and troops had become frequent. Throughout the country, against the wishes of elites, county meetings formulated resolutions and distributed petitions in favor of parliamentary reform. The meetings had also elected delegates to send to a national meeting on the reform issue, a meeting ominously described as a "National Congress." At the same time, Protestant volunteer militia companies were inviting Catholics to drill and march with them and even to take up arms in companies that were little more than the armed wing of the reform movement.

To explain this outbreak of political radicalism, Sheridan looked to recent changes in popular political ideas and practice. "No two nations," he wrote, "the most dissimilar in temper, genius, habits and opinions ever differed more from each other than the people of Ireland differ at this day from what they were, previous to the American War. I remember them even within these six years almost the direct reverse of what they now are." Here, he corrected himself, recalling his own position in Irish society and perhaps the limits of his experience; he remembered "the Protestant parts of the kingdom at least." The Protestant Ireland Sheridan recalled was a nation "servilely partial" to England and "unreasonably suspicious of their Roman Catholick Countrymen." Fearful of Catholics, convinced of their own "impotence and insignificance"

3

without British support, the security of the Protestant religion was of paramount importance.[1]

However, the change in Protestant sentiment "had been as sudden as it [was] compleat." Sheridan believed many Protestants had lost all attachment to England and had given up their fear and suspicion of Catholics to the extent that they were now "ready to share every political right and privilege." In this alliance, Sheridan feared his fellow Protestants were "blind to the necessary consequence, the subversion of Protestant government." Sheridan then turned to the causes of the abrupt change he observed. What had brought about this shift in Protestant identity? In the first place, Sheridan looked to politicization as the cause of the amelioration of relations with Catholics. He noted the curious "action and reaction of religion upon politics and of politicks upon religion," so that "which ever [was] the most prevalent at the time, whether religious bigotry, or political enthusiasm, [would] infallibly direct and govern the operations of the other." While religious feeling and fear had previously directed Protestant policy, now "the prevalence of wild and extravagant politicks appear[ed] to . . . supercede all religious prejudices." This political union across religious divides had resulted in the strange spectacle in which "the papist [went] to the meeting house; the Presbyterian to the mass, and the member of the Church of England to either indiscriminately."[2]

Above all, it was the emergence of the Volunteers that had occasioned a new type of politics. With the entry of the French into the war on the side of the rebellious colonies in 1778 and government failure to organize the militia, ad hoc local defense forces were formed throughout the country. Outside of government control and inspired in part by the example of the American colonists, this force of as many as eighty thousand men developed a national organization and soon became involved in political agitation for the removal of British restrictions on Irish trade and subsequently for a more general reform of Anglo-Irish relations, the Irish government, and the representative system. Although the force had produced national pride, this was far from its most worrisome effect. The real consequence of volunteering was "the intimate communication it produced between the lower and higher classes of the people," which had "excited the insolence of the former and sunk the consequence of the latter." Volunteer meetings had been dominated by politics and were occasions where the gentry were forced to associate with "their lowest tenants or tradesmen . . . almost on a footing of equality." Even more pernicious to established authority was the regional and national structure that the originally fiercely local Volunteers had built. Meetings and assemblies produced a general intercourse between "the lower orders of different and extensive parts of this kingdom who having never met before were till then ignorant of their strength and numbers, and when agreeing in sentiments, beholding themselves in arms, they must have felt that power in reality resides in the many and have drawn conclusions by no means favourable to the authority of the few."[3]

The experience of Volunteering had, Sheridan believed, politicized all elements of society. The farmer "who never before looked beyond the fences of his field," and the shopkeeper "whose views were confined to his counter and the trader whose speculations never passed the limits of the counting house" along with all the lower ranks had been transformed "into a nation of politicians." And this was a "nation of politicians" who had "drawn their first conception of the nature of government and of liberty, from their situation in a self created army which knew no discipline, acknowledged no rules but what they had voluntarily imposed upon themselves."[4] The consequences of this change were particularly worrying:

> The two great holds by which every government must lead and direct the public mind of the community over which it presides, I mean custom and opinion are nearly lost and in their room we find disrespect for the laws, impatience of subordination, disregard for order and contempt for parliament; the house of commons, under what is styled the present mock representatives are considered as usurpers of the power they exercise, while the press daily teems with the most infamous publications in order to inflame or mislead the people and to root out of their minds all those ideas of order, decency, and obedience without which it is impossible for civilized society to exist.[5]

Sheridan believed that in the space of a few years confessional relations had altered dramatically, patterns of deference had been overturned, and those outside the political nation had become increasingly active in politics. He was not alone in recognizing these changes. The same year, *The Voice of the People*, a pamphlet supporting parliamentary reform, also noted the recent popular interest in politics:

> That the spirit of cool investigation has kept an equal pace even among the lowest classes of people, with a resolution of asserting their rights. It will not therefore in any sort appear extraordinary or incredible that the highest authorities are now familiar to descriptions of men whose sphere of information was formerly confined to the

ploughshare. You may be satisfied that almost all the farmers and
many of the lower orders of the peasantry do at this moment possess,
a degree of constitutional knowledge which I will take upon me to assert, many in the House of Commons were ignorant of at so short a
distance back as ten years.[6]

The author claimed that the man "who possibly sold the shirt [one's]
servant [wore]" would have a knowledge of Locke and Bolingbroke
and argue "that THE PEOPLE have a right to RESIST the whole legislative power if ever that power should try to enslave them."[7]

This study examines the process of popular politicization in Ireland
between 1778 and 1784 that so alarmed Sheridan and excited the anonymous author of *The Voice of the People*. Through a focus on the Volunteers
and the organization and structures of extraparliamentary political culture, I argue that the experience of politics in these years—volunteering,
associating, petitioning, toasting, subscribing, shopping, attending the
endless round of reviews, and celebrations—was central to popular politicization. These practices composed part of a culture producing what
Sheridan regarded as a "wild and extravagant politicks." Politicization
resulted in the articulation of a more inclusive understanding of the political nation that challenged traditional limits to the social, religious,
and gendered composition of the polity. I seek to show, as Tim Harris
suggests in an examination of the "politics of the excluded," that ordinary men and women did have opinions about "how duly constituted
authority was supposed to be exercised," that these opinions were not
static, and that traditional understandings of legitimate authority were
challenged and transformed by popular political engagement.[8]

To this end, I consider the mechanisms through which politicization
occurred: novel and traditional, official and extraparliamentary, ideological and practical. This is not to suggest that most people embraced a
consistent, coherent political philosophy that can be labeled "patriot."
Political ideas were socially and culturally situated. Political arguments
were encountered by some in the legalistic formulas of pamphlet literature, arguments that relied on the plethora of political languages that
have so entranced historians of political thought.[9] Most people drew
their understandings of duly constituted authority from a multiplicity
of sources: sermons, songs and ballads, handbills, toasts, graffiti, assizes, state commemorations or processions, theater, ballads, rumor and
gossip, to name only a few of the principal ways political ideas were
encountered in everyday life. These media offered densely packed and
often simplified accounts of some of the same questions broached in

pamphlets. Interpretation of political disputes or the emphasis placed on particular aspects of an issue might vary depending on such factors as social class, gender, and religious affiliation. A letter to a Belfast newspaper, addressed to "the common people," felt the need to explain that the campaign for removal of British restrictions on Irish trade was not concerned with the complete abolition of taxation.[10] At the same time, popular Irish-language Jacobite verse could connect the patriots' free-trade campaign with the desire to overthrow the Hanoverian regime and ally with Britain's enemies.[11] The arguments of MPs and pamphleteers over tariffs and the nature of Ireland's constitutional relationship with Britain might be given a different gloss by those outside the political nation, who understood the slogan of "free trade" in terms of their own particular grievances. Patriot slogans, as refracted through popular political culture, could take on a life and meaning of their own. The worlds of elite patriot culture and popular politics were not, however, completely separate, only connected by elite manipulation or popular misunderstandings.[12] The Dublin crowd, in particular, displayed a clear grasp of constitutional issues and a knowledge of parliamentary affairs.[13] Indeed, throughout the century the aspirations of the Dublin crowd for economic and political reform were often firmly focused on events in Parliament. The world of official political culture—parliamentary sessions, elections, and assizes—was central to the aspirations of those outside the political nation.

The Sources of Politicization: The Density of Politics

A Nation of Politicians examines the ways in which those outside the political nation in Ireland became politicized in the 1770s and 1780s. The questions arise: How do we measure politicization? What counts as evidence of politicization? In discussing popular politicization, I avoid Whiggish notions of the inexorable rise of more-democratic and sophisticated forms of political culture or the emergence of the public sphere, which identify this process with one particularly novel moment, the late eighteenth century. Forms of popular politicization are clearly evident, for example, throughout Great Britain and Ireland at various moments in the seventeenth century, while the 1750s have also been identified as a significant moment of politicization in an Irish context.[14] Instead, we might think in terms of what Nicholas Rogers describes as the "density" of political culture in a given period, referring to the means through which people could obtain political information in the press; the extent of associational culture; the level of communications; the degree of urbanization, literacy, and so on that contribute to a "denser political space" at any particular moment.[15] A focus on density also opens up the possibility of a more comparative approach to particular moments in the Irish past—the 1750s, the 1790s, the 1820s, for example—that were clearly politically denser than others.

The clearest evidence of political density is obviously manifested in popular interventions, such as riots and other forms of demonstration.[16] Celebrations and commemorations could likewise bring large crowds onto the streets for political occasions. The state itself might be a vehicle for such events, calling on the people to participate in public political rituals, to justify the established order, or in the commemoration of the 1641 rebellion, the birthday of William III, or the numerous public fasts and celebrations held over the course of the American war of independence.[17] Of course, the inclusion of the people in the rites of state risked subversion or appropriation. Jacobites routinely heaped indignities on the statue of King William in College Green and participated in their own counter-theater of ritual and demonstration. Most famously, the Volunteers could appropriate William's birthday in 1779 to agitate for free trade. The Volunteers were central to the process of politicization in these years, and my discussion of this force is based in part on the handful of extant minute books of the hundreds of companies that were formed. These sources are supplemented by newspaper references to the public pronouncements of Volunteer companies, the examination of manuscript sources produced by government elites, as well as local responses to this force. The culture of the Volunteers is further illuminated through the wide range of materials celebrating this movement such as ballads, poems, prints, flags, uniforms, transfer-printed pottery, and printed linen, to name a few. Much of this material draws attention to the rich ceremonial life of the Volunteers and the material culture of politics, which has been relatively ignored for this period compared to the 1790s.[18] Such sources are also central to the examination of the commercialization of politics, which continued apace in the 1770s. The ephemera produced in the course of the free-trade campaign and in support of the patriots in general have also been little studied as a source of popular politicization or as a means by which ordinary men and women articulated political arguments through their consumption choices.[19]

The density of Irish political culture was also closely related to the distribution and consumption of print. As with any study of Irish political culture in the eighteenth century, my analysis relies extensively on contemporary newspapers. The culture of print was an inclusive instrument of politicization. The growing number of Dublin and provincial newspapers increasingly discussed local and national politics. They offered reports of patriot political activities such as Volunteer reviews, celebrations, and demonstrations and presented a vision of the nation that stressed unity across social and confessional divides. The institutions of print culture, such as the tavern and the coffeehouse, served as a location for the dissemination and consumption of "the news." This social experience of news allowed readers to imagine their place in the narratives of nation, locality, gender, and consumption, to name a few, as propagated by the press.

The notion of density in the 1770s can also be applied to the degree of participation in extraparliamentary forms of association, such as clubs and societies, as well as membership in the Volunteers. This was an "associational world" that promoted forms of masculine sociability through convivial or political clubs, charitable societies, voluntary hospitals, Masonic lodges, debating societies, benefit clubs, and societies for moral and political reform, which all flourished in the eighteenth century.[20] These forums produced dense social networks that fostered a vision of both national and moral reform. Many patriot MPs socialized outside Parliament in clubs and societies for political and convivial purposes, such as the Society of Granby Row, and, in 1779, the Monks of the Screw, where constitutional questions were debated. Members of this club also included non-MPs, such as the influential pamphleteers Frederick Jebb and Joseph Pollock, suggesting the links between MPs and extraparliamentary political culture. In Dublin, the Society of Free Citizens served as a meeting place for radicals such as Charles Lucas and Napper Tandy, as well as some radical MPs, including Edward Newenham.[21] Although not necessarily promoting radical or dissident forms of politics, these associations, by their very existence "endorsed a participatory model of citizenship which allowed private individuals to appropriate, define and channel 'patriotism' through their actions in the public sphere."[22]

Debating societies in Dublin also contributed to this mix of sociability and politics, addressing a wide range of questions on issues such as political representation and gender and racial inequality. In 1778 the

Athenian Academy for Free Debate on Moral, Constitutional, and Commercial Questions met at Shaw's Court, Dame Street, to tackle a topical question, "Are representatives in Parliament bound to obey the instructions of their constituents legally convened?" In 1781 the Universal Free Debating Society asked, "Is enslaving the Negro race justifiable upon principles of humanity of policy?" Women frequently attended these debates, including one at the Athenian Academy asking, "Is it probable that women would equal, if not exceed men in mental accomplishments and qualifications if they had equal advantages of education," which was answered in the affirmative.[23]

Forms of association also served as sites where cross-confessional alliances could be forged. Masonic lodges, for example, flourished in Ireland and served as sites where Protestants and Catholics could socialize. In many instances, a significant overlap existed between membership in these and other societies. The values and the ideals of other forms of voluntary association, such as the Volunteers, were often identified with those of freemasonry. A ballad celebrating the Volunteers proclaimed:

> At word of command
> Let each firmly stand
> And daily grow bolder and bolder;
> Like Freemason's move
> In brotherly love
> Thus acting like citizen-soldier, my boys,
> thus acting like citizen soldier.
> Like Freemason's &c.[24]

Many Volunteers were also active Freemasons. In Belfast, volunteering led to the politicization of freemasonry under the influence of Amyas Griffith.[25] Beginning in 1781, Masonic parades and pageantry in that town became more public. The chairman of the first Volunteer convention at Dungannon, William Irvine, was a delegate for the Lowtherstown Masonick Volunteers and a prominent Freemason. If some Freemasons might also have belonged to Volunteer companies, from 1782 onward many lodges simply formed companies themselves. In June 1782, the members of Lodge 547 in Newtownstewart, Co. Tyrone, formed the First Free Mason Corps, and many others followed.[26] Other forms of association encouraged cross-confessional alliances while also promoting forms of political subjectivity. The spread of friendly societies in the 1760s and 1770s, with their regular meetings, management of subscriptions, and oaths of secrecy, fulfilled a variety of economic functions for journeymen. At the same time, as David Dickson observes, these tavern-based societies "initiated a much wider circle of the urban community into para-political forms and procedures," while also apparently functioning as nonsectarian sites of fraternity.[27]

The culture of print and the forms of sociability promoted by clubs and societies flourished particularly, though not uniquely, in urban environs. This period saw in the provinces, if not exactly an "urban renaissance," at least improvement in the fabric of many towns, with the construction of assembly rooms, theaters, and linen halls; the establishment of Masonic lodges; and other evidence of urban conviviality and vitality.[28] Forms of association were central to the distinctive political culture of the town. Indeed, the historian of urban life in Ulster suggests that the Volunteers were crucial in translating the culture of Dublin throughout the province and "set the tone for a distinctive urban culture in Ulster."[29] The Volunteers became ubiquitous in cultural life, promoting sociability and spectacle in provincial towns throughout the country.

The urban world of association, print, and consumption was central to eighteenth-century politics. Yet if one focuses on relatively novel sites of politicization, in the search for the "emergence" of a modern public sphere, for example, it is important also not to ignore more-traditional media and sites of public debate.[30]

· There were a variety of other ways for people to express their political opinions. Grievances could be addressed through such traditional instruments as petitions to the parliament or the king. Petitions are important sources because of the assumptions and claims about the social and political order revealed in them. These documents reflected real political divisions among the people. The process of drawing up and circulating petitions for signature also contributed to politicization.[31] Petitions were fundamental to the expression of grievances in eighteenth-century Ireland. As the *Journal of the House of Commons* shows, petitions streamed into Parliament from all over the country from corporate bodies, interest groups such as merchants or weavers, as well as individual men and women. These petitions dealt with a vast number of different issues, from the contestation of election results, or a request from Newry for convicts to help on a canal building project, to pleas for compensation for losses suffered at the hands of the Dublin mob.[32] Petitions were routinely addressed to the Irish parliament, and more unusually, to the king, as well as the British parliament. Historians have increasingly recognized that a number of useful questions can be asked about the meaning and social function of petitioning. As David Zaret observes of petitions in seventeenth-century England, these documents "portrayed grievance as an apolitical conveyance of information" through a rhetoric of deference that emphasized the "humble" and loyal nature of the petitioners as well as the localized nature of their grievances.[33] As the authorities recognized, petitions could be used by particular groups and interests as a vehicle for the expression of political agendas.[34]

Petitions were also a vehicle for the expression of local opinion on national political issues. Signatures were usually collected at major local social and political events, particularly during assize sessions. Assizes, along with meetings of freeholders, and elections, as elements of official political culture, were key formal occasions for the expression of political opposition. Local elites and central authority acknowledged their importance in the considerable effort they expended in choreographing these events. In 1775 nearly three thousand Dublin freemen, freeholders, and merchants signed a petition to the king advocating reconciliation with the colonies. They expressed their horror at the outbreak of "civil war" and noted the colonists' grievance over the "infringement of the inalienable dominion over personal property inherent in British subjects," while also hoping for peace: "With the tender feelings of humanity and love of our country, of that great community of which Briton, Hibernian, and American have heretofore been all the happy members united under your Majesty by the strongest ties of interest and affection we lament that unnatural effusion of blood which has stained the unwilling hands of fellow subjects."[35] The same year, a rival petition, which claimed to represent "the gentlemen, clergy, freemen, freeholders, merchants, traders, manufacturers, and other citizens of Dublin," secured over one thousand signatures in support of British policy in America. This petition told a different story of events in the colonies, lamenting that colonists had "withdrawn themselves from their allegiance to [his] Majesty," under the influence of the "counsels of wicked and designing men."[36] Both petitions emphasized the signatories' loyalty to the king. At the same time, they expressed competing understandings of this imperial conflict among Dublin Protestants, while attempting to present their version of events as the true "sense of the people" of Dublin.

"Fellow Slaves": Empire and the American Example

As these competing petitions underscore, imperial politics and the outbreak of war with the American colonies in particular were central to

Irish political culture in the years after 1775; to a significant degree, the war determined the context in which the Volunteers emerged and patriot politics was played out. The war was partly responsible for the weak state of Irish defenses, economic crisis, and the fall of Lord North's administration, which were crucial factors in the rise of the Volunteers, the issue of free trade, and the winning of legislative independence, respectively. Benjamin Franklin, writing to the Irish MP and leading radical patriot Edward Newenham soon after Franklin's negotiation of the Treaty of Paris had formally ended the war, depicted American and Irish struggles as part of a broader international struggle against despotism: "It is a pleasing reflection arising from the contemplation of our successful struggle and the manly, spirited, and unanimous resolves at Dungannon, that liberty, which some years since appeared in danger of extinction, is now regaining the ground she had lost, that arbitrary governments are likely to become more mild, and reasonable, and to expire by degrees, giving place to more equitable forms."[37] Irish patriots similarly lauded Ireland and the colonies as the last bastions of manly liberty, in contrast to the despotic and effeminate culture of Britain.[38] At the same time, most Irish patriots believed that the Irish and the American situations were not completely analogous. Ireland, it was claimed, was a kingdom, not a colony. As Vincent Morley argues, it was not American ideas or political thought that inspired Irish patriots but rather "the force of American *example*."[39] The American precedent of violent protest and the successful employment of a voluntary military force against British "mercenary" forces inspired Irish patriots and raised concerns for a British government fearful of further imperial calamities. The repertoire of protest, the symbolism and rhetoric of Irish patriots, also owed much to the American example, with patriots following transatlantic events avidly; the boycott and destruction of British goods, the formation of associations, tarring and feathering, the convening of a congress, to name a few, were all obvious borrowings from North American colonists.

The culture and politics of empire—accounts of voyages and discoveries, war and militarism, theories of trade and representation, food and consumer durables—permeated everyday life in eighteenth-century Ireland. Conflict over Ireland's place in the British Empire, particularly with regard to trading rights, was central to politicization during this period. Cork and its hinterland grew prosperous from the colonial provisioning trade, supplying goods such as salt beef and butter to Caribbean plantations.[40] Limerick too benefited from the provisioning trade, while merchants in Belfast also attempted to profit from this market, building up strong connections with Barbados. Waddell Cunningham, a leading Belfast Volunteer and supporter of patriot causes, made his fortune in colonial trade, owned sugar plantations, and even dabbled in slave trading. One of the consequences of the granting of free trade in 1780 was that it gave Ireland the right to participate in the slave trade for the first time, and merchants such as Cunningham in Belfast and others in Limerick attempted to benefit from this concession by establishing slave-trading companies, though with little success. As Nini Rodgers has demonstrated, the commodities of empire (and slave produce in particular) such as sugar, tobacco, and cotton were central to government revenue but also to the much-vaunted image of prosperity patriots envisaged in the wake of free trade. Sugar refining was also important to the prosperity of the increasingly politically assertive Catholic merchants, such as the wealthy sugar refiner Edward Byrne. Disputes over sugar duties were central to the free-trade agitations of 1779 and the eventual concession of an independent Irish parliament in 1782, leading Rodgers to suggest that sugar in Dublin was not far from being as explosive as tea had been in Boston in 1774.[41]

Metaphors of empire and slavery were also central to the language of political dispute. Patriot pamphleteers frequently compared Ireland's subordination to England to forms of African slavery. Writing under the pseudonym Owen Roe O'Nial, Joseph Pollock claimed in 1779 that the erosion of liberty meant the Irish would "become perfect THINGS and cease to be PERSONS" and (alluding to advertisements for the recovery of runaway slaves) that English newspapers would soon carry notices for such slaves "LOST, STRAYED, STOLEN OR MISLAID."[42] William Drennan's *Letters of Orellana, an Irish Helot* also evoked the idea of slavery, addressing his readers as "fellow slaves," with "Helot'" of the title recalling the enslaved African prince of Aphra Behn's popular *Oroonoko*, who had inspired other slaves to revolt.[43] A letter in the *Volunteer Journal*, addressed to the radical Dublin lawyer Handy Pemberton, claimed that England was "worn out in the cruel but visionary crusade of slave-making; her people corrupted by the influx of ravished Asiatic wealth—her once hardy sons long unnerved in the course of luxury and dissipation."[44] Such a vision of a corrupt and effeminate Britain, often contrasted with accounts of the rise of a manly Irish patriotism and virtue, as exemplified by the militarism of the Volunteers, became commonplace in Irish writing during the American war.

Militarization and Politicization

An emphasis on the military aspect of citizenship is central to an understanding of density and politicization in late eighteenth-century Ireland. Tom Bartlett has drawn attention to the connection between politicization and militarization. As many as one in six adult males spent time in uniform, drilling, marching, and occasionally fighting, in either the forces of the Crown, or in voluntary military organizations. This was a formative experience for many men, not least in the modes of politics in which they engaged.[45] Indeed, historians have long noted that many United Irishmen cut their political teeth as Volunteers. Nevertheless, the automatic association of voluntary military service with later radical political activity has been challenged, with attempts to both remilitarize the Volunteers by placing them within a tradition of militia service and link the force to the yeomanry of the 1790s.[46] This work has provided a corrective to accounts that overemphasize Volunteer radicalism. In its focus on continuity, however, it ignores interactions between the experience of this voluntary military service and the articulation of patriotism and new forms of political subjectivity. In the late eighteenth century, participation in citizen militias was an important factor in politicization in revolutionary Virginia and France and among the Patriots of the Dutch Republic, to name a few.[47] A renewed focus on the Volunteers can illuminate the strands of this process in Ireland.

Studies of the Volunteers over the past twenty years have rejected the traditional orthodoxy that saw in the emergence of the Volunteers the beginnings of Irish nationalism. David Miller has offered the most sophisticated revisionist account of the Volunteers, emphasizing continuity while at the same time acknowledging the novel elements of the movement and the importance of Volunteer rituals. For Miller, the Volunteers were part of an Irish Protestant tradition of ad hoc local defense to protect against invasion and internal disorder, based on ties of deference. This policing function, which included dealing with agrarian protest, escorting prisoners, and controlling mobs, is central to his view of the Volunteers. Although the Volunteers began as an expression of traditional gentry control over their inferiors, Miller concedes that as the movement progressed, its elaborate and constant ceremonials became a site where nonelite Protestants could attempt to redefine the polity and claim membership as citizen-soldiers.[48] But he concludes that "personalistic ties of patronage . . . counted for more than any impersonal sense of 'imagined community' analogous to modern nationalism."[49]

Historians have begun to challenge the revisionist picture of the Volunteers that had all but eclipsed the nationalist orthodoxy. Renewed focus on the 1770s and 1780s, as Kevin Whelan suggests, serves as a rejoinder to the contention that the 1790s marked a radical shift in Irish politics that should be "carefully fenced off from the rest of the century."[50] This reinvestigation of the period has complicated traditional understandings of the influence of international events, above all the American War of Independence, on Irish political culture. Irish-language sources, for example, particularly the work of Gaelic poets, often celebrated Britain's imperial misfortunes. Vincent Morley has utilized these sources to suggest that ordinary Catholics were almost entirely disaffected from the Hanoverian regime.[51]

While the Volunteers emerged as a national political force in the course of the free trade dispute, the experience of volunteering was also determined by regionally specific factors, and regional studies have brought the local dynamics of volunteering more clearly into focus. Ian McBride's account of Ulster Presbyterian radicalism in the late eighteenth century also examines the impact of imperial events on domestic politics, showing the ways in which revolutionary events in America radicalized Presbyterian opinion in Ulster. Using such untapped sources as the sermons preached to Volunteer units, his study provides the most innovative account of the political culture of rank-and-file Volunteers.[52] McBride's research illuminates the radical aspects of Presbyterian involvement in the Volunteers in Ulster, moving beyond the traditional high politics of patriotism and the deferential model of the Volunteers. Breandán Mac Suibhne challenges revisionist accounts of volunteering, noting that although revisionists have displaced the nationalist account, they have developed no alternative explanation of the rhetoric and symbolism of patriotism. In his regional study of the Volunteers in northwest Ulster, he argues that this movement offered a "clear articulation of an Irish national identity."[53] Mac Suibhne contends that a decline in sectarian animosities emerged out of local structures, networks, and beliefs in a "regionally-specific process of politicization" in the northwest in the late 1770s and early 1780s.[54] These studies illustrate the ways in which the Volunteers were central to the creation of a "provincial political culture outside the constitution."[55] The Volunteers of Belfast, Dublin, northwest Ulster, and elsewhere became increasingly radical from 1780 onward; many Volunteers in other regions were relatively more restrained, a consequence of less-dense regional political cultures. Dickson, for example, in his monumental study of south Munster suggests that the timidity of volunteering in that region can be explained by the absence of both vibrant artisan guilds and "a critical mass" of dissenters (important factors in the political density of Dublin and Ulster, respectively). Moderation was further strengthened by a fear of a large Catholic population and the power of local magnates, though even here Catholics were admitted to some companies, and elite figures, such as Lord Shannon, who challenged the political autonomy of the Volunteers, found themselves the victims of popular antipathy.[56] Overall, such work reveals the ways in which this military force was a significant vehicle for politicization among Protestant men outside the political nation, and even among some Catholic men. At the same time, while volunteering was a masculine pursuit, patriotism also offered a space for women to participate in politics.

Gender and Patriotism

In 1783 Martha McTier wrote from Belfast to her brother, the young doctor William Drennan. The great political questions of the day, the agitation of reformers and volunteers, she believed, had created a situation where "politics now cease[d] to be local, and so great and open the foundation, every man [might] build upon it that ha[d] materials."[57] While McTier was advising her ambitious brother, eager to achieve fame as a political writer from his obscure post in the town of Newry, her comment on the nationalization of the local and the expanding of political horizons might have just as easily applied to the opportunities to engage in the politics of the day for women like herself. McTier's letters show that she was part of the same tradition of Presbyterian radicalism as her more celebrated brother. She read a wide range of political texts and closely following local elections and national politics. With some pride, she regarded Belfast as a "corner where [politics were] treated with manly freedom,"[58] and McTier's own politics were also "manly" in this sense. Although, like all women (and most men), she was excluded from the political nation, McTier read and thought about politics, attended meetings, and spoke her mind on the political issues of the day.[59]

A Nation of Politicians examines an area of patriot politics that has been largely neglected by Irish historians: the gendered experience of political culture.[60] In part, this focus involves an examination of women's roles in various aspects of political life in the eighteenth century and in the disputes of the 1770s and 1780s in particular. But this study seeks to move beyond the simple and unsurprising recognition that women, like McTier, had an interest in politics and participated in aspects of political life, despite their formal exclusion from the political nation. I argue that gender, the social and discursive construction of masculinity and femininity, was a central category for understanding patriot politics. The Volunteers, for example, made little sense outside a view of masculinity, or "manliness," as contemporaries termed it, that charged men with protecting an imperiled femininity against invasion, as well as the symbolic manifestation of the nation as embodied in the figure of Hibernia. The presence of women at Volunteer reviews, the consecration of colors, or the round of social occasions the force promoted was not merely decorative or symbolic, but rather suggests the way in which gender was central to both social and discursive aspects of patriotism.

Historians have begun to explore understandings of masculinity and manliness, though as Karen Harvey notes, the relationship between war, militarism, and masculinity in the eighteenth century has received little attention.[61] Conceptions of masculinity, or manhood, were central to militia forces, with masculinity associated with both individual independence and collective participation in the defense of liberty.[62] Militias justified their roles by appeals to republican concepts of liberty and the "manly virtue of republican citizens eager to defend liberty against attacks from within and outside."[63] Yet while militias had traditionally bolstered a hierarchical social order, the armed citizens-soldiers of the late eighteenth century such as the Free Corps and the Volunteers, with their national assemblies and conventions, democratic organization, and often overt interference in politics, challenged the circumscribed understanding of the political nation envisioned by traditional republicanism.[64]

Matthew McCormack, in his examination of the language of "independence," has shown how Georgian conceptions of citizenship were intimately bound up with ideas of masculinity.[65] Gender was central in defining the legitimate political subject and the contours of the political nation, and not only in the obvious sense that women were excluded from citizenship. Men deemed not "independent" due to a lack of manliness or regarded as "dependent" on a patron or landlord were by definition incapable of virtuous participation in the political nation. Protestant understandings of Catholic religious and social dependency on the will of others, their "slavishness," could justify their exclusion from citizenship. At the same time, largely as a consequence of the experience of volunteering, appeals were made through the language of independence and manliness for a broadening of the political nation as increasing numbers of men began to imagine themselves as legitimate political subjects.

Conceptions of gender could be used to justify participation in politics. Men outside the elite claimed that their manliness, as exemplified in their role in the Volunteers and their "independence," validated their role in broader political affairs and even suggested the need for reform of the political system itself. The language of manliness was concerned with issues of character and emphasized an active vision of patriotic citizenship. It was one of the fundamental everyday languages through which the issues of patriotism were understood and articulated. Likewise, women's supposed greater identification with the suffering of poor weavers, for example, could legitimate women's political actions in the campaign for free trade in 1779. Women's relation to fashion, consumption, and the domestic sphere also allowed them to participate actively in this campaign, through their consumption choices or by wearing Irish clothing and symbols as public demonstrations of their support for the patriot agenda.

The Love of Country: Patriotism and Protestantism

Proponents of a more expansive vision of the political nation justified broader political participation through an appeal to gendered categories of patriotism. This study focuses on the ideas and practices of those who described themselves as "patriots." But in describing themselves as such, what did these eighteenth-century men and women mean? What was patriotism, and what was it to be a patriot? In recent years, historians have attempted to establish a more precise meaning of eighteenth-century patriotism. Jacqueline Hill, in her study of corporate politics in Dublin, has drawn attention to the variety of political languages that informed Irish Protestant patriotism, from ancient constitution to civic republicanism, and conquest theory.[66] Rather than simply regarding it as a sort of proto-nationalism, part of the story of an unfolding Irish national identity, recent work has begun to place patriotism more firmly in its eighteenth-century Irish, British, and European contexts.[67] In the British tradition, patriotism was often associated with a Whig defense of parliamentary rights against the crown and opposition to arbitrary power in general. It also had a more neutral meaning less tied to a

specific ideological position and referred rather to a disinterested love
of one's country.

As Stephen Small notes, patriotism was concerned with liberty and
the moral and intellectual qualities that fostered it.[68] In this context, patriotism can be seen both as "the virtue of social responsibility and self-
less devotion to the common weal," such as an interest in economic
and social improvement, and in the more politicized sense of a defense
of constitutional rights against oligarchy and arbitrary rule.[69] Patriotism could be expressed through involvement in the variety of improving societies that emerged in eighteenth-century Ireland, such as the
Dublin Society, which promoted agricultural improvement. Patriotism,
then, was concerned with the defense of individual rights and liberty
against the arbitrary encroachments of government, as well as the promotion of the "public good." J. T. Leersen notes that over the course of
the eighteenth century patriotism also began to lose its Whiggish overtones and became associated with disenchantment with the amorality
of a political system based on vested interest. Along with the characteristics noted here, patriotism in eighteenth-century Ireland acquired
an anti-English aspect related to specific constitutional and economic
grievances, as well as to concerns about patronage. Of course, the use of
the term "patriot" referred to a variety of different political positions, a
self-appellation of radicals, ministers, Whigs, and improving landlords,
to name a few.[70] While opponents of government did attempt to monop-
olize the term, supporters of the government also identified their own
philosophies and actions with patriotism. John Foster, a member of the
administration and habitual supporter of government policy, certainly
saw his life of public service and his role as an improving landlord as
"patriotic."[71] And although critics believed he had abandoned the
cause and become a place seeker, Henry Flood saw no contradiction
between taking government office and his patriotism. Indeed in 1781,
when he left office, he expected to resume his opposition patriot role
with ease, and though he was not immediately welcomed back to the
fold, he did eventually restore his patriot reputation.[72]

Those involved in the political disputes of the 1770s and 1780s put
considerable energy into defining patriotism, or what they often described as "love of country," a notion particularly emphasized in sermons. Sermons provide another source for understanding the meaning
of patriotism in late eighteenth-century Ireland. Contemporaries often
emphasized the theatrical elements of the sermon, and like many

sources of politicization, sermons were characterized by their performative nature. The pulpit could serve as a significant agent of politicization. Sermons were one of the main sources of ideology in the eighteenth century as well as "one of the few expressions of popular communication expressly designed to reach every level of the populace, rich, poor, literate, and illiterate."[73] Clergy spoke to the public every week in discourses that developed theological and philosophical views. Because many sermons were subsequently published, these discourses were not confined to the immediate congregation but rather reached a more general audience.

A distinctive aspect of preaching in the 1770s and 1780s was the frequent preaching of sermons by Volunteer chaplains to their companies. Volunteering involved the performance of citizenship in a series of militia maneuvers, reviews, and mock battles, and many of these events concluded with the company marching to the church or meeting house to hear a sermon on the relationship between the citizen and the soldier. To emphasize the occasion of these performances, some sermons were later published at the request of the company. Over twenty Volunteer sermons are extant, though as the pages of the provincial press attest, many others were both preached and published. In towns such as Newry and Strabane, apart from newspapers and chapbooks, Volunteer sermons were some of the earliest attempts at printing local material, and indeed religious tracts, catechisms, and sermons made up a large proportion of material printed and distributed in the provinces in the eighteenth century.[74]

The hotly contested County Down election of 1783 between the Hillsborough and the Stewart interests demonstrates the importance of the pulpit in political dispute. The election inspired an outpouring of poems, songs, and resolutions, as well as public demonstrations of support for the competing parties. Compiling this material in the wake of the election, a supporter of Hillsborough's candidate, Lord Kilwarlin, chose to emphasize the crucial role of the pulpit in this contest. In their opposition to Kilwarlin, dissenting ministers in particular had played a very public role.[75] As the author observed,

> In any commotion wherein it may be necessary to interest the lower class of men, the pulpit seldom fails to render a considerable assistance. On the present occasion, the intolerance of religious authority overleaped the bounds of propriety and moderation: a particular sect of men seemed to have embarked their all on the success of the question.

> They prostituted the sanctity not only of their functions, but of their Houses of worship, in order to administer to their purposes.—From the pulpit itself! they assured their congregations, that morality and religion required the freeholders to adopt the political opinions of their ministers, in preference to those of their landlords; and that their eternal salvation was the pledge of their obedience![76]

Dissenting clergy were active not only in electioneering but also in justifying the Volunteers' taking up of arms and explicating the ideology of the citizen-soldier.[77] Many of these clergy, such as Samuel Barber and William Steel Dickson, were active supporters of the Volunteers. Frederick Jebb criticized Dissenting ministers, particularly the "gospel-ministers, clad in uniform, and at the head of armed citizens."[78] Rather than offering "comfortable admonition, and hope," the author of the *Historical Account* claimed, their congregation "met as well in the pulpit, as in the field, the *reverend* director of his conscience clad in armour." While the author was clear on the issue of the "Propriety and Impropriety of turning pulpits into Political Theatres for the exhibition of the Actors talents," the pulpit was a site of political dispute and for the "lower class" of Presbyterians, as well as Catholics and members of the established church, a source of political information.[79]

Preached to Volunteer companies to encourage fortitude in the face of anticipated French invasion, sermons emphasize many of the main aspects of Irish patriotism: its relation to Protestantism, the constitution, the militia, the virtuous active citizen, and a benevolent cosmopolitanism. Volunteer sermons defined patriotism as the defense of religious and civil liberties. Foremost, patriotism was associated with a love of country, an emotion that William Steel Dickson described as "a universal Principle" common to both the Laplander and his "barren rocks and howling tempests" and the Libyan with his "burning sands."[80] Likewise, James Crombie believed love of country to be a "universal passion." However, this originally "noble affection" that informed "a correct attachment to country" had been perverted throughout history by nations that sought not to simply defend their territories and their liberties but to engage in aggressive wars of expansion and enslave others. A benevolent patriotism existed in tension with expansive imperialism. In its purest form, patriotism was not incompatible with a general benevolence or "the love of mankind at large." Crombie warned against "narrower associations," which inevitably "degenerates into a vicious ambition, which aspires after conquest, and which terminates in the oppression of other states, or in the ruin of our own."[81]

Although true patriotism was a type of universal benevolence, Crombie conceded that in practice "mankind at large [was] an object too vast" to move the patriotic spirit, so that "the more interesting objects of his social affections" such as family, friends, and neighborhood, formed circles of sensible affections until "they reach[ed] that which bounds the community to which he belong[ed]." From the limits of universal benevolence then, emerged the narrower love of country. Though circumscribed, this was still a noble and "instinctive" affection. Indeed, the patriot could "regard no object with indifference that ha[d] the feeblest connection with it." Love of country also went beyond affection for other members of the community to include "the customs, manners, laws, and even to the very soil upon which the community live[d]." In particular, the constitution, on which their "existence as a free people depend[ed]," should serve as the main object of patriot interest. Of course, Crombie was not alone in seeing a balanced constitution that ensured civil and religious liberties as a particular blessing of Protestant Britain. In this context, patriotism was ultimately concerned with protecting these liberties. According to Crombie, the constitution "encircles within its bulwark every object of private and public affection" so that "to love *our* country is to revere *its* constitution."[82] Crombie and other Irish patriots, in their veneration of the English constitution, emphasized the centrality of an allegiance to an English political identity in the British Atlantic world in the eighteenth century. As Colin Kidd asserts in his account of Scottish patriotism and "North Britishness," patriotism was preoccupied with the attainment and maintenance of civil liberty, which "was measured by a calculus of institutions and laws, and was not conceived primarily in ethnocentric terms."[83]

This patriot concern with the protection of constitutional rights was not necessarily analogous with a sort of Irish nationalism; indeed, until the end of the 1750s, many patriots advocated closer integration and union with Britain as the best means of ensuring their rights. Historians have recently refocused attention on the British context of Irish patriotism. Sean Connolly notes the "strong British element that pervaded political life" in Ireland, especially among the Protestant middle and upper classes.[84] Indeed, Ian McBride suggests that Irish patriotism actually became more Anglocentric over the course of the century.[85] Such insights suggest the need to avoid a simplistic teleology focusing on the *rise* of Irishness and Irish national identity as an inevitable process. A determinism that views Ireland's failure to assimilate within a multinational British state as inevitable ignores, for example, the fact that Irish patriots acted within a British context in their campaign for parliamentary reform, corresponding with English reformers and following many of the same tactics, as discussed in chapter 8.

If Britishness was bound up with a concern with liberty, religious liberty was central to this identity. George Carson, in a sermon delivered to Volunteers at Croghan, noted that Protestants living under popish governments had everywhere been "deprived of their religious liberty."[86] Many patriot sermons echoed such fears of popery. Throughout the century, patriotism was intimately intertwined with Protestantism. The confessional basis of Irish patriotism was evident in its calendar of commemoration, particularly 4 November, William III's birthday, which clearly linked the defense of liberty and Protestantism. Toby Barnard observes from his study of sermons commemorating 1641 that there was "an essential continuity in the Protestants' fears about their vulnerability" to Catholic attack even in the 1780s.[87] Sermons reminded listeners of a bloody history of popish persecution and urged vigilance against the dangers of the popish threat from outside but also within their midst. The confessional nature of patriotism was challenged in the 1770s and 1780s as some Catholics were called to take an active role in the politics of patriotism. Yet how did Catholics relate to the ideology of patriotism, and what opportunities were there for them to share in this culture of patriotism? Catholic elites could subscribe to nonassociation agreements. They could show their patriotism and self-mastery by refusing to buy or sell English consumer goods. They were also members of many Volunteers companies. The Volunteers were initially a fiercely Protestant force in ethos and membership, continuing the tradition of insecure colonial settlers organizing for defense against the Catholic Irish. By 1782 a resolution at the Dungannon convention of Volunteers could celebrate the relaxing of the penal laws against their "Roman Catholic fellow-subjects" and encourage the admittance of Catholics to Volunteer units.[88]

Of course, suspicion and fear of Catholics did not simply disappear; most Protestants continued to oppose any formal political role for Catholics. The Catholic question was highly divisive within the Volunteers, as in most areas of Irish life.[89] Religious conflict and division have often been invoked as the essential features of eighteenth-century Irish society and politics. In such classic works as W. E. H. Lecky's *History of Ireland in the Eighteenth Century*, the penal laws, a series of acts limiting the religious, political, and economic freedoms of Catholics, were interpreted as reflecting the actual power and arrogance of the Protestant minority over the degraded and demoralized Catholic majority. In recent years, historians have emphasized the limited impact of the laws, the continuing vitality of Catholic Ireland, and the equal or greater importance of other factors in explaining the character of Irish society.[90] Nonetheless, as Karen Harvey, among others, has argued, until the contentious repeal of much of this legislation after 1778, the reality and intent of these laws indicate that religious divisions were never a marginal issue for either Protestants or Catholics.[91] And if elite and middling Catholics might bring themselves to embrace the Hanoverian regime and offer support for the goals of patriotism, the Catholic masses were not so easily reconciled to the established order.[92]

Lecky's claim, followed by subsequent historians, that the 1770s witnessed the emergence of "a spirit of tolerance" has been broadly criticized in recent years. The work of Louis Cullen and others has provided a corrective to the earlier "benign-progress school of historians" of interdenominational relations, emphasizing the persistence of anti-Catholicism and a fear of popery.[93] Hill has argued that, rather than driven by a growing toleration on the part of Irish Protestants, the dismantling of many of the penal laws after 1778 was motivated by broader British imperial and military considerations.[94] But a confessional understanding of patriotism did come under increasing pressure in the 1780s. The leaders of the Catholic Committee consistently promoted an agenda that suggested Catholicism and loyalty to the Hanoverian regime were not incompatible. This propaganda, often written by Protestants for a Protestant audience, may have had some success.[95] Although only a radical fringe of Protestants publicly advocated the extension of political rights to Catholics, Protestant Volunteer companies invited Catholics to join their ranks.[96] At the same time, Catholic companies were established, and others, such as the Dublin Independent Volunteers and the Irish Brigade, attended sermons preached at Catholic churches.[97] Even if this project was ultimately unsuccessful, it represents an attempt to reevaluate the Catholic question.

How do we explain this (admittedly transitory and limited) transcendence of traditional confessional patriotism? Contemporaries, observing this phenomenon, offered a variety of explanations. Sheridan attributed it to a "wild and extravagant politicks" that had fleetingly overcome religious bigotry. Above all, it was the distinctive understanding of patriotism embraced by the Volunteers that made it possible to cross confessional divides. Well-to-do and "respectable" Catholic men at least could demonstrate their patriotism by subscribing to the funds of local Volunteer companies. The associations promoting non-consumption gave a Catholic man what Grattan described as the opportunity of "signing himself a fellow citizen."[98] According to William Drennan, it was the experience of volunteering with Catholics that had "promoted religious liberty and liberality" among Protestants and led them to rejoice in the "common title" of Irishmen.[99] Catholic participation in armed and disciplined military associations with their Protestant countrymen was presented as compelling evidence that Catholics were capable of acting as loyal subjects and were worthy, as William Todd Jones contended, of the "privileges of citizens." Through their "practical and active exertions" as Volunteers, Catholics could lay claim to the rights of citizens, while some Protestants might envisage a more expansive role for Catholics in the political nation.

Many patriots agreed on the values and institutions that patriotism was concerned with protecting. But there was less unanimity over what this involved in practice. How was liberty to be upheld? And who was to participate in the practice of patriotism? Did it potentially include Catholics, plebian Protestants, and/or women? It was here that competing understandings of the political nation and the active citizen came into play in ways that were to define the patriot movement of the 1770s and 1780s. Patriotism was not simply concerned with articulating disparate strands of political traditions such as ancient constitutionalism and civic humanism. Indeed, the coherency of patriot ideas in terms of the standards of political philosophy can be doubted. Patriot virtue was expressed first and foremost through action. As Presbyterian minister James Crombie observed, "Speculations may amuse, but if separated from action, they contribute nothing to the prosperity and greatness of our country."[100] Or, as a letter from "Hibernicus" to the *Hibernian Chronicle* contended: "Genuine patriotism is that principle that shews itself by the practical and active exertions of our utmost abilities in the defence and common interests of our country; it is in no measure governed by metaphysical doctrine or speculative opinions, but founded on the fundamental rule of all society, self preservation, Property, and a mild constitution, are objects ever worth contending for."[101] It was through virtuous public actions in defense of liberty that the patriot demonstrated love of country. The consequences of this active vision of citizenship are the focus of this study. Despite the patriots' relative lack of success in achieving their goals after legislative independence in 1782, patriot political culture was not insignificant. It was not merely a prelude to the supposedly more significant action of the 1790s, nor simply a colorful but frivolous moment that allowed the Protestant gentry to play at soldiering. The experience of the culture of volunteering and patriotism forged a "nation of politicians" and allowed ordinary men and women to form conceptions of the political nation that challenged traditional circumscribed conceptions of politics.

"Alehouse Politicians"

The Culture of Print and the Political Nation

When I clean'd my master's shoes,
All in the morning early,
To hear the hawkers cry the news,
O how my heart goes cheerly!
Freeman's Journal—
Faulkner's Journal
Bloody news—bloody news
The shoes I black—then read good lack!
The charming, charming news.

*The Songs, Duets, Trios, Choruses, and Finales
in the New Comic Opera of the Contract,
as Performed at the Theatre Royal, Smock Alley*

THE THEATRICAL PERFORMANCE of the hawker or "news-boy" in his green apron lugging his supply of papers, pamphlets, and broadsides through the streets, colorfully announcing the arrival of the morning and evening press with a cry of "bloody news'" was a familiar sight in eighteenth-century Dublin. While the picaresque aspects of this trade have often been emphasized, the quoted song also highlights its role in the dissemination of the news, here to the delight of a young apprentice. The "news" as assembled by the press was a key mechanism of politicization in eighteenth-century Ireland. In the 1770s and 1780s print was central to the propagation of a patriot vision of the nation. Picking up a newspaper in 1783 (the year this song was performed on the Dublin stage), the apprentice could not have avoided news of the Volunteers: accounts of their parades and reviews, notices of resolutions, advertisements for Volunteer clothing and ephemera, letters debating the merits of Volunteer proposals for reform, poems celebrating the force, along with three newspapers named after the force itself. There was a seemingly insatiable appetite for accounts of the Volunteers among Irish readers, and newspaper publishers were only too keen to meet this desire.

Newspapers offered competing political understandings of the nation and the state and helped to shape local and national identities. Of the papers mentioned in the song, *Faulkner's Journal* offered near unfailing support for the government, while the *Freeman's Journal* adopted a strongly patriotic and antigovernment perspective. Dublin supported a lively newspaper trade throughout the century, and by the 1770s as many as twelve papers were published in the capital. The provincial newspaper trade also flourished in these years. By this time most substantial provincial towns sustained a printer, and many provincial newspapers were established during this politically turbulent decade. In 1771 the *Strabane Journal* was established by John Alexander. In Newry the *Newry Journal* emerged in 1761, followed by the *Newry Chronicle* in 1777. The *Kerry Evening Post* was first published in 1774, the *Drogheda Journal* in 1774, and the *Clare Journal* and the *Clonmel Gazette* both in 1778. Derry, Wexford, Cork, Limerick, Galway, Athlone, and Loughrea also saw the establishment of new papers in the 1770s, while others followed in the 1780s.

The vibrant Dublin book and print trade supplied the country trade with much of its needs and was complimented by a growing provincial trade in towns and cities involving printers, booksellers, circulating libraries, taverns, coffeehouses, and a large number of itinerant peddlers or chapmen distributing and producing such items as newspapers, pamphlets, ballads, sermons, catechisms, plays, and novels.[1] Although Dublin remained the center of this industry, the provincial trade increasingly catered to local needs and tastes.[2] This study relies in large part on the extant runs of several Dublin and provincial newspapers. Historians have long recognized the importance of print culture and the press in particular in the process of politicization in late eighteenth-century Ireland. However, the history of the newspaper has attracted little attention in recent years. The best histories of the Irish press by Robert Munter and Brian Inglis are over thirty-five and fifty years old, respectively.[3] The northern radical press of the 1790s has received renewed attention, particularly the *Northern Star*.[4] The rest of the century remains relatively ignored. Many provincial titles are no longer extant, and even those that survive have been largely neglected.[5] This chapter provides an outline of print culture in the 1770s and 1780s. It focuses in particular on newspapers, pamphlets, prints, and ballads that were among the principal sources of printed political information. It sketches the outlines of readership, the relationship between the press and its readers, and the way in which the press attempted to shape and reflect public opinion. It argues that the social, gendered, and religious contours of the culture of print were more inclusive than is often assumed and that this world was central in reimagining the political nation in the late eighteenth century.

Literacy and the Circulation and Distribution of the Press

Many contemporaries believed that newspapers were important in the spread of political knowledge. John Caldwell recalled the "electrical effect" of the *Belfast News-Letter*, the first paper in Belfast. He believed that it had "raised the curiosity of the people, set them reading and from reading to thinking and from thinking to acting and exerting their energies and their rights in sending from the counties men of their choice well qualified to represent them in Parliament. This was the first fruits of newspaper knowledge disseminated amongst the people."[6] Print increasingly permeated everyday life by the middle of the century.[7] But who could read this growing tide of printed material? Literacy rates are notoriously difficult to estimate, and no reliable sources exist for an accurate estimate of literacy in either English or Irish in eighteenth-century Ireland. Recent studies of the 1790s have stressed the role of print and literacy in the increased politicization of both rural and urban environments. English language literacy was highest in towns and particularly in the East and the Northeast. Niall Ó Ciosáin estimates that literacy rates in the 1780s were well above 50 percent among men in Ulster and Leinster, while it was as low as 30 percent in Connaught.[8] A study of literacy rates in Northwest Ulster suggests that religion and gender were central to the social distribution of literacy, with male Protestants the most literate and Catholic women the least.[9] Even where literacy rates were low, the common practice of reading aloud could bridge the gap between the literate and the oral. The chasm between English- and Irish-speaking worlds was also not as vast as is often assumed; by this time Ireland was "an intensely bilingual and diglossic society."[10] Contemporary events from newspapers often served as the subject of Irish-language poetry and song so that neither illiteracy nor inability to read or speak English were necessarily obstacles for acquiring "news" or participating in the culture of print.[11]

Those immersed in the world of print found themselves with an abundance of choices, particularly with regard to the newspaper press. As many as forty provincial papers were in business in the 1770s and 1780s, with more than half of them established during these years, while Dublin supported around twelve titles. Some of these papers were relatively short-lived enterprises, but many endured, suggesting their ability to adapt to local interests and market conditions. Newspapers were not necessarily cheap. The popular *Dublin Evening Post* cost 3½d., though the average price for other papers was around 2½d. *The Belfast Newsletter* in the middle of the century cost 4s. 4d. for a subscription in Belfast and considerably more beyond the town. A subscription to the *Newry Journal* cost 13s. a year. Subscriptions averaged between 6s. 6d. and 8s. 8d. in towns and up to ½ guinea per annum in the country.[12] Costs were increased further by the introduction of a stamp duty in 1774 and an advertising stamp in 1785.[13] Publishers constantly bemoaned the effect of such taxes on sales. However, such prices did not automatically imply a socially exclusive readership since copies were not restricted to a single reader. Circulation depended on street sales by hawkers as well as subscriptions by coffee and alehouses, with private subscriptions probably playing a relatively small part in sales.[14]

Although the idea that newspapers shaped public opinion is axiomatic among historians, it is difficult to establish circulation figures for newspapers in Dublin and even more so for those in the provinces. In 1779 the *Dublin Evening Post* claimed to have the largest circulation in the country, printing between 2,500 and 3,000 copies of each edition three times per week. Assuming that each paper had at least four readers, the paper estimated ten to twelve thousand readers for each issue.[15] The *Post* had reason, of course, to exaggerate its sales and readership, not least to attract advertisers. Based on stamps sold, Munter has estimated that the number of newspapers printed in Dublin each week between 1775 and 1785 was around 45,000, or 15,000 copies three times per week, divided between eight to twelve newspapers.[16] Assuming between four and six readers of each paper, a conservative estimate, suggests a readership of between 60,000 and 90,000 readers.[17] This was a substantial proportion of Dublin's population, which had reached around 180,000 by the 1790s, and is certainly comparable with the penetration of the press in London, the largest market in Great Britain.

When we turn to the provincial press, accurate numbers are even harder to come by. The stamp tax returns suggest that total sales in the provinces went from less than 800 to under 2,500 a week between 1775 and 1785. This is almost certainly an underestimate. Provincial newspapers also made claims about their circulation, though, as with the stamp returns, such numbers must be treated with caution. In the late 1780s the *Belfast News-Letter* alone claimed a circulation of 2,000 to 3,000 per issue.[18] A minor paper such as the *Carlow Journal* could claim in 1773 to have 100 subscribers in Dublin and as many as 1,000 in Carlow itself, though this is no doubt an exaggeration. Munter suggests that up to 1760 most newspapers, apart from the largest three or four, had a circulation of 400 to 600.[19] It seems safe to assume that these sales remained relatively constant after this period and may even have risen.[20] An imprecise estimate of the total readership of the provincial press suggests it may have been between 72,000 and 108,000.[21] This is a small percentage of the population outside Dublin, which compares unfavorably with an estimated provincial readership in England of about 8 percent.[22] It is likely, however, that newspapers had a higher penetration in urban settings than in the less literate and less anglophone countryside. Regional variation is also likely, with highly literate Ulster having a higher dissemination of newspapers than Connaught, for example. Readership would certainly have been higher in towns with populations around ten thousand that could support newspapers and the institutions of sociability, which included Cork, Limerick, Waterford, Belfast, Kilkenny, Galway, Clonmel, Drogheda, Carrick-on-Suir, and Newry.[23]

Though it is difficult to say with any degree of certainty how many copies were produced and read, some provincial papers did have extensive systems of distribution. Papers were delivered to agents in nearby towns through the post office or by couriers, while papers were also available in coffeehouses throughout the country.[24] The masthead of the *Clonmell Gazette* depicted that town as a regional hub with distribution spokes for the paper stretching out to Cork, Limerick, King's County, Queen's County, Kilkenny, Waterford, and Clare. The *Leinster Journal*, published twice a week in the town of Kilkenny, announced that it was available in all villages and towns of Kilkenny, Carlow, Tipperary, Waterford, Wexford, and Queen's County. The writer claimed that through the post office the paper was available "even to the remotest parts of the Kingdom," in Merchant's coffeehouse in Cork, Nixon's coffeehouse in Waterford, as well as in various locations in England.[25] The *Connaught Journal,* published in Galway, was available in towns up to fifty miles away, while in the 1790s, as Kevin Whelan has shown, the radical *Northern Star* established an impressive list of subscribers and a network of agents for distribution throughout much of the North.[26] An extensive network of roads, improved throughout the century, facilitated the distribution of the press throughout the country.[27] Though critical of the turnpikes, Arthur Young was surprised to observe that the Irish road system was superior to that of England.[28] The postal service, which relied on the road system and provided the main means through which the provinces communicated with Dublin and London, also become more efficient. By 1768 a thrice-weekly service on Tuesday, Thursday, and Sunday had been established throughout Ireland, which allowed for relatively dependable delivery.[29]

"Alehouse Politicians": Print, Sociability, and the Political Nation

The culture of print depended on and supported a variety of institutions and forms of sociability, such as the coffeehouse and the alehouse, which were central to the distribution and consumption of the press. Humphrey Search, the apprentice in the song at the beginning of the chapter, would probably not have bought newspapers from hawkers but found other means to peruse the press. Although some hawkers rented out newspapers cheaply (much to the exasperation of printers), most readers would have experienced the news in the comfort of the coffee- or alehouse.[30] Nearly all provincial towns sustained a coffeehouse and several taverns where local and Dublin newspapers could be read along with other literature. Since the Restoration, Dublin had supported a variety of such institutions, which were often associated with specific newspapers and political affiliations.[31] It was in such an environment that John Anketell, a northern poet studying in Dublin, encountered the "spruce apprentice from his master free" and heard the "Calls for the news" and "Is the packet come?" Anketell disapprovingly described the scene:

> Here the old dotards sip the capilaire,
> And talk of politics with lofty air;
> On state affairs importantly proceed,
> And pore on papers which they cannot read.[32]

Despite Anketell's suspicions, apprentices and others pouring over the press were probably not illiterate and viewed the conviviality and sociability of the coffeehouse or the alehouse in a more positive light than the censorious poet did. Another poem, titled "The Alehouse Politicians" published in the Cork newspaper, the *Hibernian Chronicle,* lampoons the relationship between sociability, drinking, and the news:

> A pint of purl—a glass of gin;
> What news in the Gazette?
> News? Why such news as ne'er was seen,
> —Enough to make one fret!
>
> A pot of beer—a slice of cheese;
> What news in the Gazette!
> The fleets combin'd now range the seas;
> —Enough to make one fret!
>
> Nine bankrupts—nine and forty dead
> And missing, rank and file;
> A German Princess brought to bed;
> —Enough to make one smile.
>
> Where is Sir Charles and where his fleet?
> Safe anchored at Spithead,
> Providing plenty of fresh meat;
> —Enough to strike one dead! . . .
>
> St. Vincent's, Dominique, Grenades!
> The next almost as bad;
> D'Estaing among the Isles parades;
> —Enough to drive one mad!
>
> More beer for me—more gin for me;
> Let's sit us down and sing,
> "The Devil take the Ministry,"
> Here goes—"God save the King."[33]

As this ballad suggests, the reading of newspapers in the tavern promoted a particular form of male sociability. This poem is obviously mildly satirical in referring to the clientele of the tavern as "politicians," a term mockingly applied to lower-class men who presumed to pass judgment on the political affairs of the nation.[34] At the same time, it evokes the social context of the experience of "news" that often involved the reading aloud of stories as well as comment and debate on the issues of the day, the scene described here ending with an attack on the ministry for Britain's imperial misfortunes, followed by a show of rowdy royalism. The press allowed readers to "imagine" themselves as part of national, imperial, or Protestant communities, to name a few, and to adopt a variety of identities that were not necessarily contradictory or competing.[35]

The poem also reflects the heterogeneous content of the press: accounts of imperial war and naval encounters, gossip about the European aristocracy, news of bankruptcies, and a sizable amount of trade-related news. Such accounts were blended with a mix of local events and, reflecting the growing interest in reform and accountability, detailed reports of parliamentary debates. Advertisements for both mundane and luxury goods often composed as much as a third to a half of the content of the press. Accounts of local assizes, disturbances and riots, local and national celebrations, and increasingly in the 1770s and 1780s, resolutions of grand juries and instructions to MPs contributed to an understanding of the place of local interventions in national dramas. Letters on the dangers of popery, luxury, gender roles, or government policy provided explicitly political comment. The state also contributed significantly to the content of the press. Accounts of the actions of government, Parliament, corporations, and other official bodies provided much of the news content of the press. At the same time, these bodies published notices such as proclamations and addresses, which served as a significant source of revenue for many papers. The press was responsible for publicizing the spectacle of street theater occasioned by commemorations, celebrations, riots, and civil rituals, as well as avidly relaying the activities of the Volunteers. All newspapers offered detailed accounts of the wide range of Volunteer activities such as reviews, maneuvers, effigy burnings, and conventions. Such representations were central to the way in which people could envisage the disparate activities of individual Volunteer corps as part of a "national," unified movement that transcended the particular local circumstances of their formation.[36]

This mix of practical information, imperial drama, scandal, and the banal, which has long frustrated or bored historians of the press, was central in the "social production of information" encouraging a particular view of the relation between the local, the national, and the imperial and the imagined male reader's place in these structures, as well as his ability to comment on events, to play the "politician."[37] Serial publications such as newspapers helped the reader organize a miscellaneous array of recent and past events, dramatizing and historicizing them into a form of continuous narrative that, while not always reliable or consistent, provided a lens through which to interpret information and give it meaning in relation to the reader's place within the community.[38] A song from the comic opera *The Contrast*, quoted at the beginning of this discussion, is suggestive of the social context of the press, the way newspapers could organize time, and their penetration beyond the elites and the middling sort. The song, performed at Dublin's Smock Alley Theatre, depicted the day of a Dublin apprentice, Humphrey Search. A daily routine is structured around the publication of the morning and evening papers, the cries of the hawkers, and the desire for "bloody" news. The avid pursuit of news by an apprentice may have been broadly comical. However, another song by the same character expresses a sympathetic attitude to the plebian appetite for news of current events. Search is given patriotic songs to sing. The self-styled "politicians" (the term used here to mock those advocating an exclusive definition of political participation) who claim that those of "low condition" should not be concerned with the world portrayed in the press are also satirized:

> How charming 'tis to read decrees,
> And senatorial speeches,
> Of deaths, elopements, marriages,
> And matrimonial breeches!
> But base-born clods, a scrap of news
> Will serve your low condition,
> Since 'tis not ev'ry one that chuse
> Can be a politician.[39]

Literacy and the press were a central part of the social life of urban artisans and apprentices in Ireland. Many letters were addressed directly to the "lower class of people" or specific occupations or social classes, such as weavers, or "poor protestants," while others even addressed a rural readership. In publishing a series of letters on free trade from a miller "John Allan," the editors of the *Belfast News-Letter* hoped, "[The] following shrewd thoughts of an illiterate countryman will be acceptable to that class of our readers, to whom it is addressed."[40] Written in colloquial language, the letters argued that nonelites should have as much interest in political affairs as anyone else, maintaining, "If things go wrong and the people grow poor and we have a war in the country, I lose as much as another, and more too, for if the Squire loses part of his estate, he may still gain a livelihood out of the rest. . . . But if my Mill be knocked down, and the people kilt, or made slaves of, why then I must starve." The author claimed to be a Volunteer and revealed a familiarity with the recent pamphlet literature, referencing the recent works of "Guatimozin," "Owen Roe O'Nial," and others. The first letter offered a particular version of the history of Anglo-Irish relations in order to prove that Ireland should be treated as an equal and that England was entitled to as much power over Ireland as "the parish that a landlord live[d] in ha[d] over any other parish in the estate."[41] Indeed relations within the empire as a whole could be understood in part through such local analogies, so that readers should consider Britain, Ireland, the West Indies, Hanover, and the rest of the empire as "different townlands in a great estate; and the King as landlord of them all," with the only (if striking) difference that "a landlord chooses his tenants, but the people choose the King."[42] Such language, stressing the lowly social standing and occupation of the writer, served to rhetorically embrace the lower classes and others, such as women and Catholics, and include them in a community of newspaper readership.[43]

Reading the press and the forms of sociability it supported allowed urban men from a variety of social classes to participate imaginatively in the national community. Catholic men certainly participated in the cut and thrust of tavern and coffeehouse life. Accounts of trade, war, Parliament, Volunteer parades, the affairs of European monarchs, and disputes with Britain would have appealed to literate Catholic merchants, tradesmen, and apprentices, if perhaps in mediated ways. The press was also a vehicle for promoting a vision of Catholic loyalty to the Hanoverian state. Accounts of the loyalty of middling and elite Catholics were numerous in the press, in humble addresses, subscriptions for troops, or the taking of loyal oaths. The renouncing of the "errors of the Church of Rome" and the embracing of Protestantism by Catholics was eagerly reported by newspapers as evidence of Catholicism's decline.[44] Authors identifying themselves as Catholics wrote letters to the press to proclaim their loyalty and to protest the penal laws against them. At the same time, Catholics were more often than not represented as objects of a particularly Protestant discourse in the press, as actual or potential converts or as dangerous threats to the body politic, for example. The actions of violent agrarian societies reported in the press in the 1760s and 1770s, whether directed at Protestants or not, contributed to a fear of the Catholic masses. Although letters and addresses in the press were often employed to stress the loyalty of "respectable" Catholics, the fear of popery remained and found violent expression in newspapers, particularly at moments when government proposed to remove or modify legislative disabilities against Catholics. In 1778 a bill for Catholic relief sparked a series of letters reminding readers of the horrors of past massacres of Protestants by supposedly quiescent Catholics.[45] A letter suggesting the dangers of arming Catholics reminded readers of the "Smithfield fires of Bloody Mary . . . the butcheries of 1641" along with the "sacrifices of human victims by the Inquisition" in order to alert readers to the continuing perfidiousness of their Catholic neighbors.[46] At the same time, some correspondents voiced support for Catholic relief, and Catholics cautiously contributed to this debate during the 1770s, suggesting that participation in the Volunteers warranted their inclusion in the political nation.

As the growing association between volunteering and patriotism might suggest, patriotism was repeatedly associated in the press with "manly efforts" or a "manly fortitude" and a type of activist masculinity perfectly embodied in the military practices of the Volunteers. If the press was central to the creation of "the public" as arbiters of the public good, it was a specific public imagined in terms of exclusive gender, religious, and social identities. At the same time, whatever dangers it was believed this might entail, women did in fact take part in the culture of print, as printers, readers, authors, and owners of the coffeehouses and pubs. The social environment in which the press was consumed was often conceived of as a masculine sphere. However, women were certainly present in this world, especially as owners of taverns and coffeehouses.[47] Women also worked in the print business, either in their own or in a family enterprise.[48] There was at least one female owner of a provincial paper, Catherine Finn, the proprietor of the *Leinster Journal*, printed in Kilkenny. Women also participated as readers. Martha McTier, for example, read the Belfast newspapers avidly. Along with pamphlets, letters, and gossip, the press served as her main source of political information. In her correspondence she responded angrily or approvingly to the news, letters, petitions and resolutions she read.[49] Women were frequently addressed specifically as potential readers of the press through advertisements to "the ladies" but also in letters that appealed for the expression of female forms of patriotism.

From time to time women also contributed letters to the press. Women addressing the public in print might claim that their gender entitled them "to the protection of the sensible and the benevolent" though their letters often evoked hostile responses. In the early 1770s, for example, the *Hibernian Chronicle* of Cork regularly published letters from and about women on a variety of topics such as "The Female Parliament," "Defence of the Modern Ladies," and "On Female Neatness."[50] Most of these letters, modeled on the polite style of periodicals such as the *Spectator,* either attacked the frivolity of women and their supposed concern with fashion or defended the "modern ladies" against these charges. The politics of reading the press was central to this debate. "Thalestris," responding to a letter critical of women reading, claimed the correspondent was "apprehensive that by reading [women] may be argued out of some of those pretty accomplishments so necessary to the happiness of the men; or in other words, that [women] may come to a knowledge of [their] own power."[51] This letter provoked an outraged response (probably written by a woman) that attacked "the present mode of education," which encouraged "that empire of the females." Again it was female reading that provoked the author's wrath: "The wives of mechanics are infected, and I can assure you the woman in whose house I lodge, leaves her children uncombed, hungry and dirty, til she reads your paper, and then commits such numerous misnomers you swear she was a lunatic."[52] In this vision, evoking class and gender anxieties, the reading of the press is depicted as a type of pathological addiction that caused women to neglect themselves and threatened the stability of the family itself.

Many letters to the press purported to be written by women, others by lower-class Protestants and Catholics. But who was responsible for writing letters to the press and for penning the numerous pamphlets during times of heightened political dispute? This question is difficult to answer because, as the discussion thus far suggests, many of these publications were either anonymous or pseudonymous. Pseudonyms added authority and often indicated political sentiment. Anonymity could also protect an author against prosecution if the writing attacked public figures or the government. Pseudonyms and anonymity were one means through which the "public" was constituted in the press. They indicated the author's disinterested concern with the public good as opposed to a concern with fame or reputation. Frederick Jebb, writing in his fourth letter as "Guatimozin," noted: "A periodical author, whose intention in writing is to benefit the society he lives amongst, by opening their eyes upon the true objects of their prosperity and happiness, will find perpetual advantage from the concealment of his name: the public judgment concerning his productions will receive no influence from the peculiar infirmities or advantages of his personal character, and the freedom of the general opinion will direct his future attention to the removal of such prejudices as operate against the conviction of the people."[53] The author of a proreform pamphlet published in 1784 stressed that anonymity guaranteed the integrity of the argument: "The author of an anonymous pamphlet can have no means of influence, but argument, and no recommendation to the public but the soundness and liberality of the principles he inculcates."[54]

Leading parliamentarians and political writers published anonymously or used a variety of pseudonyms. Henry Flood published in the *Freeman's Journal* as "Philadelphus" and later "Syndercombe," the attempted assassin of Cromwell, while Wolfe Tone signed himself with the classical reference "Senex."[55] The radical patriot Edward Newenham contributed to the *Freeman's Journal* under a variety of pseudonyms such as "Brutus" and "Leonidas."[56] Some pseudonyms were particularly popular, and it is difficult to determine if letters written under pseudonyms such as the regular "Hibernicus" were consistently by the same author. Disputes over attributions, or the "ownership" of certain pseudonyms, attests to the importance of building and maintaining a reputation in the republic of letters through the control of particular pen names.

Pseudonymous identities were no doubt often open secrets in certain circles, though many of the most popular and prolific, such as "Humphrey Search," "Gracchus," and "Cassius" are still difficult to attribute with any certainty.[57] Pseudonyms obviously carried political meanings, alluding to a wide variety of historical figures that suggested both the author's political allegiances as well as the type of reader at whom the letter was directed. Many addressed classically educated audiences or those familiar with the pantheon of Whig heroes. Letters from "Juba" to the *Dublin Evening Post,* calling on women to embrace the patriot cause, for example, probably referred to a character in Addison's *Cato,* a perennially popular Whig play. In this play Juba was a Numidian prince who allied with Cato. He was also in love with Cato's daughter, Marcia, whom he saves from a disguised traitor. Juba spends much of the play rhapsodizing on the beauty of Marcia and must have seemed a particularly apt figure to address "Hibernia's fair." The republican Roman figure of Cato was also a "watchword for the martyrdom of liberty" in the eighteenth century Anglo-American world, and the play was familiar to Irish audiences.[58] Frederick Jebb's letters as "Guatimozin" were originally published in the *Freeman's Journal* and were quickly collected in pamphlet form in 1779. The letters offered a strongly worded attack on British policy toward Ireland and even adopted a separatist stance. The pseudonym, Jebb explained in the pamphlet, referred to a Mexican who fought against Cortés. The appropriateness of the figure of a colonized native struggling against a mighty empire was suggested in the preface with a quote from Robertson's *History of America* describing Guatimozin's actions: "He rejected with scorn every overture of peace from Cortes, and, disdaining the idea of submitting to the oppressors of his country, determined not to survive its ruin."[59] Pseudonyms often clearly suggested an identification with Protestantism and particularly the heroes of Whig history. Letters offering a defense of liberty or the Protestant nature of the Irish state frequently occasioned such allusions. The political conflicts of the late 1770s, the ascendance of the Volunteers, and new understandings of patriotism gave rise to other identifications with the past that were less stridently Protestant in outlook. The Jacobite general Patrick Sarsfield was frequently evoked as a pen name in the Dublin press.[60] Joseph Pollock's influential *Letters of Owen Roe O'Nial* evoked the name of the leader of Gaelic Irish in Ulster during the wars of the 1640s, in order to launch an attack on English policy in Ireland and the empire as a whole.

Pseudonyms served other purposes beyond providing anonymity or alluding to political principles. They could also be part of a strategy in the forging of a literary and political status. William Drennan, a Presbyterian doctor and future founder of the United Irishmen, is an example of a young man who successfully adopted pseudonyms for all these reasons. Drennan's most celebrated work was his *Letters of Orellana, an Irish Helot*, which was widely credited with revitalizing the Irish reform movement in 1784. Drennan also achieved notoriety under the name of the Whig hero "Sidney" in 1783. His sister, Martha McTier, suggested he write these letters, which were published in the Belfast newspapers. Shortly after their publication, McTier reported from Belfast to her brother in Newry, "Sidney's letters are much admired here"; "Sidney" was referred to by some as a "second Junius" with the identity of the author a point of much gossip and speculation throughout her circle in Belfast. Drennan's identity as the author seems to have been well concealed with others, such as his friend William Bruce, suspected of writing the letters. McTier advised him to remain anonymous; "being known as Sydney I would fear much at present," she cautioned, particularly in the small town of Newry where Drennan was struggling to establish a medical practice.[61] Anonymity and pseudonymous publications served, then, to mark the patriotic and virtuous disinterestedness of the author, while at the same time, as Drennan's career suggests, helping build political reputations.

"A True Political History": The Press and the Business of Patriotism

What was the role of the press? Newspapers and those who wrote to them had particular ideas on the value of a "free press" and its social and political functions. A critical letter to the *Hibernian Journal* from "Hibernicus Jr." argued that the quality of a nation's newspapers served as a "useful gauge of its civilization." A newspaper was of particular importance in a trading nation, he believed, for "it convey[ed] to the gentlemen, the citizens, and the manufacturer necessary articles of intelligence, which the whole course of their particular connections and most assiduous enquiries could never furnish them with." The press also served a particular political function, so that while it was useful on a commercial level, it was "more so on a free and constitutional one," for it provided a "true political history of the times": "The liberty of the press is one of those invaluable blessings which the malevolence of those in power has not been hitherto able to deprive us of. By it we are able to convey to the people the true state of political affairs; by it every true friend of his country is enabled to make known his sentiments. . . . To stem the current of public vice and give the wreath to virtue are the ends to which the liberty of the press should be directed as worthy its attention."[62] Correspondents and editors frequently evoked this image of the press as an arbiter of public opinion. A letter to the progovernment *Volunteer Evening Post* from "Erasmus" proclaimed in November 1783, "[The] Liberty of the Press has done everything for this country. It enlightened the genius of the people flinted into indifference by oppression; and awakened those dormant claims which were suffered to sleep for centuries in the arms of slavery."[63]

It is difficult to know why people read newspapers or in what ways they made decisions about what to read. We know more about the ways in which the press represented its role and relationship with readers. Newspapers actively attempted to mediate and shape this relationship. New enterprises often advertised their intended aims and imagined readership in an effort to drum up interest and subscriptions. The *Independent Chronicle* declared in 1778, "Corruption and jobbing will be pointed out without reserve."[64] An advertisement in a Belfast newspaper announcing the establishment of the *Dublin Evening Journal* communicated the aims of the proprietors and the printer to the "public" in some detail. Lamenting a corrupt administration, cowardly ministers, an unjust and "bloody war," and the enfeebled state of the navy, the proprietors claimed that with "unreserved impartiality" the new paper would promote the "liberties and welfare" of the nation. Competing newspapers were dismissed as "MUTILATED GAZETTES" filled with "Ministerial Essays" operated by printers and editors who had been "bribed by places" or intimidated by threats of prosecution. The *Journal* would in contrast be "UNAWED by power and UNBIASED by any Party." While it would serve liberty, at the same time the paper would also present "particulars of the most material import to a free and commercial people." This included a variety of information increasingly regarded as "news" that filled most newspaper as formats and contents became more standardized.

The paper promised to report a wide range of events such as "the interesting Occurrences that shall happen in any Part of the inhabited Globe" as well as "Domestic Intelligence," which consisted of "Promotions, the Proceedings of Corporations, Marriages, Deaths, Accidents, Robberies, Murders, Commitments, Trials, Executions &c." as well as the debates of the British parliament (to maintain vigilance against "arbitrary measures"), reports of speeches in the Irish parliament, the arrival and sailing of ships, exports and imports, prices of grain and flour, the assize of bread, as well as essays, letters, and poetry. The publisher was particularly eager to emphasize the utility of the paper to "Merchants and Tradesmen," but it would be of equal value to gentlemen, farmers, and those in the country as much as the town.[65] Such proclamations were of course intended to attract potential subscribers and advertisers, but they also draw attention to the ingredients that proprietors believed made a paper popular and viable. Indeed, the *Journal*, soon to merge with the *Dublin Evening Post*, followed this outline closely, becoming probably the most commercially successful paper in Dublin.

Emblems were also ways of conveying the politics and the purpose of a newspaper. The *Hibernian Journal, or Chronicle of Liberty*, displayed an emblem of Liberty holding a banner and leaning on the Magna Carta. A letter to the *Freeman's Journal* in July 1780 drew attention to the emblem of that paper to explicate its meaning: "Hibernia dispensing the Wreath or the Rod with an equal hand, is truly emblematical of that unbiased impartiality which should ever influence the editors of all public papers, if they wish to support with becoming dignity the freedom of the press, that inestimable privilege to which we are not only indebted for the preservation of our liberties, the prosperity of our constitution, and the very existence of the state." The press, it was claimed, was not only responsible for upholding liberty through its scrutiny of public figures, but it could also serve to actively reform a variety of corrupt types such as the "imperious peer," the "venal commoner," or the "proud-puffed Rector."[66] The *Volunteer Journal*, established in Cork in 1782, was one of several newspapers to align itself with the popular movement through both its title and politics. The editor claimed that the paper's emblem, representing Britannia and Hibernia and the phrase "Quis Separabit" (Who shall separate us?) would "best explain [its] political creed." The paper meant to glorify the exploits of the Volunteers and their "steady loyalty to the King, love of order, and manly exertion of every public virtue."[67] The enterprise hoped to appeal to loyal and constitutional patriots. Other papers took a more activist and radical stance. *Volunteer's Journal,* established in Dublin by Mathew Carey, displayed a crowned harp, flanked by two Volunteers and the motto "Libertas et Natale Solum" (Liberty and my native land) (see fig. 1). The editor painted a gloomy picture of the "critical period" the country had reached, when the achievements of the Volunteers were "rendered doubtful by corrupt intrigue" and "a baleful aristocratic influence silently pervade[d] the nation, the object of which [was] to extinguish, if possible, the noble ardour which animate[d] all ranks of Irishmen." However, the *Journal* declared it was a patriotic newspaper "devoted to the great purposes of perpetuating and extending that Public Spirit, to which the nation [stood] so much indebted."[68]

Newspapers went to great lengths to establish their patriotic credentials and particularly to associate themselves with the Volunteers. In the 1780s three newspapers and a short-lived periodical evoked the Volunteers through their titles. The activities of the Volunteers dramatically increased the amount of attention to local news in many papers. Several newspapers proclaimed that they had established an extra news column to report on the activities of the Volunteers. The *Dublin Evening Post* announced such an addition as a means of "conveying the precision, the manly efforts and resolutions of [their] brave determined Volunteers."[69] Such strategies were certainly attempts to meet the demands for news about the Volunteers, while also clearly identifying the paper with the patriot cause. Newspapers were also commercial enterprises, of course, and a patriotic stance was good for business. In the highly competitive world of the press, newspapers struggled to attract advertising and subscribers. Newspaper proprietors hoped to profit from the interest in the Volunteers by carrying detailed reports of their activities. The resolutions of Volunteer corps and a variety of other political organizations also contributed to the revenue of newspapers. The

Figure 1 *Volunteer's Journal* (Dublin) masthead, 1784 (Courtesy of the Library Company of Philadelphia)

Dublin *Volunteer's Journal* is unusual at this time for placing radical political principles above commercial considerations; other newspapers adopted restrained opposition positions that were only rarely considered seditious by the authorities.[70]

Newspapers were usually owned by printers and booksellers as secondary concerns in small-scale family businesses that sold the newspapers by subscription, through street hawkers and booksellers or from their shops. George Faulkner, the proprietor of the *Dublin Journal* from 1725 until his death in 1775, and the publisher of Swift, is a particularly successful and well-connected example of a printer in the newspaper business.[71] Many other ventures throughout the country were more ephemeral, suggesting a highly competitive field that required more than simply plagiarizing the metropolitan press and hoping for the best. While most newspapers were run solely for profit, others had more overtly political agendas. In the 1760s the demagogic popular politician Charles Lucas, influenced by his experiences in London and the tactics of John Wilkes in particular, used the successful *Freeman's Journal* as a vehicle to publicize his patriot campaign and opposition to government. Newspapers such as this were not willing to simply report the "news" but aimed at actively shaping public opinion.

The short and colorful Dublin career of Mathew Carey, although by no means representative, is illustrative of the increased politicization of print culture in the early 1780s. Carey's *Volunteer's Journal* was an overtly political and radical newspaper. The son of a prosperous Catholic baker, Carey was apprenticed to a printer at fifteen. Even before his apprenticeship, he had been actively involved in the world of print as a "voracious reader" of "the history of Pirates, and of the Irish Rogues and Rapparees" and was a member of a circulating library. At seventeen he published his first letter in the press, an attack on the practice of dueling, and in 1779 the mere announcement of his first pamphlet, calling for the complete removal of the penal code against Catholics, caused such a stir that he temporarily fled the country. In exile in Paris, he claimed to have worked for Benjamin Franklin at his printing office at Passy. After returning to Dublin, he was briefly editor of the *Freeman's Journal,* until he established the *Volunteer's Journal* in October 1783. Carey noted the paper "partook largely of the character of its proprietor and editor" and that its "career was enthusiastic and violent." He claimed the paper was a success, with only the *Dublin Evening Post* enjoying a greater circulation, though Carey seems to have lost money on the venture. It was certainly controversial, and the *Journal's* calls for violence against leading government figures soon attracted the attention of the authorities. In September 1784, after a stay in Newgate, Carey again decided to go into exile to avoid prosecution. Disguised as a woman, he boarded a ship to Philadelphia.[72]

As the hounding of Carey suggests, in the 1780s the government became increasingly concerned with the politics of the press. Officials saw newspapers as a pernicious influence on the public and took a keen interest in their contents. In May 1779 Buckinghamshire complained of "the insinuations which [were] daily circulated in the daily prints" that he held responsible for the continuing rise of the Volunteers.[73] By late 1781 the government attempted to acquire funds to exert direct influence over the press, but funds were not forthcoming. In September the chief secretary, William Eden, informed Lord North, "[I regret that] your Lordship has not found any means to assist us in the article of secret service. The press is the principal operative power in the government of this kingdom; and we are utterly without means to influence that power."[74] By the 1780s the tone of some newspapers, particularly the *Volunteer's Journal,* alarmed the administration. Writing to Northington, Sheridan described the scene in near apocalyptic terms: "The press daily teems with the most infamous publications in order to inflame or mislead the people and to root out of their minds all those ideas of order, decency, and obedience without which it is impossible for civilized society to exist."[75]

This was not mere hyperbole. In April the *Volunteer's Journal* had published a cartoon imagining the death of the attorney general, John Scott, as well as advocating his tarring and feathering. Other papers in the capital, such as the *Dublin Evening Post*, also supported radical reform. This open sedition resulted in a sustained campaign by the government against the press, with a wave of arrests and prosecutions against printers and proprietors, as well as new legislation to limit the freedom of the press.[76] In November the lord lieutenant, the Duke of Rutland, informed London that "the excessive licentiousness of the press had not confined itself to the abuse of individuals, or the free discussion of public measures. The public papers had strained their ingenuity and invention to excite commotion, to resist the authority of the legislature, and to subvert the constitution of Church and State."[77] As well as buying off a number of opposition papers, such as the *Freeman's Journal*, in 1782 the government appears to have been involved in the establishment of the *Volunteer Evening Post*, which, it was hoped, would influence opinion in the capital. This paper was unpopular and short lived.[78] Throughout the 1780s many newspapers increasingly came under government control. Certainly, then, the government believed that the press was a powerful force in shaping public opinion, even a threat to order, particularly in Dublin.

Beyond the Newspaper: Pamphlets, Ballads, and Prints

Apart from the newspaper press, several other forms of literature, such as pamphlets, ballads, and handbills, figured in the distribution of political information and argument. Pamphlet literature has long been central to the study of public opinion in eighteenth-century Ireland, though its impact and audience have been hard to gauge.[79] Major political controversies frequently led to a pamphlet "war." The money bill dispute of 1753–54, for example, not only politicized the press and led to the creation of several patriot clubs but in 1754 alone also generated over seventy pamphlets, a literature aimed at a wide audience.[80] As a representative of the barber-surgeons and an unlikely MP for Dublin, the irrepressible Charles Lucas scribbled a vast number of tracts from the 1740s until his death in 1771 on his struggles with the Dublin Corporation as well as on national questions and more-personal obsessions. His writing in turn inspired responses from his opponents. Many of these works were brief, polemical, and often scurrilous, and certainly aimed at a wider audience than the parliamentary elite that other longer, more expensive, and politely argued writings had in mind.[81] The disputes Lucas inspired generated widespread interest. *A Second*

Address to the Citizens of Dublin by Lucas's political competitor, James La Touche, published in 1749, sold possibly nine hundred copies.[82] Other issues likewise produced a profusion of pamphlet literature. The campaign for free trade spawned an outpouring of political pamphlets in 1779.[83] In the pamphlet war of 1786–88, *The Present State of the Church of Ireland*, by Richard Woodward, bishop of Cloyne, went into multiple editions. And in the 1790s the first three editions of Paine's *Rights of Man* involved a print run of perhaps ten thousand copies, despite serialization in all the main newspapers.[84]

Notwithstanding such controversies, most historians have argued that pamphlet literature was a relatively exclusive medium appealing only to the political elite in Dublin, along with clergymen, professionals, and some merchants mainly in Dublin and Belfast. Stephen Small argues that the price of pamphlets, between six pence and a shilling, but rising as high as three shillings, meant that most pamphlets were intended for a limited audience.[85] Most pamphlets certainly had very small print runs of a few hundred copies or less. But from 1774 onward there is a clear quantitative increase in the number of broadly political pamphlets produced, with about one hundred pamphlets published annually on a variety of issues, and contentious political issues during the proceeding decade creating a number of small-scale pamphlet wars.[86] These pamphlets, such as *A Plain and Affectionate Address to the Shopkeepers, Manufacturers, Artificers, and Traders of this City and Kingdom* (1780), were often shorter and less dense than previous texts, easier to read than the tightly packed font of many of Lucas's works, and usually aimed at a readership lower down the social scale.

The government certainly believed that pamphlets were a significant form of communication and employed writers to respond to opposition arguments. Government officials closely followed the impact of particular pamphlets. At the commencement of the "renunciation dispute" in 1782, John Beresford informed Eden that Henry Flood had published his speeches on the subject and that it was "sent to all parts of the kingdom, and [would] have its operation."[87] Many of these pamphlets found a wider audience through immediate serialization in periodicals such as the *Hibernian Magazine*, as well as in a number of newspapers, creating a readership far beyond the exclusive realm of relatively expensive pamphlets. Like all forms of print culture in the eighteenth century, political pamphlets were reprinted, extracted, summarized, reviewed, and plagiarized in a variety of different media, making them more widely available than is often assumed, even before the 1790s. Some pamphlets were sold for as little as a penny, such as *A Letter to a*

Friend, on Those Caballistic Words Repeal and Renounce, published in 1782. The same year, William Molyneux's *Case of Ireland Stated* was reprinted and sold for six pence to encourage its widespread distribution.[88] Coffeehouses and taverns publicized the availability of the latest pamphlets in their establishments, providing another relatively cheap means of accessing this material. The market for pamphlets reached well beyond Dublin and Belfast by this time through a system of provincial booksellers and, at the lower end of the social scale, chapmen, as well as in the modest but growing number of pamphlets and newspapers produced by provincial printers.[89]

The process of republishing often went in the other direction, particularly from the early 1770s, with many popular or influential series of letters in the press reprinted in pamphlet form.[90] Such pamphlets often reconstructed debates that had first taken place in the press between a variety of pseudonymous correspondents.[91] The pamphlet was seen as more permanent and prestigious compared to the ephemeral nature of the newspaper. Discussing a letter to the press by the reformer William Todd Jones, whom she admired, Martha McTier wished the letter "should not have died away in one newspaper like any common information." Rather, she believed, the letter should have been given "consequence" and reprinted in pamphlet form by the Dublin Constitutional Society.[92] She gave similar advice to her brother, William Drennan, as his letters under the name of an "Irish Helot" were printed in the press in 1784, suggesting that he "let the papers be collected *all* and distributed before the convention" in order to preserve the arguments and enhance Drennan's literary and political reputation.[93] Drennan believed that complicated political arguments were more suited to pamphlets and periodicals. Likewise, discussing the plans for the publication of a new political essay in a letter to William Bruce, he doubted whether publication in the newspapers would give the essay "that air of authority which might mark it with distinction." Essays in the press, he claimed, were more likely to go unread, where "they always appear[ed] longer and more tedious than in any other place." The context in which newspaper reading took place partly explained this difficulty. The bustle of company meant that readers could "only piddle at paragraphs in a Coffee-room." Even at home, he believed, there was a "certain repulsion" in reading newspapers' essays, which might be consumed if published in the more authoritative pamphlet form.[94]

Institutions emerged that allowed greater access to print culture for those who could not afford to buy expensive books or pamphlets. Circulating libraries were established in Dublin in the 1750s but became firmly established in the 1770s, with as many as a dozen booksellers or printers advertising volumes for hire; one of these was run by a Catholic bookseller and printer, James Hoey. Stephen Colbert claimed to have over three thousand volumes in his library, with others advertising equally impressive collections.[95] At the same time, as J. R. R. Adams has shown, similar establishments were emerging in Belfast, as well as other provincial towns in the North. Books could be rented individually at some libraries, but many required an annual or monthly subscription. In the North, reading societies proliferated from the 1770s onward, providing another form of literate sociability in an associational context.[96]

The pamphlet market in Dublin was largely dominated by printers whom the historian of this trade, James Phillips, describes as the "irregulars." These printers made up a shadowy world outside the luxury and respectable trade of master printers and booksellers. Producing cheap pamphlets, chapbooks, and broadsides, as well as short-lived newspapers, they were responsible for supplying much of the ephemera for the Dublin and country markets. Phillips suggests that many of these printers were journeymen taking advantage of political controversies in the hope of establishing themselves independently. Such businesses were economically unstable and often fleeting but multiplied during times of political crisis, pouring out a stream of political pamphlets, feeding demand, and fueling controversy. The number of these businesses increased rapidly during crises such as the conflict over "Wood's halfpence" or Lucas's many scuffles in the 1750s, reaching a peak in 1782.[97] Such printers, largely located on Mountrath Street, supplied the hawkers.[98]

Ballads and other ephemeral printed material hawked by such figures were also a source of news and entertainment. Single sheets containing lampoons and squibs of opposing political candidates in song and verse were distributed during election campaigns. Although little of this material survives, the County Down election of 1783 produced an outpouring of such writing that suggests the ways in which this local, often scurrilous printed matter intersected with national issues. It also suggests the dynamism of print.[99] In this contest, in which the representative of the "independent interest,"' Robert Stewart, was defeated by Lord Hillsborough's candidates, humorous ballads mocked both sides. A particularly popular ballad, "The Sheep-Sheering," probably composed by William Drennan, accused John Blackwood, a supporter of the Hill interest, of controlling the votes of his tenants:

You know silly Sheep, that at ev'ry Election,
You are blindly to follow your Shepard's direction,
Observe, then, *my* will, if you mean to be *Free,*
And beware of all Wolves—but my Bailiff and me.

Another ballad, "The New Doddle Doo," developed a similar theme of the overbearing power of local elites on the electorate:

Have you been at the Down Election?
Where each Man shew'd *Due Subjection,*
To *their Lord,* for his Protection.

Political ballads were often rather scurrilous; "The New Doddle Doo" attacked a variety of local figures, describing one "B——rch" as a "trust betrayer," "a noted pimp," and a "pulpit brayer," among other insults.[100] At the same time, these election songs and squibs offered cheap means of propagating an ideological vision of a virtuous independent interest battling against powerful and tyrannical landed interests that exerted a domineering influence over the votes of their tenants.

Ballads were printed in newspapers, on single sheets, or collected in chapbooks. A variety of chapbooks were printed in provincial towns from the 1770s onward, focusing on local events, places, and personalities. These sources provide some of the most colorful accounts of urban culture outside Dublin. Ballads were sold in the country by traveling chapmen to ballad singers, who then performed them throughout the region. Daniel Carpenter of Newry was one of the principal printers of this genre. The subject matter of the ballads he printed ranged from celebrations of the Volunteers to accounts of British naval victories, as well as eulogies to ale and the local tavern culture of the town.[101] The market for ballads underscores the complex relations between print and popular culture. The culture of print did not simply replace "traditional" forms of culture such as the oral tradition of song, but rather became implicated in the commercialization of such popular forms as the ballad and institutions such as the alehouse.[102]

Visual culture in eighteenth-century Ireland, and the production and consumption of prints in particular, has been largely ignored, and this study attempts to take seriously the variety of political engravings produced in Dublin during these period. Although the relationship between politics and "visual ways of knowing" has received some attention, such work has focused largely on portraiture and history painting rather than on the more ephemeral print.[103] The Dublin market supported an impressive number of engravers and print sellers catering to a range of tastes. The leading scholar of political prints has argued that "Dublin prints, many of them vulgar, were for the most part social rather than political in character."[104] Indeed, picturesque scenes of the lakes of Killarney and portraits of well-known actresses seem to have dominated the market.[105] However, at the same time, a lively market for patriotic and political prints also flourished. While Nicholas Robinson is correct to assert that this print industry was in large part based on the pirating of London prints, momentous events such as the campaign for free trade and the rise of the Volunteers created a market for prints related to local political issues, not simply beholden to the magnetism of London's political scene. William Allen's print shop on Dame Street seems to have been the most productive in the city, but Isaac Colles of Capel Street, publisher of the *Freeman's Journal* beginning in 1779, and a relatively large number of engravers and print sellers competed for the market in prints throughout the 1770s and 1780s.[106]

Prints were sold individually from shops or by hawkers, and many were included in periodicals such as the *Hibernian Magazine* and Exshaw's appropriation of the *Gentleman's and London Magazine*. Alongside London prints, these periodicals included prints on imperial, English, and Irish themes, emphasizing those "beautifully engraved by the Irish artists."[107] Empire was represented through figures such as Admiral Rodney and George Washington, or representations of the inhabitants of Dusky Bay from the voyages of Cook. Prints satirizing the women at Coxheath military camp or celebrating Admiral Keppel's acquittal reflected English themes that resonated with Irish audiences. Prints produced specifically for Irish consumption included images of opposition politicians and Irish patriot heroes such as Henry Grattan and the Earl of Charlemont, often influenced by representations of the heroes of the American Revolution.[108] In a move based perhaps as much in economy as flattery, a print of the radical Napper Tandy published in 1784 made rather literal connections between Irish radicals and American heroes; the government-supported *Freeman's Journal* claimed that the print was produced by simply rubbing out the head of George Washington from an old plate and adding the head of Tandy to Washington's body, leading the paper to wryly note, "He now makes so *capital* a figure on the body of the transatlantic hero."[109] Volunteer engravings proved particularly popular.[110] Other prints were more specifically political and patriotic in purpose, such as the anti-English critique of jobbery, "The Englishman in Dublin Gaping for Preferment," by Handy Pemberton, a radical patriot, produced for the *Hibernian Magazine* in 1783.[111] Many satirical prints of contemporary political figures were also produced. In 1780 the *Dublin Evening Post* advertised "Hibernia Unshackled; or the Volunteers Revenged," which attacked two politicians described as "notorious deserters from the cause of liberty."[112]

What was the market for these prints? With some exceptions, print runs were small in London and probably smaller still for the Dublin market. At around 6d. a sheet, or 1s. colored, the print was not, for most, an item of casual consumption. Elites certainly collected prints, with Lady Louisa Conolly establishing a special print room to display her collection at Castletown House, County Kildare.[113] The production of many prints in Dublin relied on subscriptions. By the middle decades of the century, engravings were to be found in the homes of the less elevated.[114] In 1785 Martha McTier instructed her brother, William Drennan, to buy her "some rural prints, cottage-like or some good ballads, fit to line [her] porch," on his next trip.[115] It is difficult to estimate the number of prints produced and sold in Dublin or who the market for such items might have been. While engravings of rural scenes, portraits, and devotional images were produced for a broader market, some historians claim that the political print in particular was hardly an item of "popular" consumption and "made its appeal to a limited circle."[116] However, from the 1770s onward, engravings representing patriot themes or satirizing politicians and government figures were widely distributed. Although print runs were limited, a print such as "Paddy's Resource," produced in the course of the free-trade dispute, was extensively circulated and available from hawkers and also referenced and reproduced in later prints and other texts.[117] Political and patriot prints were also sold outside Dublin and advertised in provincial newspapers.[118] Prints were not cheap, but the viewing of such items was not simply the preserve of elites. Prints were sold to be displayed within the home, but they could also be viewed in a variety of other contexts, such as in coffeehouses or the homes of social superiors. Engravers adapted the same print to several different markets. For example, Edward Lyons, an engraver on Essex Street, advertised a print of the Reverend John Murphy in a variety of sizes for those unable to afford the original large print, which had been sold by subscription. The new prints were also intended to "defeat the base designs of those . . . threatening to pyrate" his original work.[119] A print from *Exshaw's Magazine* depicts a scene outside the shop of the print seller William Allen on Dame Street (see fig. 2). Images of crowds gaping at print-shop windows were a minor genre in themselves and "are not necessarily any more verisimilitudnous than

Figure 2 *View of a Print Shop, Exshaw's Magazine,* 1780 (Courtesy of the Board of Trinity College Dublin)

other representations of Georgian 'street life.'"[120] With this warning in mind, one might conclude from the print that a variety of people, from the fashionable to the criminal, could view the latest prints as displayed in the windows of various print sellers throughout the city. The prints displayed, along with surviving prints and advertisements, depict military, political, sexual, and domestic themes, with portraiture seeming to dominate. Indeed, many of the prints depicted in Allen's window are identifiable as ones actually printed by the shop, suggesting that this enterprise was more than simply the pirating of a London genre.[121]

Public displays of prints were prominent enough to cause controversy and offend polite sensibilities. In 1755 the Lord Mayor "made a general search at the Print Shops, and tore in pieces all the indecent obscene figures he found." The *Hibernian Journal* noted in 1780 that a Dublin magistrate had once again taken exception to a print in the window of Allen's shop. A satirical poem on the magistrate noted that while walking through the town "A Croud in Dame-Street he espied / At comic Pictures gazing." The paper described how this "intrepid and sentimental Praetor of [the] City" was upset by a scatological print of an engagement between Admiral Keppel and D'Orvilliers that included "the unpardonable Obscenity of shewing the Anus of a French

Admiral."[122] Prints were more numerous and widespread than has been previously allowed and, from the 1770s, were an important aspect in the commercialization of Irish political culture.

The press in the 1770s and 1780s served as a vehicle of politicization outside the metropolitan world of Dublin and reached beyond the realm of the elite and middle-class readers to those at the lower end of the social scale. Improved communications and a wider variety of institutions supporting the distribution of the press facilitated access to newspapers, pamphlets, and other cheap forms of print. These sites of sociability, along with the rituals of reading the press, promoted a particular and highly mediated understanding of the political community and the national interest. This phenomenon was effected not simply through explicit political argument but also in the more mundane and commonplace reporting of the spectacular politics of the Volunteers on the street or review field. The press was deeply implicated in the performance and practice of patriotism. The next chapter examines this intersection between print and practice in more detail, focusing on the celebratory politics of the street.

"Paddy Shall Rise"

Celebration, Commemoration, and National Identity

IN JULY AND AUGUST 1780, fresh from their successful agitation for free trade the previous year, Volunteer companies across the country gathered to honor the "dense cluster" of significant moments in the Irish Protestant commemorative calendar. On the anniversary of the battle of the Boyne, newspapers reported the unlikely sight of Catholic "gentlemen" of the Drogheda Association parading to the tune of "King William over the Water" while wearing orange cockades in their hats in celebration of the day.[1] King's County Volunteer companies— from Eglish, Leap, Birr and Shinrone, and Durrow—assembled near Birr to commemorate the battle of Aughrim with an elaborate mock battle.[2] In Derry, the lifting of the siege was commemorated by the Derry Battalion, which marched to the cathedral to hear a sermon by Rev. Harrison Balfour—the chaplain of the Londonderry Fusiliers— before engaging in a review and returning to the Diamond, where they fired three volleys in honor of the day.[3] In the midst of these commemorations, the *Dublin Evening Post* noted that traditionally "certain anniversaries frequently fomented divisions and hatred, or opened old sores which had been healing." However, in recent years the "spirit of party and of bitterness is no longer seen even in our anniversary celebrations," so that "persons of every denomination may now cheerfully join in doing honour to such days as recall events that have been favorable to liberty and property, or the establishment of a free and legal constitution."[4] With varying degrees of intensity and enthusiasm, the battle of the Boyne (1 July 1690 OS), the battle of Aughrim (12 July 1691 OS), and the lifting of the siege of Derry (1 August 1689 OS) were celebrated as part of a plebian Protestant culture.[5] Yet, as the participation of Catholics in the Boyne events and the comments of the *Post* suggest, by 1780 such commemorations were not regarded as purely sectarian triumphalist occasions. Rather they could serve as expressions of a united "national" interest, particularly in the wake of the victorious campaign for free trade. As with the memory of William, the key events of the Williamite revolution were increasingly commemorated as part of the tradition of liberty and toleration rather than one of domination and sectarianism.[6]

State-sponsored commemorations and celebrations, such as the commemoration of the rising of 1641 (23 October OS), were opportunities to promote traditional understandings of deference and authority through hierarchical processions, spectacular display, and the benevolent distribution of food and alcohol. As research on social memory and commemoration in Ireland by Guy Beiner and others suggests, popular plebian forms of commemoration offered alternative ways of remembering and challenged the historical narratives of the past proposed in the rituals and ceremonies of the state.[7] This popular social memory was manifested not only through the Jacobite counternarrative to the anxiety-tinged triumphalism of Williamite festivities but also in disputes over the meaning of the past among Protestants based on differences in both social class and religious denomination. Public rituals of commemoration and celebration could also be created or appropriated by the opposition, or even by "the people," as forms of protest through which ideas of "the nation" were mobilized to express alternative understandings of government authority, history, or the limits of the Irish polity. The streets of the capital were sites of intense political conflict in the late 1770s and early 1780s, where the staging of dramatic rituals allowed patriots to oppose the government and to articulate different notions of the political nation and the public interest. Parades, illuminations, bonfires, effigies, toasts, and the elaborate transparencies and other symbols that decorated buildings—all communicated political meanings just as surely as the patriotic press.[8]

This chapter examines the general features of Protestant public festivities in eighteenth-century Ireland. It does so first by focusing on the act of toasting as a means of expressing political sentiment through the ritualized consumption of alcohol. It then examines in detail two national celebrations and a protest during the annual commemoration of

King William III. The first celebration marked the acquittal of Admiral Augustus Keppel in February 1779 in his court-martial for misconduct and neglect in a famous engagement with the French fleet at Ushant off the French port of Brest in July of the previous year. The month of November 1779 saw the first foray of the Volunteers into national politics, with their hijacking of the annual commemoration of William III in order to demand "free trade" for Ireland. The second major celebration marked the patriot victory on this issue, with the granting of free trade by Lord North.[9] The extraordinary outpouring of joy on the acquittal of Keppel illustrates the British and imperial dimensions of Irish Protestant patriot culture. The acquittal also offered an opportunity to denounce the British government. The examination of the Volunteer protest and the free-trade festivities suggests how patriotic ideology was increasingly defined in opposition to British policies and associated with the articulation of an "Irish" identity. These two events also draw attention to the way in which celebratory and commemorative festivities, through symbols and gestures, articulated political arguments. Just as print culture was mobilized by patriots to evoke particular understandings of the nation that drew on a variety of political ideologies and historical narratives, these rites employed a disparate range of symbols that suggested a variety of identifications—with the British Empire, Orangeism, Irishness, and even Gaelic culture. During the years 1779–80 these events served as occasions for the discursive construction of patriotism and "the nation" in the public domain; these acts of construction were negotiated by a national audience.[10] This chapter also draws attention to the ways in which such symbolic action was central to the transformation of political participation in eighteenth-century Ireland by allowing a broader section of the population to identity with the patriot cause.[11]

Commemorations, as a means of mobilizing and articulating Irish Protestant understandings of history and as sites of ideological conflict, have received increased attention in recent years.[12] These events offered opportunities for large numbers of people from all walks of life to publicly express their allegiances through symbols, gestures, and even their mere presence. They generated impressive crowds not only in Dublin but also throughout the country. Those who did reflect on these forms of collective action leave little doubt that they believed them to be emotionally charged and "historic" moments. Both spectators and those involved more directly as participants in parades and military reviews had a sense of their own "historical agency" at these performances. The description of the formal elements of these events—the actions and gestures of the crowds, the flags flown, the music played, the symbols displayed—all provide important evidence of the types of arguments that participants hoped to make on these occasions.[13]

The rise of the patriot movement and the Volunteers in the late 1770s multiplied opportunities for participating in popular festivities throughout the country. While few were left untouched by such events, they would also experience them, or sometimes re-experience them, through the steady stream of newspaper accounts of particular celebrations and commemorations. Anyone who reads a late eighteenth-century Irish newspaper cannot fail to be struck by the routine reporting of the extraordinary variety of local rituals that made up this rich commemorative and celebratory calendar. Accounts of festivities in the press might be quite detailed, drawing attention to the wide range of symbols employed while also reflecting on their meaning and the wider significance of the occasion. For example, in 1780 the *Dublin Evening Post* provided a long report of St. Patrick's Day festivities in Dublin:

> Never were more honours paid to the memory of St. Patrick than yesterday: all sorts and sizes seemed emulous to distinguish themselves. Our cathedrals threw open their doors, and the oratory of the preacher was applied to him. The bells diffused their harmony; the mouths of both great and small guns were opened to shew forth his praise. The military processions, the shamrock cockades, were highly agreeable to every true-born Irishman; but particularly [agreeable were] the Goldsmiths and Colonel Talbot's Corps of Volunteers assembled on their parade, from whence they marched to Ranelagh, where they went through their evolutions, &c., with the greatest exactness; after which they returned to town and dined together. In the evening bonfires blazed with universal lustre; squibs and crackers bounced about with surprising velocity in their motion; numerous and jolly were our merry meetings, loyal and patriotic our toasts. At the conclusion of the busy scene our honest fellows were either all alive or dead drunk in honour of our hero.[14]

Radical newspapers such as the *Dublin Evening Post* were often eager to portray the unity, order, and goodwill of such gatherings of "true-born Irishmen" and to evoke the emotiveness of these occasions. Reports of some annual events (such as the commemoration of the battle of the Boyne or the king's birthday) were often more prosaic, noting simply that celebrations included "bonfires, illuminations, &c." and that "the whole concluded with the greatest joy and festivity."[15]

This relentless description of public festivities in newspapers is, of course, a main source for this account of street politics. At the same time, such descriptions are not simply windows into the actual experience and meaning of these events. As David Waldstreicher argues in his study of nationalism and ritual in the wake of the American Revolution, historians must pay attention to "the printed discourse that surrounded these events and gave them extra-local meaning." Just as festivities evoked strategic understandings of the nation, newspaper reports did not simply describe events but also transformed and nationalized scores of local rituals. Newspapers emphasized that while these celebrations might be spatially separate, they were simultaneous in time and unity of national sentiment.[16]

Protestant Rites, British and Irish

Eighteenth-century Ireland accommodated a wide range of public festivals and commemorations. These resolutely Protestant occasions recalled "national" deliverances of the seventeenth century, with King William III and the Glorious Revolution taking center stage. The Hanoverian monarchy was also the focus of a variety of celebrations. By 1760 as many as twenty days were given over to the commemoration of men and events central to forging and maintaining Protestant hegemony.[17] The form and the appeal of such occasions varied according to the specific figures and ideas that the day invoked. For example, 4 November—the birthday of William III—was central to state-sponsored ceremonials consisting of a levee at Dublin Castle, followed by a formal procession of the lord lieutenant, members of the administration, and other notables through the city. By contrast, 1 July served as the occasion for a more "popular" Protestant celebration consisting of drinking and bonfires uninhibited by state formalities.[18] This calendar was not static. James Kelly notes that these events became increasingly contested and controversial in the charged political atmosphere of the 1770s. New commemorations and celebrations were incorporated into the calendar, and old ones were transformed in their meaning and expression. Apart from the celebration of royal anniversaries and Protestant deliverances, a variety of other occasions provoked either state-sponsored or "popular" festivities. Significant events in local, national, or imperial politics sparked demonstrations of joy. Besides the festivities ignited by such charged events as the trial and acquittal of Admiral Keppel, other events, including local elections, British military victories, and the passage of important bills in Parliament, provoked rounds of celebrations with particular forms and symbols.

Central to any festive occasion were numerous toasts. They were made daily at such venues as taverns, public celebrations, and banquets.[19] The noted English writer Horace Walpole claimed that the Irish, and the Volunteers in particular, were addicted to the practice. The Trinity-educated lawyer Jonah Barrington, recalling Irish forms of masculine sociability in the 1770s, noted that "numerous toasts, as was customary in those days, intervened to prolong and give zest to each repast—every man shouted forth his favourite or convivial pledge; and each voluntarily surrendered a portion of his own reason in bumpers to the beauty of his neighbour's toast."[20] Toasting was a symbolic act central to the sociability of clubs and societies and served to express the commonality of sentiment among members as well as to articulate more-contentious political opinions. The order and content of the toasts were usually prepared in advance to minimize the risk of disharmony among the group. Toasts offered opportunities for the public expression of political sentiments, both loyal and oppositional. As early as the 1750s, during moments of intense political conflict, long lists of toasts from public festivities were published in the press along with accounts of parades and dinners. The press was a vehicle through which the sentiments contained in toasts acquired extralocal publicity and meanings.[21]

Of course, such acts of speech, especially when fueled by copious amounts of wine and ale in taverns, were unpredictable and often led to seditious words and conflict.[22] Toasts offered opportunities for the expression of royalism, or radical patriot opposition, or even Jacobitism and other seditious sentiments. In 1777 a Dublin man was tried for drinking a toast to "General Washington and downfall to the ministry [of Lord North]," although the prosecution was ultimately unsuccessful.[23] Edward Newenham, the radical MP, worried about the allegiance of "certain men" after attending an election campaign in Kilkenny city in 1778: "The tunes their pipes played and the toasts they gave were as good evidence [of disloyalty] as if given under their hands."[24] Toasts served as a particularly sensitive and public register of political sentiment. The variety of persons, events, institutions, and ideas that were toasted attest to the range of figures and ideas central to Irish patriotism in the 1770s and 1780s, while at the same time pointing to the limitations of this ideology. The Volunteers harnessed the toast as both a rite

of masculine sociability and a means of publicly expressing understandings of "the nation." Volunteer ritual, as reported in the press,
followed a well-established routine. The company would first parade
in public, going through their different "firings and evolutions," and
then retire to a local inn to dine and drink, followed by a prolonged
period of toasting—all conducted with "the greatest cheerfulness and
regularity."[25]

The number of toasts might run as high as forty. The actual toasts
proposed demonstrate the many strands of Protestant patriotism in late
eighteenth-century Ireland as well as the centrality of a shared British
political culture. Countless toasts rehearsed the commemorative calendar of Irish patriotism.[26] The king and the royal family were traditionally proposed as the first toast. The cults of King William III and the
Glorious Revolution were the focus of numerous toasts. Whig heroes
and martyrs, such as Hampden, Russell, and Sydney, were commonly
evoked. Toasts also became a vehicle for the creation of a new pantheon
of patriot heroes. The famous London radical John Wilkes, for example,
figured in many toasts for his efforts to secure British electoral reform.
Often described as the "Irish Wilkes," the patriot Charles Lucas was
also often toasted, as was Lord Charlemont, the commander of the Volunteers. British opposition politicians regarded as friends of Ireland
and liberty, such as the Marquis of Rockingham and the Earl of Shelburne, were often added to this list. Recent patriot victories, such as the
granting of a free trade, were quickly incorporated into a calendar already saturated with political commemorations.

More contentious matters, such as the American conflict, were also
frequently remembered. In Limerick city the celebrations over the concession of free trade began with "loyal toasts" to the king but concluded with more disturbing sentiments: "May England or Ireland
never feel the horrors of a civil war. The exports of Ireland. Peace with
America and war with all the world."[27] Volunteers in Enniskillen celebrating the Boyne victory on 1 July expressed their hope for "a speedy
reconciliation between Great Britain and America."[28] The imperial conflict inspired toasts predicting the defeat of Britain's "natural enemies"
France and Spain, though attitudes to the rebellious colonies were more
ambivalent. The commemoration of an election victory for the "independent" interest in County Down in June 1779 toasted peace with
America "and a hearty drubbing to the French."[29] Lord Charlemont's
Volunteers at Armagh also wished for peace while declaring their desire that "Frenchmen never be masters, nor Americans slaves, of Great

Britain."[30] Memories of imperial victories were evoked through the names of British admirals, such as John Byron and Edward Hawke, suggesting the importance of the vicissitudes of empire to Irish Protestants. Byron, who commanded the West Indies fleet, was worsted off Grenada in 1779. Hawke had failed to destroy a French convoy bound for America in 1758, though he redeemed himself with a signal victory over the French at Quiberon Bay in November 1759.

Merit Rewarded, or the Brave Keppel in Triumph

The names and fate of admirals could also provoke other forms of public demonstrations. Imperial conflict and the trial and acquittal of a prominent admiral provoked one of the largest demonstrations of national jubilation in eighteenth-century Ireland. On 11 February 1779 Admiral Augustus Keppel was honorably acquitted after court-martial proceedings that gripped the public in both Ireland and Britain. Keppel had become involved in a public dispute with one of his officers, Hugh Palliser, over the handling of an engagement with the French fleet off Ushant in July 1778. Because Keppel was a Rockingham Whig, his cause was quickly taken up by the opposition in England and provoked acrimonious debate in the press and on the streets.[31] Keppel's trial also provoked similarly intense interest in Ireland. Coverage of the trial itself demonstrates the increasingly central role of newspapers in constructing and interpreting events and the intensified national penetration of the press in the late 1770s and early 1780s. Full accounts of the trial dominated Dublin and provincial newspapers throughout February 1779, often at the expense of local and national news. Special supplements were often added to accommodate expanded coverage. Palliser's trial the following May merited almost as much attention. The commercial opportunities afforded by the trial and the subsequent public acclaim for Keppel were quickly exploited in Ireland. Ballads and prints celebrating Keppel and denigrating Palliser and the North ministry were frequently printed over the course of the trial. The *Hibernian Magazine* produced a print of the admiral and a brief sketch of his achievements. A print of Keppel titled *Merit Rewarded, or the Brave Keppel in Triumph* was "engraved by Irish artists" in Dublin and advertised in Belfast (see fig. 3).[32] The print depicts a jubilant Keppel being chaired through the streets by honest sailors, while his accusers and enemies are tormented by demons. Accounts of the judicial proceedings were

MERIT rewarded or the BRAVE KEPPEL in Triumph

Figure 3 *Merit Rewarded, or the Brave Keppel in Triumph,* 1780 (Courtesy of the National Library of Ireland)

published in Dublin shortly after the verdict and were also advertised for sale by Henry Joy in the *Belfast News-Letter.*[33]

While the trial demonstrates the importance of the press, the national celebrations that followed his acquittal show how even a figure like Keppel, an aristocratic British admiral, could be appropriated by opposition politicians in Ireland to protest against the government and British restrictions on Irish trade through theatrical street performances. Even before the verdict had been announced, Keppel's acquittal had been widely anticipated, and in many parts of Britain plans for a celebration were well under way—a circumstance explaining some of the more elaborate devices that immediately appeared in many towns.[34] The news of his acquittal, reaching Ireland a few days after it was announced in Portsmouth, was greeted with jubilation. Rejoicing occurred throughout the country, but the scenes of celebration were particularly fervent and elaborate in Dublin. The press emphasized the size of the crowds and their representativeness of the city as a whole. One newspaper commented that the "throngs of people in the streets rendered them almost impassible." The festivities brought a cross-section of society onto the streets: "The lower kind of people with acclamation gave full proof of their approbation, whilst the most respectable concourse of citizens ever known paraded through the city to testify their joy of this happy and desirable event."[35]

One observer of the pandemonium in Dublin declared, "Every street, lane, and alley vied with each other in a profusion of illumination and bonfires." The *Freeman's Journal* reported that "the NAME of KEPPEL appeared in the midst of transparent lights in various parts of the city—in others the figure of sailors and ships firing at each [other]," along with the words "KEPPEL" and "VICTORY." On Grafton Street "a very large fire was made, on the top of which was placed an effigy of Sir Hugh Palliser, and [it was] consumed amid the joyful acclamations of surrounding thousands." On the same street, Adams's toy shop displayed transparencies of Palliser suspended from a gallows, with "his diabolical friends attending to him." A house on Dame Street displayed a similar image, while all the "fashionable houses" were also finely illuminated. Nearby Stephen's Green became "a great illuminated square." King William's statue on College Green was "struck round with flambeaus, and such a number of lights were [*sic*] exhibited from thence to the Royal Exchange as seemed to turn the night into day." The Exchange itself was decorated with colored lamps "with such taste as rendered the whole a beautiful spectacle."

The celebration was not confined to the decoration of streets and buildings. From the Exchange to Essex Bridge, "and along the several quays . . . the reflection of the lights from the water perhaps could not be equalled in his majesty's dominions!" On the Liffey between the Queen's Bridge and the Old Bridge, a "floating bonfire" had also been constructed by attaching pitch barrels to a raft. The patriot press was eager to make clear that this popular jubilation was sharply different from the feelings of the government. The *Hibernian Journal* noted sardonically that the contrast with "the neighbouring darkness of the Castle," home of the British administration in Ireland, only added to the scene, while the *Freeman's Journal* commented that the building "resembled the deserted Castle of Otranto," thereby emphasizing the importance of illuminations as a public register of political sentiment.[36]

This spectacular celebration of an English admiral in Dublin, illuminating the whole city in a "brilliant scene" from Stephen's Green down to the quays, exemplifies the centrality of street politics and popular celebration in eighteenth-century Ireland. Political experience was not confined to the individual reading of printed texts. Sights and sounds, the emotional aspects of involvement in festive occasions, were central to the way in which people encountered and participated in the political life of the nation.[37] The urban landscape at times resembled a battleground where political disputes were played out through the mobilization of rival symbols and rituals. Public rituals might serve to buttress political authority, but as in the failure of Dublin Castle to join the festivities, it could also serve to illustrate the gap between the sympathies of ordinary people and of those in power. Official political culture vied with the patriot opposition and forms of popular politics for control of the meaning of the urban landscape. Competing groups attempted to fix particular significance to political events such as the acquittal of Keppel through a combination of emotive and cognitive appeals. Scenes like the Keppel celebrations that "seemed to turn night into day" played on the emotions of participants, but such episodes, through the use of textual and allegorical symbols, also made political arguments.[38]

While Dublin witnessed the most impressive celebrations, Keppel's acquittal also sparked festivities in towns throughout the country. Belfast witnessed daytime Volunteer parades, followed in the evening by illuminations, bonfires, and toasts.[39] At Newry there was "great rejoicing," along with bonfires and illuminations.[40] A letter writer from Glaslough, Co. Monaghan, noted that the acquittal "occasioned a most universal and sincere joy" in that town, with local gentlemen meeting at the local inn to drink numerous healths.[41] The town of Donaghadee in County Down was illuminated "in the most conspicuous manner possible." Volunteers paraded the streets and fired volleys, with each followed by three cheers, "as there were a number of sailors present." Like many accounts of the festivities, this report also noted that "amongst the large concourse of people, young and old, there was nothing but cheerfulness and good-humour in every countenance."[42] These assurances, common to most descriptions of oppositional patriot activity in the press, sought to emphasize that such occasions were not an excuse for drunkenness or disorder but rather were models of respectability. Accounts also emphasized that the occasion had inspired national harmony, though as the description of Dublin's celebrations suggests, behind the unity in sentiment there remained a clear divide between the "lower kind of people" and "respectable citizens" in the occupation of festive public space.

Many towns witnessed the ritual execution of Keppel's accuser. At Donaghadee, local "gentlemen" raised a subscription to erect a large gallows at the market house, where, after a procession through the town, the effigy was burned, followed by "loyal and patriotic toasts" at a local inn.[43] At Ballymena, illuminations and bonfires lit up the town, and bells were rung. Crowds assembled to watch the Volunteers parade, and an effigy of Palliser was drawn through the town on a cart and burned. Similarly, at Kildare a mock trial was followed by the burning of an effigy, along with the usual illuminations.[44] Palliser's effigy also received rough treatment in Derry.[45] At Macroom the Volunteers paraded, Palliser was burnt, and the gentlemen of the town provided alcohol for the "common people." The author of this report noted that women played a prominent role in the demonstrations and showed eagerness to take part in "this memorable day."[46] Clubs, societies, and even civic bodies also feted the admiral. At Kilkenny the members of a Masonic lodge wore blue ribbons stamped with the name of Keppel at their meeting, while "bumpers were frequently filled to the health of that brave commander with all the possible honours of masonry."[47] On 24 February 1779 Dublin Corporation presented the admiral with the freedom of the city in a box of "Shilelagh Oak."[48] By the following April, clubs honoring Keppel had also emerged in Dublin.[49] For the next several years, Keppel was repeatedly toasted at patriot and Volunteer gatherings.

But what exactly did Keppel mean in Ireland, and why did his acquittal occasion such exhibitions of joy? The phenomenon of "admirals as heroes" in eighteenth-century Britain and the factors that turned such figures as Edward Vernon and James Wolfe into national icons have received much attention.[50] Vernon had taken Porto Bello from the Spanish in 1739, to great popular acclaim in England; Wolfe had died while his troops famously seized Quebec from the French. Admirals took on a variety of meanings in popular political culture, with their exploits represented as exemplifying several competing political narratives concerning the fate of the nation and the empire. As the celebrations of Keppel's acquittal suggest, naval heroes occupied a similarly eminent place in Irish political culture. In Britain, Keppel was portrayed as both a naval and an opposition hero. On one level, his acquittal was represented as the vindication of an honorable man. But the event was also closely related to existing political divisions, with the trial portrayed by the opposition as a ministerial plot to destroy both Keppel and the very liberties of the nation. The celebration of Keppel throughout Ireland has received little attention from historians, perhaps because it fits uneasily within a framework that has emphasized the emergence of an Irish "national" consciousness. As the similarity of these celebrations in Ireland and Britain suggests, Irish Protestants drew on a common British culture to interpret these events. At the same time, they also viewed these events through the prism of local politics, Anglo-Irish relations, and their own perceived status as second-class citizens of the empire.

In Ireland the personal qualities of Keppel were celebrated in the press and on the streets. The *Hibernian Journal* celebrated the "honest unbought plaudits" and the "unfeigned demonstration of joy for the acquittal of the illustrious Keppel," which were "perhaps the most honourable testimonies that ever were given to the virtue of an individual."[51] The *Dublin Evening Post* claimed that through the celebrations "a regard to injured innocence, to approved courage, and [to] distinguished abilities was thus happily evinced, as well as a just indignation against the agents and implements of corruption."[52] The celebrations were seen as a "small tribute due for the many services he ha[d] done his country, the navy, and state."[53] Keppel was also feted as an imperial hero. The *Freeman's Journal* claimed that the national jubilation was motivated "by a just sense at the merit, bravery, and noble conduct of this illustrious character, whose distinguished spirit of enterprise humbled the enemies of Britain."[54]

The discourse of the navy as a bulwark of empire and of the admiral as defender of liberty against tyrannical ministers loomed large in the language of Keppelite festivities in Ireland. Many newspapers reported the presence of sailors at the festivities and the use of naval imagery in transparencies. The loyalism of the celebrations and connection of naval heroes and the empire were illustrated at Donaghadee, where the Volunteers marched with a band that played such patriotic tunes as "God Save the King," the naval ballad "Britons Strike Home," and "See, the Conquering Hero Comes."[55] These celebrations, along with Irish enthusiasm for the triumphs of the British navy throughout the war, attest to the high regard of the navy in the popular imagination as the safeguard of an "empire of the sea." The naval victories of Admiral George Rodney and others were routinely celebrated by Irish Protestants. Admirals and the fleet were frequently toasted at the meetings of clubs and societies.[56] Imperial heroes, especially those with Irish connections, were also feted. For example, William Blakeney, the elderly governor of Minorca, was celebrated throughout Great Britain and Ireland for holding out for seventy days against the French in 1756 before an honorable surrender. He was favorably contrasted with the supposedly cowardly actions of the reviled Admiral John Byng, who had retreated, leaving the island almost defenseless. (Byng was court-martialed, sentenced to death, and shot in 1757.) Blakeney, born in Limerick, was celebrated in Ireland for both his defense of imperial possessions and his local origins. An ode to him was published in Dublin, while Henry Dell's play on the siege of Minorca was published in Dublin and Cork. In July 1756 Blakeney was given the freedom of Dublin by the corporation and received a gold box for his part in the siege. After his death, the Friendly Brothers of St. Patrick commissioned a statue by Van Nost in his honor on Sackville Mall.[57] The celebration of Keppel's acquittal could be placed within this tradition of the veneration of naval and imperial heroes.

But in many ways Keppel was an unlikely naval hero. Rheumatic and out of service for twelve years, he hardly cut the same triumphant figure as Vernon, especially since the engagement at Ushant had proved inconclusive, despite high hopes of British success. Keppel's real value in Ireland arose from the way in which the trial and acquittal allowed the venting of antiministerial sentiments. Keppel's close association with the Rockingham Whigs allowed the celebrants and newspaper editors to portray the trial as a spiteful ministerial conspiracy against a political opponent. The *Belfast News-Letter* suggested that the celebrations were evidence of a "just indignation against the agents and implements of corruption." In Belfast, along with engaging in bonfires and illuminations, the principal inhabitants "drank many toasts expressive of their sense of such a dark, malicious, and ill-grounded prosecution."[58] Palliser was represented as a corrupt tool of government.[59] Throughout the country, his effigy was paraded through towns, hanged, and burnt on bonfires. As the folklorist Robert St. George observes, in the eighteenth century the use of effigies had deeper meanings beyond the likeness of the figure imitated. The symbolic inversion of the traditional commemorative effigy sometimes served, as it did in this instance, not only to mock the individual but also to "inflict symbolically upon the stuffed or wooden figure a punishment the 'real' person rightfully deserved."[60] The ritual subjection of Palliser to burning in effigy also represented a form of symbolic justice against the British government's pursuit of Keppel and its attack on Irish liberties.

The *Hibernian Journal* explicitly associated Keppel's acquittal with the defense of a Whig tradition of liberty. Alluding to the fact that Keppel's grandfather had arrived in England with William of Orange in 1688, the paper noted the "peculiar propriety" of the illuminations placed around William's statue in Dublin, since "the Keppel family became British subjects on our delivery from arbitrary power."[61] Keppel's fight against the supposed despotism of the British ministry could be understood in the context of a Whig struggle for liberty and, through Keppel's family history, related to the Williamite cult that was particularly strong among Irish Protestants. A few months after Keppel's acquittal, this cult of King William, and the malleability of its meaning in Protestant political culture, also allowed the Volunteers to enter firmly onto the Irish political stage.

Free Trade, or This

On 4 November 1779, King William's birthday, the Volunteers made their first, and perhaps most decisive, intervention in national politics. In the days that followed, newspapers throughout the country provided vivid accounts of their actions. In the morning, the various Volunteer companies of Dublin city and county assembled at Stephen's Green. From there, with drums beating and flags flying, they paraded to College Green, where as many as a thousand Volunteers surrounded the equestrian statue of William (see fig. 4).[62] Here they fired several volleys and discharged a rocket and some small canons. William's horse had been decorated with orange and blue ribbons, and on each of the four sides of the statue's pedestal were what one observer described as "these extraordinary words" in large capital letters:

> SHORT MONEY BILL, A FREE TRADE—OR ELSE.
> THE GLORIOUS REVOLUTION.
> THE RELIEF OF IRELAND.
> THE LOYAL VOLUNTEERS.
> QUINQUAGINTA MILLIA JUNCTA PARATI PRO PATRIA MORI.[63]

The *Dublin Evening Post* asked of this display, "Have not such national appearances also their use?" The paper suggested that now perhaps Great Britain would "learn [Ireland's] sense and resolutions respecting expected commercial privileges or the answer hoped for to [Ireland's] addresses and petitions." The meaning of the demonstration was clear, for the banners around the statue "spoke the most intelligible language; they were suitable hieroglyphics for a year big with the fate of Ireland!"[64]

William's birthday was at the center of state-sponsored commemoration in eighteenth-century Dublin. As the viceroy, the Earl of Buckinghamshire, observed in 1779, "The anniversary of King William III has

Figure 4 Francis Wheatley (1747–1801), *The Dublin Volunteers on College Green*, 4 November 1779, oil on canvas, 175 x 323 cm (Courtesy of the National Gallery of Ireland, Dublin)

always been celebrated in this kingdom with particularly solemnity."[65] By midcentury, several loyalist societies had emerged to promote and organize commemorations of William. A statue of King William, erected in 1701 on College Green, was the focal point for the Williamite cult, but it was also a place where competing interpretations of Irish history and the nature of the political nation could be expressed. The official ceremony traditionally began with the firing of volleys by the army and the ringing of bells, followed by a levee held by the lord lieutenant. After the levee came a procession by the notables of the city from Dublin Castle along streets lined with soldiers through the center of the city. The festivities ended with a procession circling the statue of William three times. Associations in Dublin devoted to the cults of William and the Glorious Revolution, such as the Boyne and Aughrim societies, paraded around the statue on one of the several days commemorating Protestant deliverances. The statue was marked with subversive political slogans and by youthful indiscretions; it suffered many indignities at the hands of Tories, Jacobites, and drunken students, decorated with green boughs and covered in mud and hay, while parts of the statue were broken off on several occasions.[66]

In 1779, however, reports stressed the particular fervor of commemorations, with one paper noting, "Never did the oldest persons among us remember the glorious 4th of November to have been so eminently distinguished. . . . If the scene during the day was busy and beautiful, the evening was brilliant and illustrious. A general illumination took place attended by every mark of real rejoicing. . . . Harmony, affection, and public spirit reigned."[67] It was not only the Volunteers who were involved in this commemoration. The crowds of spectators who attended the parade were described as "almost incredible"; they joined the theatrical protests with their huzzas at each discharge of the Volunteers' guns.[68]

Spectators stressed the order and decorum of the event. Charles Perceval commented that the Volunteers on that day were "extremely expert at military discipline and maneuvers" and made "a most beautiful appearance."[69] The Earl of Buckinghamshire recorded that the Volunteers "concluded the day at different public entertainments, where uncommon libations were made to the glorious memory; they separated quietly without giving any person offence."[70] Newspapers described the display as fitting for both the memory of William III and the dignity of the Volunteers.[71] Similar commemorations, though on a smaller scale, took place across the country. At Lisburn some 110 men of the True Blue Company of that town paraded and fired volleys in honor of the "glorious memory." The commemorations suggested the flexibility of the Williamite cult, with the *Belfast News-Letter* remarking that William was a particularly appropriate object of Volunteer veneration, for he was a monarch "whose heroic spirit led him almost from his birth to become a volunteer in the service of mankind, and to whom this country in particular [was] indebted for its liberty and everything it [held] dear."[72] Keppel could be associated with the cult of William through his ancestry, while William himself could be transformed into the progenitor of volunteering and his memory mobilized to protest against restrictions on Ireland's liberty to trade.

"Paddy Shall Rise": The Rituals of Free Trade

The campaign for free trade had resulted in the politicization of the Volunteer militia force and in considerable activity from those outside the political nation—a combination that forced Lord North to grant trade concessions on 9 December 1779.[73] "Free trade" granted Ireland equal access to markets in the American colonies, the East Indies, and Africa, as well as removing the prohibition on the exportation of items such as wool and glass. On receipt of the news, the press carried accounts of people throughout the country overcome by joy.[74] Many of the celebrations were elaborate, involving large numbers of people, transparencies, emblems, and banners. The announcement of the commercial concessions had been widely anticipated, which probably allowed for advance organization of festivities. Celebrations were undoubtedly expensive, but local elites regularly subsidized these occasions. In Queen's County the people of Cullenagh "illuminated their windows, doors, &c., in a most elegant manner, with upwards 1,800 lights in various emblematic figures and devices, expressive of their joy at that notable event; and at two immense bonfires, with some hogsheads of that genuine Irish liquor, whiskey-punch, they concluded the evening with good humour, mirth, and festivity." Festivities continued for several nights and included a joint display by the Cullenagh Volunteers, their leaders, and local weavers. The figure of the weaver was often employed as an icon of the prosperity of the nation or as an object of sentimental pity at moments of economic distress. Weavers now claimed a central place in celebratory festivities. Many commentators believed that the restrictions on Irish trade were largely to blame for the poverty and unemployment experienced by the weavers in 1778 and 1779. The campaign to wear Irish-made clothing was, among other things, also intended to directly benefit weavers by putting them back to work. The vivid account from Cullenagh captures this symbolic significance. The Volunteers received the weavers at the house of their commander, Colonel John Barrington, where hundreds of the weavers

> dressed uniformly, walking two and two; in their centre a carriage drawn by six horses (attended by martial music), on which was placed a loom, ornamented with colours, ribbands, &c., a boy at work, throwing specimens of his performance amongst the immense concourse of people, mostly dressed in the manufacture of Cullenagh. The Rangers saluted the manufacturers with a rest and three vollies; and having gone through their different firings and evolutions with propriety and éclat, were all elegantly entertained at the house of their colonel, where a plentiful collation was provided for their reception. Many glorious and national toasts were drank [sic].[75]

This scene was in many ways a display of traditional largesse by a local notable, stressing social interdependence and providing entertainment and libations to the people of the town at a time of jubilation for the community and the nation. These celebrations, not unlike the displays of corporate and artisan identities in the riding of the franchise (a ritual perambulation of the city boundary that gave public expression to the

jurisdiction and privileges of the corporation) in Dublin, also allowed
artisans such as weavers to articulate their identities as skilled laborers
who were central to the economic health of the nation.

Other parts of the country celebrated in similar style. A correspondent from Grass Hill in King's County reported that the "news of en-
largement given to [their] trade operated here like magic." The local
Volunteers paraded, and as in other celebrations throughout the country, the evening concluded with fireworks, illuminations, and ringing
of bells.[76] In Dublin, among many scenes that delighted onlookers,
there were bonfires, illuminations, and volleys fired by the Volunteers,
who "afterwards entertained a numerous concourse of ladies and gentlemen with a supper and ball, which were conducted with the greatest
regularity, harmony, and order."[77] Descriptions of celebrations stressed
the harmony and decorum of these occasions, with all the social orders,
as well as women and Catholics, united in celebration and patriot ardor.
Such celebrations and the accompanying depictions of unity concealed
real divisions throughout the country over how to react to the news
from England. What exactly had the campaign for a "free trade" meant,
and what sort of victory had been won?

Throughout 1779 the administration experienced increasing difficulty in controlling the symbolic landscape of Dublin, the center of
government. The celebration of Keppel's acquittal, riots, and particularly the Volunteer's appropriation of 4 November demonstrated the
failure of official political culture to define the limits of political participation and to control the festive representation of the nation. With the
announcement of free trade, official political culture attempted to reassert its authority with a vengeance.[78] This attempt, however, was not
without difficulties. Many radical patriots were unwilling to cede control of public space and attempted to impose their own interpretations
on the free-trade celebrations that conflicted considerably with the official view. On the receipt of the news of Lord North's proposition in England in favor of Irish trade, the lord mayor of Dublin (at the request of
the lord lieutenant) distributed notices throughout the city requesting
that "his fellow citizens will on Monday night testify their approbation
of this GLORIOUS EVENT by a general illumination."[79]

The government left little to chance and actively participated in the
illuminations in an attempt to impose a particular understanding of political events on the inhabitants of the city. On 28 December the Castle,
the Royal Exchange, and the main military barracks were all brightly illuminated, and porter was distributed to the crowds.[80] The post office

was decorated with "the most elegant transparent paintings, emblematical of the present occasion," and representing the "figures of his majesty on the throne extending this Magna Charta of commercial freedom to Hibernia kneeling—Fame, flying with a free trade over the ocean to Asia, Africa, Europe, and America—St. George and St. Patrick giving the pledge of friendship and peace by an embrace, and treading on venomous reptiles, while the Demon of Discord skulks behind."[81] The allegories these transparencies depicted would not have been difficult to decipher, even without such helpful glosses in the newspapers.[82] Ireland gratefully accepted the gift of free trade and access to the markets of the British Empire, a gift that had restored the former harmony between the two kingdoms, despite the efforts of malignant forces. Other images and texts throughout the city emphasized a renewed union of interest and sympathy between Ireland and England and the prospect of commercial success for Ireland. On Temple Lane, the house of the extravagant Thomas Ryder, actor and theater manager, was hung with colored lamps, and allegorical transparencies were placed in the windows. The first of these depicted Britannia and Hibernia "closing hands and jointly treading on the arms and family compact of France and Spain, with the sea and shipping in the background, and a cherub pouring the contents of a horn of plenty between both the figures and all over 'Ireland's prosperity, a free trade.'" Another transparency celebrated "the disinterested and upright administration of the earl of Buckinghamshire and the glorious 23rd of December 1779."[83]

In the wake of North's announcement, progovernment sentiment was not confined to the mostly government-sponsored and directed celebrations in Dublin. Many who had been swept along by the wave of anti-British sentiment and a radicalized patriot movement attempted to occupy a more moderate and accommodating stance. North's concessions were depicted as the realization of all Irish demands. The Tipperary Volunteers, for example, celebrated with a "feu-de-joy" while "the townspeople testified their approbation by general illuminations, bonfires, &c."; the revelers drank a variety of toasts, including ones to the king and constitution, to the anniversary of the arrival of Lord Buckinghamshire, as well as to parliament, the Volunteers, and an "everlasting union to the hearts and interests of Great Britain and Ireland."[84] The corporation of Naas illuminated that town, while the Volunteers fired several volleys. They also entertained "a numerous concourse of ladies and gentlemen" with a supper and ball. Similar celebrations took place in Waterford.[85] Although most accounts suggest that the celebrations involved the entire populace, in most instances the degree of popular involvement is hard to gauge. As the description of events at Naas and elsewhere suggests, there was a clear distance between the supper and ball of "ladies and gentlemen" and the celebrations of ordinary citizens in the street. Many displays were striking for their elaborateness and for the apparent expense involved, and events in Naas, as in Belfast, Dublin, Cork, and Limerick, were clearly orchestrated by local authorities.[86]

A single celebration could incorporate a variety of seemingly contradictory political messages. In Cork city, for example, the military and the navy were prominent in parading, though the Volunteers did march later in the evening. As in Dublin, sophisticated allegorical transparencies were much in evidence. The iconography depicted the familiar image of a dejected Hibernia supported by St. Patrick, who was looking up to a cherubim coming from England "with a free trade and pointing to a distant view of Commerce to Africa, Europe, and America." The Gaelic language was even employed to cement this vision of harmony restored, with St. Patrick saluting the Angel with a "Kaad meel a falthera." A second transparency asserted threateningly, "Paddy shall rise," while a third proclaimed loyally, "More success to the British arms."[87] This mixing of icon and text presented a variety of messages to the eye suggesting that an assertive Irish patriotism and loyalty to the British empire were not regarded as incompatible. The geographical diversity of such festivities also suggests that Lord North's proposals were greeted with a certain amount of acclaim throughout the country, even though the meaning of the concession clearly embodied a range of interpretations and hopes.

"The Demons of Discord"

Many patriots, however, believed that there was little to cheer about. Francis Dobbs, a leading Volunteer and pamphleteer, recalled that he and other patriots saw "the loss of a free trade in the appearance of one" and felt that "the people might be amused by a shadow till the hour in which the substance might be obtained had passed away."[88] Plans for celebrations of Lord North's announcement caused immediate controversy. Government fear of disorder scuppered the original plans for festivities. Privy councillor John Beresford had wanted "the bells rung, guns fired, bonfires [that] night, and drink [given] to the mob," but he complained, "Nothing is done."[89] Buckinghamshire observed, "Every effort has been exerted by the emissarys [*sic*] of faction, France, and America to check the gratitude which have [*sic*] had no other operation but to prevent a general illumination, as the magistrates apprehended it might have occasioned a mob riot."[90] A correspondent of the *Hibernian Journal* poured scorn on "the *bribed* illuminations and *Castle joy*" that he believed the celebrations represented. Foretelling the constitutional issues that would dominate the patriot agenda over the coming year, the author instructed readers that "the very Act of Restitution contain[ed] a shameful aggravation of unjust authority asserted by the British parliament over the Irish parliament." Regarding the concessions granted by the British parliament, he maintained, "[They will] serve to cloud and darken the benignity of our common sovereign until those restraints upon our constitution are totally done away with." This correspondent also argued that celebrations were premature: "No, you *should not*, you *will not* illuminate—it would at present be ludicrous and idle to stamp an approbation before we have reason to decide on the utility of the measure." There should be "no SUPPLIES, no REJOICING, until the parliament of Great Britain does away [with] all its acts that in any manner affect this country; then and only then can we have a free trade—then may we rejoice indeed. Until that is accomplished, may he who illuminates or rejoices be *branded* as an *enemy* to his country."[91]

Volunteer corps were also eager to emphasize their refusal to observe the celebrations. The Lawyers' Corps of Volunteers felt obliged to publish a denial of reports that they planned to mark the occasion with "some public mark of approbation." Rather, such a demonstration would be "highly unbecoming of the dignity of a Volunteer corps" until such time as a "full redress of the grievances of this country" was achieved.[92] The Newry Volunteers published resolutions stressing that the proposed easing of restrictions had not gone far enough in recognizing the sole authority of the Irish parliament. Under the very same act that would repeal the laws restraining Irish trade, the British parliament by implication would have the right to make other laws for Ireland. For those who claimed that Ireland was a separate kingdom, this was anathema because it suggested that Britain "in this instance grant[ed] a favour, not yield[ed] a right"—a favor that could be withdrawn at any time. The Newry Volunteers proclaimed that they would do "all that [could] be expected from the ardour of freemen to maintain and promote the welfare, dignity, and splendor of the British empire," but they insisted that the different parts of the empire could be connected only on the foundations "of equal liberty and sacred, substantial justice."[93] Until such times arrived, public consent was to be withheld.

Refusal to celebrate was one reaction to the perceived limits of North's concessions. As the events in Cork city have already shown, celebrations could also stress the multivalent ways in which people identified with Ireland, Britain, and the empire. An account of the celebrations at Derry, among the many provincial spectacles reported in newspapers, is perhaps most illustrative of this process; the account demonstrates as well the importance of the press in "nationalizing" and glossing such local events. The receipt of news of Lord North's announcement produced "a day of singular rejoicing, congratulations, and triumph" on which "the spirit of the people rose with the importance of the occasion and the honest feelings of independent Irishmen animated every bosom." The celebrations at Derry involved four local Volunteer companies, who paraded and fired volleys. At seven in the evening the bells were rung and "the friends of Ireland and freedom" assembled at the town hall, "each with his bottle of Irish liquor." Alcohol and its provenance, which had been an important issue in the course of the free-trade campaign, played a significant role in the celebrations. It functioned not simply as a stimulant or as part of the toasting ritual but also as a powerful symbol of unity; it was a means through which the participants could identify themselves as "Irishmen":

> Whiskey in every possible modification—currant, raspberry, mixed, and plain, &c.—was poured out in libations to Ireland's prosperity, freedom, and constitutional independence by the most numerous and respectable assemblage of true born patriot Paddies. Some drank out of the Irish noggins whilst others had the feet of their glasses broke off, and the want supplied by potatoes. The toasts were in perfect union with the spirit of the time and occasion—but the illuminations beggar'd all description; from the palace of the bishop to the cottage of the beggar was one blaze of light; the appearance of the town hall in particular was conspicuously grand and striking, entirely lighted and decorated with beautiful illuminated inscriptions, which, beginning at the south end, read as follows:

> NO NEW TAXES
> THE GLORIOUS MAJORITY 138
> A FREE TRADE
> THE IRISH VOLUNTEERS
> SPES PATRIAE [94]

This description, and the very actions of those participating in the carousing, slyly subverted traditional stereotyped representations of Irish national character, familiar in such venues as the London stage and popular prints, of paddies, potatoes, and whiskey.[95] Here, however, such markers were reappropriated and represented in the context of an Irish victory over the restrictive and monopolizing practices of the British parliament and the British ministry. The illuminated inscriptions echoed the assertive display of the Volunteers around the statue of William III in Dublin in the previous month—a demonstration that had hinted at violence if free trade were not quickly granted.

To what degree can we attribute this manipulation of symbols at Derry, and other similar scenes throughout the country, to a growing sense of nationalism in Ireland, spurred on by clashes with England, the growth of the Volunteers, and perhaps the American example? Some historians have attempted to place the Irish patriot movement in its British and European contexts and to rescue the language of patriotism from the teleology of the traditional nationalist story of the growth of national consciousness. But as Breandán Mac Suibhne has recently claimed in an effort to explain the Derry celebrations and to challenge this growing consensus, such scenes might well be seen as evidence of the growth of an Irish national identity among Protestants in Ireland.[96] His account of these celebrations is an important corrective to previous accounts in that it takes seriously the symbols and rhetoric of such crowds. It ignores, however, the ways in which such identifications were often tactical and temporary and did not prevent identification with a variety of causes and projects that fit uneasily within this understanding of a new homogeneous Irish identity.

It is worth repeating that such celebrations did not prevent Irish Protestants from identifying publicly with the cause of empire or with Protestant victories over Catholic enemies. As people in Derry were celebrating free trade, in nearby Limavady the local Volunteers were commemorating Admiral Hawke's victory over the French at the battle of Quiberon Bay in November 1759.[97] In March 1780 Admiral Rodney's victory over the Spanish off Cape Saint Vincent also prompted celebrations.[98] At the same time, the British parliament passed the bill conceding free trade to Ireland, and the king gave his assent. The *Hibernian Chronicle* reported on the explicit linking of these events in popular festivities in Cork city: "The illuminations on Friday night were the most magnificent that we ever remember to have seen. The inhabitants seemed to vie with each other in expressing their double joy, that while the abolition of coercive laws promised wealth and happiness at home, Admiral Rodney's glorious victory revenged our insults and our wrongs on a haughty foe and is a prelude to our resuming the right of empire on the ocean."[99] Similar festivities took place across the country.[100] Though many incorporated imagery critical of the British ministry, celebrations were at the same time essentially royalist and were followed by a stream of addresses to the king. An address from Cork city expressed "the happiness of being governed by the same gracious sovereign" and "connected by ties of blood and uniformity of manners and language"; above all, the framers of the address rejoiced in the mutual enjoyment of a "free constitution with [their] fellow subjects of Great Britain."[101]

Reactions to the war and empire were equally ambivalent in other contexts and produced more varied reactions than simple "joy." Victories over the French and the Spanish could unite all Protestants in celebration. The defeat of those still understood by most to be "fellow British subjects"—the rebellious Americans—occasioned little jubilation. The British victory at Charlestown a few months after the celebrations of free trade and Rodney's victory occasioned some rejoicing in Dublin by troops from the garrison, who lined the quays and fired a *feu de joie* as well as rockets and canon. But the *Freeman's Journal* reported that although large crowds observed this display, "it was to be lamented that victory could not command acclamations by the defeat of our natural enemies, as all was melancholy silence from a reflection that it was triumphing over the misfortunes of our unhappy brethren, and a deeper incision in the wounds of the empire."[102] The war with the American colonies created deep fissures in Ireland as it did throughout Great Britain.[103] The funerary reaction accorded to the soldiers' *feu de joie* on this occasion illustrates the distance between the crowd and the government as well as the complex identification of this crowd with a more extensive understanding of Britishness encompassing all subjects of the empire.

Celebrations and commemorations, with the rich array of symbols, imagery, and gesture employed by participants, were occasions for the expression of patriot understandings of "the nation." The sheer number of such events, their multifarious purposes, and the meanings evoked through the visual and aural symbols of street theater, along with their representation in the press, make them key sites for investigating the expression of political identities and ideas of "the nation" in patriot discourse. An analysis of the celebratory culture of Irish patriotism in the late 1770s and early 1780s gives the lie to any simple narrative of the "rise" of an Irish national identity. The Protestant calendar of commemoration was marked in Irish towns, as it was throughout Great Britain, by the traditional ringing of bells, lighting of bonfires, raising of toasts, and staging of illuminations. Fireworks, gunfire, and music often accompanied this visual and aural spectacle. As the earlier discussion of the celebrations of Keppel's acquittal suggests, the ceremonial landscape, particularly in the larger towns, was also augmented by a variety of other displays. Both Keppel's acquittal and the announcement of the conceding of free trade produced public spectacles, demonstrating that many Irish Protestants saw little contradiction in identifying themselves as "Irishmen" in a consciously anti-English manner while also strongly celebrating the British Empire and the monarchy. The commemoration of King William III, a decidedly Protestant hero but one closely identified with Whig notions of liberty, allowed the Volunteers in spectacular fashion to identify their own cause with this tradition. Popular rejoicings served first and foremost as expressions of political sentiment. These highly emotional occasions allowed even those excluded from the political nation to participate, in varying degrees, in such richly expressive ways as toasting, parading, and displaying symbols on their persons or homes. These celebratory occasions allowed ordinary men and women a sense of popular agency and assent in the politics of "the nation."

Shopping for Ireland

Consumption, Gender, and
the Politics of Free Trade

I must confess, that Dress, in the general acceptation of the
world is a subject of little importance; but the national dress of
our ancestors receives some consequence from the circumstances of its having been so often the object of parliamentary
consideration. Indeed the history of the Dress of any Nation
does, in some degree, involve that of the manners of its inhabitants: it is a mirror in which we can discover the progress of society; at one time we may see her falling into the depths of bar-
barism, and again emerging into the light of civilization.
    Joseph C. Walker, *An Historical Essay on the Dress*
    of the Ancient and Modern Irish

Hear this ye fair, in whose gentle breasts the fine tender feelings
of humanity are supposed to reside. Your bosoms are fit temples
for tenderness and compassion to dwell in. Should ye persist in
a pernicious fondness for foreign fopperies, against the cries of
distress, and the public welfare, ye must look contemptible even
in your own eyes, or in the end, be the enslaved victims of pride,
vanity and the caprices of fashion.
    "Juba," *Dublin Evening Post*, 21 August 1779

IN MAY 1779 Charles Bourns, a silk weaver and haberdasher, advertised a "device" in the *Hibernian Chronicle*. Bourns claimed that his
product was already a great success, worn by "Ladies and Gentlemen

of the first rank in Dublin." Should this stamp of approval from the elite not convince the reader, the advertisement offered a detailed description of the device. It depicted "a harp untuned, strings hanging loose, supported on one side by a woman assistant in the Arts of Ireland weeping; on the other by a manufacturer looking up to Heaven for relief, and both figures pointing to a shuttle lying on the Ground, neglected and unoccupied. The Motto We will support You."[1] In July a "ribband" advertised for sale in the *Dublin Evening Post* included a device depicting "a Harp and Crown with a bleeding heart on the left; and a Shamrock reversed in the right, pointing to the words 'A FREE TRADE.'"[2] Over the course of the year and beyond, merchants and hawkers peddled an impressive array of patriotic ephemera through the press, in their shops, and on the streets. Such goods allowed consumers to illustrate their sympathy for distressed weavers and support for the removal of British restrictions on Irish trade (or a "free trade," as this demand was popularly described) widely believed to have caused that distress. At the same time, a market emerged to take advantage of the national enthusiasm for the Volunteers, supplying both military accoutrements for the force and souvenirs for enthusiasts.

The flowering of Irish patriotism in the late 1770s and early 1780s has received renewed attention in recent years. For the most part, these studies have focused almost exclusively on the history of patriot ideas as articulated in pamphlet literature or on the "public opinion" of discrete confessional communities.[3] Yet popular manifestations of support for free trade have not been ignored. The spectacular interventions of the Volunteers and the Dublin mob in November 1779, as discussed in the previous chapter, are staples of accounts of the period. But the more quotidian ways in which people expressed their support for patriotism and free trade have not received the attention they deserve. The work of Toby Barnard and others has drawn attention to the rich world of goods and the culture of consumption in eighteenth-century Ireland.[4] Martyn Powell's recent study demonstrates how the practice and language of consumption were laden with political meanings throughout the eighteenth century.[5] In 1779 the worlds of patriotism and goods collided, as everyday acts of consumption became a means for the articulation of patriot affiliation. Through the purchase of Irish clothing, goods, and political ephemera, consumers demonstrated their support for free trade. This chapter attempts to situate Irish patriotism in a commercialized extraparliamentary culture and focuses on the emergence of a market for patriotic goods in the context of the free-trade dispute and the rise of the Volunteers. It examines the types of goods consumers could purchase, the symbolism of these goods, the ways in which trades and businesses could capitalize on patriotic zeal, and the gendered nature of patriotic consumption. I argue that the symbolic world of everyday acts such as shopping were as important to the free-trade campaign as the more exalted realms of parliamentary debate or the expressions of Protestant patriotism articulated in pamphlet literature.[6]

Advertisements in the press serve as an essential but underutilized source for the examination of the range of patriotic goods available and the techniques exploited to market them.[7] The ephemera these advertisements peddled suggest the everyday way in which consumers could express or encounter the arguments of patriotism through condensed and complex symbolism or simplified but emotive slogans. Surviving artifacts are also essential for understanding the material culture of politics of this period. Articles by connoisseurs and local historians have done much to emphasize the variety of materials available for study, such as pottery, flags, prints, and paintings. Few, however, move beyond formal descriptions of objects; thus this archive has not been used to address broader historiographical questions such as the social meaning of these artifacts or their relation to patriot political culture.[8] Letters to the press and pamphlet literature also reveal much about the imperative to purchase Irish goods and particularly the gendered rhetoric of consumption expressed by advocates of the boycott.

Recent work on consumption focuses on "the material culture of politics," identifying the variety of meanings attached to acts of individual consumption and the articulation of political arguments and notions of citizenship through a moralization of the language of consumption.[9] Boycotts against British goods in the American colonies in the 1760s and 1770s, the abstentionist campaign against slave-grown produce in the 1790s, and the *swadeshi* movement in India in the twentieth century, for example, all offer instances of the politicization of consumer practices in the face of contentious British imperial policies.[10] This was indeed, as T. H. Breen has described it, an "Empire of goods."[11] Concepts of identity, nation, and empire were contested and reformulated through the politicization and moralization of consumption and the commodities of empire. The language and symbolism of these movements were also heavily gendered. In these campaigns, women were represented as the defenders of the virtue and purity of the national community through their role as vigilant consumers in a morally charged marketplace. The campaign for free trade in 1779 shares many similar issues and problems with these other instances of consumer protest. At the same time, the language and symbols of this campaign emerged in a specific context of Irish patriot politics, as well as in a particular consumer culture.

The culture of consumption affected the lives of many in eighteenth-century Ireland. Toby Barnard has argued that through the diffusion of commodities and standards of taste, elites and the middling sort in Ireland "resembled more closely their contemporaries in Britain, Europe, and North America."[12] The houses of the Protestant gentry, which have received the most attention, were richly furnished with a variety of European goods, often purchased on grand tours, their tastes formed by close relations with the English nobility through intermarriage and their frequent travels across the Irish Sea. Barnard's studies of household inventories and domestic account books and Sarah Foster's analysis of newspaper advertisements demonstrate that, to a certain degree, even those Protestants further down the social scale participated in this commercialized world of goods. Women, for example, had opportunities to consume, with the wives of the gentry and middling sorts enjoying considerable purchasing power, as the range of advertisements addressed to them suggests.[13] How far down the social scale these opportunities permeated and the confessional particularities of consumption are harder to gauge. Certainly, aspects of Catholic participation in the world of goods would repay closer attention. Even in the backwater of Connaught, Catholic gentry, such as the Bellews of Mountbellew, County Galway, consumed in much the same way as their Protestant counterparts.[14] The opportunities for the mostly Catholic poor to take part in consumer culture were probably limited, though they were by no means excluded from this world.[15] More prosperous Catholics in the countryside, particularly the emerging and influential "big farmer," seem to have avoided such overt displays of wealth, adopting a frugality in marked contrast to the ostentatious lives of the displaced traditional Catholic gentry.[16] In many urban centers, the Catholic middle class became increasingly dominant in trade and were no doubt as involved in buying as much as in selling.[17]

Over the course of the century, Dublin in particular saw a marked increase in the number of luxury goods manufacturers, such as goldsmiths, silversmiths, jewelers, and silk merchants, catering to the tastes of well-to-do consumers.[18] Advertisements in the press provided lists of the bewildering range of domestic and foreign goods available in the capital, with the French and English origins of many items underlined.

Travelers to Dublin frequently commented on the profusion of English goods in the city. Arthur Young, a visitor in the late 1770s, observed somewhat censoriously, "The influx of wealth into that country brings a taste for the elegant luxuries with which we abound, and the capability of purchasing them ensures the purchase. An Englishman cannot go into a single house in Dublin, or see a person dressed, of either sex, without having this truth staring him in the face."[19] If well-off Dublin consumers looked to London and Paris as centers of fashionable consumption, as the economic center of the country, Dublin offered a cornucopia of consumer choices for provincial visitors. Many came to the capital bearing orders from family and neighbors. Urban centers, such as Cork and Belfast, provided a range of opportunities for consumption.[20]

Beyond the main cities, the world of goods also began to penetrate small towns. Market towns across the country became more closely "integrated into regional and national economies, so that ties with Dublin, the ports and hinterlands tightened."[21] The town of Armagh in 1770, with a population of under 2,000, supported twenty-nine shoemakers, twenty-five shopkeepers, five hatters and milliners, two dressmakers, five breeches makers, and eleven tailors, as well as two weekly market days.[22] Small merchants in Birr and Edenderry provided not only the necessities of life but made some concessions to fashion, carrying silk girdles and handkerchiefs, as well as a range of wigs, among their stock.[23] Satirists and moralists suggested that young women were particularly prone to the temptations of fashion. The print *The Farmer's Daughter's Return from Dublin,* for example, depicts a young woman with an elaborate wig she has evidently purchased on a trip to the capital, much to the horror of her rural family, suggesting the way in which increased opportunity for consumption also multiplied anxiety about its effects.

Eighteenth-century Irish consumers eagerly purchased a profusion of goods, but they expressed reservations about the consequences of their actions. Throughout the century, many commentators voiced a familiar concern over the harmful impact of luxury. Others focused on the damage caused to Irish industry by the desire for foreign goods. Indeed, this was hardly a new concern among patriots. Although the campaigns of nonimportation and nonconsumption in 1779 were influenced by the American example, they did not need to appropriate wholesale the language and practices of the colonists. Patriots evoked an Irish tradition of consumer politics, looking to Swift as instigator of this form of protest. In the first half of the century, during trade disputes, economic downturns, or at moments of patriotic fervor, Swift and others had periodically called for the rejection of English goods and the consumption of Irish clothing.[24] Weavers, often cast as the main victims of trade restrictions, frequently took matters into their own hands, exacting symbolic and actual violence against the wearers and sellers of foreign clothing, as well as the material itself.[25]

Concerns over the health of Irish manufactures and the negative impact of trade restrictions were still central to the language of patriotism by the 1770s. Clubs and societies, such as the radical Society of the Free Citizens, frequently toasted "free trade" and encouraged members to wear Irish clothing.[26] By 1778, in the course of an economic slump, the call for the exclusive consumption of Irish textiles and other items, such as porter, became more widespread. This economic downturn was blamed on an embargo of Irish provisions to the colonies introduced in 1776. Ireland actively engaged in colonial trade in the eighteenth century, with this trade, largely composed of provisions and linen, constituting between 9 and 12 percent of total exports. Imports from the colonies included sugar and tobacco (landed first in Britain), flaxseed, and rum. This trade was not inconsiderable, but it was Anglo-Irish trade that accounted for the majority of exports and imports throughout the century. The initial campaign for the removal of restrictions on Irish trade was largely promoted by those directly interested in colonial and English trade.[27] A Dublin committee, led by members of the Dublin Corporation, was established to encourage Irish trade, and an "aggregate body" of the inhabitants of Dublin adopted nonimportation resolutions against British goods. Although some concessions were made by Britain in 1778, these were widely regarded as inadequate, and calls were increasingly made for further trade concessions, or a "free trade."

This demand meant different things to different people. For most, it had little to do with the doctrines advocated by Adam Smith, whose *Wealth of Nations* had been published a few years earlier.[28] The campaigners were not attempting to overthrow the orthodoxy of mercantilism but rather sought to allow Ireland to participate in this system on equal terms with Great Britain. In a letter to the *Belfast News-Letter*, written in colloquial language, a "Miller" attempted to define free trade for a popular audience. He claimed, "[It is] nothing more or less, than a liberty to send our manufactures and our provisions where we please, without asking leave of the English; and to bring home any thing our customers give us in return for them, without asking their leave for that either. That's all; and isn't it very fair?"[29] This "liberty" was to be achieved through the organization of associations against English goods, enforced through sanctions such as shaming and mob violence.

Ordinary men and women also publicly expressed their attachment to political causes in practical and symbolic ways through the clothes they wore, the artifacts they bought, or the copious amounts of Irish porter they drank in local taverns. Patriots emphasized the antecedents of their campaign in the promotion of Irish manufactures by Swift and earlier patriots. However, the campaign in 1778–79 differed markedly in terms of its level of organization and national impact. This was a broad-based campaign organized around associations, mobilizing ordinary consumers across the country. Like earlier protests, the campaign initially targeted aristocratic consumers, but as the boycott gathered force throughout 1779 this plea became more generalized, appealing to a wide range of men and women to renounce English (and indeed all foreign) goods.

Supporters of free trade argued that all of Ireland's economic and political woes could be traced to England's attempts to restrict Irish imperial trade (to be sure, a symptom of a greater constitutional tyranny) and to the broader cultural problem of Irish men and women's dependence on English goods, interpreted as a further indication of "slavishness" and corruption. Although an economic downturn was a factor in motivating the campaign for free trade, commentators were quick to point out that greater political and cultural issues were also at stake. For many patriots, the history of Irish relations with England, since at least the enactment of the Woolen Act, could be interpreted as a series of restrictions and humiliations based on a mercantile theory of trade and empire that promoted British interests at Ireland's expense.[30] Trade and liberty were seen as inextricably entangled. As Henry Grattan, the leading parliamentary patriot politician argued, for a "mercantile empire" it was a short step from restrictions on trade to assaults on the liberty of the dependent nation, "under the pretence of maintaining tradelaws."[31] Many British commentators believed that the American war had called into question the morality of empire. In Ireland, the further restrictions placed on Irish trade as a result of the American crisis led many to redefine the empire as an authoritarian, monopolizing instrument of English dominance.

"Foreign Fopperies": Consumption and Patriotism

For patriots, Ireland's constitutional subordination to Britain was manifested not only in obvious ways, such as restrictions on Irish trade and commerce. Symptoms of this political malaise were also evident in the eager adoption of metropolitan notions of taste, a cultural dependency that mirrored the political. Consumer goods from England and France, as newspaper advertisements make clear, did have a certain cachet and symbolic value among consumers. Despite the periodic attempts by patriots to promote local industries, foreign goods were valued for both their quality and fashionability. One correspondent noted, "The predominance of fashion has a powerful Effect on the minds of every rank of people. . . . In our Dress we copy from the English and the nearer we approach their Manners and Appearance, so much more are we considered to advance in Point of politeness."[32] While earlier seen as evidence of progress and civility, the import of English ideas of refinement and the "accessories of politeness" came to be regarded by Irish patriots as evidence of servility and a dependence on the metropole.[33] Supporters of domestic consumption were at pains to argue that items such as clothing and porter produced in Ireland should no longer be considered second rate.[34] Others conceded that, although Irish materials might be inferior, a sacrifice of quality only enhanced the patriotic sacrifice of the wearer.[35]

During the economic downturn of 1778, addresses from weavers appealed to elite women to practice and encourage patriotic forms of consumption. With the "deepest humility," the weavers called on aristocratic women to decline the use of foreign clothing; such action, they contended, "will create a spirit of emulation amongst all other ladies of tender feelings and sentiments, to appear in Irish manufacture, by which generous and humane Condescension, your Ladyships will remove the dreary and dismal Hopes of the Poor working manufacturers."[36] These pleas were based on assumptions about the duties and responsibilities of the elite in Ireland. The Irish gentry had traditionally been depicted as particularly extravagant, spending vast sums on imported luxuries such as wine and clothing.[37] This neglect of domestic production and the consequent poverty of the producers who depended on their patronage were regarded as a failure on the part of the elite to meet the obligations their social positions prescribed.[38] Addresses to the gentry relied on the notion that elite women set the tone of fashion and taste in polite society, and alluded to the "influence" such women were believed to have over their husbands. The various addresses from ribbon weavers, silk weavers, as well as the patriot press, adopted the language of deference, while evoking this duty to consume home-produced goods.

Many elite women responded enthusiastically to these addresses. Forms of elite sociability and association that were regarded as particularly feminine spheres of influence became suffused with the symbols and rhetoric of patriotism. In May 1778 the *Dublin Evening Journal* reported that women attending the Rotunda had entered into an agreement to wear linen gowns.[39] The following year, a charitable ball at the same venue served as an opportunity for the patron of the evening, the Countess of Buckinghamshire, the wife of the lord lieutenant, to promote the wearing of Irish manufactures "to aid the poor unemployed Weavers" of the city.[40] Individual women were celebrated for their roles in promoting domestic manufactures. In April 1781 the Corporation of Weavers offered the freedom of their guild to Mrs. Newenham, wife of a prominent patriot politician, for her "earnest endeavours and constant attention to promote the sale of the Manufactures of Ireland." Newenham responded by deprecating her efforts but concluded that she felt "real satisfaction in becoming a Sister to citizens of such worth and virtue."[41]

By 1779, appeals were also made to women beyond the elite by stressing the supposed greater capacity of all women for sympathetic identification with the plight of others.[42] One such memorial, to the "patriotic ladies of Ireland" from the ribbon weavers of Dublin, detailed the extent of unemployment among their number and concluded that the cause of this misery was "too fatal a Predilection . . . for Foreign Manufactures of every Denomination." This state of affairs had placed the weavers "under the Pressure of a gloomy Despondence at seeing such a vast Import and Consumption of foreign ribbons and gauzes, which impel[ed] them to think they ha[d] not the most distant prospect of relief, which sad reflection add[ed] to their present Misery, and almost persuade[d] them that they, with their numerous Families, must inevitably perish for Want." Or, according to another correspondent, Irish women, as the "patronesses of distress," could express their patriotism through "their appearance and example." Indeed, for the author writing under the pseudonym "Juba," consumption and display were expressive of a particular female form of patriotism, as sure as "courage, love and generosity [were] the genuine characteristics of the gentlemen of the Irish nation."[43] Women were encouraged to reject foreign fashions and embrace a national simplicity: "Do your native charms require the aid of Foreign Fripperies?" asked "Patrick" in a letter to the *Hibernian Journal* in 1779. "Are these not the badge of your dependence on Strangers for the comforts of your existence? Or rather are they not the gilded chains in which your enemies hold you in Slavery."[44] Political and commercial dependency were intertwined. But in this argument, it was the desires of individual consumers, an "alienated Female taste" in particular, that led to collective enslavement. By rejecting "the faint Lustre of foreign Parade" and adopting native fabrics and styles, men and women could assert their independence in both the political and the aesthetic realms.[45]

While Irish consumers eagerly participated in the world of goods, the relation between consumption and moral decline was repeatedly emphasized in the press and alarmed sermons. Women's consumption practices were a constant source of worry for censorious commentators. But men's consumption habits were considered equally weighty. A concern with the connection between the acquisition of goods and virtue was hardly new. The political language of civic virtue was obsessed with the seemingly inexorable historical process of the rise of luxury and effeminacy, loss of virtue, and the decline of empires.[46] As one pamphleteer described this vision, those sunk in an effeminizing sumptuousness were necessarily political enemies of patriotism: "Let those who have been nursed in the lap of indolence and bred in the school of luxury, who have been enervated under a long course of sensual pleasures and physical consequences, let them arm themselves in all the female paraphernalia of sighs, tears, and entreaties; let them ascend the pulpit of *passive obedience,* and preach *patience to the people!*"[47] Such men not only contaminated their own bodies but also threatened the integrity of the body politic. As this attack on luxury suggests, gender was central to understandings of consumption. The consumption of foreign luxury goods caused indolence and enervation. Surrender to desire was a symptom of effeminacy, demonstrating an unmanly failure to master sexual or consumer appetites. Yet individual weakness had far-reaching consequences. Dissolute masculinity also resulted in forms of political slavery as men failed to assert a rational independence and instead submitted to a "passive obedience."

These dangers were believed not simply to be confined to Ireland but were rather part of a broader imperial malaise.[48] Many Irish commentators saw Britain's imperial crisis as fitting easily within a historical narrative of the emergence of dissipated forms of masculinity and the fall of empires. Such anxieties confronted patriots with a familiar problem. But in 1779 this problem was reformulated to conform with the peculiarities of Ireland's political and cultural circumstances. If trade and empire inexorably led to corruption, effeminacy, and contamination (with the example of Britain as contemporary proof), while prosperity was essential to the maintenance of liberty, how might consumption be reconciled with virtue and with patriotic forms of masculinity and femininity? The answer lay not in the complete renunciation of the world of goods but in forms of patriotic consumption. Consumer virtue, the everyday choices made by men and women while shopping, became central to this vision of patriotism.

The Commercialization of Patriotism

Men and women could exhibit this consumer virtue in a variety of ways. They could simply choose to renounce English goods. Or they could purchase and wear Irish textiles, a practice that elite Irish women had ostentatiously exhibited throughout the century. Retailers also offered an array of goods to men and women outside the elite that allowed them to declare their consumer virtue more overtly. Throughout 1779, retailers and manufacturers offered for sale an impressive array of patriotic ephemera. Patriotism provided a variety of commercial opportunities they were quick to exploit. Although many merchants and manufacturers no doubt enthusiastically embraced the patriot cause, and their motives cannot be simply reduced to notions of economic self-interest, patriotism was also good for business.[49] Potential customers were targeted in numerous ways. Newspaper advertisements were one of the most common means of alerting consumers to the availability of patriotic artifacts. The eighteenth-century press contained more advertisements than "news," and such notices were central to the promotion of luxury goods and services.[50] Printers, often engaged in a range of commercial activities, placed advertisements for patriotic ephemera, such as prints and buttons, in their newspapers. These appeals to consumers promoted a premeditated mode of consumption mediated through the culture of print.

More spontaneous and transitory forms of consumption were also central to the dissemination of political ephemera and the multiplication of commercial opportunities. Shop windows and signs served as one means to inspire impulsive shopping. A wide range of public commemorations and celebrations, particularly the spectacle of Volunteer reviews, attracted large transitory crowds.[51] These events served as ready markets for food and drink, but also for cockades, patriotic ballads, and other mementos of patriotic commitment.[52]

A number of different trades and businesses benefited from the surge in patriotic political activity in the 1770s. The printing and book-selling businesses of Dublin were well placed to capitalize on this market. Newspapers went to great lengths to establish their patriotic credentials. Several newspapers proclaimed that they had inserted an extra news column to report on the activities of the Volunteers. The *Dublin Evening Post* announced an additional column as a means of "conveying the precision, the manly efforts and resolutions of [Ireland's] brave determined Volunteers."[53] Such embellishments were attempts to meet the demands for news on the Volunteers, while clearly identifying the paper with the patriot cause. Newspapers were also commercial enterprises, of course, and a patriotic stance was good for business. In the highly competitive world of the press, newspapers struggled to attract advertising and subscribers. Newspaper proprietors hoped to profit from the interest in the Volunteers by carrying detailed reports of their activities. The resolutions of Volunteer corps, free-trade associations, and a variety of other political organizations also contributed to the revenue of newspapers.

The culture of the Volunteers also provided a range of commercial opportunities for the print trade. Periodicals and almanacs drew special attention to commemorative prints of Volunteers and the free-trade campaign included in their volumes.[54] The commercialization of patriotism was furthered through the production and sale of sheet music and prints. Numerous ballads were printed at moments of political tension, intended to spread the patriotic message to a popular audience in an engaging and profitable way. While many patriotic ballads and poems were printed in newspapers, others were sold on the street by hawkers as broadsheets or chapbooks, or in print shops. John Lee, on the corner of Eustace and Dawson streets, advertised a number of patriotic songs, including "The Volunteer Boys" and "Rouze Hibernia," both of which had been performed at the Rotunda on 4 November "to great applause."[55] The *Dublin Evening Post* advertised "The Volunteers Medley," a humorous account of various corps and commanders of Dublin.[56] Military music, central to the pageantry and color of Volunteer reviews, was collected and sold, such as the twelve "slow and quick Marches" and "favorite Irish tunes" composed by W. Jackson.[57] The Volunteers' passion for military activities created a market for instructional books for would-be soldiers. For example, *A Concise Compendium of Military Manoeuvres* (1781) was one of the many manuals published providing Volunteers with detailed instructions for the conduct of reviews, complete with engravings of various military formations.[58] Other texts were produced as guides and mementos for particular events such as field days or commemorations such as the Glorious Memory Battalion's celebration of William III.[59]

The culture of patriotism offered other commercial opportunities for the print trades. By the 1770s, Dublin supported several print sellers and engravers, who sold locally produced work as well as imports.[60] Prints offered a relatively inexpensive vehicle through which consumers could display their patriotism in a domestic setting. Although the number was small compared to the London market, prints advocating free trade or commemorating contemporary political events were produced in Dublin. Prints could be purchased individually from shops and hawkers or were included as loose sheets suitable for portfolio collections in periodicals such as the *Hibernian Magazine* and *Exshaw's Magazine*. Isaac Colles of Capel Street was perhaps typical of the opportunism of this trade. Colles advertised, among other goods, French engravings and transparencies for shop windows. He also sold lottery tickets and painted ribbons. With the emergence of the free-trade campaign, Colles made speculative forays into the patriotic market. In November 1779 he announced a "new humerous print" titled *Paddy's Resource* (see fig. 5). The image was accompanied by a patriotic verse:

> Ireland long tuned her harp in vain
> Her cannon seconds now her strain;
> Our music England would not hear;
> Our thunder let her statesmen fear.[61]

The print depicts a threatening Irishman holding a shillelagh, who proclaims, "Arrah, sure they won't give us a Free Trade—Nabocklesh," a phonetic rendering of an Irish-language phrase meaning "never mind." With a busy port in the background, the figure points to a cannon (with the caption "a short Money Bill, A Free Trade, Or Else"), muskets, and other weapons of the Volunteers. The print is not alone in using an angry, presumably Catholic, figure to represent Ireland's trade grievances. A better executed version of the same print with a Gaelic title is attributed to the pseudonymous "Owen Roe O'Nial," evoking the name of the leader of Gaelic Irish in Ulster during the wars of the 1640s, though probably referring to the same pseudonym used for the influential pamphlet *The Letters of Owen Roe O'Nial* (1779). After the granting of free trade, Colles published another print for the occasion, again mixing text and image, but this time with a more conciliatory, less aggressive

Figure 5 *Paddy's Resource, Exshaw's Magazine,* 1779 (Courtesy of the Board of Trinity College Dublin)

message. *Paddy's Resource* suggested the threat of violence might be the best way to wrest concessions from England. In the new print "The Reconciliation, with the Meeting of Hibernia and Britannia reviewing the Irish Volunteers," the Anglo-Irish relationship was represented as harmonious once more, with a "beautiful poetic Discourse" celebrating this reunion of sentiment and interest.[62] William Allen, a print seller on

Dame Street, also catered to the seemingly endless demand for souvenirs of Volunteering. In February and March 1780 he advertised Volunteer prints of "light horse, grenadier, battalion and light infantry figures" at 6d as part of a set for collectors. For 1s. 1d., the prints could be colored to match the uniforms of any corps. Allen deemed this set fitting for those who "would wish to transmit to posterity, an idea of that laudable and universal spirit, which has so eminently distinguished the present Age."[63]

Prints could serve as vehicles for the expression of political affiliation, the commemoration of national victories, and the extension of Irish trade throughout the Empire, enjoyed in the comfort of the family home. A print of Benjamin Franklin, offered for sale by Allen, exemplifies the way in which prints and affiliations were displayed, with the print forming part of "a compleat set of pleasing and entertaining furniture for a small room, peculiarly well adapted for a Breakfast room."[64] A handsome print, such as that produced by the painter and engraver William Hincks, might serve as part of a collection of "furniture" prints, usually hung in dining rooms or other rooms used for socializing. As Stana Nenadic observes, though displayed in a domestic setting, these prints were intended for "semi-public consumption."[65] Domestic interiors were spaces rich with symbolic expressions of status and taste, but they could also serve to display the patriotic affiliation of the family. At the same time, cruder, less polite prints were also produced, items more likely to be pinned to the wall of a tavern and enjoyed in a public setting to commemorate the patriot's success. Such a print might have been *Paddy's Victory or Arrogance Mortified* (see fig. 6), which depicted a threatening Irishman, similar to the figure represented in *Paddy's Resource*. Again, the Irish language is employed as part of his threat, with the figure exclaiming, "Sure you'll make laws for us—Fagh Shin," meaning "leave that." The explicit threat of the previous print has now been realized, and this figure is hanging and burning the act restricting Irish woolen exports, while a more finely dressed figure curses a six-month money bill, the instrument used by the patriot opposition to wrest a free trade from Britain.

Patriotic fervor, particularly the martial needs of the Volunteers, offered other benefits to Irish trade. In September 1780, in the wake of the joy exhibited throughout Ireland at the establishment of "free trade," a correspondent to a Dublin newspaper remarked, "The great service rendered by the Volunteers of Ireland to the manufactures of this kingdom may be seen by the following calculation—Supposing their number to

Figure 6 *Paddy's Victory, or Arrogance Mortified* (Courtesy of the Pierpont Morgan Library, New York, Peel Collection, Peel V, 026)

be only 50,000, the ribbons and cockades will amount to 2,500l. and their clothes and accoutrements to 250,000l. exclusive of arms, colours, gold and silver, lace &c."[66] While it is not clear how much volunteering actually contributed to the economy, the very practice not only required a substantial investment in time but also a significant outlay on the "accoutrements" of patriotism necessary for their round of reviews and mock battles. The outfitting of the Volunteers served as one means of marketing traditional forms of military apparel in patriotic terms. Samuel Barr of Belfast was one among many merchants who advertised such items as pouches, belts, engraved plates, and silver and gilded gorgets for the Volunteers of that city throughout 1779.[67] A large number of medals were also produced, awarded to Volunteers for their shooting abilities, and usually inscribed with the name of the company and patriotic slogans. In the course of the free-trade campaign, it became essential for corps to be seen to outfit themselves in clothes and accoutrements of Irish manufacture.

The masculine conviviality of the Volunteers belonged as much to the homosocial world of the tavern as on the review field. Publicans clearly benefited from the sociable aspects of Volunteering. Clubs and societies had long convened their meetings in taverns. They met for a variety of purposes, and while some were organized around particular political principles, most seemed to have been concerned with promoting conviviality and "fine fellowship." The Snug Club of Newry, for example, recorded in 1780, "The club dined and spent the day together with the social harmony that so particularly distinguishes the 'Snugs.'"[68] In Dublin in particular, certain taverns had been long associated with a host of clubs and societies. James Hoey's Phoenix Tavern, off Werburgh Street, for example, hosted meetings of the Free and Independent Citizens during Charles Lucas's political campaign of 1749. In the 1750s it served as a meeting place for the Grand Lodge of Masons, the Hibernian Society for the Improvement of Education, and the Friendly Florist Society. In the 1760s the tavern hosted a motley assortment of clubs, including the Prussian Club, the American Club, and the Corsican Club, which was formed to "support the cause of liberty and Paoli." By the 1770s the tavern's "great room" was the venue for the meetings and debates of the Constitutional Society.[69] At the same time, the King's Arms was the site of meetings for the Society of Free Citizens, a radical political group led by Napper Tandy.[70] The Eagle Tavern on Eustace Street was the home of the Friendly Brothers of the county of Dublin Knot and the Constitutional Club, as well as hosting the Volunteer company commanded by the Duke of Leinster.[71] The associational world of eighteenth-century Dublin, motivated by the principles of patriotism, was a lucrative one for the pub trade. Publicans were also active in this world themselves, no doubt for a mixture of patriotic and more self-interested motives. The Bear Tavern in Crane Lane, for example was kept by David Corbet, who was at the same time the leader of the band for the Dublin Independent Volunteers.[72]

The consumption of alcohol oiled the wheels of sociability. Alcohol was central to most forms of sociability and politics in eighteenth-century Ireland. While drinking need not necessarily promote the type of "social harmony" advocated by the Snug Club, alcohol had its social uses, with none more commonplace in the world of voluntary organizations than the toast.[73] By 1779 many associations were toasting "free trade" and "success to the Volunteers." Although many established clubs and societies, such as the Society of Free Citizens in Dublin and the Anna Liffey club in Kildare, had long supported Irish trade, this stance was now publicly reiterated. Other clubs and societies made public professions in favor of the campaign. Occupational groups, such as the silk weavers of Dublin, formed clubs to promote Irish trade.[74] The Society of Free Citizens publicized the fact that each "member on his admission bound himself to wear the manufactures of this kingdom" with many new societies and associations following this stance.[75] Dublin Castle became particularly anxious over the activities of "certain persons stiling themselves the Aggregate Body of the citizens of Dublin," an organization closely related to the Free Citizens, and instrumental in publishing the names of importers of English goods, whose resolutions appeared to Buckinghamshire, the lord lieutenant, "to be of such dangerous tendency" that he forwarded a copy of them to London.[76]

The rituals and the material culture of associational life were also influenced by patriot enthusiasm for free trade and the Volunteers. Although historians have identified the world of consumption as a particularly gendered sphere where women predominated, associational culture provided opportunities for men to consume in a patriotic manner.[77] Ceramics in particular were "a vital prop in the ritual performance of political allegiance and solidarity."[78] Transfer-printed jugs, punch bowls, and mugs, produced in support of free trade or the Volunteers, were intended for ceremonial use in the heavy-drinking masculine world of the tavern and were often decorated with the toasts and slogans of the associations that drank from them. Based around drinking from communal punch bowls and numerous toasts, the communal consumption of porter that followed local Volunteer meetings resembled the meetings of other clubs and societies. Many corps purchased drinking paraphernalia printed with appropriate patriot slogans and symbols along with the name of the corps. One such transfer-printed Volunteer jug was decorated on each side with a harp and the motto "TUNED / TO FREEDOM / FOR OUR / COUNTRY" along with a Volunteer and a figure of Liberty. On the other side, the patriotic principles of the company are clearly stated: "ARM'D FOR MY COUNTRY'S CAUSE I STAND / RESOLV'D, NOR E'ER WILL FLY' / BUT

LIBERTY'S SUPREME COMMAND / WILL FOLLOW TILL I DIE."[79] A verse printed on a Volunteer serving jug, accompanied by an image of Hibernia and a crowned harp (see fig. 7), exemplifies the mixture of militarized patriotism and conviviality such meetings were meant to embody:

> Ye Honest sons of Irish Oak
> Who fear not thunder or fire or smoke
> But boldly for your country stand
> Nor fear the threats from foreign lands
> We drink and sing, laugh and joke
> With one accord draw in our yoke
> And thus we pass our time in glee
> Hibernia's sons will never flee.[80]

Given the centrality of drinking and tavern culture to patriots, it was inevitable that this sphere of consumption would become politicized. In particular, it was through the consumption of porter, so the argument went, that members of clubs and societies could most clearly display their patriotism. The free-trade campaign intensified the already-strong relationship between patriotism and the culture of drinking. Correspondents in the press noted the irony of Irish patriots toasting the success of Irish trade while drinking London porter. Irish beer, it was argued, now rivaled that produced in England. In 1778 the *Hibernian Journal* noted that a host of clubs and societies gathered in taverns throughout the city each evening. At these meetings members bemoaned the state of their trades and professions and reflected on the causes of the nation's economic stagnation. Might the real cause of the countries woes, the paper asked, be the fact that the same men were "ballasted home every night with the dregs of two, three, or four Quarts of LONDON porter?" Progress was being made, however. The paper claimed, "The principal Societies and Clubs, &c. in this city have resolved to discontinue the use of London Porter, and obliged their Hosts and Hostesses to supply them with Irish, which is now found to be, in general, so good that the Use of it must shortly become universal in this kingdom to the great credit of its inhabitants."[81] The following year a correspondent noted, "All Clubs and Public meetings in Tap houses, Porter Houses and Taverns do publish their resolutions not to drink London Porter or any kind of English beer."[82] The Volunteer corps of Cork entered into resolutions to consume only Irish porter, following similar resolutions by clubs and societies in Dublin.[83] Alcohol, then, was central to the activities and the rhetoric of patriots. Taverns

Figure 7 Volunteer jug (Courtesy of the National Museum of Ireland)

throughout the country benefited from the custom of local Volunteers. Patriot clubs, societies, and associations provided similar opportunities for tavern keepers to profit from the surge of patriotism, while brewers no doubt benefited from the politicization of alcohol consumption. At the same time, the rites of drinking, along with the artifacts in which alcohol was consumed, promoted a vision of patriot conviviality and sociability in which everyday acts of consumption acquired political significance in the context of the campaign for free trade.

The rituals of drinking were gendered. If men, in the space of the tavern, performed an array of rituals around the consumption of alcohol, there were also feminine rituals and spaces of consumption. Again,

Figure 8 Volunteer
tray (Courtesy of the
National Museum of
Ireland)

these activities offered opportunities for the retailers of patriot goods.
Items such as teapots belonged to the feminine and domestic world,
based around the polite rituals of tea drinking.[84] Like jugs, teapots were
printed with such slogans as "May Ireland Flourish with a Free Trade"
or "Success to the Independent Volunteer Societies of the Kingdom of
Ireland," along with images of a volunteer, Hibernia, and a crowned
harp.[85] These artifacts mixed the symbols of Irish patriotism with other
imagery. One Wedgwood teapot depicted a Volunteer and Hibernia on
one side and a rural scene on the other. Another depicted the famous
scene of the death of General Wolfe along with more local concerns,
suggesting that unsold stock was successfully recycled by Wedgwood
for the Irish patriot market.[86] Irish patriotism, ironically, offered opportunities for English manufacturers. At the higher end of the market, but
again for domestic consumption, a tray was engraved with an image of
a Volunteer presenting Hibernia with a free trade (see fig. 8).[87] The production of fabric, printed with scenes of a Volunteer review, also shows
how household furnishing could display support for the patriotic cause
within the domestic realm (see fig. 9).[88]

Symbols of patriotism decorated household objects, such as pottery,
jugs, teapots, prints, and fabrics, with images of Hibernia and the Volunteers and proclaimed support for free trade and the Volunteers. The

Figure 9 Volunteer fabric, depicting a scene from a Volunteer review (Courtesy of the
Grand Lodge of Ireland, Dublin)

press also called on men and women to engage in patriotic consumption, basing their appeals on a gendered division of patriotic labors. Gender was central to much of the language of patriotic consumption. While Irish newspapers routinely carried advertisements addressed "To the Ladies," merchants in Dublin were quick to capitalize on the demand by women for a variety of symbols to express their patriotism. Women could decorate their hair and clothing with patriotic ribbons and cockades. Advertisements promoted items such as the devices discussed earlier, which, it was claimed were "so much worn by the fair daughters of Ierne, who wish[ed] to encourage the manufactures of their own country," along with a variety of items, such as cockades and ribbons.[89] In July 1779 John Magee advertised a new die, struck by "one of the most ingenious Irish artists in this Kingdom, with the following DEVICE":

> Industry with her distaff, in the character of HIBERNIA reclining upon a wool-pack, surrounded with raw materials, the Gift of bountiful Providence, and the natural Produce of her Isle, but which, by the cruel, monopolizing and compulsive Hand of Power, she is prevented from using, for the Employment of the Industrious cloathing [sic] of the naked, or even as the very Means of support for her children, while the poor, ragged manufacturer, struck with the dreary prospect, drops from his nerveless Hand, the shuttle that formerly furnished a comfortable support for a tender wife and a numerous, Beloved offspring: with the other Hand, he struggles to uphold poor Hibernia's Harp, broken and unstrung, from which he cannot strike even one single note of Harmony. In this complication of woe, every Breast must be touched by their plaintive, humble Request, *Assist* or *we perish;* while every Irish Heart re-echoes back the joyful sound, *We will protect you.*[90]

These complex allegorical representations of the meaning and effect of trade restrictions were powerful everyday expressions of patriotism. The language and symbols of such ephemera also suggest popular understandings of patriotism, based on the language of sentiment and sympathy for the weaver and his family. Throughout the nonimportation campaign, such sentimental representations of the economic plight of weavers symbolized the patriots' political campaign and served to represent the plight of the nation.[91]

Although the call for the nonconsumption of British goods in 1779 was addressed to the nation as a whole, campaigners made their appeals in specifically gendered terms. A female figure, in the shape of poor Hibernia, served as a symbol for the free-trade campaign. Actual women played an active role in the campaign, and their participation was seen as crucial to the success of the boycott. Women's desires were traditionally represented as resulting in the spread of luxury and the effeminacy and decline of public virtue that inevitably followed. In the course of the free-trade campaign, a more positive account of the relation between women, consumption, and Ireland's commercial prospects was proposed by advocates of patriotic consumption. Likewise, men could demonstrate their patriotism through virtuous consumption. Spheres of feminine and masculine sociability, such as the tea table and the tavern, became sites of politicized consumption.

The concession of free trade at the end of 1779 was widely believed to mark the beginning of what the patriotic poem "The Association" envisioned as a new era of Irish freedom, wealth, and "Imperial sway":

> On ruins tott'ring verge Ierne spied,
> a gleam of hope, a spark of virtuous pride;
> Her Sons arraying in their own defence,
> Her Daughters cloath'd in native elegance,
> Prizing the offspring of their arts and trade,
> Happy to wear, with honour, what they made;
> From whence would emanate a glorious ray,
> Of wealth, of freedom, of Imperial sway.[92]

Newspapers emphasized the national dimensions of these celebrations by drawing attention to numerous local manifestations of joy and unity. At the same time, they drew attention to a new wave of patriot ephemera celebrating this victory. The campaign for free trade and the rise of the Volunteers involved an extraordinary mobilization of ordinary men and women throughout the country. Commitment to this cause was in part based on common understandings of how individual consumer choices symbolized political commitment. Patriotism was experienced and understood through the quotidian world of ephemeral items sold in shops or on the streets. The politics of material culture also allowed for what William Drennan described as "the immediate agency of the people" in the free-trade dispute.[93] Associations were formed, oaths were taken, merchants were threatened and attacked; foreign goods were forgone, replaced by native equivalents. Patriotic fervor created a market for a vast array of goods carrying slogans and symbols that disseminated popular understandings of the patriot cause. A commercialized extraparliamentary political culture allowed even those outside the political nation to fashion a patriot identity and to act like political subjects, imagining themselves "sole agents" in an unprecedented, and ultimately successful, mobilization against restrictions on Irish trade.

The New Magna Carta

*Voluntary Association, the Crowd, and
the Uses of Official Political Culture*

WHILE THE CONSUMPTION practices of ordinary men and
women were a central focus of the patriot campaign for free
trade, a variety of other means were promoted to pressure the British
administration to concede patriot demands: the formation of associations; the issuing of addresses, instructions, and petitions; and the violence of the crowd. The years 1778–79 witnessed an unprecedented
degree of association for both the extension of trading rights and the
defense of the nation. Military forms of association were initially the
preserve of respectable Protestant men. However, association based
around the politics of consumption was characterized as a way of overcoming sectarian, social, and political divides and of forging a patriotism that was truly national. Although free-trade associations were often
initiated by such solidly Protestant and gentry-dominated bodies as
county grand juries, respectable Catholics were encouraged to subscribe, while correspondents in newspapers also lauded the patriotism
of others excluded from the political nation, including lower-class Protestants and women.

The free-trade campaign has received much attention from historians
and has often been seen as a turning point in the creation of an "Irish"
national identity. However, it is usually examined in relation to its parliamentary expression or with regard to its consequences for Anglo-Irish
relations.[1] Although aspects of the popular dimensions of this movement have been studied, the rhetoric of inclusion and the relationship

between "respectable" patriotism and those outside the political nation have not received the consideration they deserve.[2] This chapter focuses on these elements of the campaign by examining three distinct but related aspects of the extraparliamentary agitation for free trade: voluntary association, the appropriation of instruments of official political culture by the opposition patriot movement, and the politics of the Dublin crowd. It argues that the political language of association and free trade, as articulated through such media as newspapers, pamphlets, ballads, petitions, poems, and handbills, was crucial in redefining the limits of political participation and offering new models of citizenship. Political languages do not simply reflect social experience or gendered and national identity but also serve to actively constitute it.[3] The formal political nation excluded the vast majority of the population based on religion, gender, or economic status. The sphere of voluntary association was represented as a space where extraparliamentary solidarities could be formed for patriotic purposes. At the same time, the representative structures of national and local government, such as the parliament and the grand jury, were hardly marginal to this campaign. The appeal to the culture of official politics, as well as the use of unofficial means, generated heated debates over the nature and legitimacy of the "people" interfering in the politics of the nation. No aspect of this involvement was more controversial than the often violent participation of the Dublin crowd. While a focus on spectacular crowd interventions can be criticized for producing an episodic account of popular politics, I argue that the actions of the crowd reveal both underlying assumptions of duly constituted authority as well as the relation of the crowd to the broader aims of the patriot movement.[4] Rather than focusing on the well-worn topic of debate and allegiances within Parliament, I examine how these three aspects of this campaign intersected and the ways in which the campaign for "free trade" by these disparate groups transformed understandings of the political nation.

Print, Patriotism, and Association

Letters to the press advocating the consumption of Irish manufactured goods, as the last chapter suggests, initially concentrated on influencing the consumption habits of the elite through the language of deference. "Hibernicus" argued that in order to improve Ireland's economic position, readers "must enter into Association to give that preference to

[Ireland's] own manufacture of every kind which [would] create consumption." But he addressed his pleadings in particular "to the great": "Let me conjure them to assist poor Ireland in promoting its manufactures. Let me intreat them not to use English goods, when they can get manufactures of their own country. We have cloths and silks; we have tabinets and poplins in which they may appear with Splendor."[5] Besides such traditional appeals, other types of pressure were applied to encourage the elite to do their patriotic duty. The *Hibernian Journal* noted, "We are assured that the manufacturers of this city are determined to publish a list of the names of the patriotic nobility and gentry, who shall appear on the Birthday at the Castle dressed in the Fabricks of Ireland."[6] By June the nobility and gentry were conspicuously dressed in Irish manufactures at the Castle celebrations of the king's birthday. Although such "castle patriotism" had been common throughout the century, in the summer of 1778, letters to the patriot press put particular pressure on the elite (long criticized for either preferring foreign goods or residency) to make a show of their patriotic credentials through their habits of consumption.[7]

Beginning in the spring of 1778, letters to the press had called for the formation of associations to encourage the consumption of Irish clothing and porter, and for the public to enter into "a non-consumption Covenant."[8] Voluntary associations were a central feature of eighteenth-century life, particularly for urban elites and the middling sort. In Ireland, many associations, such as the Dublin Society, were formed with a view to economic "improvement."[9] As James Livesey argues, these societies also represented a new form of sociality and a set of values that offered an alternative to the language of sectarianism.[10] The associations promoted in 1778 were limited in their aims, following a British tradition of association whereby individuals pledged to join together to secure a specific end. As the many references to "covenants" suggest, these forms of association were religious in origin, but political associations were a significant issue during the reign of Charles II, with Shaftesbury's supposed association burnt on occasion by Tory crowds.[11] Williamite political associations also emerged in the 1690s. Loyal associations were formed throughout Ireland during the crisis of 1745.[12] Associations were often formed to suppress agrarian protest movements, such as a general association organized in Enniscorthy in 1776 to suppress local Whiteboy "outrages," attracting over one hundred subscribers.[13] Others, such as an association in Cashel, were organized to prevent the abduction of young women.[14] Association usually involved a public ceremony at which the "covenant" or association agreement was signed.[15] Subscribing to an association morally bound participants to persist until their end had been achieved.[16] Binding forms of obligation, such as oaths, were commons features of ritual life in Ireland, widely administered by agrarian protesters, combinations, freemasonry, and later, the United Irishmen and the Defenders. In the case of both Catholic and Presbyterian clergy, oaths were also a means of expressing consent or disaffection with the political order.[17] This form of public assent to the principle of nonconsumption would not have been taken lightly.

While extraparliamentary political association was still a relatively controversial development, the formation of single-issue "patriot" associations also had antecedents in Ireland. During the money bill dispute of 1753, a countrywide network of patriot clubs emerged to promote the opposition cause. The dinners, toasts, and public celebrations of these clubs, as well as the ways in which the opposition used the press and other forms of print culture to publicize their cause, in many ways anticipate the associational culture of the 1770s and 1780s.[18] Over the course of the free-trade campaign, and in subsequent attempts at economic and political reform, association was lauded as the most patriotic of activities. "Paddy Churchill" prefaced a poem celebrating the "patriotic sons and daughters of Ireland" by exclaiming "ASSOCIATION!—glorious word!—'tis this will lead us, if we tire not, to SAFETY, WEALTH, and LIBERTY! Let us pursue it with unwearied assiduity! 'Tis no Phantom, but a substance, a bulwark of defence, that may raise us high, when England is no more."[19] Such panegyrics to forms of voluntary association were common by 1779. The free association of private individuals for the public good was characterized by several letters writers in the patriot press as the ultimate expression of patriot activism. A pamphlet, *A Scheme for a Constitutional Association,* defined the principles of association: "By a constitutional Association, I mean that all true friends of their country should stand forth and avow themselves and their Principles; subscribe a solemn Covenant and Declaration; and bind themselves to co-operate in all constitutional Measures for the public Good."[20] "Swift" urged readers, "This day associate—now is the moment—resolve, and shew your churlish, niggard sister, that you can be free—and throw off her long worn Tramell—enter into a non-importation Covenant of all goods of what nature or kind soever that can be had at home."[21]

Correspondents extolled voluntary association as the surest way to protect public liberty, with "Sarsfield" claiming, "Associations will

soon be as dear to them as Magna Carta, and our Children will hereafter join in on a grateful Sound of *Liberty* and *Association*."[22] One letter
writer described this vision of association in June 1779: "Associations in
a public cause should be held more sacred than the Tenor of the laws,
passed thro' interested Views, and perhaps made to serve particular
Purposes. An Association of the People is the dernier resource, which,
though it may be marked with some disturbance, like a fever in the
Blood, tends to remove an Evil from the Public body—it therefore is the
noblest Virtue to associate for the general good, and the worst of treason
to interrupt its progress."[23] While patriot writers such as "Sarsfield,"
"Swift," and "Hibernicus" celebrated association in extravagant language, the actual practice of associating was publicized and reported in
newspapers in more prosaic but nonetheless significant terms. By the
spring of 1779, calls to associate became more pronounced as grand juries across the country began to adopt nonconsumption resolutions. Associations were established and resolutions drawn up at the important
local occasions of the county assizes. Articles of association and resolutions were further publicized through announcements in metropolitan
and provincial newspapers. The daily reporting of patriot resolutions
and the emphasis placed on the respectable nature of subscribing situated the local actions of grand juries in the context of a broader national
initiative so that the press did not simply describe events but transformed them in the act of reporting.

   The rhetoric of the press promoted a particular vision of association,
consumption, and retailing that at the same time emphasized the problems inherent in a campaign that depended on individuals mastering
their desire for profit or consumer goods. A letter signed "Mollyneux"
claimed that the success of the campaign had thus far rested on "the
noble ardour" of "the middling ranks of men." It was elites and the
fashionable who had given in to their desire for foreign goods, providing merchants with an incentive to sell them.[24] Henry Grattan recognized that controlling these desires would not be an easy task. He was
well aware of the "foreign magnificence" of British goods, a superiority
fostered by restrictions on Irish trade and manufactures. He hoped
the demand for the rich variety of fashionable foreign goods would be
replaced by "the merit of exhibiting the rude efforts of our own country."[25] Individuals might choose to refuse British goods of their own ac-
cord. But such "internal resolutions," according to Grattan, were inadequate: "The very violence with which they entertain them now, secures
their departure from them. Many will be influenced to break them by

the same power which makes such people reluctant to sign them; many will be tempted to forsake them by the bribe of a bargain; many will consider their own insignificance and in a strain of affected humility, give themselves a criminal latitude. . . . Thus a spirit not regulated nor communicated, nor perpetuated by covenant, violent in some places, indolent in others will evaporate in all."[26] The temptations of consumer society were manifold, and consumers were apt to give in to desire. For Grattan, a public renunciation of British goods was necessary to bind individuals to the cause of free trade.

The practices of merchants and importers were particularly open to suspicion. Letters to the newspapers bemoaned the methods devised by merchants to flout the agreement. According to "Sarsfield," "Some pitiful individuals, preferring their own mercenary views to the good of Millions, still continued to render our Associations nugatory and ineffectual, by importing goods from England in the very hour that opposite conduct must have procured us all we wanted from the Parliament of Great Britain."[27] Even those who had entered into associations might not be trusted. Patriot writers warned readers to take care to differentiate between "true" patriot merchants and those opportunists donning patriotic garb to exploit a popular cause. Joseph Pollock feared that many merchants were publicly advocating nonimportation while secretly breaking the agreements. Casting doubt on the patriotism of those involved in trade, he asserted, "Drapers and mercers are of no country or party."[28] How were consumers to engage in patriotic consumption in the face of merchant duplicity? In a letter to a Cork newspaper, "Pro Patria" suggested shopping should be a rational patriotic activity; goods were only to be purchased from shopkeepers who entered the solemn engagement.[29] A "Friend to Ireland" went further, suggesting that traders who had pledged themselves to nonimportation should affix evidence of their subscription on the door of their shop, so that consumers could differentiate between genuine patriots and the "Enemies to their country."[30] "Sarsfield" believed that a type of social ostracism was necessary to "fix some degree of Reprobacy on all who act[ed] against the society they live[d] in—some shameful Stigma, or common Resolve of excluding such Men from the Commerce of their fellow citizens. What neither Honour nor Coercion could bring them to might be effected by public Contempt without giving loose to the Dictates of Indignation."[31]

Even these measures by vigilant consumers might not be enough to overcome the resourcefulness of scheming merchants, who found a

variety of ways to counterfeit a patriot identity. *Magee's Weekly Packet*
claimed that "principal importers of English manufacture, as a protection to their property, and to cover their future practices" had enlisted
in various Volunteer corps in order to forge patriot credentials so as to
"injure [Ireland] with impunity."[32] Some merchants and hawkers in
Cork, it was claimed, were attempting to pass off English goods as Irish.
The *Hibernian Journal* observed that some fifty woolen drapers, "many
of them wealthy and eminent in trade," had declined to enter into the
association. The paper claimed that they continued to import British
goods "under the names of obscure and insignificant men who [were]
employed about their houses and to whom no public ill-consequence
[could] ensue, while others (and those of no small consideration) receive[d] English goods through the hands of English riders."[33] It is hard
to gauge the extent of this activity. However, the printed returns of English imports from the custom house, printed in the patriot press, confirm that some merchants were willing to risk the wrath of patriots in
their pursuit of profit.[34]

The campaign in the press promoting association, along with the resolutions of the grand juries, inspired a variety of responses. The press
claimed that the campaign had crossed social and confessional divides.
A print produced in 1779, reflecting on Britain's imperial difficulties,
suggests this is how the campaign was perceived in London. *The Political Raree-Show* (see fig. 10) depicts the "citizens of Dublin" creating an
association and signing a resolution against English manufacture. As
some citizens support the expiring figure of Hibernia, another declares,
"Though we differ in religion we will unite for our country." The *Hibernian Journal* noted, "The different Classes of Society have adopted the
same patriotic resolution" as the grand juries to promote Irish manufactures, along with "Free Masons, friendly brothers" and "every order of
the community, who are capable of feeling a generous indignation for
the injuries done this Kingdom will no more contribute to feed the Peli-
can which devoured the Bowels of their country."[35] Patriot writers were
eager to promote associations as a way to unite the whole nation and
erase distinctions of party, religion, and social class.[36] Henry Grattan
urged Catholics to participate in the campaign, claiming that association would give the Catholic "an opportunity of signing himself a fellow
citizen": "The association is a measure wonderfully calculated to unite
all descriptions of men, and inspire that union. . . . It is that question
where Whig, Tory, Dissenter, and Roman Catholic, country gentlemen

Figure 10 *The Political Raree-Show* (detail) (Courtesy of the Lewis Walpole Library, Yale University)

and courtier, must agree; they unite to prefer property to poverty, and trade to the want of it. So much does the association keep clear of all division, and apply to the common interest of all persuasions, that it might be moulded into a form of prayer, and all religions might join in it."[37] Frederick Jebb, under the pseudonym "Guatimozin," likewise argued, "If men of all denominations in the kingdom shall unite against the common oppressor, no doubt can be entertained of success."[38] Some put this vision into practice; Catholic gentlemen and local Protestants associated in Meath against English goods in a public ceremony, and it is likely that this was not the only instance of such an alliance.[39] Although most Protestants remained profoundly ambivalent over the issue of extending any political rights to Catholics, the sphere of association was represented as a space where Catholics and Protestants could unite in a campaign in which the values of trade and utility overcame confessional divides.

Clubs and societies made public professions in favor of the campaign. The Society of Free Citizens published their resolutions specifying that "each member on his admission [had] bound himself to wear the manufactures of this kingdom."[40] Dublin Castle became particularly anxious over the activities of "certain persons stiling themselves the Aggregate Body of the citizens of Dublin," an organization closely related to the Free Citizens and instrumental in publishing the names of importers of

English goods.[41] Occupational groups, such as the silk weavers of Dublin, formed similar associations.[42] Volunteer companies drew attention to their uniforms of "Irish manufacture" and adopted resolutions to support free trade.[43] Women were also called on to form their own patriotic associations. The preceding chapter identified the ways in which women's private domestic actions could be considered acts of patriotism; some authors suggested that women should also make public declarations of their support for the nonconsumption campaign. These acts were seen as useful for the positive moral influence they might have on men, with one author claiming, "And you, ye fair-born daughters of Ierne, who set the bright example of wearing your own manufactures, continue to enforce YOUR patriotic Associations. 'Tis a national virtue, that makes your beauty shine with double lustre! 'tis a virtue, that has influenced every rank of men to adopt your measures 'tis a virtue that will place you above the Roman and Spartan dames."[44] Another proclaimed, "You, my fair countrywomen, whose superior charms require no adventitious aid, may signalize your public spirit at this interesting period, by liberally Associating to wear and patronize manufactures of your own Country."[45] In April 1779 a newspaper reported that women calling themselves "the Hesperians" had formed an association and adopted resolutions to support the use of Irish manufactures; other women seem to have formed similar associations.[46]

While resolutions and associations proliferated throughout the country in the spring of 1779, Ulster was a notable exception to this pattern. This failure did not escape the attention of contemporaries. The *Belfast News-Letter* observed, "It is remarkable that though the western counties of this kingdom have nobly [*sic*] entered into associations of non-importation yet the northern parts which have been deemed the most independent and wealthy look on, with a tameness that does no great honour to their feelings as men, or to their patriotism, as the most populous part of the kingdom."[47] Ulster had not been as badly effected as the rest of the country by the economic problems of 1778, and historians have plausibly explained the lack of activity in that province as resulting from fear of British retaliation against their thriving linen trade. Still, a lively debate did ensue in Northwest Ulster over the issue of association and nonimportation. The campaign to use Irish goods exclusively appears to have had some success in that part of the country.[48] However, despite calls in the *Belfast News-Letter* for the establishment of associations, many shopkeepers continued to advertise English goods in that paper with seeming impunity.

The growing intervention of the Volunteers in political affairs was also central to the success of the free-trade campaign. The usurpation of 4 November by the Volunteers, discussed earlier, was their most dramatic and celebrated intervention in the campaign, but they were also involved in the local organization of the boycott. In many instances, such as in Meath, the formation of an association against English goods was followed by the adoption of resolutions to form local armed defense forces. "Mercantile and military associations" went hand in hand.[49] Consequently, considerable overlap existed between the membership and leadership of both types of associations.[50] A meeting of the "Gentlemen and Freeholders" of the County of Dublin in July also illustrates the interconnectedness of the two forms of association. The meeting resolved "at this Crisis" to raise Volunteer companies for the defense of the county and at the same time "owing to the impolitic restrictions on [Ireland's] Trade" subscribed to organize a meeting on a nonimportation and nonconsumption agreement. That the organizers included such respectable opposition patriot figures and prominent Volunteers as Henry Grattan and Luke Gardiner, as well as such radical demagogues as James Napper Tandy, also shows the unlikely political alliances that the issues of 1779 produced.[51]

The Appropriation of Official Political Culture

Grattan characterized associations as a type of "civic prayer" that crossed sectarian boundaries. However, this political reform did not require the complete rejection of the institutions of the state. Assize grand juries were central to the promotion and the organization of the nonimportation and nonconsumption campaigns. Although it has often been assumed that such solidly Protestant bodies were pliant tools of local elites or the central administration, by the 1770s patriot sympathies were expressed by grand juries throughout the country.[52] The assize served as a significant social occasion and as an opportunity to perform the theater of magistracy. At the same time, as the most recent historian of local government in Hanoverian Ireland has observed, "Grand juries both provided a local stage for the re-enactment of national political conflicts and represented a crucial avenue of communication between the provinces and the central government."[53] Buckingham viewed each spring assize with anxiety, as "many political discussions, many tests, associations, and electioneering objects [were] put off to that period."[54]

Calls to associate against English goods had been common in the patriot press throughout the economic crisis of 1778, but only with the adoption of resolutions by local grand juries at the spring assizes of 1779 did the campaign gather national momentum. The Galway grand jury was the first to adopt resolutions against English goods, thereby setting the tone for subsequent measures. Widely reprinted in newspapers across the country, the Galway resolutions specifically targeted Manchester manufacturers, who had petitioned strongly against trade concessions for Ireland. These manufacturers, the jury believed, had "ungenerously and ungratefully opposed every effort made in the British parliament, for the extension of the trade and manufactures of [Ireland]." This, the grand jury asserted, was contrary to "the principles of sound policy" as it tended to "disunite two Kingdoms, whose mutual interest it [was], to preserve and maintain, inviolate, that Harmony so necessary to make [the Irish] happy at home and respectable abroad." Such action not only constrained Irish trade but also was inimical to the commercial interests of the British Empire as a whole. In response to the narrow vision of these "ungenerous proceedings," the grand jury resolved to boycott the manufactures of Manchester.[55] A vision of the unified interests of the empire as a whole could be mobilized against the narrow policy of specific interests.

This body, along with the high sheriff and freeholders of the county, also addressed the king in the deferential language of the petition. Describing themselves as "dutiful and loyal subjects," they emphasized "the readiness which [they had], on every occasion shewn to chastise foreign foes, and suppress intestine commotions." However, the current crisis had brought them to despair. They asked the king,

> To whom, Sire, shall we apply for succour, in the hours of danger and distress; but to the common father of his people? . . . And, we further humbly beg leave to assure your Majesty, that we would not, at this time of public distress, presume to approach the Royal presence with a representation of our unhappy situation had we not been forced thereto by the sad and moving spectacle of thousands of our manufactures, and artificers, reduced to extreme indigence, the natural though unhappy consequences of decayed manufactures and a ruined trade![56]

Similar pathetic scenes of the poor "half naked and starving" were presented to the king by the Wicklow grand jury the same month.[57] In the months that followed, resolutions, addresses, and petitions were drawn up by grand juries throughout the country. The grand juries of

Mayo, Meath, Tyrone, and Monaghan soon imitated the example of Galway in resolving to use Irish manufactured goods.[58] The Cork grand jury resolved to refuse foreign clothing for seven years.[59] In all, twenty-two county and city grand juries adopted such resolutions by the late summer of 1779.[60] These resolutions and pleas were published prominently in provincial and Dublin newspapers, promoting a vision of a unified nation supporting the campaign and offering further publicity for the cause of free trade.

By October, meetings of freeholders began instructing MPs to vote for a short money bill rather than the traditional two-year bill. As with the creation of nonimportation associations, Galway was among the first to issue instructions.[61] Others were quick to follow; Dublin freeholders adopted similar resolutions the same month. They justified their instructions by evoking the catastrophic affects of trade restrictions: "the critical situation of affairs, the loss of public credit, and the almost total annihilation of our trade and manufactures, rendered the more alarming by a certain increase in the national debt and by unjust, impolitic and oppressive laws passed by an assembly which possesses not the smallest right or authority over Ireland."[62] In Cork, noting the recent address of the Commons to the king calling for free trade, freeholders addressed their representatives Richard Longfield and John Hely-Hutchinson: "The distresses of this Kingdom, by the impolitic and unjust restraints on our trade, are too well known to need being described, and too severely felt to be fully expressed. The TRADE OF THIS CITY IN PARTICULAR droops under the calamity, and commerce deplores the loss she must sustain, if not relieved by the public spirit of a virtuous parliament. These considerations have determined us to recommend to, and instruct you, Our Representatives, to exert your utmost efforts in Parliament, for obtaining our speedy and effectual relief."[63] As in Galway, the freeholders called for a six-month money bill. Instructions to MPs for such a bill were prepared around the country, including in Ulster, which had been relatively inactive during the formation of the nonimportation associations. The town of Carrickfergus noted that the present restraints were not only unconstitutional but "contrary to the general Interest of the Empire at large."[64]

The practice of issuing instructions was not novel. Instructions had been a central part of the money bill dispute of 1753–54.[65] But this form of address remained contentious, outlining as it did a controversial theory of representation.[66] Belfast, for example, instructed its representatives, being "fully convinced of the attention and respect which the representative body owe[d] to the opinion of their constituents."[67] MPs routinely responded to the instructions they received from their constituents, with both usually published in the press. Radical MPs, such as Edward Newenham, frequently responded enthusiastically to instructions.[68] Some MPs, while acknowledging the right of constituents to issue instructions, disagreed with the specific measures advocated or declined to commit themselves.[69] Others felt uncomfortable with the very idea of being instructed by the electorate, suggesting competing understandings of representation.

"A Petition in One Hand and the Brand of War in the Other"

Over the course of this campaign, the patriot press presented a vision of a nation united, with all former differences subsumed by the desire for free trade and opposition to oppressive British policies. Nevertheless, the increasingly assertive nature of bodies dominated by patriots, as well as the tone of patriot rhetoric in print, afforded critics of the movement an opportunity to attack the campaign. The rhetoric of unity evoked by patriot writers eluded the fact that even many self-professed patriots were distinctly uneasy with elements of the campaign. The formation of political and military associations, the issuing of instructions and petitions, as well as an appeal to "the people" were all controversial forms of political action, and some questioned the legitimacy and even the legality of these tactics. Patriots dismissed attacks against them out of hand as the scribblings of "castle hacks," and many historians have been inclined to do the same.[70] Although the government appears to have lost the argument in this instance, in what ways did such writers attempt to discredit the patriots and counter the tide of patriot opposition? In an effort to discredit the free-trade campaign, critics focused their attacks on the alleged illegality of reform tactics and their similarity to the schemes of American rebels; they and also played on fear of invasion and antipathy to the French. Letters to the press debated the legality of association. In response to doubts about the legitimacy of such organizations, "Causidius" asked, "Will any man say, that a body of men, legally assembled, associating to wear the manufactures prepared by their relations, their friends and their neighbours, in preference to those sent to them by men whose intercourse with them is contempt, and whose government of them is oppression, has any tendency towards an insurrection against LAWFUL authority?"[71] This debate dominated the letters section of newspapers such as the *Freeman's Journal* in April and May, as well as provoking a stream of pamphlets.

At the beginning of 1779, as calls to associate against English goods appeared in the press, the *Belfast News-Letter* suggested that the French should be the real target of Irish hostility:

> The prohibition of the French King, respecting British and Irish manufactures, should animate proper resentment and retaliation. Our destructive imports from France, are, confessedly infinitely superior to our exports thither. Did Ireland cease to bring wines, brandy, and numberless fripperies (not to say smuggled cambricks, laces, silks &c.) from that vain, perfidious nation, it would not a little distress their trade. . . . A free generous individual doing this is not what is meant: Anti-Gallican aggregates should be assembled through the kingdom, and the most spirited resolutions entered into, relative to supporting our own consequence and manufactures.[72]

The pamphlet *A defence of Great Britain against a charge of Tyranny in the Government of Ireland,* by "An Irishman," also evoked hostility toward the French as well as toward recent events in the colonies. The author went further; the leaders of the free-trade agitation wanted nothing less than a break from Great Britain, harboring "schemes of Independence under the auspices of France." Focusing on the similarity of Irish and American methods of protest, he continued: "Their politics, which are nothing less, than under a plausible popular call, for an association to wear our own Manufactures, to spread disaffection through the nation, imitate the American non-importation agreement, and in the end like them, accept of *Freedom* from the House of Bourbon. They seem to me to resemble scavengers who collect dirt from the different dunghills, and then scatter it indiscriminately on all they meet."[73] Denying that Ireland's commercial difficulties were related in any way to British policies, "An Irishman" suggested, "Our distresses proceed from ourselves" (anticipating some recent economic historians), and then continued to equate the free-trade movement with republicanism, separatism, and French sympathies: "I will take it upon me to say that redress in our commercial laws, would be the greatest disappointment some individuals, who have promoted the present Associations could meet with, as it would take from them every excuse, for plunging the nation into scenes of blood and confusion, by which alone they think they can accelerate the independence of America. . . . To expect a free trade without contributing to the general exigencies of state, is what an Advocate for

American independence only could think of."[74] It is likely that not only supporters of government feared such radicalism, real or imagined. Few patriots were openly separatist by 1779. The widespread alarm in 1778 over a feared French invasion had not only inspired the creation of local volunteer militias but also provoked a stream of loyal addresses to the George III. In August of that year, the high sheriff and grand jury of Monaghan, for example, assured the king, "When a war is in prospect with the natural enemies of your Majesty and of these your Majesty's kingdoms, . . . [we are] ready to exert ourselves to the utmost of our abilities in support of your majesty's crown and dignity."[75]

Reports from across the country also raised doubts about Catholic loyalty. Colorful accounts of the conspiracies and dark ulterior motives of reformers appealed to worries that the Irish Catholic masses were unrepentantly disloyal, simply waiting for an opportunity to over-throw the established order. In June 1778 the government received news that the Catholics in the west planned to revolt with "a view to overturn the present government by the aid of the French and the Span-iards," and it was widely believed that, in the event of an invasion, the Catholic masses would rally to support the French.[76] Critics of the free-trade campaign could appeal to real fears of Protestant men and women, and such scaremongering may have been more effective than historians have traditionally assumed. The patriot writer "Sarsfield" responded to these accusations of subversion or republicanism, reassuring moderate supporters of reform: "Our Resolutions are humble, though manly; and a decent fortitude marks the features of our Associations. We hold not, after the manner of the English republicans, a petition in one hand, and the brand of war in the other."[77] Accusations continued throughout September and October, however, as letters supportive of the govern-ment attempted to represent "Sarsfield" and the leaders of the campaign as republican separatists.[78] By this time, the actions of the Dublin crowd provided ammunition for these claims and threatened to bring the pa-triotic campaign into disrepute.

"The Very Lowest and Poorest Class of People": The Crowd and Patriot Politics

Association was initially regarded as the preserve of the "respectable" elements of Irish society: the Protestant gentry and urban elites. But it quickly came to encompass a wider spectrum of society, including merchants, tradesmen, respectable Catholics, and women. The campaign also appealed to those who fell outside even this more inclusive vision of extraparliamentary political participation, particularly the urban poor, whose welfare the patriots professed to champion. The patriot campaign invoked the power of the crowd, and the crowd in turn developed a type of "plebian patriotism" legitimating popular association.[79] Intimidation and violence were essential elements of this campaign, particularly in Dublin, where the "mob" had a history of intervening in political issues.[80] "Respectable" patriots routinely denounced attacks on suspected importers or sellers of English goods, but the publication in the press of the names of importers by associations such as the Committee of the Aggregate Body suggests there was at least tacit acceptance and even promotion of such activities.[81] Indeed, the lord lieutenant believed the practice of publishing these names was "probably calculated for the abominable purpose of drawing the indignation of the mob upon individuals."[82]

The participation of those the lord lieutenant described as "the very lowest and poorest class of people" in the free-trade campaign has often been regarded as motivated by both economic concerns and elite manipulation and bribery.[83] To be sure, much of the crowd was composed of weavers residing in the Earl of Meath's Liberty, an area deeply affected by economic downturn. And elites did often provide alcohol and spectacle to attract and direct the crowd, but dismissing this as simple "bribery"' ignores the centrality of alcohol to all forms of politics in the eighteenth century.[84] The campaign of violence and intimidation also reflects the increased politicization of the "mob" as they appropriated the language and agenda of Protestant patriotism. For the weavers, the economy and "bread-and-butter" issues were intensely political, and the actions of the crowds reveal much about underlying assumptions about right order and political authority. As the preceding chapter suggests, the idea of trade and industry as foundations of national prosperity had become central to popular understandings of the economy over the course of the American war, making it difficult to separate purely "economic" motives from political ones.[85]

In many cases the direct action of the crowd anticipated the calls of the patriot opposition for nonimportation. The economic downturn of 1778 initiated a wave of crowd action. In June a mob "paraded the streets of the city and indiscriminately abused all they met" and reportedly killed John Kelly, coachman, off Castle Street. One newspaper contended that the economic woes of the weavers might be alleviated "if the handicraftman of the respective branches in the Woollen and Silk Business &c. would apply but half their time in the improvement of their manufacture, which they consume[d] in idle meetings, riot and every species of dissipation."[86] The same month, the lord lieutenant noted a crowd had broken the windows of two woolen drapers and "did some mischief" in a haberdashers' shop, before being dispersed by the magistrates and military.[87] In July the *Freeman's Journal* reported that "a disorderly, enraged multitude went from house to house destroying English goods wherever they could meet with them; they stove and spilt all the English porter they could find; and not content with this, they seized some casks of whiskey which they drank, and were proceeding in their outrage, when the guards came and dispersed them."[88] Such acts of violence became widespread; on 17 July "a riotous mob" of between four and five hundred people attacked the property of a Henry Maunsell, a tavern keeper in Stonybatter. Seizing the woolen cloth they found there, along with a large quantity of other cloth appropriated from a house on Pill Lane, they proceeded to Weaver's Square, where the cloth was ceremoniously burned. The Castle claimed that the crowd had also destroyed 505 pounds worth of goods, belonging to the Cavan linen manufacturers Henry Patterson and Hugh Cleary. A reward of two hundred pounds was offered for the apprehension of the rioters.[89]

A "Friend of the poor Manufacturers" reproached the weavers for their "unwarrantable, foolish, and self-destructive riots." When they had "continued quite," he claimed, "everyone beheld [them] with compassion; they pitied [their] distresses; they lamented the decay of trade which caused them." Deferential addresses and dignified suffering that provoked elite sympathy, rather than the ritualized destruction of English goods, it was suggested, would best serve the weavers' cause.[90] The following year, as the campaign for free trade became a political force, larger crowd actions took place. In June, an estimated crowd of three thousand "demolished" the windows of the house of Mr. Ball, "a silk-man," on Nicholas Street; they meted out similar treatment to the house of Peter Callage on College Green before being driven up Grafton Street by a party of Volunteers.[91] In July a mob attacked the house of Nicholas Mahon on Bridge Street, firing a pistol and taking away "several pieces of English cotton."[92] In November the house of a Mr. Hughes, a woolen draper at the Corner of Cock-hill and Michael's

Lane, was attacked by an armed mob because he was suspected of selling English goods.[93]

Publishing the names of those suspected of breaking the nonimportation agreement provided convenient targets for the wrath of the crowd. Although this tactic was criticized for promoting riot and disorder, the increasingly violent rhetoric of the patriot press could provide a justification for crowd action. Denunciations served to redefine the boundaries of community, depicting merchants who broke the agreement as both monstrous and treacherous. One newspaper, emphasizing the relation between print, the mob, and "traitors," warned merchants "that their names and places of abode [would] be given at large to the public, to shew what regard these vultures ha[d] for the distresses of the nation."[94] A letter signed "Mollyneux" asked, "[Why] in the name of common sense, will people encourage those canker-worms, who gnaw [against] the general interest . . . by importing foreign articles?"[95] "Hibernicus" went so far as to imagine the deaths of those breaking the agreement:

> Thus abused and insulted, with the gates of mercy shut against us, the patriot sons of Ierne resolved against commercial connexions with their oppressors. However, gentlemen, I detest the barbarous inquisition, I confess I should not be sorry to see those monsters in human shape, led along to the place of execution amid the hisses and imprecations of the starving manufacturers, with each a san-benito on, and a label fixed to his breast with the following inscription in capital letters, "Here goes the traitor to meet his just fate, who pampered the people of another country while he not only suffered but caused his own to starve."[96]

The patriot press routinely condemned crowd actions; but such representations of importers of foreign goods as monstrous traitors cannot have helped prevent further attacks nor the diffusion of the notion that many merchants were conspiring against "the general sense of the People."[97]

By October the attorney general, John Scott, claimed, "The People talk sedition and write treason everywhere."[98] On 15 November 1779, over a week after the Volunteer demonstration on the birthday of William III, the Dublin crowd engaged in some theater of their own, this time aimed at MPs and the government rather than unlucky merchants. The lord lieutenant wrote of a "violent disturbance which happened [that] day in this city":

This morning early, as I am informed, a drum was beat throughout that part of the city which is called the Liberties which is inhabited by great numbers of the lower classes of the people, viz weavers, dyers, tanners, skinners and such like, who thereupon gathered in a very large body, many of them armed with bludgeons, cutlasses and pistols and about twelve o'clock assembled before the Attorney General's house in Hanover Place and finding he was gone to the Four Courts, part of them attacked the front windows, doors &c with stones and brick bats, whilst another part went to the Four Courts and filled the avenues demanding the Attorney General to be delivered up to them who had escaped from thence to the castle. . . . They then assembled before the Parliament house and as the members came hither they made them get out of their chairs and coaches and administered an oath to them to vote for the good of Ireland, for a free trade and a short money bill.[99]

Newspapers accounts of the incident estimated a crowd of between five and eight thousand, noting that MPs "who approved themselves friends to their country, were received with the loudest acclamations of joy and gratitude;—the women joined in the repeated shouts of a Free Trade, Short-Money Bill."[100]

The lord lieutenant stressed that "the persons concerned consisted principally of the very lowest and poorest class of people who were so intoxicated with liquor as to be utterly insensible of the violence they were committing and of the danger to which they exposed themselves."[101] The patriot press presented a more sympathetic portrait of the crowd, drolly claiming that the crowd had "serious business to transact" with the attorney general. The crowd did indeed have specific targets in mind; Scott was the main object of their wrath, with one description claiming a "very great body of them ran to the Four Courts" in search of him "to assassinate him." Only the intervention of the popular politicians Samuel Bradstreet, an MP for Dublin, and Alderman Nathaniel Warren had prevented the crowd from destroying Scott's house, though windows were broken. Habitual government supporter John Monck Mason, MP for Saint Canice, Co. Kilkenny, and (during a brief dalliance with the administration) Sir Henry Cavendish, MP for Lismore, were also intended targets; the crowd even engaged in the symbolically unambiguous act of carrying a coffin for Mason through the town, though troops protected both their houses and persons from harm.[102] Patriots expressed misgivings over such interventions by the people. The Lawyers corps attended the protest unarmed; afterward they distributed a handbill throughout the city and Liberties stressing their support for a short money bill and free trade but warned, "Nothing is so likely to prevent the success of it as assembling again at the parliament house as you did this day."[103]

The government unsurprisingly represented the crowd as a homogeneous mass: drunk and idle, the dregs of Dublin society. But what else can be said about the composition and motives of this free-trade crowd? Although it is clear that the mob was increasingly active in Dublin from the spring of 1779 onward, it is harder to recover the motives of this crowd or the type of ideology that justified their actions. Women certainly seem to have been present at the larger crowd actions, but the extent of their participation in the violent aspects of "riot" is not known. The occupational composition of the crowd is easier to establish. This crowd appears to have been composed of weavers, dyers, tanners, skinners, and others affected by the economic downturn. But others were also involved. In June, a group of twenty butchers, an occupational group traditionally involved in ritualized street fighting in Dublin, participated in violent attacks on two woolen drapers.[104] By the 1770s the population of Dublin and the Liberties had become increasingly Catholic, and it seems likely that Catholics made up a good proportion of this and other instances of crowd action in 1779.[105] This is further suggested by a pastoral letter read at Catholic churches throughout Dublin on 23 November; the letter warned congregations to "avoid running with tumultuous or riotous meetings which [could not] but be offensive to magistracy and government and which by consequence must draw their severest frowns and censures upon them."[106]

If the Dublin crowd was confessionally and socially diverse, in what ways did this heterogeneous crowd relate to the wider patriot campaign? Was the crowd motivated by the language and symbols of the patriots that had dominated public debate throughout the year? Or can such actions be seen in the context of more "traditional" crowd violence, as part of a vision of a "moral economy"? Although most reports of attacks on the houses, property, and persons of merchants and traders accused of breaking the nonimportation agreement stressed the "disorderly" nature of the mob's actions, it is clear that these actions were "an expressive form of planned symbolic violence" on a group represented in the press as both monstrous and treacherous.[107] Attacks usually involved the seizing and destruction of suspected English goods. Windows were frequently broken during such raids. Elite politicians who failed to support free-trade demands were also targeted by the crowd in 1779 with only the intervention of popular politicians preventing the destruction of the attorney general's house; again windows were targeted in symbolic acts of violence against perceived enemies of free trade. Members of the crowd legitimated their intervention in the political affairs of the nation by claiming they had been called into action by patriotic members of parliament. Handbills purporting to be from a MP and "written in a very inflammatory style" had been distributed throughout the Liberties in the days prior to the riot. When a popular member of the house attempted to disperse the crowd, he was asked, "If you do not want us, why did you send for us."[108] This exchange indicates that the crowd believed, or at least claimed, that their actions were legitimated by MPs. It also draws attention to the central place of the Irish parliament for patriots at this time as the defender of liberty.[109]

Although occupational groups such as weavers used both the language of deference and threats of violence to draw attention to their economic plight, they were unquestionably familiar with the slogans of the free-trade campaign. In October a crowd organized around the cry "a free trade or death, and confusion to all importers."[110] In June a letter from "Sarsfield" to the *Hibernian Journal,* discussing the actions of the crowd, recommended "to those persons who ha[d] bound themselves by foolish [ties] and ridiculous ceremonies on the common in Kilmainham to return to their dwellings."[111] Such actions suggest that those involved in crowd activities engaged in formal ceremonies, perhaps in imitation of the public ceremonies that cemented the associations of their social betters to support nonimportation and nonconsumption.[112] Apart from such dramatic crowd interventions, more low-key acts of subversion and sedition continued apace throughout November; such acts continued to give the administration cause to worry about the political power of those out of doors. John Beresford wrote in late November:

> For you have no idea of the tyranny which is exercised over weak minds by the terrors of the mob. There are serious and premeditated acts, tending to put in jeopardy the rights of both kingdoms. There are also many trivial circumstances which also show the disposition of men's minds at this time, and which, although unworthy of notice at any other, yet at the present I think you ought to know; such as that very improper toasts are drank at public meetings, which I do not choose to repeat; that healths which used to be drank are now refused.[113]

As Beresford noted, drinking toasts might have been relatively unremarkable at other times, but in the context of heightened political tensions such acts took on more-charged and threatening meanings.

Patriots utilized a variety of tools to enforce nonconsumption and promote free trade. They appropriated the organs of official political culture: the county meeting, the grand jury, and the parliament. Association, the swearing of oaths, the threatening publicity of the press, as well as the mobilization of the people were all employed for similar purposes. In December, Lord North's announcement in the British parliament of proposals removing many restrictions on Irish trade has often been cited as a great victory for the patriot movement. However, many contemporaries were not so sure, and the problem of securing and furthering these gains became the focus of patriotism in proceeding years. The campaign for free trade promoted short-term association over a single issue; other, more enduring, forms of association also emerged. The Volunteers in particular promoted patriot sentiments and ideas of active citizenship for Protestant men. The remaining chapters will examine the politics and culture of the Volunteers, and the way in which this force transformed Irish patriotism, challenged confessional divides, and allowed large numbers of men (and some women) to participate in national politics.

5

A Rage *Militaire*
The Volunteers

IN AUGUST 1780 land agent John Moore of Clough, Co. Down, wrote to his employer Arthur Annesley on the subject of this swift rise of volunteer militia companies in his locality. Moore regarded this voluntary militia force with a mix of suspicion and apprehension. He admitted that while he "at first no means liked the scheme," after witnessing a large review he could no longer withhold his amazement and admiration: "I am so surprised at what I see that I can scarcely trust the evidence of my own senses. To observe a large body of men assembled in every part of the country compleatly armed, under Voluntary control only, put to enormous expense in their various appointments, drawn from their trades and professions, paying implicit obedience to officers of their own election and guarded by a sense of honour and emulation only, against every irregularity incident to mobs, is almost without parallel in History."[1] Moore's change of opinion captures many of the features of this movement that seemed novel, worrisome, or awe inspiring to contemporaries.

Protestant men had joined voluntary military organizations throughout the century for defense against invasion or to quell local disturbances. The Volunteers emerged from this tradition and were organized in the context of fears of a French invasion in 1778. Initially, many companies were under the command of traditional grandees and borough patrons, such as Lord Shannon in Cork and the Duke of Leinster in Dublin. As Moore observes, however, they were also innovative in many regards. They were military bodies independent of the government, organizing themselves in many instances along democratic lines, electing officers, and bearing much of the expense of military practice themselves. Grandees too eager to assert their influence or wary of Volunteer interference in politics could find themselves humiliated and marginalized, a fate that eventually befell both Shannon and Leinster.[2] By 1779 the Volunteers numbered forty thousand, and this figure may have risen as high as an extraordinary eighty thousand by the middle of 1782.[3] They came to encompass Protestant men from all social classes and eventually even Catholics, while overcoming the localism of their origins to create a regional and national structure and emerging as a powerful political force in their own right.

Many historians have stressed the continuity between the traditional militia and the Volunteers. Padraig Ó Snodaigh in particular has attempted in numerous local studies to "remilitarize" the Volunteers and relate them to the militia in opposition to what he sees as the excessive attention historians have given to their role in contemporary political conflict. Focusing exclusively on the officers of these forces rather than the rank and file, he argues that the Volunteers should be placed in "the pattern and tradition of loyal, local, military service" and has persistently portrayed the Volunteers as heirs of the militia and ancestors of the yeomanry.[4] In addressing the origins of the Volunteers as a loyal defense force against foreign invasion as well as their role in maintaining local law and order, Ó Snodaigh and others have indeed provided a valuable corrective to accounts that overemphasize Volunteer radicalism and even nationalist separatist tendencies. This narrow focus on the militia and the Volunteers as a military force nevertheless ignores the interaction of military and political cultures. Much recent work has examined the complex interactions between the experience of part-time soldiering and military ceremony and the articulation and negotiation of national identities, patriotism, and others forms of political subjectivity.[5]

The Volunteers were, of course, a military force but at the same time a form of voluntary association. They were part of an "associational world" along with convivial or political clubs, loyal societies, charitable organizations, voluntary hospitals, Masonic lodges, debating societies, and benefit clubs, which flourished in the eighteenth century.[6] Many companies emerged from these very forms of associational life, with existing Masonic lodges and political and convivial clubs particularly well represented.[7] Some lodges simply embodied themselves as Volunteer companies, as did existing patriotic and loyal clubs.[8] Although the Volunteers clearly emerged out of traditional forms of military organization and social interaction, in their internal regulation they instituted structures that were often democratic and self-financed through the associational instrument of the subscription. They created rules to organize and discipline themselves that were also martial and associational. Like other associations, they socialized in local taverns, raised funds for charitable purposes, disciplined negligent members, and publicized their activities in the press.

Participation in these local voluntary defense forces, which were sustained for several years, provided many men a type of civic education that moved easily from a focus on defense to the formulation of political resolutions. For many, their status as a citizen and a soldier were intimately related, as outlined in sermons preached to companies.[9] The Volunteers also served to reduce the social distance between the merchants, farmers, and artisans, who comprised much of the rank and file, and the gentry. Henry Joy, a member of the First Belfast Volunteer company and proprietor of the *Belfast News-Letter*, noted, "The cords of Society were drawn more closely together in the daily musters of the People under arms; and an approach was made between its several orders that had long been wanted in this country."[10] And while the "generality of interests" created by volunteering is no doubt romanticized by Joy and others, a force that emerged within traditional structures of hierarchy could both bolster and redistribute power and authority. In some instances associational principles had radical political implications, particularly when the principles and rules of these organizations were at odds with those of a gentry-dominated society and served as an implicit critique of existing structures of power.[11] This chapter first examines the origins of volunteering. Drawing largely on surviving minute books of individual companies, I then consider how companies organized, financed, and disciplined themselves as voluntary defense forces. Finally, I outline the debates that emerged over the legitimacy and consequences of this force, its impact on social relations, and the role of Catholics in the Volunteers. The next chapter elaborates on the variety of Volunteer spectacle that so entranced John Moore, the relation of participation in the Volunteers to understandings of masculinity, and the politicization of this movement and its apotheosis in popular culture.

The Origins and Rise of the Volunteers

A strong tradition of local amateur military service existed in eighteenth-century Ireland, both under the auspices of the government and as a parallel system of ad hoc voluntary forces. A militia emerged after 1660 as a makeshift body of Protestant men organized for local defense. Only after the Williamite settlement did the militia become a fixed element of Irish life, under government control and embodied to meet a variety of external and internal threats.[12] The Militia Act of 1715 regulated this already-existing militia force further; all Protestant men between sixteen and sixty were required to muster four days a year. The force turned out sporadically throughout the first half of the eighteenth century, with the threat of a French invasion in 1756 prompting the last major array.[13] Lieutenant governors of the counties were responsible for distributing arms and nominating officers to these forces, who were drawn from among the local gentry and notables. The governor of Cork wrote in 1691, "The greatest care was taken to place beloved officers over the men, which prudent conduct drew the men into the service of their country with all their hearts. The men were not to stray far to look for their officers, their officers were picked out of their landlords, friends, and neighbours."[14] Such elite understandings of the militia supports Sean Connolly's view that service in the militia was "a perfect expression of vertical social bonds," with men serving under a local leader and relations reinforced through displays of hospitality and sociability.[15] In this view, the militia was a stabilizing and conservative force that bolstered the authority of local elites and taught subordinates their proper duty.

Although it may have worked well as an institution cementing social relations, the military value of this force has been questioned by historians. The militia certainly suffered a chronic lack of arms and equipment; in 1760, when called upon to meet Commodore Thurot's invading French force at Carrickfergus, many of the men carried scythes because weapons were either in short supply or in a state of disrepair.[16] Alongside the official militia force, there existed a parallel force described as "volunteer" or "independent" companies, which seem to have been encompassed within the structure of the militia, their officers commissioned in the usual way. In 1753 the lord lieutenant of Antrim, the Earl of Antrim, reviewed the "volunteer and independent companies" of that county, suggesting little conflict between the varieties of amateur military bodies.[17]

The organization and function of the militia was understood in the context of a broader debate throughout Great Britain and Ireland over the role of standing armies.[18] The cost of the army in Ireland was frequently denounced in Parliament. Opposition to the army was also based on actual experience of its excesses, particularly a number of military outrages in the 1760s.[19] Others drew on a long tradition of antipathy to a standing army, based on their supposed connection with tyranny. The desire to reinvigorate a neglected militia force became a central issue for the nascent patriot party in parliament, with Henry Flood sponsoring several militia bills in the 1760s, largely in response to government plans to augment the army.[20] In 1768 Charles Lucas, who shared a traditional Whig suspicion of standing armies, contributed to this debate in a pamphlet against augmentation. While noting the expense of the military establishment, he feared that an increase in the size of the army in Ireland would inevitably "prove Fatal to Civil Liberty."[21] A standing army, particularly during peace time, was seen as a threat to liberty and the first step toward despotism. Alexander Haliday, a leading Belfast radical, wrote to a friend in 1771 condemning "the spirit of administration who certainly want[ed] to put fetters on [the Irish] and to have them riveted by a standing army." This was possible due, in Haliday's words, to the "selfish views of our representatives and the dastardly disposition of our degenerate gentry, who would rather indolently scheme for protection and a fallacious security . . . than exert themselves with a becoming manly spirit." This sorry situation would lead to a disarming of Protestants and a further augmentation of the army.[22]

As critics maintain, the rise of the Volunteers has often been placed rather narrowly in the context of the emergence of a Protestant nationalism in Ireland. But the experience of volunteering was not exclusive to Ireland. Throughout Great Britain, though on a much smaller scale, the creation of volunteer companies as local defense forces to augment regular troops and militia was common.[23] In the course of the War of American Independence, besides the large numbers in the army and navy, as well as the English and Welsh militia and the English and Scottish fencibles, as many as thirty thousand men may have been embodied in ad hoc volunteer units throughout Britain, numbers that no doubt fluctuated depending on the circulation of rumors of imminent invasion.[24] The British and imperial context is, of course, essential for understanding the emergence of Volunteer companies. In 1776 the war with the America colonies depleted regular forces in Ireland. Many patriots renewed their call for the revival of the militia, which had been neglected since 1760; fiscal difficulties prevented the government from implementing a militia bill in 1778, though at the same time it seems many favored a voluntary force over a more coercive and onerous militia service.[25]

The wider British context of volunteering is also apparent in the relationship many radicals observed between military and political participation; Volunteers could serve as a "people's army" guarding against the dangers of tyranny.[26] British radicals, who were to the fore in advocating military associations, observed developments in Ireland with interest. Although British volunteering did not become a significant political force, some radicals hoped that Ireland might provide a model for a similar English force. In 1780 John Cartwright wrote to the leading Volunteer Francis Dobbs, "I do not yet see any prospect of corps similar to those of Ireland becoming sufficiently numerous in this country to render any essential service to the cause of freedom: but as our foreign enemies increase it is possible that external danger may yet give rise to them." If such a force did emerge, Cartwright hoped that Dobbs might provide practical advice on "associating, arming, clothing, training and supporting a volunteer corps, in order to be prepared for shewing the easy practicability of the thing and to remove all difficulties."[27] Militarization and politics were related in other ways. Forms of popular protest throughout Britain and Ireland since at least the Restoration frequently modeled themselves on marital examples.[28] Earlier forms of popular protest in Ireland had also embraced the trappings of military organization. The predominantly Catholic rural protest movement, the Whiteboys, which emerged in Tipperary in the 1760s, organized themselves in military formation.[29] The Hearts of Oak, a largely Presbyterian movement protesting tithes and taxes in Ulster beginning in 1763, created "companies," adopted colors, and openly marched in array, accompanied by bands. Indeed, this "militia" aspect of the movement seems to have reinforced the Oakboy's sense of their own legitimacy. A similar movement, the Hearts of Steel, likewise organized along martial lines.[30]

Organization and Finance

Advocates of Volunteering might claim that every citizen should be a soldier. At the same time, volunteering involved considerable expense and organization. Organizational and disciplinary rules, along with articles of association, were drawn up. Expenses could be considerable. Uniforms, arms, and other equipment were needed, so funds had to be raised. The minute books of a handful of companies permit a reconstruction of these organizational aspects of volunteer in its early stages, as well as illustrating tensions that existed between traditional social hierarchy and some of the more democratic aspects of these military associations.[31] The volunteer companies of 1778, while clearly emerging from a Protestant militia tradition, differentiated themselves from the past in several ways. First, many companies entered into a written "Association" that defined their purpose and clearly outlined their internal organization. The Newry Volunteers in their "Association" of September 1778 declared their objective: to defend the country against foreign and domestic enemies, to uphold the constitution, and to acquire expertise in arms.[32] They declared that "every Citizen whose health [was] not infirm or situation very peculiar should be, in some degree, a soldier." Traditional militia companies had been under the control of the government, which commissioned the officers. Many companies, particularly those in the North, now emphasized both their "independence" from government as well as their democratic organization. Indeed, while much recent scholarship has attempted to trace the continuity between volunteering and the traditional militia, it overlooks the fact that many companies rejected government control from their inception. In August 1779 the government did offer commissions, but by this time the idea seems to have been unpopular.[33] As early as March 1778, the Belfast Volunteers pledged to be governed by a majority of the company and to refuse government commissions and therefore the basis of the militia structure.[34] The Newry Volunteers likewise stated, "We engage to bear our own expenses, accepting neither pay nor commission from the Government."[35] There were a variety of reasons for opposing a government-controlled militia. James Hamilton, regarding the rise of volunteering in Derry with apprehension, recalled a conversation he had with a Volunteer who informed him that his company would not take commissions from government, for "if they had they might have been called on to go elsewhere."[36] The Rathfriland Volunteers also emphasized the local and independent nature of their company, proclaiming that they would "keep the peace in [their] town and neighbourhood" and would only subordinate themselves to the military discipline of their officers "where they commanded [them] within the county of Down."[37] Such attitudes reflected a widespread fear that a militia force would be called on to serve outside its locality.

Companies also stressed their democratic structure. The Rathfriland Volunteers admitted new members only through a ballot supported by three-quarters of the company.[38] Many companies elected their officers. In August 1779 the Doneraile Rangers resolved, "No subordination shall be between officers and men, except under arms."[39] The Armagh

Volunteers underscored this democratic aspect in their articles of association, declaring, "We will be governed in every case that may arise by the declared sense of the majority, saving that on actual service we will be solely commanded by our officers."[40] The Newry Volunteers also declared, "We will in all things be governed by the laws of the Company to be determined by the majority."[41] The right to vote, as in other forms of association, was reserved for those who paid their subscriptions in a timely manner.

The idea of "independence" from official interference was valued by many companies. In other ways, particularly with regard to the supply of arms, the Volunteers were as reliant on the government as the traditional militia. But companies now hoped to acquire government arms without placing themselves under official control. Many companies suffered from a chronic shortage of arms and petitioned the government and the county governors to distribute arms reserved for the militia. This caused difficulties for the representatives of central and local government. In Armagh, as governor of the county, Lord Charlemont was responsible for storing and distributing militia arms; as a consequence, he was inundated with requests for arms.[42] He doubted the legality of distributing arms to independent associations and was at first uncertain how to deal with such requests. After he consulted the lord lieutenant, his fears were confirmed, and he initially refused to release any weapons. Until June 1779 Buckinghamshire had turned down applications, but by the end of that month he abruptly changed policy and requested authority to issue arms; given the unpopularity of plans for commissions and the sheer weight of demand for arms faced by the lord lieutenant and the governors, Charlemont claimed that the government decided to "steer with the current which they could not stem."[43] Eventually the government issued sixteen thousand weapons, with five hundred distributed to each county through the county governor. Neglected since the 1750s, many of these weapons were in a state of disrepair. William Brownlow, MP for County Armagh, wrote from Lurgan in July 1779 requesting arms, noting that he had one hundred muskets and bayonets from 1760 that were now "unserviceable."[44]

The availability of arms was significant in the appeal of particular companies. When Edward Tipping arrived in Armagh to array the company of Upper Fews, he found "a great many of that company particularly the young fellows had entered into different corps near them where they got arms despairing of getting any in the Fews."[45] There was intense competition between companies for the limited supplies of functioning arms available from official sources. With arms scarce, a number of factors determined to whom they were distributed, particularly reputation and social status. The perceived respectability of a company was critical in reviewing requests for weapons. In response to Charlemont's queries on the character of one Volunteer requesting arms, Alex McCullagh informed him, "I do not know much of Mr. James Black of Derrynoose, Armagh as to say whither he is a proper person to entrust with arms but am informed that about twenty creditable young men (tho' not freeholders), tenants and tenant's sons under Lord Farnham . . . have associated with Mr. Black but that it is not likely the company will be respectable unless Lord Farnham gives his concurrence."[46] This involvement of a local notable was critical in the establishment of a "respectable" company that could acquire arms from the government, though such individuals often took no real active part in the life of the company.[47]

Volunteer companies were eager to maintain their independence and avoid government control, though it seems reliance on official sources for arms was not regarded as compromising this independence. Volunteer relations with members of the local gentry were equally ambivalent; companies were often dependent on the wealthy for funds and the stamp of respectability but anxious to avoid falling under the sway of notable individuals. Many companies were almost completely financed by the local gentry, who assumed command. John Barrington raised and outfitted two companies, the Cullenagh Rangers and the Ballyroan Light Infantry in this capacity, while his son commanded the Kilkenny Horse and the Durrow Light Dragoons. In June 1779 Mr. Crooks of Lurgan offered to "clothe and arm such of the mechanics" of that town who desired to volunteer.[48] Others were equally generous. In October 1779 Richard Johnston of Gilford, Co. Down, wrote that he planned to embody and clothe "good Protestants" on his estate and many others seem to have done the same.[49] James Stewart of Killymoon gave a hundred guineas, colors, and two pieces of canon to the Volunteer companies he commanded.[50] In February 1780 the Wexford Independent Volunteers thanked Henry Hatton for "his liberal support in clothing, arming, and accounting a number of men whose limited circumstances otherwise would have prevented them standing forth at this important period."[51] A month later the same company addressed Vesey Colclough to acknowledge his "unbounded liberality" through which he had "embodied, clothed and disciplined" the company at his own expense.[52] Such actions were equally represented as part of traditional patterns of largesse serving to bolster hierarchical relations based on ideas of deference.[53] It also allowed those without substantial means to outfit themselves and participate as citizen-soldiers and so helped to broaden the social profile of volunteering.

Many of the gentry threw themselves enthusiastically into military theatrics. Others were less eager, though often had little choice in leading and outfitting companies. James Hamilton, agent for the Earl of Abercorn, complained that Volunteer companies were forming in Strabane, noting, "They at the same time offered me the command and have press'd me to write to our Representatives to endeavour to procure for us from government a hundred stand of Arms colours, drums &c."[54] Hamilton, like many other local notables called on to lead local companies, viewed volunteering as a bothersome, time-consuming undertaking, but one that it was difficult to avoid. As volunteering began to expand rapidly in late 1779, many men intent on entering companies lacked the financial resources to participate fully. In February 1780 Richard Charleton, of the Barony of Strabane Battalion, informed Abercorn that new companies were being organized in Strabane; as many of the men associating lacked the finances for clothing, arms, and accoutrements, they had resolved to "apply to every nobleman and gentleman who had property in this barony in hopes of obtaining a certain subscription from each."[55] Pressure to contribute to local companies could be considerable. The bishop of Derry complained, "The companies of Volunteers are multiplying: contributions are more than solicited—they are in a manner exacted and non-protection denounced against those who do not contribute."[56] Subscriptions were a principal means of raising money for local companies. In September 1779 it was reported that in King's County a "liberal subscription" was made to meet the cost of raising men for local defense. In February 1780 the Ennis Volunteers thanked those who "liberally and voluntarily subscribed to aid [their] fund."[57] At the same time, they asserted menacingly that "gentlemen" who did not either attend company meetings or subscribe would not "merit the protection" of the company. By 1783 the company was threatening nonsubscribers with the sanction of publishing their names in the local press.[58] Again, it is not always clear how "voluntary" such subscriptions were; intense social pressure was often placed on local residents to subscribe to the cost of supporting companies.

Although David Miller claims that the Volunteers should be defined in terms of "personalistic ties of patronage," companies were often just as wary of elite influence as they were of government control.[59] The

Lawyers and the Merchants Volunteer companies in Dublin were praised in the *Dublin Evening Post* for "excluding all men of high rank from holding any dominion over them" through the practice of rotating the highest commission throughout the company. The correspondent congratulated them for "scorning to be a feather in the cap of any nobleman," suggesting that other companies were viewed in such a light.[60] Companies with limited means could assert their independence by refusing any offers of assistance. In November 1779 David Bell, a captain in the Newry Fencibles in Armagh (a company composed of fifty-four of "the principal gentlemen of this place"), noted that a similar number of tradesmen had requested to join this company. Unable to afford arms, they had nevertheless refused Bell's offer to purchase them and had rather requested government arms.[61] For many men who lacked the means to become uniformed and armed volunteers, the only options were to accept the largesse of the local elites, appeal to the government for a share of the militia arms, or open local subscriptions. These methods were often combined, and the preferences of particular companies depended on a variety of factors, chiefly relations with local gentry and the degree to which the corps believed such funding would compromise their "independence."

Volunteering involved a variety of expenses. The Men of Mourne Company recorded an expense for the cost of lodging and food for Samuel Youart in Newry, where he went each week to learn the fife, while James McBride was also sent there "to learn the art of drumbeating."[62] The cost of drill instructor, drummer, and fifers comprised a large part of companies' general expenses as they strove to emulate the regular army in the performance of their military exercises. Over a few months in 1778 and 1779, the Ennis Volunteers paid out £10 in expenses relating to the hiring of drill sergeants, drummers, and fifers; the purchase of powder, ribbands, drink, and turf added to the expense.[63] Subscriptions helped finance these general expenses; officers of the Ennis Volunteers paid a fee on joining the company ranging from £2 16s. 10½d. for a lieutenant colonel to 11s. 4½d. for an ensign. Members were required to pay a further 1s. 1d. each month to cover expenses.[64]

Companies created an elaborate system of fines to support general expenses and to enforce the military discipline to which companies aspired. In the Ennis Volunteers, nonattendance at meetings or reviews merited a 6d. fine, while the same offense warranted 2d. in the Rathfriland Company. This company proposed similar fines for nonattendance at "publick worship" and for "speaking, laughing or behaving disorderly while under arms." Drunkenness on the day of a public meeting was punished with a fine of 1s. 1d., with fines doubled for offending officers. The importance of discipline was also emphasized through other regulations and methods of punishment. The Portaferry Volunteers established rules for, among other offenses, "the punishment of mutiny, disobedience of orders, drunkenness on parade or during field days or exercise, slovenlyness in arms at any time and persons and arms on field days, non-attendance on duty, misbehaviour under arms, vis speaking in the ranks, and looking giddily behind and about contrary to that graceful and steady deportment, so proper and necessary for a disciplin'd Volunteer to conduct himself by." The punishments for offenders were not simply pecuniary but also focused on the public honor of company members, a sanction believed to be effective across the social spectrum. For the Portaferry Volunteers, this included "drumming out privates from the company and shooting of them in effigy as a mark of disgrace," followed by publication of their offense in the *Belfast News-Letter*.[65] Other companies employed this mode of public shaming, with one correspondent lauding its effects on two privates in Connaught, even though "the Delinquents were of the lower class."[66] In Kilkenny a dispute between Sir John Blunden and local Volunteers resulted in a paper war and concluded with the burning of Blunden in effigy while he was said to warm himself at the fire.[67]

A variety of other techniques were also employed to enforce discipline. The Rathfriland Volunteers stated that while swearing could "scarcely be supposed to happen in an Independent Company," if it should occur "let there be no fine but an universal [hiss] of abhorrence." The Rathfriland Company set down a system of court-martial to deal with disobedience and disorder, composed of officers as well as a number of privates chosen by ballot. Deserters were a particular focus of this form of discipline and were to suffer "ignominy and contempt" of the company for this offense. No company seems to have initiated a system of corporal punishment in imitation of regular forces, and, indeed, the Rathfriland Company explicitly rejected such practices.[68] As voluntary organizations, of course, beyond a system of fines companies had few disciplinary options open to them apart from the ultimate sanction of expulsion, which seems to have been used relatively frequently, perhaps reflecting the problems with attendance and subscriptions endemic to associational culture.

Along with establishing discipline, uniforms were central to Volunteer conceptions of the citizen-soldier. Nearly all companies wore the traditional scarlet coat, though some wore the blue of the regular artillery or the green of rifle units while white, buff, and gray were also worn.[69] Each company customized their coats with its own facing colors for the cuffs and lapels and other accessories. These colors were carefully recorded in minute books or printed in articles of association in the press. Facing colors proclaimed the distinctiveness of the company.[70] Volunteer companies expended considerable effort and expense in their attempts to look the part of a military force, adopting the paraphernalia and technical language of the regular army.[71] Although frequent doubts have been cast on the Volunteers' potential as a defensive force, as the next chapter describes in more detail, many companies certainly looked the part. Along with a strong commitment to order and discipline, they provided an impressive spectacle.

Equipping a volunteer was an expensive undertaking. Flintlocks cost between 28 and 38 shillings.[72] The Men of Mourne Company paid 7s. a yard for the scarlet cloth of their uniforms.[73] Most companies also required swords, belts, gorgets, cartouche boxes, and bayonets, which all added to the cost of becoming a citizen-soldier. It was estimated in 1782 that equipment for horsemen cost as much as £80, while for foot soldiers it was about £20, figures suggesting that volunteering required substantial means.[74] Good materials were often hard to acquire, particularly outside the large towns, but companies expended considerable effort. In May 1780 the Men of Mourne Company corresponded anxiously with Thomas Carson of Downpatrick about the price and availability of a range of soldierly accoutrements, eventually agreeing on a price for fifty sets. Stuart Moore, the secretary of the company, reminded Carson that the clasps and buckles of the bayonet belt "be well executed" and bemoaned the fact that the leather was too buff.[75] To ensure the "strictest uniformity" in the clothing of the company, a committee was established to "treat with the several Master Taylors in the Barony of Mourne" and to agree on an appropriate cut and price for the material.[76] Of course, not all Volunteer uniforms were equally gorgeous, with the prohibitive cost putting many accessories or the more expensive cloth outside the reach of most Volunteers. At the same time, it does appear that most Volunteers were well turned out and cut a pleasing spectacle at reviews and other formal displays. As described above, wealthier members of companies often helped defer the costs of outfitting those of more modest means, thus expanding the social profile of volunteering beyond those initial recruits who could have afforded such a costly undertaking.

Choosing a uniform was a serious undertaking; the issue increased conflict as companies began to form battalion and regimental structures and act outside their local communities. In January 1780 Benjamin Bell wrote to Lord Charlemont from Armagh concerning such a dispute. Unsurprisingly, given Charlemont's stature in Armagh and his role as de facto leader of the Volunteers, Bell had assumed that the united companies of that county would adopt the colors of Charlemont's company. Yet he found that James Dawson, captain of the Orior Volunteers, had chosen a black facing for their uniforms and "declared he could not insist on his men changing their uniform." At the same time, he discovered that the officers of the Old Armagh Company were "violently determined against" the facings of the company commanded by Alexander Patton from the nearby village of Clare and refused to send a major until the uniforms were altered. Bell's dispute with Dawson and Patton perhaps reveals some underlying social tensions between the different companies. Bell continued, "Every company of our battalion are uniform and we will not receive any other corps in any other dress, and almost every officer in our battalion are men of property in their county and the whole of the other battalion, Mr. Moore excepted, have not an acre of estate in the county; except the Lieutenant-Colonel, I might give them the widest expanse."[77] Uniforms and other martial accoutrements not only were the cause of dispute among companies but could also promote harmony and a sense of common purpose. Items such as gorgets, belt plates, and helmets were often inscribed with the name of the company as well as its motto. The gorget of the Kilworth Volunteers was inscribed with the motto "Vis Unita Fortior" (Union is strength; see fig. 11), that of the First Armagh Company with "Pro Patria Non Timidus Mori" (Not afraid to die for my country). The gorget of the Belfast Volunteer Company was decorated with a harp and crown and the motto "Devotum Morti Pectus Liberae" (Death in freedom's cause). The Killymoon Volunteers proclaimed "Pro Patria" (For my country), while the Portaferry Volunteers emblazoned theirs with "Pro Rege et Lege" (For king and the law).[78]

Colors were central to the pride of any company, serving as the main focus of Volunteers' public ceremonies. The presentation of the stands of colors was accompanied by elaborate rituals including orations and consecrations.[79] Protection of colors in the course of combat had been a traditional preoccupation of the regular army. Volunteers, while never troubled by actual service in the field, adopted the rhetoric of devotion to their colors and bravery in their defense. In 1781 the Ormond

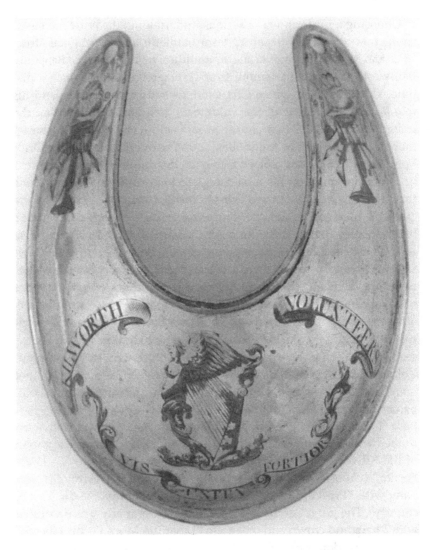

Figure 11 Gorget of the Kilworth Volunteers (Courtesy of the National Army Museum, London)

Volunteers, after the presentation of new colors, published their resolution "never to abandon them, nor suffer their lustre to be tarnished in [their] hands by any dishonorable act."[80] The colors were often made or embroidered by wives of officers, but some were produced by local painters.[81] Colors were of ornate design and, as with gorgets and medals, were embroidered with the motto of the company and symbols that

Figure 12 Guidon (flag) of the Mayo Legion (Courtesy of the Irish Georgian
Society, *Bulletin* 33 [1990])

often reveal much about the ideology of different companies.[82] Many
banners displayed fairly conventional sentiments, expressing their attachment to patriotism, the king, and Protestantism. In August 1780
Colonel Roche presented the Imokilly Horse company with new colors
emblazoned with a crowned harp and the mottoes "Dieu et nos Droits"
(God and our rights) and "Libertas et Natale Solum" (Liberty and my
native soil).[83] Many included mottos that were ambivalent in their loyalty, such as "Pro Rege saepe, pro Patria semper" (For my king often,
for country always; see fig. 12).

"A Republicanism of Spirit"

Public ceremonies, such as the presentation of colors or the donation of
clothing and weapons, often emphasized the unity of purpose among
Volunteers and between the social orders, but volunteering also put
considerable strain on relations between elites and their social inferiors.
Although the traditional militia has been represented as an expression
of harmonious hierarchy, local elites were often reluctant to become involved in the Volunteers and uncertain of their power over this force. A
traveler in the North wrote approvingly of a dispute in October 1780:

"You have seen that the companies will not be *officer-rid*, since some of them have protested against their proceedings and resolutions at large, others against the election of even a chaplain without their consent, and a third have got their officer to declare his signature a forgery. I am heartily glad to see such gentry exposed when they would pretend to give the sense of the people."[84] James Hamilton had been distinctly ambivalent about the value of Volunteer companies in his locality since their emergence in July 1778. He had reluctantly accepted the command of the Volunteers in Strabane in order to exert a moderating influence over them and prevent their "going to very improper lengths." In December 1779 he was approached by Andrew Leitch, the son of a tenant, who informed Hamilton that Leitch himself and twenty other young men, swept up in the military enthusiasm of the previous summer, had been practicing military exercises for the past month. They now hoped to form their own company but first wanted Hamilton's guidance on the matter. Hamilton was unsure what advice to offer the young man. As he explained to his employer: "Had I advised him much against it, he certainly would have told it, and as certainly I would have been in the papers declared an enemy to my country, for there was a resolution offered at one of our meetings last week, that the person who did not take some active part, should be stigmatized with that epithet."[85] The democratic structures of companies equally troubled Hamilton. The same month he despaired: "Now I find it that those who they call their commanders, must obey their orders; they are their constituents and their orders must be observed."[86] Buckinghamshire, the lord lieutenant, also viewed such practices with alarm. In October 1779 he claimed, "There are some companies whose principles are determinedly republican." His concern went further: "From every quarter . . . more corps are forming, as whatever may be their professions and avow'd principles they are in general independent of their ostensible leaders, that tho' sober people reluctantly speak out, they are in fact uneasy respecting the line of conduct which the spirit of the moment may induce them to adopt."[87] Hamilton was to experience this independence of the rank and file from their supposed leaders firsthand. With the eleven companies of the barony of Raphoe forming themselves into a battalion, he informed his company of his choice for a commander of this force, a Mr. Hamilton: "I was astonished to find a person dissenting from it, as civilly as they could they gave their reasons against it" and instead proposed the son of the Stewarts of Killymoon.[88]

Often members of the local gentry became involved in volunteering in order to exert some influence over companies or to shore up their electoral interests. Charlemont believed that the majority of gentlemen took leadership of companies "from interested and more especially electioneering schemes."[89] Hamilton, in 1780, wrote that he thought it "pretty evident that more attention [was] given to Volunteers on account of the approach of election."[90] William Steel Dickson claimed that "many gentlemen of landed property who, at first opposed, or barely tolerated, the measure; and even some who seemed to dread the armament of the people as much as they hated American independence . . . assumed the uniform of their country." Dickson believed this change of heart occurred "merely to keep their tenantry under control" and also because volunteering had become fashionable.[91] Elite attempts to influence the companies they patronized did not always have the desired effect. In 1780 the Duke of Leinster was involved in a public dispute with the radical Napper Tandy when he attempted to limit the political role of the Dublin Volunteers. Although Tandy was eventually expelled (and went on to form the Independent Dublin Volunteers), the duke's authority among Volunteers was greatly diminished.[92] Even such a figure as the Earl of Shannon failed in his efforts to direct the local company.[93]

Many believed that the Volunteers had inspired a dangerous independence and hostility to deference. Richard Musgrave, writing after the 1798 rebellion, saw in the Volunteers the origins of many of Ireland's woes, for the body had "destroyed subordination, so essential to the existence of social order; for persons of low rank, associating with their superiors, lost that respect which they had entertained for them, and were inspired with leveling principles."[94] Hamilton and Musgrave were not alone in recognizing the relationship between volunteering and a spirit of independence. Supporters of the movement also offered eulogies on this aspect of volunteering. William Drennan, in a pamphlet addressed to Edmund Burke, offered one of the most forceful accounts of the democratic consequences of volunteering and the way in which it had "levelled" social distinctions:

> The emulation of individuals in the use of arms, the frequent meetings of collective bodies which produce military attachment and coincidence of political opinion; and the leveling of social distinction of rank and fortune, necessary in martial evolution and manoeuvre, concur in giving the lower ranks of the community an independence and

republicanism of spirit, that will have much influence on their future
conduct; will tend to remove that servile awe of estated tyrants which
is incident to the lower orders of men; and will secure the free and unbiased election of the representative body.[95]

Drennan, like many other commentators, believed that volunteering resulted in a greater social intercourse between classes and that those at
the lower end of the social scale developed ideas of political independence through the practice of volunteering. The organization of quasi-
democratic, disciplined companies; the drafting of petitions, addresses,
instructions, and resolutions; and their appropriation of the ceremonial
life of the nation gave such men what another author described as "consequence." Volunteering reduced distinctions between Protestants of
different social classes. It also had an impact on confessional divides.
As Sheridan's remarks in the introduction suggest, many commentators
asserted that the force had ameliorated relations between Presbyterians
and members of the established church. Relations with Catholics were
also said to have improved. Yet the question of the relationship of the
Volunteers to Catholics was a vexed one from the beginning. The problem has continued to preoccupy historians, though much of this has
focused on high politics and Volunteer attitudes to the "Catholic question."[96] The next section examines the role of Catholics in the Volunteers and the debates this provoked.

Catholic Volunteers

On 1 August 1780 the Volunteers of Dundalk gathered in the Market
Square to celebrate the Hanoverian succession, firing twenty-four volleys, before marching to the King's Arms for a dinner, which was followed by many "loyal and patriotic toasts." The evening concluded
with "the greatest mirth and happiness." Such a scene was hardly unusual in 1780, with the press reporting hundreds of similar events
throughout the country. However, as the author noted "with singular
pleasure," this company included several Catholics. Not only were
Catholics central to this company, but the author averred, "Not a Volunteer Corps in the kingdom assembles with more cheerfulness, unanimity and harmony."[97] Catholics were also conspicuous in the rituals
of other companies, participating in events in Dingle and Longford,
among other places.[98] Although it is impossible to estimate the extent of
their involvement, Catholics participated in the movement in many

areas well before their influx into the force in 1784. And while some Volunteers, and many subsequent historians of the movement, represented the period in terms of the decline of prejudice and the forging of a new unity across confessional divides, the participation of Catholics was contentious.

Many companies excluded Catholics. William Steel Dickson recalled how in Ulster, Catholics "in great numbers, and with great zeal offered themselves as Volunteers, in common with their Protestant and Presbyterian neighbours." However in most of the province, their offers were rejected "not without insult."[99] In 1780 the formation of the "Catholic Division of the Tyreril Volunteers" in Sligo led to a confrontation outside Sligo town and the disarming of the Catholics by the Sligo Loyal Volunteers.[100] In Wexford the issue of arming Catholics was divisive. George Ogle, leader of the Wexford Volunteers, also organized the General Association against Whiteboyism, which focused on prosecuting Catholics in possession of arms. Ogle was also at the fore in resisting Catholic participation in the Volunteers in Wexford in 1781.[101] Protestants in County Meath proved particularly resistant to the idea of Catholic Volunteers.[102] In July 1781 a meeting at Trim presided over by the county sheriff sparked considerable controversy by adopting resolutions explicitly condemning the participation of Catholics in companies in that county. In doing so, the group stressed the legal soundness of its position: "That according to the laws now established it is not lawful for any papist to carry arms unless he be licenced by the chief governor of this kingdom and the Privy Council thereof to carry such arms as are appointed by the same." As a consequence, it concluded that Protestant Volunteers in Meath should refuse to attend reviews along with those of the "Popish persuasion."[103] Protestants in Meath had been criticized in the press in 1779 for associating with and arming Catholics. "A Protestant" in Trim noted sardonically, "Let no man be alarmed—in these times when we freely admit of a tolerant *Somnolency*, nothing can be more apprehended from putting Arms into the hands of Papists!" and concluded, "Let the Legislature alone be the judge whether the principles sucked in by the papists at the breast and enjoined by the merciless tenets of their religion, are so blunted as to entitle them to the liberties of Protestant subjects."[104] The following year the Grand Jury of Meath entered into resolutions against Catholics bearing arms.[105]

These resolutions provoked much debate in the press. A letter from "Hampden" in the *Dublin Evening Post* was particularly vehement in defense of Catholic participation. Catholics, the author argued, had long since demonstrated their loyalty to the king and government through both their "peaceful demeanor" and "in their readiness to defend the kingdom against all invaders." He was certain the gentlemen of Meath would revive the memory of "the Irish massacre dressed up in the most bloody of colours" in order to justify their resolutions. Against this divisive vision of the past, "Hampden" argued that it was "high time to bury all remembrance of religious discords in the grave of oblivion." In Munster and Connaught, he claimed, Catholics made up two-thirds of Volunteers, and even outside heavily Catholic regions Protestant and Catholic Volunteers drew "together in the greatest amity and friendship."[106] "Juvenis" wrote from Kilkenny to condemn the Meath resolutions, noting that "no distinction of religion" was known between Protestant and Catholic Volunteers in that town.[107] Volunteers in Meath did eventually unanimously resolve to admit Catholics to their different companies. However, certain conditions were applied. Before admission, in order to certify that the candidate was "a person of character and property," a Catholic was required to take the oath of allegiance and be approved by the majority of the corps.[108] By this time, many Catholics in the area had accepted an invitation to join the Drogheda Volunteers in neighboring County Louth.[109]

For many of the same reasons as their Protestant counterparts, the Catholic gentry were often eager to partake in the enthusiasm for volunteering; for some, it was also a means of expressing their loyalty to the regime. In July 1781 Charles O'Conor of Belanagare noted that local Catholics had been invited to join Volunteer corps there and that "they prided in the circumstance of being trusted in active service at a time of threatened invasion." At the same time, he suggested there was an element of compulsion for some Catholic tenants; many found it difficult to decline these invitations "without disobliging their Protestant landlords." As one of the ever-cautious leaders of the Catholic Committee, O'Conor expressed misgivings over Catholic participation in the Volunteers, favoring a return to "the *passive* state prescribed to them by the laws of their country."[110] Writing to fellow Catholic Committee member John Curry, he asked, "Was ever any conduct more improper and indiscreet than incorporating ourselves with Protestant militant associates, with the laws of our country so express and so penal against us for meddling with arms?"[111] Catholic volunteering was also viewed askance by many Protestants. Local notables attempted to use their influence to prevent Catholics from volunteering, particularly if those companies were outside Protestant influence. During an invasion scare in May

1779, the Earl of Tyrone wrote to his brother: "On the Alarm here of the French landing I found from their Zeal that the Roman Catholics in all parts of the country were full of forming themselves into independent companies and that in a neighbouring county it was actually begun, the variety of consequences which must attend such an event, tho' I am convinced well intended, are so obvious." Tyrone eventually convinced local Catholic leaders to halt their plans in order to avoid alarming Protestants, but the question of Catholic volunteers continued to cause tension throughout the country.[112]

As the discussion of Catholic Volunteers in Meath makes clear, the issue of Catholics bearing arms was particularly sensitive. Protestants had long feared the consequences of weapons falling into the wrong hands. In 1760 Catherine Ball wrote from Ballymoney of her Uncle William: "He is ever dreaming of plots, conspiracies, and rebellions, and since the year 1715 when he received a Commission from the Whig Ministry of Queen Anne to search the houses of Roman Catholics or suspected Roman Catholics for fire-arms, he thinks he sees a murderer or assassin in every unfortunate Papist that he meets." Indeed, Ball suggested that her uncle was not unusual, noting of others who received commissions, "Severely did they exercise the power entrusted to them."[113] Again, Protestants in County Meath were particularly vigilant in this regard, with the grand jury offering a reward for those successfully prosecuting Catholics in possession of arms. In 1776 the assize at Trim indicted Edward Flood, a Catholic, for carrying arms, though he was subsequently acquitted.[114] Numerous letters to the press in 1779 and 1780 also reflected on this issue, the actions of the Meath Volunteers in particular provoking a fierce debate in the press.[115]

The arming of Catholic volunteers assumed such significance not simply because of concern with legality or from a fear of Catholic revolt, though neither factor was unimportant; they also possessed a symbolic power. To possess arms, or to be trained in their use, served to assert membership in the polity, particularly for poor Protestants, Presbyterians, and also for Catholics. The rhetoric of the "citizen-soldier" was central to the ideology of Volunteering, with the bearing of arms a central aspect of this character. William Drennan wrote, "The possession of arms is indeed the prime distinction of a freeman from a slave. He who has nothing, and belongs to another, must be defended by that other, and needs no arms: but he who thinks he is his own master, or has any thing he can call his own, ought to have arms to defend himself, or otherwise he must live precariously and at discretion." Drennan believed the bearing of arms was an essential feature of citizenship; it also created unity across traditional social divides: "Arms made Irishmen worthy of their weight, and necessity made all ranks of men unite in a common cause; and every rank rose in self-consequence and attained greater elevation in the scale of society."[116]

Participation in a voluntary militia could serve as a civic education, putting into practice the vision of the citizen soldier. Hundreds of companies formed from 1778 onward, organizing themselves along associational lines, engaging in military training and discipline, establishing quasi-democratic structures, and by the end of 1779, coordinating themselves along "national" lines into a Volunteer army. The associational structure of this force challenged existing hierarchical structures and justified political participation by those outside the polity. The free-trade campaign allowed the Volunteers to bring their considerable weight to bear on political issues, and from this point on they became increasingly assertive as an extraparliamentary force. The next chapter examines this increasing politicization by focusing on the way understandings of "manliness" were vital in legitimating the political role of the Volunteers, as well as the spectacle of volunteering and the wider cultural implications of the force.

"Playing the Man"

Invasion, Masculinity, and the Citizen-Soldier

Be of good courage, and let us play the men for our people, and for the cities of our God: and the LORD do that which seemeth him good.
2 Samuel 10:12

THE VOLUNTEERS took seriously their self-appointed military role as defenders of the nation. As the last chapter demonstrated, they expended considerable time and effort in equipping, organizing, financing, and disciplining their companies. In the context of Britain's imperial crisis, this military enthusiasm also had broader cultural and political implications. With the entry of the French and the Spanish into the war on the side of the colonies, fear of invasion gripped the nation. Among many Protestants this revived suspicions over the loyalties of Irish Catholics. At the same time, patriots offered a competing vision of the nation under siege, united across social and religious boundaries against a common enemy, based on a vision of a shared Irish identity. Defense of the nation was depicted as a particularly masculine sphere of endeavor. Volunteer sermons serve as sources for the articulation of contemporary understandings of what it meant to be a man. A heroic masculinity, as embodied in a citizen-soldier army, was considered vital for defense against impending invasion. The traits of manliness also encouraged the cultivation of personal "independence" and could ultimately justify participation in the affairs of the nation. Manliness was placed in opposition to servility and slavery, with the Volunteers ideally positioned to express an independent "manly virtue" through the very organization of their companies, their spectacular military displays, and their political resolutions. This chapter examines both the practice of volunteering and the ideology that validated this force. These factors are explored in the particular instance of the mobilization of the nation against feared invasions beginning in 1778, when the French entered the war. Then, through an examination of Volunteer sermons, it considers the representation of masculinity in relation to the expansive ideal of the citizen-soldier. This ideology justified a broader vision of political participation that, by 1783, led some companies to recruit Catholics en masse and advocate radical parliamentary reform.

The politicization of an independent armed force was controversial. Although the emergence of the Volunteers has often been depicted as the moment when the middle class begin to play a decisive role in Irish politics, the way in which this new role was represented has received less attention.[1] The ideology and practice of volunteering were important in justifying their political role. Manliness, as a sign of disinterested public spirit, was a crucial factor in the politicization of the force as the Volunteers became involved in the political controversies of the day, such as free trade, legislative independence, the reform of Parliament, and the place of Catholics in the political nation. The mobilization and politicization of the Volunteers had consequences for articulations of national identity, with many Protestants adopting an "Irish" political and cultural identity characterized by manliness and at times defined in opposition to Britishness.

"A Cargo of Priests, a Pope's Legate, and a Consecrated Standard": Invasion Fears

Writing from Cork in October 1779, Richard Pigott observed, "Apprehensions of invasion continue strong in the minds of the people here. Should such a misfortune happen, I trust and believe we shall show ourselves men."[2] Volunteering emerged in the context of an emergency, the threat of invasion in the course of an international conflict. This crisis shaped the political and cultural evolution of the Volunteers. With the entry of the French into the war on the side of the rebellious American colonies in 1778, followed by the Spanish in June 1779, there was a palpable apprehension of an attack on Great Britain and Ireland.

Stephen Conway has recently argued that this fear was an important factor in the emergence of a British identity, for it "engendered a sense of beleaguered Britishness."[3] How did this fear influence identities in Ireland? Among Irish Protestants, though they remained divided over the war with the colonies, as well as other issues such as the rights of dissenters and the need for political reform at home, the fear of invasion did produce a united front against a common foe. But this did not necessarily result in a shared Protestant Britishness. Mobilization also resulted in the formation of local voluntary defense forces, later to coalesce as a potent political citizen army. The Volunteers were central to efforts that tested and redefined the limits of both Britishness and Irishness.

That local defense forces were deemed necessary at all derived from the removal of many British troops to fight in the war and the failure of the government to mobilize the traditional militia. For many balladeers and pamphleteers, the exigencies of war and colonial policy had led Britain to abandon Ireland to its own defenses; thus the Volunteers were represented as an expression of the triumph of a besieged Irishness.

The threat of invasion also offered Catholics the opportunity to declare their loyalty and contribute to national defense. The press readily published details of cooperation across confessional lines as evidence of this new national unity. At the same time, many Protestants remained suspicious of Catholics' ultimate loyalties. The language of antipopery was far from dead; the possibility of attack served to remind many of the threat from within, which though quiescent of late, had not gone away. The fear of attack acted in complex and contradictory ways, uniting Irish Protestants in a manner that shares much with an identity of "beleaguered Britishness." But it also suggested the limits of identification with Britishness, opening up debates over the meaning of "Irishness." Alarm over invasion led many to promote an understanding of Irish identity that attempted to sublimate confessional and social divisions and replace them with a rhetoric of national unity.

Invasion fears captured the imaginations of people throughout Ireland. Popular literary and theatrical culture attest to the theme, with an outpouring of ballads, poems, and plays focusing on various themes: the military camps established all over Great Britain and Ireland; the efforts of men and women to prepare for the arrival of the French; and the patriotic enthusiasm the threat aroused. On the stage, Frederick Pilon's *Invasion, or a trip to Brighthelmstone* was produced in Limerick and elsewhere in 1779.[4] George Farquhar's perennial favorite *The Recruiting Officer,* a comedy concerning questionable recruiting practices, was once

more revived.[5] Richard Sheridan's successful play *The Camp* was
performed in Belfast in 1779 and in Dublin in 1780. This topical piece
provided a spectacular account of Coxheath, one of the largest military
camps in England. The play served principally as an excuse to present
military drills and patriotic songs against a backdrop of spectacular
scenery. Besides the central love story between a soldier at the camp
and his cross-dressing sweetheart Nancy, the play also focused on British fears of French attack and infiltration through networks of spies. Of
particular interest to an Irish audience would have been the character
of O' Daub, a blundering Irish painter, who arrives to paint scenes from
the camp (for use in theatrical sets for a play on military camps). His
sketches arouse suspicions, however, and he is mistaken for a spy. His
nationality and religion further enflame their fears; the soldiers assume
he is an Irish Catholic sympathetic to the French. As one soldier describes it, he has been accused because "he has an O to his name."[6]

Ballads and poems also focused on invasion. A ballad published in
the *Hibernian Journal* is representative of this genre:

> When Frenchmen and Spaniards so vainly did boast
> Of Landing their Armies on our Irish Coast,
> Hibernians did laugh at the Dons and Monsieurs,
> Defended by Heroes, the brave Volunteers.
>
> When Britain cried out, that poor Ireland was gone,
> And could give us no help, but must save number one;
> That their Fleet could not cope with the Count D'Orvilliers,
> Why, then did associate our brave Volunteers.
>
> . . . .
>
> Tho' some may behold them with a jealous eye,
> And in Self-defence rank Rebellion may spy;
> Courtiers may conjure, with Sieve and with Shears,
> To discover the meaning of brave Volunteers.
>
> But the Irish for Courage and Loyalty fam'd,
> Or rebellion or Treason they never yet dream'd;
> In Defence of their Country to weld their strong Spears,
> Is the honest intention of the brave Volunteers.

Like much of this invasion literature, the ballad pours scorn on the
threat posed by the Spanish and the French, while also celebrating the
bravery of the Volunteers. It emphasizes the loyal nature of volunteering, and accuses those who question their motives of being "courtiers."
The ballad ends by suggesting a sexualized notion of patriotism, urging

women to withhold their affections from "cowardly Coxcombs" and give their attention instead to Volunteers.[7] Significantly, it also accuses the British of deserting Ireland in its moment of need, suggesting the ways in which a common British identity could fracture when faced with the demands of war.

Rumors and alarms of invasion made mobilization a common experience for men and women in communities across the country. The press trafficked in reports detailing sightings of enemy vessels, wild rumors of invasion and espionage, and accounts of army and Volunteer mobilizations. Fears mounted over the affects of this sensationalist reporting. "Hibernicus" suggested that rumors alone put the lives of Irish women at risk, "it being the lot of the female sex to experience that weakly state in which the impressions of terror [were] often inevitable death."[8] Despite such condescending concerns, Martha McTier, whose husband, Sam, was a leading Volunteer, noted in September 1778: "We are kept in a constant state of alarm night and day, and the terrors of a visit from the French give rise to no other conversation. This is one of the things gives me no dismay, though Sam was raised at two o'clock on Sunday morning by an alarm from the coast, that assembled all the officers and put most of our women to pack up plate etc."[9] Such preparations show that mobilization impinged on not only Volunteers and the army, but also women like McTier preparing their husbands for defensive duties and reviews.[10] As a citizen army, the Volunteers were related to specific localities and households. Many sermons and ballads placed particular emphasis on their role as defenders of the nation, property, and women's virtue. The social world of volunteering, while often represented as masculine and homosocial, was also rooted in sphere of the family and community sociability.

Invasion scares served to demonstrate the unity of local communities, involving not only Volunteer companies but also women, Catholics, and the lower orders. In June 1779, as Volunteers in Cork, including the Boyne, Aughrim, and Culloden companies, celebrated the king's birthday with exercises and maneuvers, a letter arrived claiming that several ships had been sighted in Bantry Bay. As with many such reports, this was a false alarm. But the report of the scare in the local *Hibernian Chronicle* emphasized local unity and the participation of local Catholics in the mobilization: "A great number of Roman Catholic gentlemen immediately offered themselves as volunteers, to join with their fellow Protestant Citizens, and were well received . . . as they readily seized this opportunity of testifying their loyalty to the King, and

great zeal for the protection of our country."[11] A letter to the same newspaper claimed that mobilization in the face of invasion was central to
the emergence of patriotic sentiment and led to the "generous Youth,
the veteran Citizen, the Protestant and Papist uniting in the common
cause."[12] The same month, Catholics in Derry were praised for their
readiness to help during an invasion alert in the course of a celebration
of the king's birthday in that town. Reports and notices of thanks from
Sligo and Clonmel also took care to laud Catholic offers of assistance.[13]

Lower-class Protestants could also share in this enthusiasm. Volunteering in its early days has often been portrayed as a rather socially
exclusive phenomenon. This is perhaps unsurprising given the cost of
purchasing uniforms and the various accoutrements on which many
companies insisted. Yet as early as August 1778, as the first companies
were forming around the country, Protestants lower down the social
scale expressed their patriotism through mobilization. A letter from
Wexford noted that the "lower class of Protestants" was forming a company in imitation of the other companies in the town. The correspondent acknowledged that "they performed their exercises tolerably well"
and were addressed as follows by their captain: "Boys it is true we are
not dressed in scarlet but why should we not fight as well in any other
colour? Consider we are fighting for our liberties and if we are con-
quered we shall have nothing but French slavery, Popery and small beer;
if we conquer, we shall have liberty, property, and good Irish porter and
strong beer."[14] Ordinary Protestants could utilize the fear of French invasion to express their own relation to the nation: a distinctly Protestant
and anti-French understanding of liberty. Fear of invasion might promote a rhetoric of national unity, but it could also stimulate still-vital
Protestant fears of popery.

Apprehensions of invasion were ultimately groundless, but this did
not make them any less terrifying. Sermons reflected this fear, encouraging vigilance and depicting the disquieting consequences of conquest by a foreign power. In August 1779 James Crombie, a dissenting
minister, addressed an audience that included the Belfast Volunteers on
the role that a love of liberty and the constitution could play in motivating patriots: "To be forced to surrender up the invaluable privileges of a
free constitution, to be stripped of our inherent rights, to become the
vassals of a despotic monarch exhibit a prospect, that must rouse all the
sensibilities of men accustomed to nobler ideas, and born to the freedom of regarding no laws but such as they themselves have made." For
those who lived under "despotic sway" and "knew no law," conquest

would be of no real consequence, Crombie claimed. However, for Irish Protestants, "[to] fall in the last expiring efforts of this honourable contention, would be infinitely preferable to our surviving the liberties of our country."[15] Crombie was not alone in offering such a catastrophic vision. John Rogers, preaching before Volunteer companies at Lisnavein in June 1780, was particularly exercised by the threat conquest posed to religious liberty. Rogers believed that the "safety and security of religion should be preferred to [their] very lives." But invasion by France or Spain would lead to the establishment of popery and an end to all religious liberty. Rogers had little time for the conciliatory language of some of his coreligionists who "in this *enlightened* and *catholic* age" distinguished between loyal Catholics and others: "For Papists, as such, must be enemies of the Protestant interest."[16] While others observed that some Catholics had taken the oath of allegiance to the king, Rogers pointed out that many had not. He had misgivings over the loyalties of the Catholic clergy in a war with Catholic powers. More menacing, Rogers believed, was the insolence of lower-class Catholics: "Our wives and children know very well how they were insulted by common vagrants, many of whom would presume to affix a certain day, before which the French would invade us."[17] Fear of common cause among Catholics across national boundaries remained among Protestants despite protestations of loyalty by associations such as the Catholic Committee.

Even in the unlikely event that Irish Catholics remained loyal, Rogers argued, an invasion of the French and the Spanish would bring with it the horrible sight of a "cargo of priests, a pope's legate, and a consecrated standard." William Nevin rehearsed the many deliverances "wrought by God" on Great Britain and Ireland over the centuries, from the Spanish Armada to arrival of "our glorious Deliverer" William III. However, even with God firmly on their side, Protestants should still "exclude all confident Presumption" in the face of current enemies. Protestants needed to be active in their own defense. Like Rogers, Nevin expressed doubts about the loyalty of Catholics in the event that "a foreign enemy of the same religion erected his standard," but was sure that French popery should be "resisted unto death."[18] Many shared Rogers's misgivings. Government officials in Dublin had little doubt about the political leanings of Catholics. In 1777, authorities in London were informed: "Should an enemy there invade this island, the attempt is most likely to be made in the South and South West parts of the Province of Munster" as this would enable them to transport "arms to distribute among the inhabitants there who are by far the greatest part papists."[19] In June 1778 a letter was received outlining "a plot for a revolt in the west of Ireland among the Roman Catholics, with a view to overturn the present government by the aid of the French and the Spaniards."[20]

Mindful of the Protestant paranoia fueling accusations of French sympathies, Catholic leaders maintained a strongly loyalist position. Professions of loyalty, as a means of achieving relaxation of the penal laws, had long been the policy of the Catholic Committee, and in the late 1770s and early 1780s, Lord Kenmare continued this careful strategy. In June 1779, as free-trade protests raged, the committee sent an address of loyalty to the king and another to Buckinghamshire.[21] At a local level, Catholics across the country drafted addresses to George III stressing their loyalty in the event of invasion. Some of these efforts were organized by nervous members of the Catholic Committee, eager to assure the government that Catholic participation in the Volunteers was a loyal undertaking. Charles O'Conor, in his role as a member of the Catholic Committee, was involved in organizing a loyal address from "the principal Catholics" of Roscommon in order to legitimate Catholic involvement in the Volunteers in that county. Leading Catholics in Limerick presented a similar address.[22] An early expression of allegiance came from the Catholics of Enniskillen and County Fermanagh in May 1778. They addressed the king, assuring him, "We will to the utmost extent of our person with our lives and fortunes support every measure that will tend to maintain the rights of the constitution, to secure the dignity of your crown and to disappoint the designs and punish the perfidy of your enemies."[23] The entry of the French into the war in 1778 produced a flood of loyal addresses to the king including several from Catholics. In Waterford, Catholics joined with their Protestant neighbors to reaffirm their steadfast attachment to their monarch.[24] In April the Catholics of Newry held a public meeting where over four hundred men signed an address to the king. They declared their loyalty and support for the war, as well as their willingness to fight for the king, if only the law permitted Catholics to acquire arms: "We humbly beg leave to assure your majesty that the undutiful, obstinate and ungenerous perseverance of America gives us heart-felt grief; we feel for the distresses of the parent-state like afflicted sons, and weep that tears are the only arms allowed us to prove our attachment to your royal person."[25] In August 1779, Catholics attended a town meeting in Drogheda and offered their assistance, with forty-seven of their number signing an address asserting they were "firmly attached to His Majesty as subjects" and proclaiming, "[We are] ready at this critical time (or at any time it may be necessary) to risk our lives and properties in defence of the peace of this kingdom against all enemies whatsoever."[26] Catholics in Galway expressed similar sentiments in September 1779.[27]

Father Arthur O'Leary, a Capuchin, was particularly concerned with ensuring the loyalty of the Catholic lower orders in the event of invasion.[28] In September 1779 he addressed his pamphlet against aiding an invading force to "the common people of the Roman Catholic religion," advising them to "remain peacably in [their] cottages." An invasion, he claimed, would not result in greater freedom or the recovery of ancient estates, arguing, "Whatever distinction the laws of this kingdom may make between Protestant and Papist, a conqueror's sword makes none. War levels and confounds all religion." He noted that the French had not joined the Americans out of love for "Presbyterians" (suggesting how the rebels were regarded), but rather "all religions are alike to a political people, whose only aim is interest and conquest." Protestant generals, he observed, were now commanding the French army, further evidence of the lack of their fidelity to the Catholic cause. While recognizing that ruined castles and the names of old estates inspired "sentiments to which the lower class of people in other countries [were] entire strangers," O'Leary argued that the French could not be relied on to undo ancient grievances. In a Protestant kingdom, loyalty and Catholicism were not necessarily incompatible. Prussian, Dutch, and Hanoverian Catholics, who all lived under Protestant governments, could join their sovereigns against Catholic powers. Irish Catholics, he believed, were also capable of such loyalty in defense of their king and nation.[29]

"Playing the Man": The Volunteers and Military Masculinity

As the main bulwark against an anticipated invasion, the Volunteers embodied and celebrated a particular brand of militarized masculinity. Masculinity in eighteenth-century Ireland had long been demonstrated by displays of lavish hospitality, hard drinking, fighting, and dueling among the gentry, as immortalized in the recollections of Jonah Barrington and his colorful tales of "fire-eaters" and "half-mounted gentlemen." Heavy drinking and extravagant hospitality do seem to have characterized masculine behavior among certain sections of the Irish gentry, as attested by Barrington as well as numerous English travelers.[30]

Middlemen in particular were targets of criticism. The agriculturalist and travel writer Arthur Young (who briefly served as a resident agent to leading Volunteer Lord Kingsborough on his estate at Michelstown, Co. Cork) famously described Munster middlemen as those who "hunt in the day, get drunk in the evening, and fight the next morning."[31] Yet although such commentators were eager to note how far Irish practices deviated from British standards of civility and politeness, it seems that in general the lifestyles of the Irish gentry did not differ markedly from that of their British counterparts.[32]

A code of honor was also central to notions of manliness. Although, once again, the extent of this practice was not as different from British and European patterns as contemporaries imagined, it did reach the height of its influence in the 1770s and 1780s.[33] Personal honor and public reputation were central to the identities of gentlemen in Ireland as in other societies dominated by an "honor culture." This obsession with honor was not simply confined to the elite but was widely diffused, with varying degrees of acceptance, among professionals, the lesser gentry, and the commercial interest. A code of honor was influential across the social spectrum. The *Dublin Evening Post* reported in 1780, "So prevalent is the practice of duelling become and so fond are the lower orders of people grown of cutting each other's throats, in imitation of their betters, that two journey-men card makers in New Row having some altercation a few days ago, agreed to decide it in an *honourable way* the next day."[34] The journalist's mockery of lower-class pretensions suggests that honor was regarded as a socially exclusive attribute. However, such incidents indicate that a plebian code of honor did exist, vigilantly defended by the duel.

Opposition to dueling emerged in the press in the late eighteenth century. The convivial society the Friendly Brothers of St. Patrick was established throughout the country to oppose the practice.[35] Yet such opposition proved largely ineffective in reducing the number of duels. Periods of intense political conflict increased the likelihood of dueling as political quarrels degenerated into personal insult and attacks on individual honor.[36] Electoral contests contributed to a large proportion of such duels.[37] Patriot politicians, such as John Hely-Hutchinson, were particularly prone to dueling. Patriots and Volunteers in parliament, including Edward Newenham and Isaac Corry, or street demagogues, like Napper Tandy, were also involved in highly publicized affairs of honor. The most notorious matter of honor of the century occurred between the leading lights of Irish patriotism and the Volunteers,

Henry Grattan and Henry Flood, in 1782. Political divisions between the two led Grattan to launch a blistering personal attack on Flood in the Commons, in which he concluded, "You are not an honest man." Although a duel in this instance was narrowly averted due to the attention of the authorities, it illustrates that for patriots personal honor was central to political reputation.[38] Volunteers initially seem to have refrained from dueling, and some were involved in antidueling societies. But as conflict increased within the movement over issues such as parliamentary reform or the establishment of the fencibles, so did incidences of dueling.[39]

Volunteering then did not simply displace prevailing notions of masculinity associated with a code of honor. Nor did it supplant traditional recreations associated with manliness, as evidenced by the drinking culture that characterized Volunteer sociability. It did, however, offer the opportunity for the expression of a different form of manliness that, although based on concepts of honor and courage, understood these traits in terms of patriotism, participation in the political life of the nation, and the ideal of the citizen-soldier. Volunteer masculinity, as an aspect of national identity, could also be contrasted with English national character; recent imperial misfortunes suggested an inexorable decline of British military manliness.[40] The Volunteers stressed a disciplined form of masculinity that, for example, frowned on drunkenness while engaged in military maneuvers.[41] Reports of Volunteer reviews and crowds in the press consistently emphasized the good order and lack of violent incident among Volunteers' ranks. The masculinity of the Volunteers was expressed through sartorial display, military discipline, the bearing of arms, and a language of virtue permeating all aspects of public life.

Volunteers were eager to emphasize the manly nature of their endeavor. A letter from "Sarsfield" defending the actions of the Volunteers in 1779 proclaimed, "Our resolutions are humble though manly; and a decent fortitude mark the features of our Associations."[42] In speech and in writing, "manly" expressions were those associated with freedom and forthrightness. Martha McTier described her native Belfast as a town where politics was "treated with manly freedom." Political resolutions that met her approval were characterized as "manly and noble."[43] The rhetoric of manliness permeated political discourse in eighteenth-century Ireland. What was the military manliness of the Volunteers thought to consist in? For William Drennan in his *Address to the Volunteers of Ireland* (1781), the active maintenance and pursuit of liberty was a central and agreeable aspect of patriotic manliness: "There is a pleasure that noble minds feel, even in pursuit of liberty, that its possession could not communicate to slaves. This earth can supply us with few objects more illustrious than a great and active spirit, moving onward in the all-sufficiency of manly virtue, and with zeal that strikes fire from disappointment, to a practicable perfection of public freedom."[44] Forms of subjection, and particularly slavery, were frequently equated with "unmanliness" in patriotic discourse. If the English subjection of Ireland could be understood in terms of the "unmanning" of Irish patriots, then the Volunteers were represented as a reassertion of manliness or the "active spirit" of "manly virtue," as Drennan describes this zeal for Irish liberty. Patriot attitudes toward Catholics were also understood in terms of manliness and slavery. Discussing plans by radical patriots to ally themselves with Catholics in order to push for parliamentary reform, William Todd Jones described Catholic men excluded from the political nation as living "a precarious, unmanly despicable existence."[45]

The discourse of masculinity was also central to sermons preached before Volunteer companies that reflected on the meaning of manliness and courage in the context of war and the threat of invasion.[46] In these sermons a number of Volunteer chaplains chose to explicate a passage from the second book of Samuel, in which Joab leads the army of Israel to repel the forces of the Ammonites and exhorts them to "play the men." The use of this passage was commonplace in Ireland and Britain during war, threats of invasion, or national days of fasting and humiliation.[47] Volunteer chaplains saw a clear analogy between the besieged Israelites and the dangers facing Ireland, with James Crombie extending the comparison to the Volunteers, describing Joab's forces as composed of "the chosen citizens of Israel."[48] For George Carson, as discussed above, the need to "play the men" was of particular urgency given the danger of invasion from popish foes, whose dreadfulness he demonstrated by recounting their "barbarities and cruelties" in recent history. Though the phrase was principally addressed to soldiers, Carson understood "Be of good courage, and play the men" as applicable to everyone, "for in time of danger, every one should be a soldier, or at least know the duty and discipline of one." In particular, "to play the men" meant to "exert every ability and resolution [one was] capable of, in defence of these invaluable rights and privileges" consisting of civil and religious liberties.[49] Those who refused to fight for these liberties were "not only unworthy of life, and the noble name of MAN," but

should be branded cowards, "the most degrading epithet among all nations." Civil liberties involved not only everything that could "render
life *supportable* but even [that which rendered it] *comfortable* and *easy*."
To depict the awfulness of the loss of these liberties at the hands of
popish invaders, Carson asked his audience to imagine the horror of
enforced solitude on "desolate shores," emphasizing the "sociable" nature of man.[50] Aspects of manliness acquired meaning only through the
practice of these values in the context of society. Religious liberties too
were in mortal danger: popery had "always marked her steps, wherever
she trod, with blood,"' which he illustrated with lurid descriptions of
the history of popish persecution. Given the interest of every man in
preserving these liberties produced by the "great chain of society," it
was imperative in this time of danger for each man to consider "the
public interest as his own."[51]

Central to Carson's understanding of "playing the man" were displays of courage, the ability to "contend for those things that [were] so
dear and valuable to [Irish Protestants], that even life itself is not life, in
point of enjoyment, without them."[52] Courage led men to lay down
their lives for their country and religion. Opposed to what Carson saw
as true courage was the danger of "effeminacy." He speculated that "all
nations whatsoever have lost their courage and liberties, and become
effeminate, in proportion as they have departed from virtue and true
religion."[53] Failure to behave in a manly fashion, then, was not simply a
private matter but one of vital interest to the health and security of the
nation. As Carson implored, with regard to manliness, "Let the names
public and *private* be blended together."[54] The public spirit and the bravery of the Volunteers were for Carson the "life guards" of the nation
against such dangers. Spreading throughout the country "like a stroke
of electricity," volunteering had promoted fraternal bonds of manly affection. Volunteering, he assured his audience, would not only protect
the nation against "perfidious enemies" but would at the same time
"fan the flames of brotherly love" among them by encouraging "disinterested feelings of refined passion" among those men "fighting for
the same cause, the same religion, the same liberty."[55] Throughout the
world, he believed, freedom was on the wane; the decline of British imperial fortunes served as the clearest example of this trend. But a manly
defense of the values of freedom and liberty had not been entirely ex-
tinguished. If called into the field to fight, the Volunteers would be defending "these glorious and immutably happy privileges [for which]
the Americans [were] now pouring out their lives and fortunes," while

the Swiss cantons also offered examples of "boldness and public spirit" that might inspire Volunteers.[56] The ultimate expression of true manliness for Carson was heroic death in defense of the nation; such a fate was more heroic than to "spin out a life of misery."[57] Andrew Alexander, in a sermon preached at Urney, argued that military instruction would likewise protect against tyranny at home and guard against a "designing Prince . . . bent upon destroying the liberty of his subjects."[58] This could be demonstrated by the example of the history of Rome or, Alexander suggested, closer to home in the display of Protestant bravery in the course of the siege of Derry.[59] Contemporary events also served to illustrate his argument. Revealing his sympathies regarding Britain's imperial woes, he suggested that the actions of the colonists could be interpreted as a similar type of heroic masculine endeavor, noting, "It is scarcely to be doubted, but the present time will enable posterity to add another of the same kind on the other side of the ATLANTIC, as illustrious and memorable as any that history can afford."[60]

For John Rogers, manliness was likewise an essential component of Protestant patriotism. Again, vividly depicting the base intentions of popery, a threat from both without and within, he concluded, "It is better to die freemen, than to live as slaves: our bodies groaning under cruelty, and souls destroyed by idolatry."[61] Manliness was central to the defense of the nation. Courage was "that fortitude of mind whereby a man [could] oppose the greatest dangers, without being disconcerted, or incited to commit base actions." Men should "act like rational creatures, not hurried on by natural instinct, like a ravenous beast upon his prey." True manliness was a moderated passion or "the medium between timidity and rashness." For Rogers, to "play the men" necessitated action: "Many can talk like men, who can not play the men." A courageous man, he contended, "talks little, especially of himself, and brags less: He is not the hero of his own tale, but rather loves the silent language of the hand, and to be seen than heard." This was a gendered understanding of courage. Such men would clearly differentiate themselves from women, who were "volatile, taken up with shews and trifles, and too often deceived with outward appearances."[62]

The idea of a manly character could also serve to legitimate the participation in politics of men beyond the formal political nation. Andrew Alexander also believed that throughout history luxury ("that bewitching Sorceress") was responsible for the degeneration of masculinity and the decline of empires.[63] He regarded volunteering, and particularly a knowledge of the use of arms, as central to the expression and revival of a patriotic manliness. In the first place, military exercises disciplined the bodies of young men: "Whoever has attended to the many branches of the military exercise, must allow, that the different attitudes of the body, and the various motions of the limbs that it requires, tend to give youth the free and ready use of their bodily parts, by which they must insensibly acquire an EASY MANNER, a DECENT EXTERIOR, and a MANLY PORT." Volunteering would also serve as a means of socialization for young men, particularly those "bred up in the shades of obscurity." Use of arms would also instill a personal and political independence, fostering in these youth "a manly spirit and just sense of their own importance." With this knowledge they would not be "easily intimidated or overawed into any measure whereby their own, or the credit or interest of a friend [might] suffer."[64] Not only would they oppose "insolent invaders," but the Volunteers could also transform social relations within Ireland. Citizen soldiers would "assert their rights as men and members of society" and "oppose the arbitrary encroachments of such as [were] meanly inclinable to lord it over their weaker neighbour." Knowledge in the use of arms would educate men in their "natural rights" and teach all "orders of men" to "treat other persons who [were] naturally equal, tho' neither on point of outward fortune, nor mental endowments, yet upon a level ALL, in their claim to humane and equitable treatment from one another to the free use and full enjoyment of all those rights that NATURE or social compact allow[ed] them." It would be particularly beneficial to "the subordinate classes of mankind" that had previously been regarded as "a timid, weak and spiritless herd, fit only to be led or driven, as the mere will of the superior dictate[d]." They could now "acquire an importance in society" to which they had been "in a great measure, strangers."[65]

Presbyterian preachers celebrated the Volunteers while also suggesting the force served as a sort of school for civic virtue and political independence; Church of Ireland sermons, on the other hand, were more circumspect, particularly as the Volunteers became a radical and politicized force. In 1779 Francis Turner had preached what he pointedly titled "A Constitutional Sermon" to the Enniscorthy Buffs in County Wexford. Before the same company in 1784 he praised the Volunteers for their role in defending the nation from invasion but reminded his audience, "You took up arms not to reform the constitution, but to defend it." Turner questioned the ability of the people to guide the "ship of state," suggesting such a complex task was best left to traditional elites. As the radical convention met in Dublin, Turner lamented that the uneducated "lowest artisan" assumed to direct the ship of state "without chart or compass." As a consequence of this constant debate and assembly, he feared, "They will new-model the constitution."[66]

Much of the patriots' criticism of the government and its supporters was couched in terms of an attack on their "servile effeminacy." Such language was hardly novel and did not involve a wholesale assault on the aristocracy. In March 1780, during a dispute with lower-class and more-radical members of the company, the Dublin Volunteers feted their leader, the Duke of Leinster, for his "manly and truly patriotic conduct" in parliament, and Volunteer leaders were routinely praised for displaying manly political principles.[67] Lord Charlemont, the leader and hero of the Volunteers, although a committed Whig, was more at home in the world of aristocratic connoisseurship than on the review field. A sickly man, he was also a poor public speaker, lacking the widely acclaimed eloquence of other patriot heroes such as Flood and Grattan. This unlikely hero was celebrated in numerous poems as a valiant military leader, though his ill-health was not ignored. One poem, for example, published in *The Volunteer* in 1781, feted him as Ireland's liberator:

> Lov'd Charlemont's approach; much honour'd name,
> To all Hibernia dear—FREEDOM'S chosen star,
> Shining in all the dreadful pomp of war;
> While her bright satellites around him move,
> Bright in the orbit of their country's love.
> IN vain disease would on his vitals prey,
> No; LIBERTY preserv'd him for this day;
> Sent her own SON to heal the God-like man,
> And fill up all the outlines of his plan.

The poem concluded that in judgment of Charlemont and the Volunteers, history, "wielding high the far illum'd pen / with exaltation points out, 'these are MEN.'"[68]

À la *Militaire*: Volunteer Uniforms

From this leader and hero to the lowliest Volunteer, a central aspect of the Volunteer citizen-soldier was sartorial display. A common feature of almost every private or printed account of observing a volunteer spectacle was the impression made by the finery of uniforms. Volunteer uniforms were not only on display at reviews or drills; the craze for military dress injected militarism into everyday life. Uniforms were worn at balls, at the theater, and on the street. MPs were not immune to this fashion for military uniform; Wheatley's painting of Grattan's famous speech in parliament attests to the importance of the Volunteer uniform as a public marker of patriot affiliation. Prints and paintings of Volunteer leaders emphasized a heroic, assertive masculinity.[69] Charlemont and many other aristocratic Volunteers sat for portraits dressed in the splendor of a military uniform. Beyond the elite, uniforms were equally conspicuous, with less-elevated subjects than Charlemont sitting for portraits as Volunteers. These portraits served as a means of representing the status and patriotism of the sitter. Portraits were not concerned with representing the "likeness" of the subject in a "realistic" sense. The process involved discussion and negotiation between painter and sitter over posture, the props, and the background of the painting, all of which were part of a process of self-fashioning. Clothing was perhaps the central way through which status and identity were represented in eighteenth-century portraiture.[70] Clothing, as David Kuchta argues, "was not merely an inert political symbol—some static afterthought of power that manifested preformulated ideologies." Clothing itself was "a form of power, enacting the articulation, negotiation, and personalization of power. Manners and material culture gave shape to ideological processes; material signs formed and informed systems of power, rather than standing outside them in some exterior symbolic realm."[71]

The symbols of a heroic masculinity embodied in the Volunteer uniform served as a means for the contestation of political authority and legitimacy, a way for elites to reassert their claim to leadership, but also for those outside the elite to appropriate the aristocratic ideals of masculine character and integrity to outline a broader vision of the political nation. This is evident from the importance placed on uniforms by many companies, as described in the preceding chapter, as well as in the market that emerged for portraiture of the middling sort in their uniforms. Hugh Hyndman, a lieutenant in the Belfast Third Volunteer Company, chose to portray himself in uniform, along with the accoutrements of his successful tobacco company (see fig. 13). Hyndman was painted by Joseph Wilson, a successful local artist who also painted the Earl of Antrim in his Volunteer uniform. Another prosperous merchant, Waddell Cunningham of the Belfast First Volunteers, was painted by the well-known Dublin-based portrait painter Robert Home.[72] These individuals, among many others, chose to represent their social position in their portraits through a variety of different signs such as the

Figure 13 Joseph Wilson (fl. ca. 1766–93, d. 1793), *Lieutenant Hugh Hyndman*, ca. 1782 (© 2009 Ulster Museum, Collection of Ulster Museum, Belfast; photograph reproduced courtesy of the Trustees of National Museums Northern Ireland)

trappings of their businesses or their homes, but most prominent among these was the uniform that informed the viewer of their role as citizen-soldiers. The rejection of Volunteer props by a sitter likewise had symbolic significance. Disillusioned by the rapid decline of patriot and Volunteer fortunes, William Drennan declined to wear his beloved Volunteer uniform when he sat for Home in 1785 and chose instead a shell, the ancient Greek symbol for ostracism, to represent his relation to politics.

The desire to parade in uniform was often regarded as an important factor inspiring participation in the Volunteers. In July 1778 Amyas Griffith, a leading Volunteer and Freemason, noted mockingly, "To such a vast height is our military disposition arrived that incredible numbers of Papists are every day recanting in this province in order to get into different associations, and be entitled to dress and walk *à la militaire.*" The spread of military dress also served to blur social categories. Griffith himself had recently mistaken a tailor for a "certain lieutenant-colonel." This fashion for military dress had brought about a near sartorial revolution; Griffith wrote that it was "really astonishing to see quondam ragged wretches who would formerly no more wear ruffles and cue-wigs, than they'd wear halters, now strutting in regimentals, sword, or bayonet, tailed wig, edged ruffles." Women, he believed, were particularly at risk over this transformation and the possible misidentifications it might cause: "The ladies are ruined by this unlucky spirit's prevailing, for, as gentlemen of the army were the chief objects of their attention, it may happen now in walking, or in public meetings, Miss may be engaged in small chat with a good military cobbler, in regimentals, whom the dear innocent had taken for a major, and whom she would not so much look at, were he not *en garbe militaire* from head to foot."[73] The supposed sexual appeal of the Volunteer uniform is a common theme in many discussions of the movement, another way in which Volunteering could reinforce masculinity through enhancing the sexual potency of those in uniform.

An interest in dress was not confined to the well-off, who could afford the often expensive accoutrements of soldiering. Francis Dobbs claimed that even among the "lower orders of men, the smartness of those who had enrolled themselves, became an object of envy and emulation."[74] Uniforms not only embodied masculinity but also served as markers of changing expressions of Irish nationality. Although for the most part Volunteers wore the scarlet coats of the regular army, in 1784 the radical *Volunteer's Journal* asked, "Does not every independent nation clothe her army in the same colour of her national flag?" Furthermore, the paper claimed that the scarlet cloth had been "polluted by the bloody massacre committed on [their] friends and brethren in America." An azure green cloth, as worn by the Kilkenny Rangers, would be more "elegant and soldier-like" and serve to honor the national flag. Uniforms served to identify true, manly Irishmen.[75]

"Such a Town as We Have Just Now!":
The Spectacle of Volunteering

Volunteers saved their finest costume for their rounds of reviews, maneuvers, and conventions, which served as local and regional spectacles as well as political and social occasions. These reviews began in 1778 with many companies preparing themselves for impending invasion. Companies also participated in local commemorations, celebrations, and festive days that made up the Protestant ritual year and provided opportunity for popular political activities. These occasions attracted large crowds, sometimes of several thousand spectators. Such events had a considerable impact on those who observed them. A correspondent wrote from Belfast in July 1780, "Such a town as we have just now! Nothing to be heard from seven in the morning til evening, but fifes and drums of the different corps marching in for the review tomorrow and Wednesday."[76]

As with militia companies before them, the Volunteers participated in the pantheon of Irish Protestant commemorations and celebrated the Hanoverian regime and British military triumphs.[77] At the same time, they added their own repertoire of performances to this calendar and, in the process, refashioned the meaning of traditional occasions. The festivities of the Volunteers contributed to the articulation of an Irish "national" identity that was forged through the "practice of patriotism" at local and regional events. Hundreds of such occasions, attracting sizable crowds, were described in the press throughout the first years of volunteering. A commemoration of the battle of the Boyne by Volunteers in Enniskillen in Southwest Ulster is typical of the structure of these occasions. In the morning the company and the local inhabitants assembled, alerted by the ringing of bells. Led by their captain, Lord Viscount Enniskillen, the Volunteers then marched through the town to the commons; before a crowd of two thousand, the company went through its maneuvers, firing volleys in honor of the day. The press report stressed the unanimity of the occasion, noting that "every distinction of party and religion here [had been] long laid aside." After the military performance, the company adjourned to the courthouse, where an "elegant dinner" was served, followed by numerous toasts that articulated the local, national, and imperial political sentiments the occasion embodied. Such dinners were often provided by the officers, particularly in the first years of volunteering. After the traditional toasts to the royal family and the "glorious and immortal memory" of

William III, toasts also addressed contemporary political controversies, mentioning the English opposition figures the Duke of Richmond and Admiral Keppel, as well as hoping for a "speedy reconciliation" between Great Britain and America and defeat for the French and the Spanish. The local importance of the linen industry was recognized with a condemnation of its "enemies," while the "independent electors" of Fermanagh were feted and contrasted with the "venal tools of a corrupt ministry."[78]

By 1780 the Volunteers had begun to establish extralocal structures through the creation of regiments and battalions. This enabled companies to cooperate beyond the local level and established their own calendar of spectacle in the shape of regional reviews and field days (see fig. 14). These took place over several days and involved an impressive array of social, military, and political events. In March of that year, Volunteers in Galway gathered for such an event over the course of five days. The review involved the 300 men of the Galway corps, 230 of the Clanricarde cavalry, and 280 of the Loughrea infantry. A hectic week of mock battles and socializing concluded with a *feu de joie* to celebrate Admiral Rodney's victory over the Spanish. A newspaper account of this review drew attention to the respectable nature of those in attendance, noting, "The property of the gentlemen who compose the corps amounts to between four and five hundred thousand pounds per annum."[79] But the round of Volunteer dinners, assemblies, and reviews offered some opportunities for social mixing between elites and those lower down the social scale. These entertainments were not without their social tensions and elite condescension. Dorothea Herbert recollected a "grand dinner" held at Curraghmore, Co. Waterford, for local Volunteers. She remarked, "Many were the laughable stories told of them—One ate salt with his grapes and sugar with his walnuts—Another offer'd Lady Tyrone a well aired chair, which he (a very fat man) had sat on."[80] A socially exclusive occasion was encountered by the young Quaker Mary Leadbetter, who, while attending school in Dublin, observed a Volunteer exercise in 1779. At first unsure whether "going to see such a sight was quite proper," on arriving at the Duke of Leinster's grounds with her master, she discovered only Volunteers and "genteel women" were being admitted to the review ground. This caused some anxiety for the young girl, "not knowing whether [she] should be looked on as one of the latter," and she eventually took her place "on a rising ground amidst a crowd of vulgar people." Although the restricted view had caused her to hurt her neck through stretching,

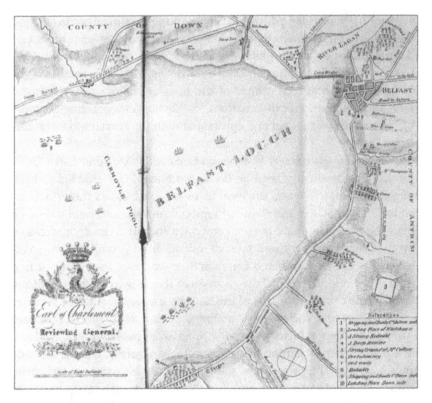

Figure 14 "A Plan of the Attack and Defence of the Town of Belfast," *Dublin Evening Post,* July 1781

Leadbetter concluded that the exercise was a "fine sight."[81] As Leadbetter's experience suggests, Volunteer spectacle was hardly as inclusive and unifying as much rhetoric suggested. Yet while hierarchy and social exclusivity were not forgotten in this patriotic enthusiasm, even the "vulgar people" could observe this military spectacle as an exciting day out and perhaps, at the same time, as a patriotic experience.

By 1780 the Volunteers had introduced the paramilitary funeral into their repertoire. In Kilkenny, Volunteers marched in their uniforms along with a number of "respectable citizens" in a funeral procession for Thomas Waters, who was "interred with every military honour" with three volleys fired over the grave.[82] Many accounts stress the solemn and honorable aspects of these occasions, but others were not so generous. Mary Roche wrote to her husband from Limerick in April 1783 recounting the Volunteer funeral of a local dyer. She noted the presence of the son of Edmond Sexton Pery, speaker of the House of

Commons, as well as "some honest traders" known to her and re-marked on "the splendor of their dress and arms and the richness of their furniture." Roche concluded, rather uncharitably, "I could not help fancying that the Volunteers were not sorry for the death of their Brother which enabled them to display such military parade."[83] Despite such mockery, military spectacles, reviews, mock battles, funerals, and demonstrations all served as opportunities for the Volunteers to exercise a manly public virtue and for large crowds to experience the excitement of a patriot nation in arms.

Moral Reform and the Practice of Volunteering

Volunteering stirred up considerable controversy over its legality, utility, and compatibility with religious virtue. Sunday exercises by Volunteer companies were particularly divisive. A letter from a "Protestant Dissenter" to the *Dublin Evening Post* argued for the legitimacy of Sunday exercises, claiming, "I consider exercise in the field, as much part of duty as worship in the church." Military training was of use because after men had "thanked god for the possession of [their] lives and liberties," such training increased their "capacity of defending them."[84] The following week, a letter to the same paper, from a "Sincere Christian," conceded that volunteering was necessary but opposed exercises on the Sabbath. While the Volunteers themselves recognized the extraordinary nature of their meetings, the author claimed such a spectacle would have a detrimental effect on the lower orders, for "on their returning home, they [would] be apt to think it no great breach of the Sabbath to yoke their horses, and proceed to plough, or bring home their harvest."[85] As late as March 1781, when the Volunteers were well established, James Crombie devoted an entire sermon to the problem in *The Propriety of Setting Apart a Portion of the Sabbath for the Purpose of Acquiring Knowledge and Use of Arms in Times of Public Danger.* Samuel Butler also attempted to reconcile religious virtue and military endeavor in a sermon preached before the Goldsmiths' Volunteers in Dublin. He argued that "to insinuate the Incompatibility of the Duties of War and Religion, approache[d] nearly to Blasphemy: the Lord Teaches Men's Hands to war, and their fingers to fight: What man [should] hesitate to practice what the almighty teaches."[86]

As Volunteer companies began to form in 1778, there was also uncertainty about their legal status. Until the government had issued commissions and called out the militia, these armed companies were technically illegal. As the Volunteers became increasingly involved in politics throughout 1779, pamphlets and letters to the press argued for the legitimacy of this armed extraparliamentary force. Their uncertain legal status offered a pretext for opponents of the force to proceed against them. A "Poor Protestant" wrote in August 1778 of a conflict over the legality of volunteering, suggesting local divisions over the desirability of the force. Two companies "well disciplined and well armed" had been established under the command of colonel Hungerford and his sons. However, the author lamented, as the drums beat to assemble the companies for exercises, "the Rev. Mr. ———, who ha[d] some authority in this borough, ordered the drummers, at their perils, not to beat; for that their associations were illegal and unconstitutional; and that he would indict every soul who should in future assemble under arms by beat of drum."[87] Others defended the legitimacy of the Volunteers; in 1779 the author of *A Defence of the Armed Societies of Ireland with Respect to their Legality* argued that they were nothing more than "protestant inhabitants, armed and disciplined, so as to assist the civil magistrates when called upon, and also to defend their country whenever attacked by a foreign enemy." Citing the jurist Edward Coke, the author claimed that the assembly of this armed force was not illegal in itself as the men were not assembled to perform any unlawful act.[88] The politicization of the Volunteers was also controversial, even among those who accepted their military role. In 1781 a pamphlet by Frederick Jebb and Robert Johnson criticized the Volunteers' involvement in politics, noting, "If the legislature is influenced by the authoritative resolutions of armed bodies of men . . . the legislature is then superseded by the compulsion of the armed force, and its authority transferred to a new power."[89] Volunteering as an emergency defense against invasion or as a pastime was something to be tolerated; its role as an extraparliamentary pressure group was a different matter.

In 1780 the author of *A Volunteer's Queries* criticized the Volunteers through a series of questions. The author was particularly concerned with the social and economic consequences of this force. He complained that if men did not restrain their passion for Volunteering, "the consequences [might] . . . be ruinous to many of themselves and their families and also to the kingdom at large by the idleness and dissipation which even witnessing of their exercises occasion among the lower ranks of the people."[90] Likewise, a letter to the *Hibernian Journal* lamented, "The ambition of appearing *en Militaire* has led many weak young men to neglect his [*sic*] means of subsistence." To the detriment of these men and their families, the author claimed "the shuttle and the needle have been laid by for the musket."[91] "Sarah Dealwell," who claimed to be a country shopkeeper, wrote to the *Freeman's Journal* satirizing this *rage militaire* and suggesting the inappropriateness of merchants engaging in military practices at the expense of their businesses. Arriving in Dublin to purchase stock, Dealwell had entered one familiar shop on High Street only to see behind the counter "a person whom, at first view, [she] supposed an Officer in the Corps of the Artillery." She soon recognized the figure as an old friend, "Mr. Clout Serge." On previous encounters she had found him "dressed as other citizens [were], and not mortifyingly above the degree of a country-dealer." On this occasion he was dressed in "an exceedingly smart blue frock lined with a scarlet, with buff waistcoat and breeches, his hat . . . was ornamented with a cockade, and his shoulders with what, [she thought] were epaulettes." When Dealwell inquired into the reason for this elaborate costume, she was informed that the "imminent danger of public affairs required the universal exercise of arms," though the shopkeeper intended to combine the character of citizen and soldier. When "Mr. Clout-Serge" presented his customer with the cloth yard for her inspection, the display turned into a peculiar mixture of retail display and his "drill manoeuvres" in a "variety of strange attitudes and changes of situation: now to the right—then suddenly to the left—to the right about again; then advancing in a quick, equal pace—next retiring in a low solemn movement." Dealwell expressed shock at this "metamorphosis" and warned other "amphibious readers" to avoid similar displays or risk losing her custom.[92] The rage for Volunteering and particularly the donning of uniform were frequent subjects of such satire. Dealwell's experience plays on the inappropriateness of a shopkeeper acting the part of the soldier and the ridiculous lengths to which such pretensions could go.

Defenders of the Volunteers represented the force as an instrument for social and moral improvement rather than degeneration. Company minutes and articles of association often expressed a concern for ensuring moral fortitude. In 1781 Francis Dobbs countered criticism of the force in his *Thoughts on the Volunteers*. Rather than taking "the Manufacture from his Loom—the Farmer from his plow," participation in the Volunteers, he argued, as well as the observation of Volunteer spectacle, had become a recreation for the common man. Indeed, it was now a substitute for morally suspect forms of masculine sociability, such as "cockfighting, horseracing, and the various amusements to which [the

Volunteer] was formerly addicted." While such pursuits were associated with "rioting, gambling, and drunkenness," volunteering promoted "sobriety and good order." The Volunteer was to be doubly applauded according to Dobbs, for he saved "both to the Nation and to
himself."[93] Henry Joy also claimed that volunteering had resulted in a
reformation of manners: "Idleness and despondency among the working classes at once gave way to an honest pride of appearing as well ap-
parelled in the ranks as those of superior condition; and in order to be
so they had to recourse to great exertion of industry."[94]

   Andrew Alexander noted in a sermon that instead of spending their
"vacant hours" in guilty pursuits, men now spent this time perfecting
the military arts, which tended "to secure their morals."[95] Others observed this happy unity of patriotism and moral reform at work. On 4
November 1779 the 110 members of the newly formed True Blues of
Lisburn, like Volunteer companies throughout the country, paraded in
honor of the day. An admiring observer noted, "Though this company
consists chiefly of tradesmen yet their conduct shews them to be animated by the purest love of country." Such patriotism had apparently
failed to interfere with their industry. To ensure that their military endeavors did not get in the way of their businesses, the men would rise
early and work late. As a consequence, the correspondent declared,
"The idle become industrious; the irregular become regular. In short, if
they persevere, they will exhibit an example of public spirit rarely to be
found."[96]

The masculinity of the Volunteers, as a social and discursive construction, was expressed both through a language of independence and public virtue and through the practice of parading and drilling in uniform,
a militarism that emphasized physical deportment, discipline, and
good order, so that the Volunteers were believed to embody the masculinity celebrated by patriot politicians. Between 1778 and the establishment of legislative independence in 1782, because of their sheer size
and popularity and the successful identification of the force with public
spiritedness, no real attempt was made to disband or replace the Volunteers, despite their ambiguous constitutional position. In their military
capacity at least, a vote of thanks for their service from both houses of
Parliament went a long way to offering official endorsement of the
force. The "respectability" of the Volunteers was also aided in no small
part by the leading part taken by such figures as Lord Charlemont. His
reputation in particular made it difficult for opponents of volunteering

to portray the force as mere rebels and troublemakers. At the same time, the language of manliness, an emphasis on discipline and good order among their ranks, and the assent of the large crowds attracted to elaborate and lengthy military reviews, helped legitimate the prominence of a citizen army outside government control. In their martial language and practice, the Volunteers also defined a type of virtuous masculinity based on the exercise of public virtue and the cultivation of "independence." The language of manliness could justify increased participation in politics, and, as Alexander described the effect of this involvement, allow those outside the political nation to "acquire an importance in society." A broad notion of manliness embraced men outside the political nation, who were called on to display their virtue and independence through drilling, sartorial display, and the bearing arms. "Respectable" Catholic men too could lay claim to the language of manliness through this voluntary service. The concept of patriotic masculinity embraced by the Volunteers served to justify the participation of a broad spectrum of men in the affairs of the nation, allowing them to "play the men."

7

Petticoat Government
Women and Patriotism

THE IDEOLOGY of patriotism propagated by the Volunteers was profoundly gendered. Patriotism and masculinity were intimately connected. This can be seen in the heroic masculinity celebrated in Francis Wheatley's well-known Volunteer paintings, particularly *The Dublin Volunteers on College Green,* which captures the demonstration on that date, but also in his *Irish House of Commons,* which depicts Henry Grattan making his famous speech supporting a motion for legislative independence on 19 April 1780. Wheatley's paintings commemorate moments of manly patriotism, but they also suggest much about the role of women in Irish patriot politics. Women are present in nearly all of Wheatley's Irish Volunteer paintings; in *The Dublin Volunteers on College Green* (see fig. 15), well-dressed women look down at the protest from windows above the scene; in the *Irish House of Commons* (see fig. 16), women, observing Grattan's speech, crowd the best seats in the public gallery, a familiar site in the Irish Commons, unlike in its British counterpart. His other Volunteer paintings, such as *Lord Aldborough reviewing the volunteers at Belan, County Kildare,* likewise suggest women were certainly present at the key moments of Volunteer politics.[1] But what does the presence of women in these paintings reveal about their place in the patriot movement? Were women mere spectators, marginal to important manly matters of parading and orating? Or were they more central to the politics of patriotism than previous accounts suggest?

This chapter examines the role of women in patriot politics and demonstrates that women engaged with the patriot construction of the nation. I argue that the rise of the Volunteers provided increased

Figure 15 Francis Wheatley, *The Dublin Volunteers on College Green*, 4 November 1779 (detail) (Courtesy of the National Gallery of Ireland, Dublin)

Figure 16 Francis Wheatley (1747–1801), *The Irish House of Commons*, 1780, oil on canvas (© Leeds Museum and Galleries [Lotherton Hall], U.K. / The Bridgeman Art Library)

opportunities for women to engage in politics and consider themselves good patriots. Wheatley's paintings show that women were present at Volunteer ceremonials. In a recent account of women and politics in Georgian England, Kathleen Wilson rightly admonishes historians for conflating women's presence with their influence in public life.[2] This is a corrective to more-recent celebratory accounts of women's role in the Georgian public sphere. At the same time, it is important not to confound women's formal exclusion from the political nation with their unimportance to patriot politics or to dismiss their presence as merely decorative. Women made up a sizable proportion of the large crowds of spectators at local and regional Volunteer reviews, an action that offered public assent to the force. Along with other groups excluded from the political nation, women could also display intense interest in political affairs, such as electoral campaigns, parliamentary proceedings, and the politics of the Volunteers. Aristocratic women had traditionally played a role in electoral politics, canvassing electors on behalf of their family interest in a parliamentary seat. Previous chapters have shown that women participated in the campaign for free trade through their consumption choices and the display of political symbols. They were also active in the world of print culture. The rhetoric of patriotism repeatedly evoked a dynamic sense of interrelation between women and men in the project of renewing public virtue. Such language drew on broader cultural understandings of gender that stressed the complementary roles of men and women.[3] As the discussion of invasion scares suggested, notions of the family and gender relations were central to the culture and ideology of volunteering. Although limits remained on the degree of political participation or "gender disorder" that would be tolerated by male patriots, women were nonetheless central to the culture of volunteering and the politics of patriotism.

Recent research on the 1790s and the rebellion of 1798 in particular has begun to uncover the role of Irish women in the politics of loyalism and republicanism.[4] This period has received increased attention, but with the exception of Mary O'Dowd's general history of women in early modern Ireland, women's political presence before the French Revolution has been all but ignored.[5] This is somewhat surprising given that historians of eighteenth-century Britain have emphasized how the challenges of war and empire provided women with a wide range of opportunities to "act like political subjects within the commercialized world of extra-parliamentary politics," well before the 1790s.[6] And historians of revolutionary America have long recognized that the

crisis of war "pulled women into political relationships and forced un-
familiar political choices."[7] Stephen Conway, in a recent examination of
the myriad ways the War of American Independence impacted life in
Great Britain and Ireland, concludes tentatively that the war "might
have enhanced the status of women," and that few were left untouched
by its impact.[8] Opportunities to participate in extraparliamentary political culture increased for women beyond the elite, but the social acceptance of their excursions into politics was variable. National crisis
and war also often "intensified the strident masculinism of patriotic
discourse."[9]

Maidens of the Atlantic Shore: Women and Patriotism

What was the consequence of this masculine discourse and the gendered ideology of politics more generally? If the gendering of politics
was merely an ideological construction, as much recent work contends,
it was nevertheless powerful in shaping the actual behavior of women
and the way in which they experienced the world. Ideology could structure experience.[10] Political thought throughout the Anglo-American
world expressed considerable ambivalence about women's participation in politics. National crisis did not necessarily exclude women from
the political realm. Certain forms of participation were acceptable; in
times of national danger and intense political conflict, women were
called upon to act as "patriots."[11] Commentators looked to both classical and recent history to demonstrate that, especially in times of national emergency, women were capable of engaging in patriotic activity.
William Crawford, in a sermon preached in Strabane in 1779, claimed
that in the past British women, "forgetting the natural softness and timidity of their sex, ha[d] catched the patriotic spark and fought in defence of liberty with a spirit of manly fortitude."[12] Women could display
"manly" characteristics. Martha McTier of Belfast, for example, viewed
manliness as an important quality of political pronouncements. When
the resolutions of the Tralee Volunteers were read aloud at a mixed-sex
social gathering in her native Belfast, McTier noted how she "got the
start of all and boldly pronounced them manly and noble, lamenting
that the Belfast sentiments had not been so worded, and that then they
would have been faultless." McTier's approval of the Tralee resolutions
might be seen as "manly" behavior in itself. And indeed she suggests
her awareness of the boundaries between acceptable and transgressive

forms of female public speech, noting of her performance, "This *seemed* to be allowed."[13]

Although women might display positive "manly" traits as an expression of their patriotism, most accounts were modeled on a vision of Roman women's contribution to public life, which regarded their main task as motivating the actions of men.[14] William Preston's account of the patriotism of Greek and Roman women, in a poem celebrating the Volunteers, is typical of this vision:

> And you, fair daughters of th' Hibernia soil,
> Shall you be wanting to the patriot toil?
> In story'd volumes lives the immortal praise
> Of virtuous dames, in Greek and Roman days.
> Did public danger private aid demand,
> They gave their jewels, with no sparing hand;
> They met their husbands, red from glorious wars,
> And kist with weeping joy their honest scars.
>
> . . . .
>
> For her with pride the gallant heart shall bleed,
> For her ev'n cowards dare the mighty deed.[15]

Preston defined female patriotism largely in terms of male heroism, with women's role as one of passive inspiration for acts of chivalry. But there was also a more active definition of women's political involvement; the efforts of women in other nations, particularly in the American colonies, were cited to support this understanding of female patriotism. One author noted, "The virtue of the American ladies during the late unhappy war, in purchasing the plainest dresses wrought in their own States, rather than the most gaudy ones of the mother country, has often been mentioned to their honour, and will make . . . a splendid figure in the history of American emancipation. Is not an Irishwoman less capable of love for her native country than an American?—certainly not." By following the American example and forming associations Irish women could prove "that [the Irish people's] public virtue is not confined to sex, but pervades every description of inhabitants."[16]

The little-known anonymous novel *The Triumph of Prudence over Passion*, published in 1781, offers both a rare example of a literary work set in the Ireland of the Volunteers and an account of a gendered understanding of patriotism, purportedly from a woman's point of view. The epistolary novel recounts the relationship between Miss Mortimer and Miss Fitzgerald and examines the negotiation of gender relations in the institution of marriage, the nature of Anglo-Irish constitutional affairs, and the gendered politics of patriotism. In a discussion of a Volunteer review, Fitzgerald proclaims herself as "public spirited as any Roman Matron" and argues that women too can be taught the "disinterested love of their country" that fosters a greater degree of patriotism among the men. Among the Greeks and Romans, she believes, "the women were just as warm in their country's cause, as the men: and history has applauded them for it; though now people affect to think those things above our capacity."[17] Mortimer replies that she can see "no reason why women should not be patriots; for surely, if tyranny and oppression are established in a country, they are most liable to suffer from it both in their persons and properties than men, because less able to defend themselves: it therefore concerns them much to use all their influence in opposing it; and doubtless that influence is more powerful than people are aware of."[18] Women then can and should be patriots, she concludes, "as the welfare of [Ireland] is of as much consequence to women as men." Mortimer and Fitzgerald's epistolary dialogue suggests that women could feel and act like patriots. But what avenues were open to women to express their patriotism, and what were the gendered limits of this practice?

Electoral Politics and "Petticoat Government"

Electoral campaigns were occasions when women could exert influence or express political affiliation, and they can serve as an introduction to the possibilities and limits of women's participation in politics. From the 1760s onward, Irish elections grew more frequent and contested with the emergence of an "independent" interest, as well as a nascent parliamentary reform movement. Elite women participated in the world of electoral politics between and during electoral battles through their attendance at a wide range of social events, from race meetings to dinners and balls.[19] The victory of John O'Neill in the Antrim election in 1783 saw "chairing rejoicings, ball illuminations etc," with the ball opened by his wife.[20] The numerous subsequent toasts included an extended eulogy to the "public and private virtue" of Mrs. O'Neill, whose "every nerve [was] strung with the sentiments of liberty" that united them that day.[21] Elite women, although excluded from the franchise, took active roles in electoral politics; they served as overseers of a borough interest throughout the course of a son's minority; they engaged in canvassing and petitioning.[22] A satire on women's involvement in the politics of patriotism, though hostile, is indicative of the ways in which elite women maintained their political influence and canvassed in election campaigns. The satire suggested that in support of parliamentary reform, a group of elite women made the following resolution: "that such of us as are possessed of any *borough* which returns *members,* or of any interest in the half or the quarter or the eight part of a borough do *sacrifice* the same at the altar of liberty . . . and that we will not, for the future, by *entertainments, sweet looks,* or *sugared speeches* or any undue influence, endeavour to make any man vote for representatives in parliament, otherways than as stern patriotism directs."[23] Often criticized as forms of corruption by contemporaries, and indeed by most historians, this social politics of electioneering aimed at cultivating the family electoral interest and was both common and expected of elite women.[24]

Elite women participated in the ceremonial and social aspects of electioneering, but involvement beyond an acceptable and circumscribed role could provoke censure. A short pamphlet titled *Petticoat Government, Exemplified in a Late Case in Ireland,* published in 1780 and possibly written by Robert Day, told a tale of intrigue, deception, and perhaps even murder among the Kerry aristocracy. The work recounted the story of Lady Anne Fitzmaurice's unnatural quest for power: how she destroyed an ancient family, the lives of countless people (including her husband), and brought the borough of Dingle under her tyrannical rule. The author narrates how Lady Anne married Maurice Fitzgerald, the Knight of Kerry and, with the "Love of rule, the general passion of the fair sex," proceeded to reduce her husband to a state of "abject slavery."[25] Lady Anne's most contemptible crime, according to the author, was to engage in a scheme to wrest exclusive control of the borough of Dingle by creating large numbers of freemen, all at the expense of her husband's uncle, Robert Fitzgerald. Unlike women who have "a proper feeling for decency," she did not conceal her dominion over her husband from public view but rather flaunted it as she exercised "her sovereign authority."[26] In spite of all the best attempts of the burgesses and freemen of the town to counteract her plans, this "Machiavel in petticoats" carried out her scheme with ruthless determination. She reduced her husband to a hopeless drunk, created a despotic rule over a corporation that had governed as "a well united family, bearing sincere affection for each other," and destroyed the name and estate of an ancient family. In short, Day, the nephew of Robert Fitzgerald, tells us, a "total revolution had taken place under her influence."[27]

In the 1780s this image of tyranny and the treatment of a parliamentary borough as private property would no doubt strike a chord with reformers obsessed with corrupt electoral practices. The pamphlet was also concerned with gender and the boundaries of gendered action. The veracity of this attack, concerned as it is with familial politics and property, might be doubtful. But Day's condemnation of Lady Anne in many ways illustrates the limits of aristocratic women's involvement in politics. It was acceptable for such women to exert a certain degree of private influence over their husbands in political matters. They might also participate in a variety of legitimate electoral rituals and festivities and engage in the social politics of patronage. The public and aggressive search for "dominion," which Day attributes to Lady Anne, was beyond the limits of propriety. For a man such as the Knight of Kerry to fall too much under the sway of a woman's influence in political matters, evoking images of a courtly decadent and sensuous world, could be represented as a failure to uphold a prescribed masculine role and a drift into effeminacy. There was, then, an implicit danger in women's involvement in politics.

Beyond the wives of candidates or aristocratic women oiling the wheels of patronage, women outside the elite could also participate in electoral politics in a variety of ways. The often-lavish entertainments and spectacles provided by candidates in municipal and parliamentary election campaigns not only targeted those with a vote but often courted popular opinion as well. Even for women not involved in an election through familial connections, it was difficult to avoid the balls, parades, and dinners sponsored by candidates as part of the treating that extended well beyond the enfranchised. In Newry, Ann Blair sent the songs and farces of the 1774 election in that town to her brother in New York, informing him that both sides illuminated the town and gave balls "to the ladies," which Blair and her mother attended. Blair concluded that she had "laughed at both parties" while at the same time "took care to give offence to none."[28] Forms of ceremony and largesse also accompanied a candidate's victory, in which women might be both spectator and spectacle. The success of James Wilson in the Antrim election of 1776, regarded as a victory for the Presbyterian "independent interest" in the face of the combined forces of the landed interest of that county, was widely feted with numerous toasts in Belfast and an elaborate parade in Ballymena.[29] Along with a large number of Freemasons, Wilson's victory celebration included a group of five hundred young women in white, with blue ribbons, carrying green boughs. A female band followed, with the "animated daughters of liberty" playing such tunes as "Britons Strike Home" and other "patriotic songs."[30]

Women's interest in electoral politics could also take on a more ideological complexion. Historians have long noted the oligarchic nature of Irish elections and their basis in familial and local ties of patronage. At the same time, especially from the 1770s onward, many elections acquired an ideological complexion, with national issues and the idea of "independence" coloring more-specifically local issues and loyalties.[31] Martha McTier took a great interest in the politics of her hometown, Belfast, as well as several other heated electoral battles throughout Ulster. As the wife of an election agent and the sister of William Drennan, writer of electoral pamphlets and squibs, McTier came from a political family. She also took a more active role at times, distributing her brother's pamphlets to the people of Newry during the election of 1783 and perhaps even contributing material to radical newspapers. Her angry letters to her brother over the merits of parliamentary candidates for Belfast along with her vision of the qualities a member of parliament should ideally possess suggest the way in which the unenfranchised could engage passionately with national electoral politics.[32]

The Nation Embodied: Hibernia and the Volunteers

As the role of young women in Wilson's electoral celebration suggests, women were often central to political ceremony. Female allegories were also central to patriot language and symbolism.[33] The patriot campaign was frequently characterized as an attempt to defend Hibernia, the female personification of Ireland. Similar to the figures of Liberty and Britannia (and often described as the sister of the British symbol), the figure of Hibernia became more widely disseminated in the course of the eighteenth century.[34] Hibernia was probably adapted from the traditional figure of Liberty and was usually depicted wearing the cap of Liberty and carrying a pike or spear. A palm branch, a symbol of victory, was frequently included with the figure of Hibernia, as was a crowned harp with a winged maiden fore pillar.[35] The government utilized this symbol to represent a unified nation. Hibernia appeared in a variety of other contexts: on coins, trade cards, frontispieces, prints, and the mastheads of newspapers. It was the rise of the Volunteers, however, that transformed Hibernia into the main symbol of patriot and opposition politics. Local Volunteer companies adopted Hibernia as a patriot symbol on their banners and flags. Many of these elaborate colors were

Figure 17 The Caledon Volunteers banner (© 2009 Ulster Museum, Collection of Armagh County Museum; photograph reproduced courtesy of the Trustees of National Museums Northern Ireland)

made by local women, usually the wives of officers. Other accoutrements of volunteering, such as the medals awarded for their shooting abilities, along with drinking jugs, were also decorated with images of Hibernia. Many of these local banners present forceful images of Hibernia. The flag of the Caledon Volunteers of Tyrone presents a classically draped Hibernia naked to the waist holding a palm branch and a pike covered with the cap of Liberty (see fig. 17).[36]

For patriots, the fortunes of Hibernia served as an allegory for the fate of the nation. The figure proved endlessly adaptable. As Joan

Landes observes, "The embodied female figure stands apart in its power to evoke feelings of affection and intimacy," and the patriots took full advantage of this emotional resonance.[37] In the course of the struggle for free trade, for example, Hibernia was repeatedly represented in allegorical descriptions and prints as bound in chains, with her harp "broken and unstrung."[38] When free trade was granted, a variety of new images presenting Hibernia in a different light were produced to celebrate this victory. William Moore, a jeweler on Capel Street, advertised a seal in June 1780 that interpreted this political transformation. The seal depicted

> Hibernia leaning on a Harp rested on a Pack of Linen, a wool pack at her feet, in the Front Ground, on the Wool Pack, Nov 1779; near which is a lion, who has hold of the wool pack with his paw, as if drawing it [slyly] to him; in the Centre is a Volunteer fully accoutred, with his Bayonet fixed, who while he gently raises Hibernia with the one hand, rests the butt of his Musket across the paw of the lion, so as effectually to prevent his taking the Wool, Hibernia, in a manner of surprise, raises her Head off her Hand, and looks at her Deliverer. Motto, "Armed for your Defence."[39]

A crude print from 1782 titled *The Rescue, or a Volunteer delivering Hibernia from the Claws of the Lion* (see fig. 18) adopts the same imagery, this time in favor of the repeal of Poyning's Law, which patriots argued limited Irish constitutional liberties.[40] In both images, it is the heroic masculine figure of a Volunteer who saves the poor, defenseless woman from the clutches of a voracious English lion attempting to destroy her commercial and constitutional freedoms. In such images, Hibernia is presented dressed in classical garb and in a noble pose, a virtuous but vulnerable maid. Lewis Perry Curtis has described Hibernia in the eighteenth century as a static and passive figure "possessing dignity, inspiring veneration rather than pity," and indeed in many images Hibernia's passivity is reinforced through her need for protection from a Volunteer. Hibernia was also often depicted as a dejected, broken figure allegorizing Ireland's economic and political oppression at the hands of England in a way that foreshadows nineteenth-century nationalist imagery.[41]

At the same time, representations of Hibernia were not homogeneous. For example, the figure of Ireland as a woman could also be sexualized for satirical purposes. Although English colonists had long imagined Ireland as an available woman, Hibernia also became common in English representations of Ireland in the late eighteenth century. A

Figure 18 *The Rescue, or a Volunteer delivering Hibernia from the Claws of the Lion*, 1782
(© Trustees of the British Museum)

satirical print *Suiters [sic] to Hibernia on her having a Free Trade* (see fig. 19)
plays on the sexual overtones of "free trade" and depicts Hibernia (a
shield making her look more like Britannia than usual) as a sexually
available women. As the divorced wife of "John Bull," Hibernia, courted
by Dutch, French, Portuguese, and Spanish men, now has "license"

Figure 19 *Suiters [sic] to Hibernia on her having a Free Trade*, London, 1780 (Courtesy of the Lewis Walpole Library, Yale University)

with her ports "free for all Mankind to enter."[42] A figure behind a tree claims that only Britain's difficulties in America have allowed the Irish to achieve commercial concessions. The satire suggests that Irish agitation was a form of infidelity; just as the colonies had allied with Britain's enemies, now Ireland, in the figure of Hibernia, might become equally promiscuous with her affections.

Hibernia was not only represented as vulnerable to English tyranny or European advances. The striking *Hibernia attended by her Brave Volunteers* (see fig. 20), by William Hincks, was advertised for sale in May 1780; it foresees a new era of Irish prosperity based on trade within the empire. The print is described in an advertisement as representing Hibernia "exhibiting to the world her commercial freedom, attended by the Volunteers. Europe, Africa and America are offering their treasures. At her feet the Harp is laid out with a Cornucopia pouring its riches on it, and in the background vessels sailing in and out of port & c. emblematic of extended commerce."[43] In this scene, the Volunteers, though still serving as protectors, are relegated to the background,

Figure 20 *Hibernia attended by her Brave Volunteers Exhibiting her Commercial Freedom*, 1780 (Courtesy of the National Library of Ireland)

with Hibernia clearly a more central and confident presence. The patriot victory is represented by a joyous young woman in flowing garb, with a similar figure representing Europe, while America and Africa are depicted as native men offering up the treasures that it was hoped would follow the removal of restrictions on Ireland's trade.[44] As an embodied symbol representing the nation and the patriot cause, Hibernia was not neutered.

In her study of the visual representation of women in revolutionary France, Landes draws attention to the much neglected erotic aspects of patriotism and the ways in which the "depiction of the nation as a desirable woman may have eroticized men's bonds to that nation."[45] Hinck's Hibernia is the central focus of his print, an appealing young woman accepting the riches of globe trade.[46] Likewise, the language of patriotic balladry and poetry emphasized the erotics of patriotism, promising manly patriots the affections of the "fair daughters of Hibernia" as a reward for their martial endeavors on behalf of the nation. Hibernia could also stand more specifically for the bodies and virtue of Irish women. With the threat of invasion, commentators and preachers implored their male readers and listeners to contemplate the horrors that would befall Irish women should French invaders succeed. The defense of the nation was conflated with the defense of vulnerable female bodies by heroic men in splendid uniforms. And participation in the Volunteers itself was often advocated as a way of stimulating female desire. Women were encouraged to withhold their "favors" from men who failed to volunteer or express a proper manly patriotism.

The Rites of Volunteering

The threat of invasion and the ceremonials of the Volunteers, described in the previous chapter, not only evoked feminine symbolism but also offered women the opportunity to publicly contribute to the patriot cause in concrete ways. In 1778 the "general Apprehension of Invasion" and the emergence of local Volunteer companies created occasions for many women to exercise their organizational abilities and express their patriotism in public ways.[47] The outfitting of a voluntary military force, whether for reviews or for potential engagement with the enemy, required a good deal of labor. It was the wives and daughters of Volunteers who "the dread habiliments of war prepare," as one poet described women's patriotic task.[48] Women contributed to the material

culture of the Volunteers in other ways, for example, weaving orna-
mental colors, which were presented at public ceremonies.[49] Women
were central to many of the ceremonial aspects of Volunteer culture.
The presentation of the stands of colors by wives of officers and patrons
of companies was often accompanied by elaborate rituals and orations.
In County Meath in 1781 the Moyfenrath Light Dragoons thanked Mrs.
Loftus of nearby Killyon for the presentation of an "elegant standard,
the embellishments of which [did] not less distinguish her taste, than
the manner of giving it [did] honour to her politeness."[50] The presentation of another "elegant stand of colours" by Mrs. Prittie to the Ormond
Volunteers served as an occasion for the corps to address the role of
women in the patriot movement: "The smiles of the fair have ever been
deemed a most prevailing incentive to generous and gallant deeds.
While therefore we look to our colours, calling to mind the hand by
which they are committed to our trust, we cannot fail of being inspired
with the resolution never to abandon them, nor suffer their lustre to be
tarnished in our hands by any dishonorable act." The elaborate flags
and banners of the Volunteers, often depicting female characters such
as Liberty and Hibernia, certainly added to the pomp and authenticity
of the Volunteers as a military force. Such ceremonies allowed women
to publicly display their support for the patriotic cause beyond the passive, inspirational patriotism envisaged by some commentators. At the
same time, women's actual participation in the patriotic public sphere
could take on a symbolic currency. The address from the Ormond Volunteers continued: "And, while we are thus justly proud to be ranked
among the protectors of this Isle, we cannot overlook its loveliest orna-
ments, nor forget, that it is the happiest privilege of bravery in our
bolder sex—to protect those gentle virtues that charm us so much in
yours."[51] As this Volunteer address suggests, paraphernalia produced
and presented by women could symbolize the duty of a manly virtue to
protect female honor.

"Ye Amazon Ladies!" (Cross-) Dressing for the Public Sphere

Representations of the gendered nature of political participation were
not hegemonic. A variety of languages existed for the representation of
women in the political sphere, with the degree of acceptance of or ambivalence about their actual presence determined by context. Indeed,
as many historians of gender have come to recognize in recent years,

gender categories were often permeable. The language of patriotism in Ireland could serve as the means for a variety of women to negotiate a gendered politics. The fashion for cross-dressing, with women adopting military-style clothing, illustrates this point. The stage was one site where the boundaries of gender and identity could be negotiated and performed. In the theaters of Dublin, Cork, and Belfast, sites of political dispute throughout the century, the relations between women and the political culture of the Volunteers were regularly played out. While few original plays were produced on the Irish stage during these years, the prologues, epilogues, interludes, songs, dances, and occasional pieces that made up the average bill of theatrical fare enabled the incorporation of a wide range of material adapted to local circumstances that often commented on local events.[52] Irish audiences would have encountered representations of the Amazon and women cross-dressing in military uniforms on stage. In 1780, at the Theatre Royal, a "pantomimical Musical interlude" called "The Female Volunteer" was performed, which no doubt included women dressing in military costume and performing drills.[53] Writing from Cork in 1779, a correspondent in a Dublin newspaper noted proudly that a martial spirit "prevail[ed] through all ranks of the people" there. This spirit had been exemplified during a recent visit to the theater, where, to great applause, "Mrs. Smith, one of the heroines of the stage, appeared in the dress of a volunteer, and by the beat of a drum, went through their manual exercise, with that exactness and dexterity which would do honour to the oldest veteran in the King's troops."[54] Sheridan's play *The Camp*, as discussed in chapter 6, included military songs and much drilling and parading. It also incorporated much cross-dressing, satirizing elite women who attended the camps in military-style clothing.[55] The main plot centered on a young woman passing as a soldier and provided opportunities for female actors to perform convincing military drills. A wide variety of plays and occasional pieces likewise incorporated military themes.

The blurring of gender boundaries could be tolerated, even celebrated on the stage; cross-dressing women also participated in the theatrical and militarized world of the Volunteers. Francis Wheatley's *Lord Aldborough reviewing the volunteers at Belan, County Kildare* (see fig. 21), though less celebrated than the heroic moments captured in his *Dublin Volunteers on College Green* or *The Irish House of Commons*, depicts a more everyday moment in the ceremonial world of the Volunteers. Edward Stratford, Lord Aldborough, presides over a review of his Aldborough legion; in the background, the smoke of the gunfire rises over the troops on the left, with the camp established on the right of the scene, his seat

Figure 21 Francis Wheatley (1747–1801), *Lord Aldborough reviewing the volunteers at Belan, County Kildare*, 1782 (Courtesy of Waddesdon, The Rothschild Collection [The National Trust]; photograph by A. C. Cooper, © The National Trust, Waddesdon Manor)

at Belan Park in the background. Central to the painting, however, are the female observers of the spectacle; in the foreground, seated in the carriage, are Aldborough's mother in uniform and her daughter Hannah. To the right, Aldborough's wife, Lady Barbara Herbert, is on horseback and dressed in the style of a Volunteer, illustrating how some women adopted the uniform of the Volunteers as a fashionable statement of their patriotism.[56]

Although there appears to have been a general fashion among elite British women at this time for styles regarded as masculine, this tendency seems to have been most pronounced at military camps and reviews.[57] Scenes of elite women dressed in military costume were not uncommon in Volunteer culture. The practice of volunteering created opportunities for the gathering of large crowds to witness the parades, reviews, sham fights, and conventions that were a ubiquitous part of the social calendar in Dublin and throughout the country from 1778 onward. Camp culture, as discussed in the previous chapter, rather than being unique to Ireland, was also a phenomenon throughout Great Britain. In 1778 a *rage militaire* also spread throughout England. As evidenced in numerous satirical prints, a fashion emerged for the adoption of military-style clothing by women visiting the camps in England. A letter from Bridgetown in August 1778 notes that this military fashion had spread throughout Ireland: "The very Ladies are in uniforms; and in this town, every women has a scarlet gown, edged with green, green petticoat, and green stomacher and apron, to match our regimentals, which are scarlet, faced with green, and buff waistcoat and breeches, edged with green."[58] A print titled *Frolic, or the Female Volunteers*, published in Dublin in 1780, suggests that the practice was widespread enough in Ireland to merit commercial exploitation.[59]

It might be assumed that the public cross-dressing of women at military events produced a certain ambivalence, or even hostility; was it necessarily a form of transgression, as much work on cross-dressing suggests? Many descriptions of such scenes were mildly satirical, such as William Drennan's reference to the "dress militaire" of "Amazon ladies" in a comic ballad describing the Belfast Volunteer review, discussed below. The figure of the Amazon and the female warrior were common in ballads and on the stage throughout the eighteenth century. "Amazon" women were more likely to be celebrated in literary and dramatic contexts than condemned, and the term "Amazonian" had not yet acquired wholly negative connotations.[60] These figures and the prevalence of cross-dressing women on stage, celebrating female bravery, suggest the ease with which gender boundaries could be crossed. In many accounts of Volunteer activities, militarized women become as much a spectacle as the martial maneuvers. A satire on volunteering, published in 1780, describes the participation of militarized women in the Volunteer displays:

> The fair thus are tickled, and boast 'tis their pride,
> To be with such fine gallant heroes ally'd.
> And Amazon-like, round the Standard they flock,
> And plume themselves up with a fierce martial cock.[61]

A "Song on the Volunteers" also describes these female patriots. While gently mocking the current fashion for military dress, it envisions female warriors defending the country against French invasion:

> Encamp'd so like soldiers, hair power'd and frizzled,
> To decide which was which they'd be monstrously puzzled.
> Let no sour grey beard deride their intention,
> Any lady among them could vanquish a Frenchman.[62]

While serving mainly to ridicule the military prowess of both the Volunteers and the French, this verse also refers to the supposed gender confusion created by this fashion at the camps.

This ambiguity led to the suggestion that the presence of women at these military events offered sexual possibilities.[63] In an unpublished ballad, William Drennan described the Belfast Volunteer review as a site of female cross-dressing, gender ambiguity, and sexual display:

> Ye Amazon ladies! whose dress militaire,
> Make our Hearts beat a ruffle to bid us, Beware;
> Smooth fac'd little fellows that keep such a Pother
> To persuade us you're neither one sex or the other
> Masquerade it about, for where is the sin
> To coquet it without, when you're constant within?
>
> Ye Damsels (like some since the late Revolution)
> Who think more of Free Trade than a sound Constitution,
> Take your visiting rounds—'tis the same with us all,
> For the fashion of sliding came in with the Fall.
> . . . .
> For here we can boast what ne'er was surpast,
> Our Volunteer lads, and the Belles of Belfast.[64]

Volunteering is here described as a form of patriotism fueled by an economy of desire, with the hope of inspiring the "envied precedence" of women serving as the stimulus for this military rage.[65] Drennan's verse also suggests that women had become politicized by the reform movement and the Volunteers. At the same time, a demand for "free trade" implies a sexual license among those women attending Volunteer political and social gatherings and is opposed to a "sound constitution," an allusion to both female chastity and political reform. This satirical song was probably written to be performed at a mixed social gathering after reviews and balls. The ballad expresses little anxiety over the dress of these "Amazon ladies," who are "neither one sex or the other." Rather than suggesting concern over the blurring of boundaries, this and other accounts by male commentators, in their playful descriptions of the permeability of gender boundaries, suggest a certain *lack* of anxiety over the ultimate durability of existing structures.[66]

Reviews and maneuvers were not without their sexual dangers and anxieties. Newspaper reports associated the large crowds drawn to these events as potentially sexually charged sites dangerous to the morals of impressionable women. In 1781 *Faulkner's Journal*, depicting women as the victims of predators rather than as sexually aggressive themselves, warned, "No female who regards her reputation, should go unprotected, for not only the arts of seduction will be put in practice, but from the various inclinations predominating in such an aggregate mass of persons, little decorum need be expected."[67] At the same time, women were not regarded solely as objects of unwanted and dangerous advances. A bawdy ballad, "The Manual Exercise," uses the language of the various textbooks published to instruct these amateur soldiers in the finer points of military discipline, as well as the notions of Volunteer patriotism and duty, to describe the sexual instruction of a young Volunteer by Kitty, a "fair maid." In order to teach her young lover the "Volunteer exercise," Kitty instructs him to

> Fall to your exercise without delay
> Make ready your cartridge observe what I say
> And also your firelock for that's my desire,
> be quick with your motions present and give fire.

As the young Volunteer is put through his paces, he "observe[s] well his motions and fire[s] rounds three." However, Kitty proves a hard task master, and the Volunteer finally pleads with her:

> Your orders being hasty you soon do me tire,
> that this time once more I'm not able to fire,
> and my ammunition now fairly spent,
> with three rounds dear Kitty you should be content,
> for want of a charge now my firelock dies,
> so that I'm quite weary of my exercise.
> if that all generals were like unto you,
> the volunteers surely would dread a review.[68]

Such ribaldry suggests that even the language of popular cultural forms, like the chapbook and the ballad, were influenced by the culture of volunteering and its obsession with military professionalism and discipline. If the military culture of the Volunteers was at times presented as an erotically charged site, erotic language could simultaneously also be militarized, with humorous effect. Cross-dressing or "manly" women, observing military maneuvers, could be celebrated in song and ballad or witnessed on the stage.

Gender Disorder and the "Political Family"

The emergence of the Volunteers offered women a wide variety of opportunities to participate in public ceremonies and the festive culture this movement forged; however, the acceptance of their excursions into the political realm was contingent and limited. From late 1783 onward, the politics of gender and the issue of women's participation in politics, especially as the demands of reformers grew more radical, were evoked to discredit the program of political reformers and the Volunteers. Opponents of reform claimed that the agitations of the reformers risked destroying cherished notions of citizenship. Class and gender anxieties were combined in criticisms of the National Convention, an alternative representative body elected by the Volunteers in 1783. Prerogatives of legitimate political participation, based on social, confessional, and gendered exclusivity, were threatened by the politicization of the urban poor, Catholics, and women. The *Volunteer Evening Post*, a government-supported newspaper, was particularly active in associating the efforts of Volunteer reformers to politicize the people with disordered social and gender relations. A satire on the convention, for example, claimed an analogous body had emerged to promote women's rights. According to the *Post*, this "Female Committee" was to meet at the same site as the Volunteers' convention: the Rotunda, a maternity hospital, described as "a place suitable to our sex." The "Committee," it was claimed, had issued their own resolutions "to assert [women's] inherent rights, and no longer patiently to be excluded from a share in the legislature of the kingdom."[69]

In February 1784 the same paper carried a warning from a distressed Mr. Rig, a "Common Council Man" of Francis Street in Dublin. The council man had been an associate of the leading Dublin radical, Napper Tandy. He had devoted himself to the politics of reform, attending the National Convention with family in tow, even at the expense of his business. However, his participation in the politics of the nation had disturbing consequences for the politics of the household. The writer's wife had recently prevented him from "going to the club to drink porter," which she was "pleased to call a parliamentary reform and a restoring of the principles of the ancient constitution." His wife expanded on this conflation of reform in the home and the nation, arguing, "Women are formed to be the companions of men; the term companion implies equality; ergo women and men are formed equal, now on the principles of equal representation, as Mr. Flood told us the other day, it is very plain, that if men have their clubs women ought to have their cosherings." Thus the language of parliamentary reform from the convention could be appropriated to argue for greater equality for women. The rebellion of his wife and loss of his porter were not to be the end of Rig's woes; soon his daughter, his son, his old maidservant, and even the tea boy all engaged in varieties of insubordination using the language of reform as propagated in the convention to usurp his authority. The final insult came when he learned that his daughter planned to marry ("throw herself away on") a tailor's apprentice, seduced by his membership in the National Convention. Rig concluded with the grave warning: "[Such] are the distresses of a political master of a political family; everything which I most revered, has in some shape conspired to my vexation; all the maxims to which I was most bigoted, have been employed to throw my family into disorder." To drive home the point of this cautionary tale, Rig concluded that such disorder led him to think of "foresaking politics" and instead "minding [his] shop."[70] As in the campaign for free trade, the domestic and the political were again represented as entangled, with women seen as central to the process. Now, however, the politicization of the domestic realm and women's (and apprentices') political actions were represented as the source of social and gender disorder, rather than the mainspring of public virtue.

The representation of women as political subjects became particularly charged as those outside the political nation became increasingly involved in politics from 1783 onward. Women's participation in politics and the crossing of gender boundaries were associated with sedition and disorder by conservative critics of reform.[71] However, I do not intend here to reiterate in an Irish context a familiar narrative of decline, from "golden age to separate spheres."[72] The rise of the Volunteers, as well as intensifying concerns over constitutional issues, allowed women to participate in the gendered world of politics in a variety of ways. This military culture and its subsequent politicization offered a variety of sites where women were increasingly visible. In some ways, the rhetoric of patriotism was based on traditional assumptions of masculine heroism and feminine domesticity. The campaign for free trade in 1779 certainly charged women with keeping the domestic sphere free of the taint of English goods. But it also offered opportunities for ordinary women to display their allegiances publicly through their consumption choices and the symbols displayed on their clothing. In other ways, women's presence in this patriotic public sphere, as well as representations of a gendered politics, could allow them to identify with the cause and language of patriotism. Did the attempt by government supporters to taint the campaign for parliamentary reform with the supposed subversion of existing gender relations lead to a hardening of gender categories? Such questions are difficult to answer while the history of gender relations in Ireland in the late 1780s and 1790s remains obscure, but public action by women remained significant, for example, in such moments as the antislavery campaign.[73] It also seems likely that women played as much a role in the politics of loyalism in the 1790s as they did in the politics of republicanism, though both topics require further research.[74] Rather than being governed by hardening oppositional categories of domestic and political spheres, gender relations and categories were often permeable and always contingent. The political realm intruded on the domestic in ways that allowed some women to act or to imagine themselves as political subjects. The moral authority women could evoke at moments of political crisis depended on a particular construction of patriot femininity that, while legitimating women's roles, clearly delineated the limits of their participation. A fine line separated "fair Hibernian patriots" and a "petticoat government."

8

"A Democratical Spirit"

*Reform, Protectionism, and
Popular Politics*

IN JULY 1784 Edward Cooke, a government official, reflected on politics in Dublin: "The party here consists of some Volunteer corps of shopkeepers and apprentices who fancy that red coats make them heroes and accordingly are open to the instigations of the wild, the desperate, the enthusiast, and the villain." He noted that these plebian Volunteers were in league with "papists" and the poor manufacturers, who were an "instrument to try the temper of the city."[1] The social and confessional composition of popular politics was transformed between 1782 and 1784, largely due to the intervention of the Volunteers. This chapter examines that transformation by focusing on demands for parliamentary reform and the introduction of protective duties, as well as the way in which these interrelated campaigns transformed the social and confessional composition of the Volunteers. The campaign for reform was ultimately unsuccessful, and in raising of the Catholic question, exposed the confessional limits of patriotism; by 1785 the movement was in disarray, and the Volunteers were no longer a force in Irish political life. Paradoxically, the splintering of the Volunteers in some ways speaks to the success of radical efforts at politicization, for they fashioned a patriotism that appealed to those beyond the political nation. An initially limited ideology, concerned with a confessionally and socially exclusive polity, patriotism was embraced by those outside this narrow definition of the political nation as a more inclusive vision of an "Irish" patriotism.

A Patriotic Frenzy: The Politics of Renunciation

With the granting of legislative independence, the Volunteers had achieved their greatest success. In the wake of this achievement, the movement immediately found itself divided over two major disputes. The first concerned the issue of "renunciation" and centered on the meaning and limits of legislative independence, though it was as much a personal clash between Henry Grattan and Henry Flood. The second contentious issue addressed the government's scheme to raise the militia-like fencibles as a rival to the Volunteers. Underlying both disputes were different visions of the role of "the people" in the politics of the nation. After the achievement of free trade, many moderates hoped that the drama of the past year was over and that traditional elites could reassert their control over politics, with "the people" and the Volunteers exiting the stage of national affairs. Several disputes in subsequent years frustrated this hope. In April 1780 the issue of legislative independence was famously broached by Grattan in parliament as a means of securing trade concessions and to prevent future British interference in Irish affairs. Further reform was also on the agenda of the Volunteers. Even before Grattan's speech, the Newry Volunteers had issued resolutions supporting legislative independence. In December 1781 the Southern Battalion of the Armagh Regiment of Volunteers met and published a number of strongly worded resolutions, including one that looked forward to the issue that would dominate the political agenda for the next three years: "that to avert the impending danger from the nation, and to restore the constitution to its original purity, the most vigorous and effectual methods must be pursued, to root Corruption and Court influence from the Legislature body."[2]

On 15 February 1782 a meeting of Ulster delegates took place at Dungannon, attended by the representatives of 143 Volunteer corps.[3] This marked a decisive moment in the politicization of the Volunteers. The resolutions drafted by the delegates reasserted the contested right of the Volunteers to participate in politics, resolving that "a citizen, by learning the use of arms, [did] not abandon any of his civil rights." The resolutions renounced the British government's right to exercise authority over Irish affairs and called for legislative independence, an amendment of Poyning's Law, and a limited mutiny bill. They also issued their well-known resolution: "that as men and Irishmen, as Christians and as Protestants, we rejoice in the relaxation of the *Penal Laws* against our *Roman Catholic fellow-subjects*, and that we conceive the measure fraught with the happiest consequences to the union and prosperity of the inhabitants and Ireland."[4] Although this proposal seems to have been resolved unanimously, the Catholic question was to prove the most divisive issue among Volunteers over the course of the campaign for reform.[5]

In the wake of Dungannon, support for the resolutions was widespread.[6] Volunteer companies, freeholders, grand juries, and others held hundreds of meetings throughout the country to offer their endorsement; resolutions were published in the press, offering publicity to a vision of the nation united behind the Dungannon principles.[7] Many other bodies issued opinions on the question of reform, though such resolutions were not without controversy. In March, Lord Muskerry lost command of his Volunteer company in Limerick for refusing to adopt the Dungannon resolutions.[8] Across the country, local elites attempted to check the language of the resolutions, particularly at assize and county meetings.[9] The lord lieutenant, the Earl of Carlisle, wrote to Shelburne in London: "Because the endeavors of the friends of government having been remarkably strenuous at those Assizes, and having nevertheless failed of success, your lordship will from thence be able to judge with what degree of ferment the popular expectation has been raised upon the subject of a declaration of right." While government supporters represented "the most decided superiority of County interest, sufficient to quell every other attempt that might be disagreeable to His Majesty's Government," Carlisle concluded local elites were unable "to silence the people upon the point of independent legislation."[10]

Local elites in many parts of the country encountered difficulties in controlling patriot proclamations. In Tipperary one of the MPs for that county, Francis Mathew, a supporter of the government, bemoaned his inability to influence the county assize. As "foreman of the Jury, as a representative for this County and without vanity believe may [I] say at the head of the most ancient and most considerable property in it," Mathew had expected to win over the majority; instead even erstwhile supporters refused to follow him, since he advocated a more moderate set of resolutions. Mathew concluded that this turn of events was merely an expression of a "patriotic frenzy" that had "seized upon almost every body and the strictest ties of friendship [gave] way to this frantick [sic] zeal of passing resolutions."[11] The resolutions supporting the Dungannon proposals were published with the support of the other local MP, Henry Prittie, an advocate of the Volunteers. Mathew composed and published his own "more moderate" resolutions in response,

Figure 22 *The Goose Pye Defil'd, Exshaw's Magazine,* 1782 (Courtesy of the Board of Trinity College Dublin)

but the episode showed the strength of feeling over the Dungannon resolutions as well as the potential threat of patriot politics to local elites. National politics, and particularly the issue of legislative independence, intersected with, and occasionally overrode, local political loyalties.[12]

As with the campaign for free trade, British politics precipitated a patriot victory in Ireland: with the fall of the North government in March 1782, the strong national support for legislative independence left the new Whig government with little choice but to capitulate to the patriots' demands. In May the British government agreed to repeal the Declaratory Act and to modify Poyning's Law.[13] However, this victory was followed by increasingly bitter divides among patriots over the issue of "renunciation." On the face of it, the renunciation dispute seemed little more than a semantic quarrel as well as a struggle for predominance in the patriot movement between Henry Flood and Henry Grattan, which is indeed how a scatological print, *The Goose Pye Defil'd* (see fig. 22), represented the contest. Flood and his supporters argued that a formal renunciation of its power to legislate for Ireland by Westminster was necessary to make legislative independence secure. Grattan claimed that a "simple repeal" of the Declaratory Act was adequate protection.[14]

Initially Grattan's position found favor with many Volunteers. In June, delegates meeting at the Volunteer National Committee in Dublin expressed satisfaction with the adequacy of a simple repeal.[15] Similar sentiments were voiced by the delegates of over three hundred corps at another meeting at Dungannon three days later. However, Volunteer companies in Belfast, led by the First Volunteer Company of the city, soon began to question this position, claiming, "The rights of this kingdom are not yet secured, nor even acknowledged by Britain" without a renunciation. Concerns were also raised that the delegates had not received instructions from the companies they represented.[16] The Volunteer review of July 1782 became an important site for this dispute and demonstrates the degree to which the Volunteers had become politicized by this time. William Drennan wrote to William Bruce, "Innumerable were the Knots of every denomination of people that every Evening during the Review agitated the great national, and very knotty question of Renunciation or Repeal satisfaction or discontent. . . . Papers of all sorts, and sizes, some penned by Griffith, some by Bryson, and some by Flood were every hour distributed thro' the camp and the Garrison."[17] Francis Dobbs, a supporter of simple repeal, described the review: "Anonymous papers in thousands were dispersed through the camp and garrison. Every private was taught, that he was competent to legislate, and consequently to express his sentiments on the most speculative points. Declaration—Renunciation—Simple Repeal—Legal Security—Better Security, and Bill of Rights, were all before them—and they were to instruct their Delegates on these important points."[18] Dobbs's condescending view of the ability of ordinary men to deliberate on political questions reflected the opinion of many leading Volunteers on the role of the Volunteer rank and file in politics. With legislative independence secured, Dobbs, Charlemont, and others believed politics should now be left to the politicians. Acknowledging that a "great occasion" had inspired the Volunteers "to legislate," Dobbs contended that the emergency had passed and "the people at large" should now avoid engaging in "speculative points."[19] But the passions inspired over renunciation dashed hopes that the Volunteers would retire quietly from the political scene.

As support for renunciation gathered pace, those who had hoped to direct the movement saw themselves increasingly vilified and their patriot reputations sullied. Former Volunteer heroes witnessed their patriot stock swiftly drop. Grattan, who had reached his apotheosis as a patriot hero with legislative independence, was attacked in the press for his position; as Francis Dobbs remarked, "Had any man foretold, that a Grattan should in a few weeks become the object of the grossest and most illiberal abuse . . . he would probably have fallen a victim to his temerity."[20] At the same time, Flood was attempting to rehabilitate his patriot reputation, damaged after he had taken up a government post. The dispute would lead to a reversal in their fortunes and demonstrates the fragility of patriot reputation and the passions such seemingly inconsequential issues could generate. Flood's patriot stock rose swiftly; John Beresford wrote from Dublin, "Flood's doctrine is, I think, pretty universally adopted"; Volunteer companies issued addresses of support and offered him honorary membership in their companies.[21] Previously celebrated patriot figures were vilified; according to Beresford, "[A] universal flame seems to me to be kindling, which will soon break out; the lawyers' corps are to meet, I understand, to censure Grattan," while it was even rumored that the hero of the Volunteers, Charlemont, was to be "ungeneraled."[22]

Beating Up for Fencibles

The divisive renunciation campaign was quickly followed by further conflict over the politics of patriotism and the Volunteers. Since the emergence of independent volunteer companies in 1778, the government had been determined to dispense with the force and replace it with a regular militia. The plan eventually adopted was to raise several regiments of "fencibles." This force was to differ from the regular army in that recruits would not serve abroad or be drafted to regular units.[23] Local elites, as well as some prominent Volunteers, accepted commissions in the proposed new force, and six regiments were eventually established.[24] Most Volunteer companies reacted with indignation to the establishment of the new force; Lord Charlemont recalled, "Recruiting parties were insulted, their drums cut. The very children were taught to lisp scurrility; and 'Fencible' was the universal word of reproach."[25] This general opposition to the fencibles is also reflected in a locally produced

Figure 23 *Beating up for Fencibles, Exshaw's Magazine*, 1783 (Courtesy of the Board of Trinity College Dublin)

print from 1783, *Beating up for Fencibles* (see fig. 23), which depicts a less-than-respectable group of men, eagerly groping for the purse held out by a recruiting officer, suggesting that those involved were mercenaries and of little consequence.

The scheme provoked violent language from many Volunteer companies. The Galway Independent Corps of Volunteers claimed that the fencibles were intended as an attack on the Volunteers, who were more useful to national defense than "new-raised mercenaries." Anyone accepting a commission in this new force, they resolved, was "justly entitled to [the] severest censure."[26] A meeting of the town of Belfast, attended by many leading Volunteers, resolved to "hold in contempt and abhorrence every man who [should] engage in any fencible corps as officer or private"; such men would be deemed "unworthy of the name Irishmen, and enemies to their country."[27] While Belfast was a hotbed of radical Volunteers, even companies who had expressed relatively moderate support for the patriot opposition or avoided political discussion altogether strongly condemned the fencibles. In October the Ennis Volunteers criticized parliament's support for the measure, resolving that it was "inimical to the cause of freedom and replete with ruin and oppression." They also condemned any of their members who might "accept the mercenary wages" of the new force. In December it was discovered that the company chaplain, James Kenny, was involved in recruiting fencibles, for which he was expelled as "an apostate to the Volunteer cause." When Lord Inchiquin, the commander of the Ennis Volunteers, took command of a fencible regiment in Munster, criticism from the Volunteers forced his resignation.[28] Rev. Richard Godley was court-martialed, then shot and burned in effigy by Dobb's Tyrone Ditches and Acton Volunteers after voting for a fencible colonel at an election.[29] Newspapers carried lists of those expelled from the Volunteers for accepting fencible commissions, while also detailing the supposed government machinations to gain support for the scheme.[30]

Disturbances were frequent, as Volunteers clashed in violent feuds with fencibles and recruiting parties. In October 1782 a battle took place at Drogheda between Volunteers and a fencible party, lasting two days and resulting in four deaths.[31] The regiment involved in this clash, led by Colonel Talbot, was still the subject of scorn over six months later after another violent incident in Kilkenny. In April 1783 the Belfast Society drank to a "Speedy justice" to this regiment: "May the fencibles and their friends never enjoy the benefits of freemen. May Ireland never want hemp to exalt all Fencible commanders who deserve it."[32] The violence of this toast reflected the passions that the fencibles aroused and the bitterness created among Volunteers when many former members defected. Although a government-sponsored militia force might possibly have found widespread support before the emergence of the Volunteers, by 1783 a similar scheme resulted in personal and political animosities as well as threatened and actual violence against supporters of the new force. The fencibles engendered fierce opposition because they were viewed (rightly) as a government attempt to undermine the Volunteers. To a certain degree, the divisions over the fencibles mirrored those of the renunciation dispute. William Drennan, a critic of the fencibles, writing of the support of his friends Crombie and Haliday for the force, concluded that the "defence of the repeal system led them to this position."[33] The *Hibernian Journal,* which had taken Grattan's side over his support for simple repeal, supported the new force. The unfortunate Francis Dobbs again found himself on the wrong side of popular opinion. His hastily composed pamphlet *A History of Irish Affairs* served as a lengthy justification for both his support of simple repeal *and* his subsequent decision to take a commission in the fencibles.[34]

A variety of reasons explain the support given by some to the fencible scheme, from miscalculation of the popular mood, as in Dobbs's case, to more mundane considerations. Charlemont believed that the conflict had been stirred up by individuals with interests in the upcoming elections.[35] Drennan offered other reasons: a powerful local family, the Stewarts, he believed, had "perceived a Spirit of independence and self-government arising among their tenantry which they [were] afraid, [might], as it ha[d] already done in some particular instances, become vexatious to them as Land-lords, and leading men of the County." Fearing the consequences of the "Democratical Spirit" that Volunteering had unleashed in the North, elites were "endeavoring to collect the reins which ha[d] lain floating on the Necks of the Multitude and to accustom them once more to that proper Discipline and Subordination."[36] Despite their efforts, elites largely failed to rein in the Volunteers. Instead, middle-class reformers in Dublin and Belfast began to assert greater control over the Volunteers agenda. Many moderate Volunteers responded to the constant politicking of 1782 by simply withdrawing from the movement, and after reaching a high point in 1782, the rate of participation in the force went into steady decline.

The Politics of Reform

In April 1783 the British government passed a bill that satisfied the Irish patriot opposition as a final renunciation.[37] After the successful campaign for legislative independence and the bitter disputes of 1782, the issue of parliamentary reform increasingly came to dominate the patriot agenda, with the Volunteers for the first time taking the lead in a political campaign. Over the course of 1782, relations between the Volunteers and Parliament had become strained, and while the Volunteers never completely renounced parliamentary authority, they convened a series of 'anti-parliaments" to represent the real "sense of the people."[38] With the loss of many "respectable" elements from the movement, the hostility of Parliament, and the divisiveness of the Catholic question, this reform movement was ultimately unsuccessful and by 1785 was a spent force. At the same time, the extent of politicization in the course of this campaign, particularly among the increasingly plebian and

Catholic support base in Dublin, deserves consideration, not least for its legacy of radical politics in the capital.

A call for parliamentary reform was scarcely innovative. Reform was a central aspiration of political and moral campaigns in eighteenth-century Britain and Ireland. In the 1780s in particular, there were a variety of campaigns for both reform and (a related term) improvement that garnered widespread support.[39] In the 1760s, influenced by the Wilkite movement and events in America, campaigns had emerged in Dublin to make more representative a parliament perceived as increasingly corrupt. This campaign, led by the apothecary Charles Lucas, was largely concerned with guaranteeing regular elections and restricting the government's ability to use patronage to ensure a parliamentary majority. Many of these issues differed little from the concerns of British country ideology with its focus on the virtue of representatives; Irish reformers diverged, however, with their claim that constitutional subordination to Great Britain was the font of Ireland's political woes.[40] In 1768, as a concession to patriots, the Octennial Act was passed. This act ensured elections were held at least every eight years rather than only on the death of a monarch. In the 1770s, led by Edward Newenham, many reformers campaigned to make representatives more responsive to the wishes of electors. As Peter Smyth observes, "Radical analysis located parliament at the centre of the social system and equated its reform with a transformation of society."[41] Associations such as the Society of Free Citizens of Dublin held debates that served to popularize the language of reform. At the same time, they put pressure on MPs and prospective candidates to follow the instructions of electors and continued to criticize corruption, particularly electoral entertainments. In the 1776 election, reformers even succeeded in returning some reform-minded candidates.[42]

Influenced by the association movement in Britain, some Volunteers had broached reform in 1780, with Francis Dobbs engaging in a correspondence with leading British reformers such as John Cartwright and John Jebb.[43] By 1783, Ulster was foremost in advocating reform. Reform became a central issue in the hard-fought elections of that year, with the "independent interest" achieving several victories in the province. In 1783, aided by the reforming Lisburn Constitutional Club, the Volunteer officers William Todd Jones and William Sharman defeated the candidates of Lord Hertford in that town. In County Antrim, two Volunteers, John O'Neill and Hercules Rowley, were returned unopposed.[44] Their victory was celebrated with a dinner for 250 freeholders, who drank to "the independent interest" and "a more equal representation of the people."[45] Reformers in Ulster did not have everything their own way; aristocratic interests attempted to reassert their authority in many contests. In the County Down election, the representative of the "independent interest" Robert Stewart was defeated by candidates favored by Lord Hillsborough, the most substantial landowner in the county and a supporter of the government. The Down contest resulted in a vigorous campaign, with an outpouring of literature and mobilization of the people through parades and meetings.[46]

As Ian McBride observes, the idea of independence had a number of connotations in eighteenth-century politics. It referred to an independent freeholder, to the coalition of smaller landowners against the great electoral interests of a county, and to the popular notion of opposition to aristocracy and rejection of electoral deference.[47] Independence was often a trait associated with manliness, a virtue opposed to servility that could be cultivated through participation in the Volunteers, removing, in Drennan's phrase, "that servile awe of estated tyrants."[48] The "independence" of Volunteer companies from government and local elites accentuated their virtue and public spirit. If electors should be independent, so too should their representatives. This suggested they should at least be propertied and free from government influence. At the same time, a representative should embody certain moral qualities or be "respectable."[49] A focus on the personal qualities of representatives had long been part of British country ideology. But how could this independence of both elector and elected be guaranteed?

By 1783 some sort of parliamentary reform seemed to many the best safeguard of political liberty. Many radical supporters of reform began to focus on notions of popular sovereignty and the rightful role of "the people" in choosing of representatives. After a series of provincial meetings addressing the question of "a more Equal Representation of the People" followed by correspondence with radical reformers in England, elected delegates gathered as a national convention at the Rotunda on November 10.[50] Many radicals increasingly placed their hope for reform in this "anti-parliament" of Volunteer delegates while denouncing the parliament itself. Recalling the free-trade protests of 1779, the placards displayed around William's statue during the annual 4 November Volunteer parade again served as barometers of political feeling: "The Volunteers of Ireland overturned the Cadaverous simple repeal must now Effectuate an Equal representation of the People."[51] The radical press offered extensive coverage of the convention and attempted to legitimate delegates as the true representatives of the people. Whole editions were devoted to the proceedings, and special supplements were issued recounting the delegate's debates. The *Volunteer's Journal* was particularly insistent in emphasizing the virtues of the convention over the parliament. On 14 November the paper proclaimed, "Every day serves more clearly to shew us the absurdity of expecting any redress of grievances from our CORRUPT, PROSTITUTE, PARLIAMENT." Rather than relying on this body, the paper suggested, "THE PEOPLE must therefore, to use the emphatical words of a celebrated writer, WORK OUT THEIR OWN SALVATION!" At the conclusion of the convention in December, based on the delegate's resolutions, Henry Flood, dressed as a Volunteer, introduced a bill for parliamentary reform in the Commons. Many MPs expressed outrage at being dictated to by an extra-parliamentary armed body. Much to the outrage of the radical press, the bill was easily defeated.

With the failure of the convention, reformers turned to other methods to promote their agenda. From the end of the year onward, they initiated a national petitioning campaign as a more legitimate means of obtaining their ends. Of these tactics, Rutland, the lord lieutenant, noted, "It seems advisable to treat it with more delicacy and respect, than was used when it was introduced from the convention."[52] Petitions were organized on a county basis; over thirty petitions were presented to Parliament, the majority from county meetings of freeholders.[53] In Tyrone, "gentlemen and freeholders" met at Omagh on 16 January and declared their loyalty to the king as well as their aim to "rescue out of the hands of a dangerous aristocracy, powers which [were] equally inconsistent with the rights of the crown and the rights of the people."[54] Counter-petitions were also presented from several counties, protesting the legitimacy and representativeness of the reformers.[55] County Down in particular witnessed a fierce struggle between supporters and opponents of reform based on petitioning. Local politics again intersected with the issue of national reform, with Lord Hillsborough once more taking an active role through the circulation of a counterpetition. Despite his electoral victory the previous year, by 1784 he was encountering serious difficulties in opposing calls for reform. In February he complained of Newry: "That town is very little short of the factious violence of Belfast and altho' I have an estate in it, I have not been able to procure above fourteen signatories to the protest against the petition of this County."[56] The insolence of the residents of Newry notwithstanding, by the end of the month he had used his considerable influence to obtain over three thousand signatures from freeholders and many of the foremost gentry in the county.[57]

In March, following the presentation of these petitions, another bill for reform was introduced by Henry Flood but once again was defeated. In the wake of a new setback, many reformers became convinced that reform would not be forthcoming through Parliament. Beginning in April, county meetings and other bodies circulated petitions to the king seeking redress. Such tactics illustrate the attachment to the British monarchy and the essential loyalty of even the most radical reformers; in April the Donegal Grand Jury at Lifford, stressing their "lively affection, duty, and attachment" to the king, addressed him, claiming that the parliament had "forfeited the confidence of the people." They hoped that he might direct his ministers to ensure that the Commons would become "the real, not the nominal representation of the people."[58] In July a petition from "the Freemen, Freeholders and Inhabitants of the city of Dublin" presented a similarly strongly worded address to the king: "The grievance your distressed subjects thus humbly presume to lay before Your Majesty is the present illegal and inadequate representation of the people of this kingdom in parliament—illegal because the returns of the members for boroughs are not agreeable to the charters granted for that purpose by the crown:—Inadequate because there are as many members returned for each of these boroughs by a few voters as are chosen for any county or city in this kingdom."[59] The petitioners blamed the "Aristocratic influence" in the nation for these abuses and connected these problems with the issue of the protection of trade, an assault on the liberty of the press, and attacks on the charters of Dublin. This concern with charters and corporate rights in many ways places the petitioners within the tradition of ancien régime Protestant patriotism propagated by Charles Lucas decades earlier.[60] At the same time, reform of the parliament and the system of representation was central to their argument. Ideas of the sovereignty of the people were formulated and the importance of extraparliamentary activity emphasized in ways that moved beyond traditional corporatism or country ideology.[61] Rutland dismissed the Dublin petition, claiming the meeting had been called by "a few desperate and violent men of no real weight in the state, of no fortune or reputation to give them influence."[62] In the wake of the Dublin meeting, campaigns to collect signatures were also organized in the North. Both Belfast and Lisburn sent petitions in July, though the first of these, delivered by William Brownlow, was rejected.[63]

In September a requisition was made to the sheriffs of Dublin to hold a meeting to select representatives for a national meeting, similar to the national convention; on this occasion, however, delegates were to be chosen by freeholders rather than by an armed force. This worried the government, not only because the requisition was signed by several Catholics but because the October meeting was designated the "National Congress," a clear echo of American events.[64] Although Rutland may have mocked the social origins and the religious persuasion of those involved, his patronizing account nonetheless illustrates the increasingly important role of Catholics and artisans in driving reform in Dublin by mid-1784. Rutland claimed that the signatories of the Dublin petition included seventeen butchers, seven hatters, as well as weavers, tailors, tinkers, stay makers, carpenters, mercers, hosiers, a shoemaker, and a ballad seller. Also represented were three attorneys, a counselor, and two "bankrupts." Of the sixty-two signatories, eighteen were Catholic, including the printer Peter Hoey.[65] This motley group in many ways represents the changing composition of extraparliamentary politics. Throughout 1784 a coalition of radicals, the lower classes, and Catholics was increasingly politicized by petitioning, meetings, crowd action, the press, and crucially, volunteering. As Jim Smyth notes, this was a critical moment, anticipating in many ways the radicalism of the 1790s.[66]

"The Dregs of Society": Opponents of Reform and the Catholic Question

The government expended considerable effort in opposing reform. Many Dublin newspapers benefited from government patronage. In 1783 the *Volunteer Evening Post* was established as a mouthpiece for government policy and to counter the radical reform advocated by the *Volunteer's Journal*. Government patronage also supported a series of antireform pamphlets that emphasized the unsuitability of the lower orders to participate in the electoral process, the alarming consequences of extending the vote to Catholics, and the machinations of radical Presbyterians. Adopting the rhetoric of patriotism, *A Reform of the Irish House of Commons Considered* (1783) attacked the reformers for canvassing the ideas of English reformers and for slavishly following English reform ideas with little consideration of Irish particularities. The reformers' plans to expand the franchise in towns and cities were also ridiculed; the urban world, it was argued, consisted of "low tradesmen, mechanics and apprentices." Such men were "the most licentious, drunken, and profligate of any in the community." As with many attacks on reform, respectability was a key term in discrediting their plans: "I lay it down as a fundamental and incontrovertible maxim that respectable constituents will alone return respectable representatives."[67] "Respectability" referred to those of landed property, but it also had a moral meaning implying political independence. Property gave men the independence to act in the public good.[68] The lower orders could not hope to aspire to such independence. Indeed, reform of the franchise would inevitably lead to even greater corruption: "The lower orders of the people set no other value on a vote than as it procures them money or interest, the merit of candidates is no part of their consideration."[69] Letters to the government-supported *Volunteer Evening Post* attempted to discredit reform by claiming that the campaign was the work of violent republicans intent on inflaming the passions of the poor. A satire on plebian politics in February 1784 asked, "How vain may that country be that can boast of the meanest peasant being (one might say) fitted for the important task of legislation, which is at the present the case?"[70] Throughout 1784 the paper continually associated reform politics with the overturning of social and gender hierarchies, casting reform as the cause of insubordination among the lower orders and women.[71]

At the same time, the *Post* represented itself as the guardian of the achievements of the Volunteers and the Dungannon meeting of 1782. Radical reform, the paper claimed, put all these gains at risk. To protect this legacy, unity was needed between the landed and the trading classes, suggesting that many members of the latter had been misled on the merits of reform. As the national convention was taking place in Dublin in November 1783, letters in the paper advocated a limited reform, while emphasizing the relation between property and representation. The paper represented itself as the true friend of reform and the constitution in opposition to the extravagant proposals of some delegates to the convention. "Trenchard," for example, called for the abolition of "rotten boroughs" and somewhat more vaguely for "an uninfluenced, independent parliament."[72] A letter from a "Dungannon Delegate" argued that the first principle of the constitution was "that it [was] property represented in parliament." The logic of reformers' schemes meant there could be "no solid reason given why every man in the kingdom, who [was] not a pauper or a malefactor, should not be entitled to a vote for a representative in parliament." This contradicted the intent of the constitution, for the vote was "not a right annexed to the person, but to the property possessed by the person."[73] The following month a letter from "A Friend of Ireland" offered a different line of argument, addressing enfranchised members of the lower class. Reform, he suggested, was actually an attack on their existing electoral privileges.[74] Similarly, "Crito" argued that political rights of the lower orders were "particularly struck at" by the resolutions of the convention.[75]

Reform and the Catholic Question

As discussed earlier, the dangers of popery were frequently evoked in the 1770s and 1780s by Protestants across the political spectrum. The reform movement itself was sharply divided on the Catholic question. Opponents of reform seized on this division to portray reform more generally as an effort to institute popery through the back door. Conceding the vote to Catholics while excluding them from sitting in Parliament, as some reformers proposed, would not protect the Protestant nature of the state. According to one author, those professing a religion that "dispenses with oaths" and acknowledges a "foreign jurisdiction" would have few scruples in "pretending conformity in Protestantism" in order to take over the Commons and subvert the Protestant church and constitution.[76] Many pamphleteers portrayed the reform movement as an unholy alliance between Presbyterians and Catholics in an attempt to overthrow the established order. *The Alarm* (1783), addressed to members of the "Church of Ireland as by Law Established," offered perhaps the most hysterical account of this plot, inciting a minor pamphlet war in the process. The author claimed that the "Puritans and Roman Catholics" had joined together and "openly declared that they [would] attempt by force of arms to change the established constitution in church and state."[77] Armed and trained in Volunteer companies, they were now executing their plans through a "council of war," the national convention. Although this body pretended to advocate nothing more than the reform of the House of Commons and extension of the franchise to Catholics, the result of this campaign would be that "the estates, real and personal, of every Protestant of the Established Church, and probably of the Puritans themselves swept away in a moment; and that their lives [could] be no otherwise secure than by speedy flight from their native country."[78]

While opponents of reform played on fears of popery to discredit plans to alter the franchise, reformers themselves differed markedly on the place of Catholics in their reform schemes. Most remained implacably opposed to any extension of political rights to Catholics; others favored a gradual extension of rights, though only to relatively wealthy Catholics. Few advocated complete equality for Catholics and were content to leave plans somewhat vague, aware of the potential divisiveness of the issue. An "Independent Volunteer" described the tactics of the "castle emissaries," who, he claimed, "[instill] their apprehensions and fears of catholic parliaments, popish inquisitions, and I know not what phantoms, which their tortured imaginations conjure up."[79] Supporters of Catholic rights faced strongly entrenched ideas of antipopery that associated Catholics with tyranny and the slaughter of Protestants. Reformers countered these traditional fears by claiming that Catholics were indeed capable of liberty. Such claims become increasingly insistent throughout 1783 and 1784 as the issue of parliamentary reform inevitably led to questions of the place of Catholics in the political nation.

Handy Pemberton, a lawyer and a Volunteer, wrote as a "True born Irishman" in the press, asserting the right of Catholics to vote and attacking Charlemont's opposition to Catholic enfranchisement: "A love of liberty is innate in all mankind, and there is no case, in which it appears, this love has not glowed with as much warmth in the bosoms of Roman Catholics, as of any other people whatever." Support for Catholic rights, he argued, would at the same time strengthen the cause of reform.[80] "Memmius," in a pamphlet titled *The Voice of the People*, also supported political rights for Catholics, arguing that the tenets of Catholicism did not make its adherents "necessarily less capable of enjoying the benefit of a free government."[81] Peter Burrowes, lawyer and pamphleteer, argued that as "Irishmen" living in a "period of liberation," Catholics had "caught the love of freedom" from Protestant patriots and should now be admitted to the franchise.[82] Burrowes was willing to concede the vote to Catholics meeting the 50s. freehold qualification; however, there could be no question of admitting them to the legislature. To avoid any threat to the established church, the franchise was "the proper boundary between toleration and policy."[83] Admitting the small number of qualified Catholics to the franchise, Burrowes believed, would have very little practical effect. The real benefit would be more psychological: "Every Protestant considers himself as free, not because he votes for a representative, for few have that privilege, but because he may arrive at it by a certain exercise of industry and attainment of property." That Catholics were unable even to hope for such an aspiration would "either debase their nature, or render them disaffected to the Constitution under which they live."[84] The vote for Catholics would inspire loyalty to the Protestant state, while support for this measure would provide an ally in the campaign for reform.

Addressing the Volunteers in July 1784, William Todd Jones, the radical MP for Lisburn, also argued for Catholic enfranchisement, stressing the importance of Catholic support for the reform campaign. Jones believed it was an "incontrovertible" position that Catholics should share "the privileges of citizens." Although the legal position of Catholics had improved, without reform of the franchise they would be "confined to their present vassalage, unprivileged, unemancipated, legislated for and taxed by others; and only indulged at the will of their lords."[85] He believed the extension of the franchise would cure Catholics of their "habit of slavery" as a freehold, and the vote would offer them "consequence and independence."[86] Todd Jones looked to history for instances of "Catholick public virtue" to prove they were indeed capable of liberty. His account is unusual in that it suggests Catholics might be the true heirs of Irish liberty and the originators of Irish patriotism.[87] His examples of this tradition included the remonstrance of Catholics to Charles I in 1642, which demonstrated a "spirited and natural defence" of their religion and "the liberties of their country."[88] Inspired by legitimate grievances and English oppression, Catholics in this instance asserted "the independence of the Irish constitution one hundred and forty years before the Protestants ventured to do it—opposing a British faction whose only object was the subjugation of this country."[89]

Most of all, Todd Jones believed, Catholics had shown their worth by participating in the Volunteers. He claimed, "They have for a considerable time past carried arms, become disciplined, and formed a part of that army which would have honoured Rome in the zenith of her liberty and simplicity."[90] The relationship between the Volunteers and the Catholic question has long been a staple of celebratory nationalist historiography. Discarding the intolerant principles of the penal laws, the Volunteers were credited with forging a more inclusive patriotism and a new understanding of Irish national identity.[91] There is in fact much to recommend this account. For example, McBride has shown that among many northern Presbyterian Volunteers there was a softening in attitudes toward Catholics.[92] At the same time, as has been emphasized throughout this study, care should be taken in assuming a general growth of tolerance and the decline of anti-Catholic feeling among Irish

Protestants. The threat posed by Catholics, their capacity to exercise political rights, and their role in the Volunteers were all deeply divisive issues in the political nation at large and within the Volunteer movement
itself. As described in chapter 6, from 1778 onward some Volunteer
companies had admitted individual "respectable" Catholics, though
this had engendered much debate. A pamphlet titled *Thoughts on the
Conduct and Continuation of the Volunteers of Ireland* (1783) explained the
logic of this early recruitment of Catholics:

> To permit the use of arms to all Catholics would have been madness.
> To confine it to men of certain property was a project full of difficulty
> and offence. . . . We wished for some mode of judging which applied
> not to property only but to fitness and character, by which a worthy
> Roman Catholic might and such one only, be trusted with the use of
> arms, and attached to his Protestant fellow-subjects. Volunteering has
> done what the law could not do. The Catholic who wishes to carry
> arms, proposes himself to a Protestant corps. His character is tried by
> his neighbours; he is admitted to an honour and a privilege.[93]

Respectable Catholics could be recruited using a careful vetting system
based on local knowledge of individual character.

By 1784, particularly in Dublin, many companies were openly
recruiting Catholics en masse, as well as making appeals to poor Protestants. In May, Rutland reported that the Liberty Corps had begun advertising for recruits and that two hundred of the "poorer manufacturers . . . with cockades in their hats" from the largely Catholic Liberties
had escorted the company to their place of exercise outside the city. One
pamphlet offered a hysterical account of this Catholic volunteering: "In
the city of Dublin, under the nose of the government a body of men,
chiefly Roman Catholics have regimented and armed themselves and
publickly and frequently paraded through the streets at noon day in
military order. . . . They have assumed the name of the Irish Brigade
being the title of those desperate set of renegades, who, deserting their
country have continued to fight against it, under the banners of the
French King."[94] These new recruits inspired some companies to reassert
the social and religious boundaries of volunteering. Rutland was convinced that companies who "pique themselves as gentlemen upon their
manners and appearance and upon being men in substantial circumstances" would balk at uniting with the "meanest and poorest rank."
Indeed, the Dublin Volunteer Company did meet to express their opposition to the admittance of Catholics, and later that month a meeting of
delegates from the Volunteer companies of Dublin rejected a resolution

to clothe and arm "persons of every rank." A compromise resolution was reached declaring "that the training to the use of arms every honest and industrious Irish man however moderate his property or distressed his situation would be a measure of the utmost utility to this Kingdom."[95]

Other companies soon followed the lead of the Liberty Corps, arming and drilling Catholics. Again, they recognized a clear relationship between the right to bear arms and the rights of the citizen. That companies throughout the country were willing to arm Catholics does suggest a more common acceptance of the identity of "Irishmen" that crossed traditional confessional boundaries.[96] Catholics were also being drilled and trained in other parts of the country. The Belfast First Company had been one of the first to allow all denominations to enter its ranks, and the Newry First Volunteers soon followed suit.[97] A Volunteer company in Dundalk raised fifty Catholic recruits and advertised for fifty more.[98] The dean of Armagh noted that in that county, John Blackhall, a justice of the peace, had advertised in the Belfast newspaper for "persons of whatever description" to join the Loughall Volunteers. In July, Blackhall had led his company to mass, "armed and drilled several papists," and brought them to the Armagh review. This brought him into conflict with several other companies that refused to drill with Catholics and suggested that Blackhall should be ducked. He was forced to dismiss the Catholics.[99] Some companies, such as the Wicklow Forresters, resolved explicitly against the admittance of Catholics.[100]

A "secret return" of the Volunteers ordered by Rutland in 1784 attests to the recruitment of Catholics, while at the same time charting the overall decline of volunteering. The return, a county-by-county analysis of the strength and composition of the force, noted the presence of Catholics in almost every county in the country. This influx of Catholics caused open confrontation in places. In Boyle, the Royal Boyle Protestants had refused to allow the Barrony Cohort Catholic company to march through the town with arms. But elsewhere, Catholic companies were raised. In Donegal, the Raphoe Battalion was found to be composed of fifty Catholics, though it seemed Catholics were not among the officers of any company. Catholic companies were being raised in Carrickmacross and Shercock. The report from Roscommon and Leitrim noted that the Mohill corps, the Leitrim Rangers, and the Strokestown corps were now all mixed companies. By the end of 1784, Catholics made up well over 30 percent of the total force of just under nineteen thousand men.[101]

In part, the recruitment of Catholics was no doubt a practical response to the problem of decline. Many "respectable" Volunteers and local notables began to withdraw from the movement, as alarm grew over the increasing political involvement of the force and the bitter divisions within the movement. Those middle-class radicals who remained looked to Catholics and lower-class Protestants to revive the force. Other companies, however, justified their recruitment of Catholics on more ideological grounds. In August a letter from Newry noted that an invitation had been issued in that town "for all nominations to enroll themselves under the banner of liberty." A number of corps had been formed as a consequence "without distinction of religion." The association for one such company, the Newry Brigade, declared this unity:

> We whose names are hereunto subscribed associate together as a military body under the title of the Newry Brigade—we associate as Volunteer soldiers in order to maintain our rights as citizens. We are sensible of the value of liberty and we all wish to possess the power of preserving it. . . . We associate although differing in religious opinions because we wish to create the union of power and to cultivate the brotherhood of affection among ALL the inhabitants of this island which is the interest as well as the duty of all. We are all IRISHMEN; we rejoice and glory in the common title which binds us together.[102]

Despite such resounding declarations of unity, many former leading Volunteers were appalled at this alliance with Catholics and lower-class Protestants. Grattan, the most noted critic, famously asked if the Volunteers had become the "armed beggary" of the nation rather than the armed property.[103] These new recruits also offered a ready opportunity for the government press to demonize the Volunteers.[104] A pamphlet defending John Foster in 1784 argued that the Volunteers had erred in "inviting and receiving plebeians, and the dregs of society into their corps." The author claimed it was impossible to civilize such recruits and that participation in the Volunteers would fill them with "imaginary ideas of independence and equality."[105] The recruitment of Catholics and the general disorder over "protecting duties" and reform were represented by opponents as evidence of a wider conspiracy. In October the Earl of Mornington informed the chief secretary, "The language of the papists is insolent to the last degree; they are in possession of several of the newspapers, and I need not tell you what powerful engines the newspapers are in this foolish nation." He claimed they would not rest until they had achieved a parliamentary reform in favor of Catholics.[106] The Earl of Hillsborough reported from the North that he had observed three Volunteer companies march through town "each with an ill-looking fellow at their head carrying a large axe. This [was] said to be aimed at the king." When these Volunteers were asked what their aim was, it was discovered they expected "shares of the forfeited estates." Hillsborough blamed such notions on "independent parsons" who "preach[ed] up the principles of Republicanism."[107] For many members of the elite, the events of 1784 revived fears of Catholic and republican conspiracy and simply confirmed the dangers inherent in involving "the people" in politics.

"Transatlantic Materials": The Dublin Crowd and Protectionism

The fears of opponents of reform were given further credence by a wave of disturbances and alleged plots in the capital. The renewed nonimportation campaign of 1784, which sparked this disorder, illustrates the appeal of the language of the patriot movement and the links between middle-class patriotism and the politics of the Dublin crowd. Beginning in April 1784, Napper Tandy, who had been instrumental in transforming the confessional and social basis of volunteering in Dublin, along with John Binns, led an effort to promote new nonconsumption and nonimportation agreements. These efforts were considerably more violent than the campaign of 1779. Tarring and feathering was the threatened punishment for those failing to observe the agreements, and the threat was carried out on a number of occasions. Violent crowd action, as well as increasingly incendiary language in the newspapers, characterized the campaign. A number of municipal issues added fuel to demands for parliamentary reform and protective duties. Crowd action culminated with an attack on the parliament and several threats against the lives of members of the administration.

While moral and physical pressure to support the agreements gained momentum, the campaign for parliamentary reform was once more renewed with a round of meetings, resolutions, and petitions. The campaigns were closely related, and the figure of Napper Tandy looms large in both. Tandy was part of a dense network of radicals in Dublin; this group chaired meetings of political clubs and societies, endlessly adopted resolutions, published pamphlets, wrote letters to the press, and actively participated in the Volunteers. Tandy had been involved in the civic politics of Dublin on the Common Council throughout the

1770s; he was a leading member of the reform-minded Society of Free Citizens and had been instrumental in establishing the nonimportation campaign of 1779. An enthusiastic Volunteer, he was expelled from the Dublin Volunteers in 1780 for proposing that the Duke of Leinster, the commander and leading patron of the company, should be ousted from his position for his parliamentary conduct.[108] Tandy responded by establishing his own corps, the Independent Dublin Volunteers, which became one of the most politicized companies and contributed in no small part to the transformation of volunteering by admitting lower-class Protestants and Catholics. He was, then, well versed in controversial alliances with the Dublin "mob."

The administration had a low opinion of Tandy, whom one correspondent described as "a bankrupt room-keeper in Cornmarket."[109] A government document titled "Descriptions of Demogogary [sic]" offered a less-than-flattering characterization of him and other radicals in 1784 particularly emphasizing their lack of respectability. The portrait of Tandy offered a more detailed and colorful account of his story: "Stiling himself Esq. tho' neither House Keeper or Freeholder lodger we hear this month in Abbey Street having formerly when an Ironmonger in Cornmarket try'd for his life for shooting a Butcher, his attachment to that fraternity is very remarkable ever since."[110] As James Kelly argues, radical reform in Dublin was led not by the dregs depicted in Castle propaganda but rather by professionals and the merchant classes, with the "demagogues" described by government including three members of the Common Council of the Corporation, six attorneys or notaries, and two members of the Catholic Committee. By 1784 political reform was increasingly under the sway of such figures as the early predominance of gentry figures or parliamentarians faded.[111] The government believed that all the disturbances originated with Napper Tandy, John Binns, and their associates. It was claimed they held meetings as the Free Citizens at which they drank "the French King on their knees" with the purpose of separation from England and "the establishment of the Roman Catholic religion."[112] Despite such unlikely scenarios, it is clear that Tandy and Binns were involved in coordinating the reform and protectionist campaigns by April 1784.

As in 1778, economic distress in Dublin did play some role in motivating crowd actions in 1783 and 1784. In May 1783, Northington (during his short-lived lord lieutenancy) noted, "I do believe the distress of the poor manufacturers to be very great and to require some speedy relief."[113] Unemployment was rampant throughout the city. Many bodies such as the Dublin Corporation and the guild of merchants claimed protective duties were needed to shelter Ireland's distressed industries against competition from British imports.[114] But it was not only economic motives that inspired the actions of the Dublin crowd. Economic grievances, as well as attacks on municipal rights and the liberty of the press, were consistently linked to the wider problem of a corrupt and unrepresentative parliament. "A Manufacturer," comparing the Irish experience to that of Mexico under the Spanish, described this well-worn argument: "We too, having been deprived of laws and constitution, have been afterwards despoiled of our manufactures."[115] A parliament under British sway could hardly be expected to enact legislation promoting Irish industry at the expense of British competition. Letters to the press, particularly in the radical *Volunteer's Journal*, consistently claimed a reformed parliament was a precondition for economic prosperity.[116]

Initially, advocates of protective duties based their hopes on parliamentary measures, and to this end the crowd attempted to intimidate MPs and members of the administration into supporting such legislation. In November 1783, as the national convention was meeting to discuss reform, a crowd gathered outside the parliament in anticipation of action following the report of a committee on the question of protective duties. Northington claimed the crowd was drunk, and although no violence occurred, he noted, "Enough was heard to drop from them in conversation with each other to denote their resentment against particular members of the House of Commons."[117] A mob also gathered outside Henry Grattan's house, though again, there was no violence. The administration was alarmed enough, however, to increase guards and patrols in the city and issue a proclamation in the press. In March 1784 a bill for protective duties was rejected by parliament. This sparked a menacing intervention of the Dublin "mob." Beresford wrote while the disorder still continued, "Behold all of a sudden a storm has arose, the end of which cannot just now be easily foreseen." He believed that a variety of issues had combined to inflame the crowd; protective duties, the prosecution of the printers of the *Volunteer's Journal* for sedition, a new bill attacking the liberty of the press, and the rejection of reform after a national petitioning campaign all inspired popular action.[118]

The immediate context for the crowd action was a meeting of "the citizens at large" against the Paving Bill. The meeting originally convened to prepare a petition to parliament against the bill but was postponed due to a poor turnout. The following day, Monday, 5 April, a large crowd turned out and resolved in favor of a petition, again to be

presented by "the body of the citizens" rather than simply by freeholders. That evening, as with the crowd action of 1779, handbills "of a very
inflammatory tendency" were distributed throughout the city. Thomas
Orde, the chief secretary, claimed that money was also dispersed in the
Liberties "to intoxicate some of the poor manufacturers" and that the
mob then set off for Parliament.[119] The crowd proceeded to force its way
into the House and performed the rituals of parliamentary procedure
as a form of mockery that, at the same time, served to legitimate their
grievances; after taking possession of the gallery, "they elected among
themselves a speaker." The question was put, "Foster should be
Hanged?" and then according to Beresford, they "declared it carried in
the affirmative, nem. con."[120]

Contemporaries, such as Rutland, were convinced that the Paving
Bill and the perceived attack on the rights of the corporation were related to the wider questions of parliamentary reform and protective duties. In May the bishop of Killaloe wrote of the serious nature of their
"commotions." He believed that "the discontent [lay] entirely among
the lower orders." The decline of the woolen manufactures was one of
their principle grievances, while the Paving Bill and another to limit the
freedom of the press caused further exasperation. This combination of
grievances had incited the lower classes in Dublin so greatly, the bishop
believed, "that order of the people [was] so dissatisfied as to be almost
disaffected." Such developments on their own were alarming enough,
but economic grievances were intertwined with broader political concerns. The principle issue remained that of reform: "The reformation of
the parliament is a point which the whole People seem to have more at
heart than ever; I scarce meet with any man out of parliament who does
not declare himself a warm friend to it upon principle and I am afraid
that the case is pretty much the same in England." The bishop was convinced that regular correspondence with British reformers was in fact
directing Irish reform efforts. At the same time, he noted the presence of
"a great many French and American Emissaries," who were "notoriously active to keep up the general dissatisfaction" by offering Catholics "hopes of a triumphant Establishment under the liberal protector of
France."[121]

Rutland and other members of the administration were equally
convinced that there were plots and conspiracies afoot.[122] Their fears
were fueled by an increasingly seditious press and the apparent discovery of actual plots against them. The same day the crowd invaded the
parliament, Mathew Carey's *Volunteer's Journal* advanced its campaign

against the government. While describing the commons as a "den of thieves," the paper saved its real vitriol for John Foster. A mock advertisement announced

> in a few days will be published
> in the WEAVER'S SQUARE
> The whole art and mystery of TARRING
> And FEATHERING a TRAITOR
> Dedicated to the rt. hon. John FOSTER.

Beneath a woodcut image of "Jacky Finance" (as the *Journal* referred to Foster) hanging from a gallows, the text described a starving mob of manufacturers attacking the commons, seizing Foster, and leading him off to be hanged (see fig. 24a).[123] It promised to dedicate further editions to John Scott, and on 9 April it repeated the threat, this time with an image of a dead Foster (see fig. 24b). The paper was immediately condemned by the Commons, where it was declared a "false, scandalous and seditious libel on the proceedings of this house, tending to promote discontent amongst his majesty's subjects, to create groundless jealousies between this kingdom and Great Britain, to alienate the affections of the people from his majesty's government, and to excite opposition to the laws of the land."[124] The government ordered the arrest of the printer and introduced a libel bill to limit the freedom of the press. A reward was offered for the apprehension of both author and printer.[125] At the same time, rumors circulated of plans to assassinate leading members of the administration. The government took these threats seriously enough. Rutland claimed, "Every discovery we make tends to confirm it and the glorious idea is kept alive by the encouragement of the newspapers and the [papists]."[126] The episode also hints at a determined and violent political underworld among Dublin artisans, located in the largely Catholic weaving districts, such as the Coombe.

As with the campaign for parliamentary reform, the failure of Parliament to support their demands led protectionists to look to extraparliamentary means to achieve their aims. Letters to the press had advocated such a campaign from the end of 1783 onward, and great hopes were held for its success.[127] A variety of different Dublin trades came out in support of this agreement. Public oaths were administered throughout the city. As in 1779, the names of those supporting the agreement were published in the press. In April many Dublin parishes resolved to support nonconsumption, as did many clubs and Volunteer companies.[128] The campaign garnered some support outside Dublin; the same month

Figures 24a and 24b "Thus Perish all Traitors to Their Country," *Volunteer's Journal*, 1784 (Courtesy of the Library Company of Philadelphia)

the Grand Jury of Cork published resolutions supporting nonconsumption and nonimportation.[129] In May the woolen drapers of Cork also enacted a nonimportation agreement. Likewise, various voluntary associations supported the campaign.[130] Unlike the campaign in 1779, this effort also received support from the North.[131] The campaign in 1784 had many parallels with the successful pressure for free trade in 1779. Women's support was again portrayed as particularly essential for the success of the nonconsumption campaign. Women were constantly commended in the press for their "tenderness" and "sympathy" toward the starving children of the manufacturers.[132] In May a newspaper reported that "several ladies of distinction" had resolved to wear riding habits of Irish manufacture and were already wearing dresses made from Irish materials.[133] A letter in a Cork newspaper from "an Irishman" appealed to his "virtuous countrywomen" to support nonconsumption.[134]

Furthermore, this campaign was likewise enforced through public pressure and oaths. But the 1784 campaign was considerably more violent than the last, perhaps suggesting less than unanimity in support for protective duties. Tarring and feathering was the main source of punishment for those suspected of breaking the new nonimportation agreement. While journeymen weavers had periodically attacked wearers of foreign cloth and clothing in times of economic distress, attacks in 1784 were far more concentrated and organized, given legitimacy by the campaign for protective duties, and even celebrated in the radical press. These attacks caused considerable anxiety for the authorities. On 19 June a crowd of about three hundred from the Liberties attacked the house of Alexander Clark, a master tailor of Chancery Lane. Some of the crowd "entered the said house with horrid oaths and imprecations" and dragged Clark, almost naked, to the Tenters' Fields, where he was tarred and feathered.[135]

Events in Dublin took an even more violent turn in mid-July when, in an attempt to rescue Plowman, a woolen draper, from a tarring and feathering mob, Sheriff Alexander Kirkpatrick received near-fatal blows to the head. Many Volunteer companies, including the Lawyers and the Merchants corps, issued resolutions against the crowd's actions and offered rewards for the capture of the guilty party.[136] Despite the censure of respectable Volunteers, attacks continued apace. A few days after the assault on Kirkpatrick, the *Volunteer's Journal* offered a defense of the attacks on those breaking the agreements; actions against importers, unlike those in 1779, were justified by explicit comparison to events in

America: "However the hacks of the government may decry tar and feathers, as they think a jacket of such transatlantic materials would be a dress too warm for their delicate nerves in summer; all persons must acknowledge, that this institution, which originated in America, proved so serviceable to that country, was the most beneficial article of commerce yet imported into this kingdom."[137] The government had hoped that a proclamation issued in the wake of early attacks would end matters, but outrages continued.[138] Although the exact motivation of the crowd is not always clear, it seems that those suspected of breaking public oaths received particularly harsh treatment, indicating how seriously these pledges were taken.[139] The authorities found that those who were objects of violence or threats were less than willing to provide information due to the intimidation of "the mob."[140] Orde reported in August that the "tarring and feathering committee" had created such fear that the authorities "vain endeavour[ed] to prevail upon those who have suffered by them to make any depositions against their tormenters."[141] Even when charges were brought, convictions were not forthcoming.

In August a journeyman shoemaker named Richard Gossan did accuse a fellow journeyman, Samuel McKeon, of tarring and feathering him. However, what the *Volunteer's Journal* described as a "virtuous jury" acquitted him.[142] Either the jury supported this popular violence, or the intimidation of the crowd reached beyond importers and merchants. Near the end of August the government finally managed to convict one member of the crowd, Garrett Dignam, who was sentenced to be publicly whipped. Fearing a rescue, a large military guard escorted Dignam through the streets, which were "excessively crowded." Before his punishment was completed, the crowd attacked the guards with stones. Soldiers opened fire, killing one protester and injuring several others.[143] Not surprisingly, this provoked outrage in the press and condemnation from some Volunteer companies. Radical Volunteer companies suggested crowd action was not without justification. The Independent Dublin Volunteers claimed such action was the inevitable consequence of the "bloodthirsty appetite of [their] tyrants" and "their mercenaries."[144]

A print published in the *Hibernian Magazine* in August at the height of the tarring and feathering in many ways encapsulates this movement (see fig. 25). In a daring act of reportage, the engraver of the print, William Esdall, a frequent contributor to the *Hibernian Magazine*, had executed the sketch in July while present at an actual tarring and feathering at Tenters' Fields. In an incident revealing of the degree of antipathy

Figure 25 *Tarring and Feathering: The Reward of the Enemies of Ireland*, 1784 (© Trustees of the British Museum)

between the government and the crowd at this time, the unfortunate Esdall was taken for a government spy by the crowd who "laid violent hands upon him."[145] The print depicts a man who has been stripped of everything but his breeches about to receive his punishment. The accompanying text in the magazine observed how the manufacturers had been driven "to desperation by the rejection of the protecting duties" and had as a consequence "adopted the example set them by their American brethren of tarring and feathering such persons as refuse to enter a non-importation and non-consumption agreement." In the background we see cloth hung on lines, on the Tenters' Fields in the heart of the textile industry most affected by the economic depression, where victims were dragged to receive their punishment. He is surrounded by a surprisingly respectable-looking gang of tormentors. One man, brandishing a brush, admonishes his victim: "This will teach you Humanity for Thousands of Starving Manufacturers, driven almost to desperation, by the United efforts of Foreign and Domestic Enemies." Another man holds a bucket of tar inscribed "for the enemies of Ireland." He encourages his colleague to "Anoint him well" and notes "I have tar enough for the whole tribe—Parasites, Pl[a]cemen, Pens[i]onrs [*sic*], mock Patriots, Paragraphers—Blackguards and all—and a Speedy Exportation to the whole—Hurra, Boys, Hurra!" Behind the victim stands a woman holding feathers, warning, "You shall be well fledg'd. Tho' I strip my old Gander for it." The final figure on the left holds a bag of feathers, which were "real Irish Cloathing for Apostate Patriots," and recites a popular Volunteer ballad:

> Was not you very dull, when you took off our Wool
> To leave us so much of the leather, the leather
> It ne'er enterd your Pate, that Sheep-skin well beat
> Would rouze a whole Nation together, together.

This ballad, "The Volunteer's March," celebrated the role of the Volunteers in securing free trade in 1779 and the way in which the military music of Volunteer companies had inspired a national patriotism against British trade restrictions.[146] The ballad quoted by one of the "'mob" in a print in a respectable periodical illustrates the link that was seen between the ideology of patriotism propagated by the Volunteers and the violent protectionist campaign of 1784. By this time, much of the Dublin crowd was probably Catholic, though lower-class Protestants were surely involved. The image suggests that the broad coalition of plebian Catholics and Protestant men (and even some women) that emerged on Dublin's streets in favor of nonimportation was inspired in part by patriot rhetoric and the militant actions of the Volunteers. At the same time, this increasing violence turned many respectable supporters of the protective duties against the crowd. By mid-August, parish meetings called by the lord mayor and magistrates in Dublin began to adopt resolutions against the actions of the crowds.[147]

The campaigns for reform and protective duties were to serve as the political swan song of patriotism and the Volunteers. In many ways, it was a pitiable epilogue to a process that had begun in 1779. The various companies of Volunteers had initially regarded themselves as a purely defensive force; however, the participation of the Volunteers in the partisan politics of these years, through such practices as the adoption of resolutions, the signing of petitions, and the election of delegates to alternative forms of political assembly, made it increasingly difficult to maintain the fiction that they were above politics and advocates of an impartial patriotism. The issues of renunciation and the fencibles, closely followed by the more explosive conflicts over parliamentary reform, Catholic enfranchisement, and protective duties, firmly enmeshed the Volunteers in politics. This period immediately following legislative independence has often been portrayed as the undoing of the Volunteers, marking the beginning of their decline and culminating in a failure to achieve any significant reform. In the final literary flourish of the patriot movement, a disillusioned William Drennan dismissed the Volunteers as a "transient political phenomenon," motivated by vanity, fashion, and "a boyish fondness for the semblance of war."[148] Yet in terms of a focus on the process of politicization, a more positive assessment of their achievements can be made; even the splintering of the force can be regarded as a measure of the achievements of those advocating radical reform measures. Clearly many moderate or conservative Protestants retired from the force after 1782, for a variety of reasons, not least due to uneasiness with the involvement of a large armed body in political affairs and fears over radical definitions of "the people." But the rump of reform-minded Volunteers still maintained significant support, while also expanding the social and confessional base of the movement, recruiting considerable numbers of lower-class Protestants and Catholics throughout 1784. Now, for the first time, it was a "non-gentry, urban, part-catholic, part-dissenter group" at the forefront of this "nation of politicians."[149]

Conclusion

Poor Ireland, whose chief pride had been the white shirt that covered, and scarcely covered her nakedness, looked wondrous well in her red cloth and her gold-lace. Her story is a short one. About six years ago the honest gentlewoman awaked from a trance; drest herself by way of frolic in regimentals, entered as a volunteer into the English service to supply the place of invalids that were sent to guard our coasts, marched up the *Mons sacer* of Dungannon, marched down again, became a strolling player, went to "enact Brutus in the capitol," *totally forgot her part*, threw off her warlike attire, and sunk down again—a wretched woman.

William Drennan, *Letters of Orellana, an Irish Helot*

ETWEEN 1778 AND 1784, the rhetoric, symbols, and practices of patriots and the Volunteers promoted a vision of the political nation and of political subjectivity that, in the face of class, confessional, and gender inequalities, legitimized sustained extraparliamentary participation by a broad cross-section of society. While the political narrative of this period is familiar, the process by which people became politicized, with some notable recent exceptions, has too often been attributed to the brief flowering of a "national spirit" requiring little analysis in itself.[1] Through a focus on the myriad ways in which ordinary men and women encountered and appropriated political ideas and symbols, *A Nation of Politicians* has attempted to demonstrate that the extent of politicization was far more extensive and understandings of the national identity more complex than have been previously realized. This conclusion suggests ways in which the approach taken here might be applied to the study of Irish political culture in a comparative context, while also briefly outlining the decline and legacy of the Volunteers.

"A Wretched Woman": The Decline of the Volunteers

Writing toward the end of 1784, as she witnessed the decline of volunteering and the failure of campaigns for reform and protective duties, Martha McTier noted a widespread disillusionment with politics. McTier asked, "What is become of that torrent of patriotism which, in a rush over the whole land, promised to bear down all before it had it reached its height?"[2] Patriotism was indeed on the decline; in October 1784 the National Congress met in Dublin and was ultimately a dismal failure, with several counties and towns neglecting even to send delegates. Many moderate reformers had withdrawn from politics by this stage, while others argued that efforts for reform should proceed through constitutional means rather than such "anti-parliaments." Radical Presbyterians from the North strongly influenced proceedings.[3] Poor attendance resulted in an adjournment until January the following year, when the Catholic question was deferred to avoid the collapse of the whole reform movement. Attendance was once again poor, and little was achieved. In the wake of the congress, the reform movement spluttered to a halt and declined, despite the efforts of some to revive it. The Volunteers, the main advocates of reform, were also on the wane. The summer reviews of 1784 had been poorly attended. In May, Richard Woodward, the bishop of Cloyne, noted that the spirit of volunteering had "worn out among people of rank and fortune."[4] The same month, Rutland confidently claimed, "The spirit of volunteering is much on the wane" in spite of the attempts of radicals and the press to inflame the people.[5] In July, the Earl of Hillsborough reported to the lord lieutenant that fewer than 1,700 Volunteers attended the review in Belfast and that "this dangerous folly" was wearing away.[6] By this time, the government's "secret return" of that year suggests there were fewer than 20,000 Volunteers.

With the failure of the campaign for reform, the patriot movement limped through 1785, briefly buoyed by a campaign against Pitt's commercial propositions; compared to the campaign for free trade in 1779, this effort was distinctly lackluster, prompting only a handful of counties to petition against the measures.[7] And while Volunteer reviews continued, they were now fairly desultory and poorly attended affairs; by 1786 the Volunteers were a spent force. A variety of factors precipitated the decline of the Volunteers after 1783: Peace and demobilization led to the return of British troops and divested companies of their defensive, ceremonial, and law-and-order functions. The Catholic question was clearly a divisive issue; large-scale recruitment of Catholics and the broaching of the Catholic question provided further ammunition for opponents of radical reform. Protestant suspicion of Catholics, without and within, remained a vital force in Irish politics. Professions of loyalty to the state by Catholic leaders and the admission of Catholics into many Volunteer companies did lead some patriots to consider a rapprochement with "respectable" Catholics at least.[8] This policy proved highly divisive, even for those patriots who advocated a broad notion of "the people," suggesting the limits of Protestant toleration and of the political nation. By the mid-1780s, traditional Protestant arguments against Catholics were revived with vigor, particularly in the course of the pamphlet war over the Rightboy disturbances, in which the concept of "Protestant ascendancy" was clearly articulated.[9] In Armagh the laws against Catholic ownership of firearms were used as a symbol against further concessions to Catholics, and raids began on Catholic houses, leading to violent disputes in that county.[10] This resurgence of sectarian divisions led to the formation of the Peep O' Day Boys and the Defenders and fierce clashes that prefigured the conflict and polarization of the 1790s.

Yet divisions over the Catholic question on their own were hardly decisive in the decline of volunteering; while the role of the state in the politics of the 1790s has received renewed interest, the state's assault on radicalism in the 1780s requires further research.[11] State repression of radicalism did not begin in the 1790s, and comparisons can clearly be made between the two periods. As David Dickson observes, between 1780 and 1786 the role of the Irish state was significantly enhanced through a range of new initiatives and legislation by both parliament and the Castle, including a policy of industrial relocation of Dublin's radical weaving population, an independent Irish post office, and in 1786 a new centralized system of police in the capital.[12] Several of these projects were responding specifically to the unrest in Dublin during 1784; other reforms, such as the improved efficiency of the post office, offered incidental enhanced powers for the surveillance of radicals. From 1784 onward, the administration also initiated a sustained assault on the newspaper press, prosecuting several printers and publishers and imprisoning Matthew Carey and John Magee, the proprietor of the

Dublin Evening Post. At the same time, the government stepped up attempts to buy the support of several newspapers, including the *Volunteer Evening Post* and the *Freeman's Journal.* New legislation was also used to cow the patriot press into submission; the Press Act of 1784 made it more difficult for newspaper owners to conceal their identity, and, more worrying for newspaper owners, a new Stamp Act in 1785 increased the duty on newspapers' stamps and the advertising tax.[13] Efforts to muzzle the opposition press were largely successful and were not unimportant in the decline of unrestrained radicalism and the dense political scene of the first half of the decade. The Stage Act of 1786 also attempted to reign in the raucous theatrical culture of the city, long an important site for the expression of radical and antigovernment sympathies.[14] The mass politicization of the previous decade did not simply wither away in the face of the Catholic question; the state was instrumental in suppressing the public sphere and driving many radicals out of national politics or out of the country.[15]

"A Short and Crowded Story": Comparative Densities and Volunteer Legacies

Drennan's disappointed retelling of the history of the Volunteers as the story of a cross-dressing Hibernia ignores the achievements of the force, particularly their role in advancing politicization as well as the legacy of this period. A focus on mass politicization has been, as Jim Smyth notes, the "master theme" of recent studies of the 1790s.[16] By focusing on political density, *A Nation of Politicians* has argued that this theme can be traced back to at least the previous decade. This study has also sought to raise broader issues about the extent of politicization and the ways in which this "master theme" might relate to the study of Irish political culture between the 1740s and the 1820s. If we are to avoid focusing simply on the inevitable "rise" of the public sphere, with the 1790s as the ne plus ultra of this process and 1798 as its nadir, we need to consider why some moments are political denser than others and to explain the great pulses of politicization at certain times that seem to subside at others. To suggest that some moments are more politically dense than others, then, raises questions: What do these moments of political density share? What differentiates them from more quiescent periods? In what ways would a comparative political density change our understanding of the long eighteenth century? Other times in eighteenth- and early nineteenth-century Ireland that witnessed a high degree of politicization, such as the 1750s, the 1790s, and the 1820s, despite their many differences, share a variety of features with the period examined in this study. In the 1750s the money bill dispute, while originating in elite factional struggle, served as a key moment in popular politicization: the dispute was rapidly nationalized by a dense political culture centered around patriot clubs, which carefully organized toasts, dinners, celebrations, and addresses to MPs, all publicized through the press. As is well known, the 1790s too witnessed widespread politicization, with the propagation of both republican and loyalist ideologies facilitated by wide-ranging networks of sociability and association encompassing clubs and secret societies. Until the suppression of the force in 1793, radicals in Dublin and Belfast hoped to enact parliamentary reform and Catholic emancipation through a revival of the culture of the Volunteers and the appropriation of the contested legacy of 1782. Associations such as the Volunteers, the United Irishmen, and the Defenders were not only important for the dissemination of political propaganda, but as Bartlett observes, also provided members, including the Catholic peasantry, with "experience organizing, acting, and identifying grievances."[17] Participation in the military, loyalist militias, yeomanry, or the shadowy world of paramilitary secret societies also drew in a socially and regionally diverse range of Protestant and Catholic men from outside the formal political nation in explicitly politicized military cultures. After the experience of defeat and repression in the wake of 1798, the mass politicization of the "Catholic nation" in the 1820s was based on the publicity of the press and a focus on association, public meetings, and spectacle that served to reclaim public space for Catholics. The politicization of consumption and the commercialization of politics were likewise integral to all these moments;[18] the popular mobilization of the 1790s and the 1820s were both based around a gendered politics that has only begun to be explored.[19]

The ideology of radical separatist republicanism in the 1790s and Catholic nationalism in the 1820s seem far removed from the patriotism of the 1780s; yet at the same time, radicals in the 1790s clearly looked to the legacy of the radical and egalitarian aspects of the culture of voluntary citizen militias as much as to the French Revolution; a Volunteer celebration of the anniversary of the fall of the Bastille in Belfast in 1792 mixed revolutionary imagery with more traditional patriotic rhetoric and images, including a representation of a Volunteer freeing a shackled

Hibernia.[20] A transparency in one window, referring to the Dungannon Convention of Ulster Volunteers and the subsequent failed national convention, suggested unfinished business from those heady days: "8th September 1783.—Armed Citizens Spoke. 2nd December 1783.—Their Delegates Ran Away."[21] The memory of the 1780s, if nothing else, was central to the propaganda of the United Irishmen, even if it involved a "radical reworking" of earlier forms of patriotism.[22] Likewise, O'Connellite campaigns were infused with the iconography of the Volunteers; O'Connell helped found societies known as the Irish Volunteers and the Eighty-Two Club, which were still toasting the bishop of Derry and Grattan's parliament in 1845.[23] O'Connell often wore military-style costume with buttons inscribed "1782," while the iconography of Repeal processions included portraits of Henry Flood and Henry Grattan (alongside St. Patrick and Brian Boru), surrounded by the motto "Remember 1782."[24]

Looking back at the first success of the patriots, William Drennan wrote,

> History can supply us with few examples of so great a change taking place by the immediate agency of the people, with so much rapidity, and so little violence. *Magna Charta* was extorted by a few domineering barons, the people being then the mere furniture of feudal tenures. The *petition of right* was wrested from the crown by a set of able and artful men, who led the nation even to the principle of anarchy; and the so much boasted *revolution,* was rather a donation to the commonalty, than the reward of their own exertions. But in the revolution of [17]80, a whole people have been the prime, or rather the sole agents.[25]

In writing this "eulogy to the lower and middling ranks of people" in the wake of the free-trade campaign, William Drennan characterized contemporary Irish events as part of a new type of popular revolution. In doing so, he drew attention to the commonplace observation that in a brief period of time, the nature of politics had perceptibly altered. The factors that contributed to this politics and the density of political culture were varied. The culture of print served as a prime vehicle for the promotion of a more inclusive vision of the political nation. The institutions of print culture, the tavern, and the coffeehouse were places where a socially and confessionally diverse cliental experienced "the news" in a more concrete setting than the idea of an "imagined community" or idealized public sphere usually suggests. The content of the press, a heterogeneous mix of advertisements, local items, and news plagiarized from Dublin and London papers, analyzed and debated by "alehouse politicians," encouraged readers to conceive of the news in terms of a broader narrative of national patriotic action.

Although the press was key in promoting the festive culture of patriotism, ordinary men and women also experienced these events firsthand. Tens of thousands of Protestant men actively participated in the onerous military rites of volunteering. These occasions often attracted massive crowds of spectators, who, according to press reports, gave their enthusiastic assent to the force. Celebrations and commemorations offered other instances where large numbers of men and women occupied public space. The meanings of these events were mutable, and participants and spectators often challenged official interpretations or commandeered ceremonies for their own purposes. Whether a person illuminated his home, for example, in the course of celebration announced his political affiliation and often resulted in broken glass. The silence of the Dublin crowd in 1780 in the face of the official celebration of the British victory at Charlestown shows that official events offered opportunities to express opposition to British policy in the colonies. The Volunteers' usurpation of 4 November in 1779 offers the most celebrated moment of appropriation of an annual ceremony for a political protest, evoking William III's association with Protestant liberty in order to advocate free trade. The symbols, slogans, and rituals of patriot festive culture were emotive occasions through which politics was experienced by men and women far beyond the boundaries of the formal political nation. At the same time, the celebrations of free trade in particular demonstrate the way in which the rites of patriotism were both stirring experiences *and* media "events" constructed by the press as inclusive, national episodes that overcame divisions based on religion and class.

A focus on the culture of patriotism also draws attention to everyday ways in which political ideas were encountered. The politicization of consumption in 1779 allowed those beyond the political nation to assert their patriotism through their choices as consumers. This campaign for free trade acquired national dimensions with the formation of associations and the adoption of resolutions by grand juries; the goods men and women consumed, or perhaps more strikingly, those they chose to forego, became significant indicators of patriotic virtue. The emergence of a market for patriotic commodities meant that the everyday world of goods was further politicized. By controlling their desires, by abstaining from the consumption of English goods, men and women could demonstrate their public virtue; commitment could be reinforced through binding public rituals.

Few displays of public virtue were as conspicuous as those of the Volunteers. This project has been largely concerned with a reconsideration of this force as a vehicle for politicization in Ireland between 1778 and 1784. The Volunteers were represented as a virtuous "people's army" protecting the nation against foreign invasion and the machinations of British and Irish ministers. This outbreak of public-spiritedness and martial enthusiasm was seen as a sharp contrast to the waning military spirit and corrupted masculinity that were widely believed to be at the root of Britain's imperial malaise.[26] Much work on the Volunteers has attempted to cast this force in terms of traditional relations of patronage and gentry control, and focused on the Volunteers' time-honored function as a Protestant militia policing a recalcitrant Catholic peasantry.[27] Yet in their articles of association, internal organization, and public pronouncements, many Volunteer companies represented themselves as forging a new type of politics. Drennan claimed in 1781 that Volunteers "associated for some other purpose, than to be the body-guards of a Servile Aristocracy." He recognized the danger of such "Military Vassalage" particularly among rural companies, but this could be avoided through democratic forms of association and by confining voting rights "in every matter of importance to the association at large." Rather than serving as "Livery Servants" for elites, Volunteers such as Drennan advocated a type of public virtue whereby the worth of men could be measured not by birth or wealth but by putting "a firelock in their hands."[28] The internal organization of many, though certainly not all, Volunteer companies was based on the type of democratic principles encouraged by Drennan. The experience of volunteering was a formative political experience for tens of thousands of Protestant men. Although local notables frequently commanded and helped finance companies, they often played a minor role in the everyday affairs of the company, and James Hamilton was not alone in observing that commanders were often dictated to by their "constituents."

The language and symbolism of the Volunteers, as much as their military presence, were significant in the creation of a space legitimating the political involvement of the force. The actual bravery or effectiveness of the Volunteers was never tested by foreign invasion, but the notion of the citizen-solider as the exemplar of public virtue remained central to the ideology of volunteering. While some contemporaries argued that the Volunteers should remain outside politics, others

claimed that the role of citizen and soldier were all but indistinguish-
able. This conflation of the two was justified by an appeal to the language of manliness that lauded the active martial patriotism of the Volunteers but also valued independence of mind and political sentiment.
A "manly" character was not the exclusive preserve of those within the
political nation; participation in the Volunteers could demonstrate the
manliness of Protestants across the social spectrum, and even that of
some Catholics. The language of manliness could also be transposed
into the public realm to justify the political actions of those "out of
doors." Not least among the factors encouraging the admission of Catholics (aside from the symbolic aspect of carrying arms) was the definition of patriotism as a form of virtuous public action. Participation in a
voluntary "national" army encouraged what one critic of the force described as "imaginary ideas of independence and equality" among both
Catholic and Protestant Volunteers.

It was this practice of patriotism that allowed those outside the political nation to "imagine" themselves as political subjects and to act as
citizens. And although it is now difficult to see the Volunteers as the
progenitors of modern Irish nationalism, in creating a broad-based extraparliamentary movement that appealed to a more inclusive vision of
the political nation, this "nation of politicians" contributed more significantly to the organization of later mass politics than previous accounts allow. In recent years, historians have emphasized the limits of
the achievements of the Volunteers and the patriot movement. It is certainly true that in terms of achieving their goal of parliamentary reform
or effectively addressing the Catholic question, Volunteer reform failed.
Even the celebrated achievements of 1782 were hardly an unqualified
success. However, the significance of popular political action cannot
be measured solely in terms of legislative successes. The campaigns
for legislative independence, parliamentary reform, and protective duties involved significant extraparliamentary organization that at times
forged cooperation across traditional social and confessional boundaries. Forming associations, drilling and reviewing, voting on resolutions, signing petitions, buying "patriotic" goods, and the myriad other
activities of ordinary men and women were all vehicles for popular politicization.[29] Such practices were also central to transformations in
understandings of national identity; as Charles Sheridan described this
change, it had resulted in both Catholics and Protestants feeling "a silly
pride as *Irishmen*."[30]

Notes

Abbreviations

BL	British Library, London
BNL	*Belfast News-Letter*
CEP	*Cork Evening Post*
DEP	*Dublin Evening Post*
FLJ	*Finn's Leinster Journal*
FJ	*Freeman's Journal*
HC	*Hibernian Chronicle*
HJ	*Hibernian Journal*
HO	Home Office Papers
JHC	*Journals of the House of Commons of the Kingdom of Ireland*
NLI	National Library of Ireland, Dublin
NMI	National Museum of Ireland, Dublin
PRO	Public Record Office, London
PRONI	Public Record Office of Northern Ireland, Belfast
RIA	Royal Irish Academy, Dublin
SP	State Papers
UM	Ulster Museum, Belfast
VEP	*Volunteer Evening Post*
WHM	*Walker's Hibernian Magazine*

Introduction

1. C. F. Sheridan to Lord Northington, Aug. 1784, National Library of Ireland (hereafter citied as NLI), Bolton Papers, MS 16,350 (4). Sheridan was also an officeholder, writing here in his capacity as undersecretary in the Military Department of the chief secretary's office.

2. Ibid.

3. Ibid.

4. Ibid.

5. Ibid.

6. *The Voice of the People in a Letter to the Secretary of his Grace the Duke of Rutland* (Dublin, 1784), 12–13.

7. Ibid.

8. Tim Harris, introduction to *The Politics of the Excluded, c. 1500–1850*, ed. Tim Harris (New York: Palgrave, 2001), 6.

9. Stephen Small, *Political Thought in Ireland, 1776–1798* (Oxford: Oxford University Press, 2002).

10. *Belfast News-Letter* (hereafter cited as *BNL*), 7 Jan. 1780.

11. Vincent Morley, *Irish Opinion and the American Revolution, 1760–1783* (Cambridge: Cambridge University Press, 2002), 257–58.

12. The term "elites" is used throughout to refer to the aristocracy and gentry, as well as substantial merchants. Although such terms are not completely satisfactory, the problem of social classification, not to mention ethnic identification, has continued to perplex historians of eighteenth-century Ireland. For an attempt to unravel these social categories among Protestants, see Toby Barnard, *A New Anatomy of Ireland: The Irish Protestants, 1649–1770* (New Haven, CT: Yale University Press, 2003). On the problems of categories such as popular and elite, see S. J. Connolly, "'Ag Deanamh Commanding': Elite Responses to Popular Culture, 1660–1850," in *Irish Popular Culture, 1650–1850*, ed. James S. Donnelly, Jr., and Kerby A. Miller (Dublin: Irish Academic Press, 1998).

13. Jim Smyth, *The Men of No Property: Irish Radicals and Popular Politics in the Late Eighteenth Century* (New York: St. Martin's Press, 1992).

14. For earlier evidence of politicization, see Raymond Gillespie, *Seventeenth-Century Ireland: Making Ireland Modern* (Dublin: Gill & Macmillan, 2006). For the 1750s, see Bob Harris, *Politics and the Nation: Britain in the Mid-Eighteenth Century* (Oxford: Oxford University Press, 2002). For a British context, see John Walter, *Understanding Popular Violence in the English Revolution: The Colchester Plunderers* (Cambridge: Cambridge University Press, 1999), 321–22; Tim Harris, *London Crowds in the Reign of Charles II: Propaganda and Politics from the Restoration until the Exclusion Crisis* (Cambridge: Cambridge University Press, 1987).

15. T. Harris, introduction, 22–24; Harris advocates the application of the term "density," coined by Nicholas Rogers in a discussion of English political culture in the early nineteenth century, *Crowds, Culture, and Politics in Georgian England* (Oxford: Oxford University Press, 1998), 234.

16. Peter Jupp and Eoin Magennis, eds., *Crowds in Ireland, c. 1720–1920* (New York: St. Martin's Press, 2000).

17. For the role of the state in fostering rituals, see Jacqueline R. Hill, "National Festivals, the State, and 'Protestant Ascendancy' in Ireland, 1790–1829," *Irish Historical Studies* 24, no. 93 (May 1984): 30–51; James Kelly, "'The Glorious

and Immortal Memory': Commemoration and Protestant Identity in Ireland, 1660–1800," *Proceedings of the Royal Irish Academy* 94, C (1994): 25–52; T. C. Barnard, "The Uses of 23 October 1641 and Irish Protestant Celebrations," *English Historical Review* 106, no. 421 (Oct. 1991): 889–920; Raymond Gillespie, "Political Ideas and Their Social Contexts in Seventeenth-Century Ireland," in *Political Thought in Seventeenth-Century Ireland: Kingdom or Colony,* ed. Jane H. Ohlmeyer (Cambridge: Cambridge University Press, 2000), 107–27. On the importance of symbolic forms of political practice, see James Vernon, *Politics and the People: A Study in English Political Culture, c. 1815–1867* (Cambridge: Cambridge University Press, 1993); Lynn Hunt, *Politics, Culture, and Class in the French Revolution* (Berkeley: University of California Press, 1984), 52–86.

18. For an attempt to address this neglect, see Martyn J. Powell, *The Politics of Consumption in Eighteenth-Century Ireland* (New York: Palgrave Macmillan, 2005). On politicization in the 1790s, see J. Smyth, *Men of No Property;* idem, "Popular Politicization, Defenderism and the Catholic Question," in *Ireland and the French Revolution,* ed. Hugh Gough and David Dickson (Dublin: Irish Academic Press, 1990), 109–16; L. M. Cullen, "The Political Structures of the Defenders," in Gough and Dickson, *Ireland and the French Revolution,* 117–38; idem, "Late Eighteenth-Century Politicization in Ireland: Problems in Its Study and Its French Links," in *Culture et pratiques politiques en France et en Irlande, XVIe-XVIIIe siècle,* ed. Louis Bergeron and Louis M. Cullen (Paris: Centre de Recherches Historiques, 1991), 137–57.

19. On the relationship between commercialization and politicization in other contexts, see T. H. Breen, *The Marketplace of Revolution: How Consumer Politics Shaped American Independence* (Oxford: Oxford University Press, 2004); Neil McKendrick, John Brewer, and J. H. Plumb, *The Birth of Consumer Society: The Commercialization of Eighteenth-Century England* (Bloomington: Indiana University Press, 1982); Hunt, *Politics, Culture, and Class.*

20. For an account of this world throughout the British Empire, see Peter Clark, *British Societies and Clubs, 1580–1800: The Origins of an Associational World* (Oxford: Clarendon Press, 2000). For the democratic implications of various forms of association, see Margaret C. Jacob, *Living the Enlightenment: Freemasonry and Politics in Eighteenth-Century Europe* (Oxford: Oxford University Press, 1991); Jürgen Habermas, *The Structural Transformation of the Public Sphere: An Inquiry into a Category of Bourgeois Society* (Cambridge, MA: MIT Press, 1991). On the forms of association in Ireland, see Toby Barnard, "The Languages of Politeness and Sociability in Eighteenth-Century Ireland," in *Political Discourse in Seventeenth- and Eighteenth-Century Ireland,* ed. G. Boyce et al. (Basingstoke: Palgrave, 2001), 193–221; David Dickson, "'Centres of Motion': Irish Cities and the Origins of Popular Politics," in Bergeron and Cullen, *Culture et pratiques,* 101–22.

21. On Newenham's politics, see James Kelly, *Sir Edward Newenham, MP, 1734–1814: Defender of the Protestant Constitution* (Dublin: Four Courts Press, 2004).

22. Kathleen Wilson, *Sense of the People: Politics, Culture and Imperialism in England, 1715–1785* (Cambridge: Cambridge University Press, 1995), 67.

23. *Freeman's Journal* (hereafter cited as *FJ*), 14 July 1781; 28 March 1778; 11 April 1778. The Trinity College Historical Society debated similar issues. See Morley, *Irish Opinion*.

24. *Dublin Evening Post* (hereafter cited as *DEP*), 23 Sept. 1780.

25. Petri Mirala, *Freemasonry in Ulster, 1733–1813: A Social and Political History of the Masonic Brotherhood in the North of Ireland* (Dublin: Four Courts Press, 2007).

26. Philip Crossle and John Heron Lepper, *History of the Grand Lodge of Free and Accepted Masons of Ireland* (Dublin, 1925), 247.

27. D. Dickson, "Centres of Motion," 120.

28. On an urban renaissance in South Munster, see David Dickson, *Old World Colony: Cork and South Munster 1630–1830* (Madison: University of Wisconsin Press, 2005). On assembly rooms see Constantia Maxwell, *Country and Town in Ireland under the Georges* (Dundalk: Dundalgan Press, 1949), 242–43; Barnard, "Languages of Politeness."

29. W. H. Crawford, "The Evolution of Ulster Towns, 1750–1850," in *Plantation to Partition: Essays in Ulster History in Honour of J. L. McCracken*, ed. P. Roebuck (Belfast: Blackstaff Press, 1981), 140–56; Peter Borsay and Lindsay Proudfoot, eds., *Provincial Towns in Early Modern England and Ireland: Change, Convergence and Divergence* (Oxford: Oxford University Press, 2002).

30. Tony Claydon, "The Sermon, the 'Public Sphere' and the Political Culture of Late Seventeenth-Century England," in *The English Sermon Revised: Religion, Literature and History, 1600–1750*, ed. Lori Anne Ferrell and Peter McCullough (Manchester: Manchester University Press, 2001), 208–34.

31. Walter, *Understanding Popular Violence*, 321–22.

32. In most cases the *Journals* simply record the receipt of a petition, the group or individuals concerned, and its general subject. Unfortunately the bodies of petitions are not recorded, though some petitions were published in the press. Other important petitions and addresses from throughout Ireland survive in the Public Record Office, London.

33. David Zaret, "Petitions and the 'Invention' of Public Opinion and the English Revolution," *American Journal of Sociology* 101, no. 6 (May 1996): 1513–17. Zaret argues that the petition was central to the emergence of a "public sphere" in seventeenth-century England.

34. Mark Knights, *Representation and Misrepresentation in Later Stuart Britain: Partisanship and Political Culture* (Oxford: Oxford University Press, 2006).

35. Public Record Office, London (hereafter cited as PRO), Home Office Papers (hereafter citied as HO), 55/7, fol. 4.

36. PRO, HO, 55/12, fol. 10.

37. Benjamin Franklin to Edward Newenham, 2 Oct. 1783, Packard Humanities Institute: The Papers of Benjamin Franklin, http://www.franklinpapers.org.

38. William Preston, *The Contrast; or, a Comparison between the Characters of*

the English and the Irish in the year 1780 (Dublin, 1780); *Ireland's Glory; or, a Comparative View of Ireland in the Years 1776 and 1783* (Dublin, 1783).

39. Morley, *Irish Opinion*, 331.

40. D. Dickson, *Old World Colony*.

41. Nini Rodgers, "Ireland and the Black Atlantic in the Eighteenth Century," *Irish Historical Studies* 33, no. 126 (Nov. 2000): 174–92; idem, *Ireland, Slavery and Anti-Slavery: 1612–1865* (New York: Palgrave Macmillan, 2007).

42. [Joseph Pollock], *The Letters of Owen Roe O'Nial* (Dublin, 1779), 22.

43. As Stewart observes, in eighteenth-century atlases, the Amazon River was referred to as Orellana after Francisco de Orellana. A. T. Q. Stewart, *A Deeper Silence: The Hidden Origins of the United Irishmen* (Belfast: Blackstaff Press, 1998), 134–35. For another address to "fellow slaves," see *Hibernian Journal* (hereafter cited as *HJ*), 22 Dec. 1779.

44. "O'Nial," *Volunteer's Journal* (Dublin), 8 Dec. 1783.

45. Thomas Bartlett, "Militarization and Politicization in Ireland (1780–1820)," in Bergeron and Cullen, *Culture et pratiques*, 125–36; idem, *The Fall and Rise of the Irish Nation: The Catholic Question, 1690–1830* (New York: Barnes & Noble, 1992).

46. Pádraig Ó Snodaigh, "Notes on the Volunteers, Militia, Orangemen and Yeomanry of County Roscommon," *Irish Sword*, no. 12 (1975–76): 15–35; idem, "Notes on the Volunteers, Militia, Yeomanry and Orangemen of County Waterford," *An Cosantóir* 35 (1975): 319–22, 341–47; idem, "The Volunteers, Militia, Yeomanry and Orangemen of Co. Kildare in the Eighteenth Century," *Journal of the County Kildare Archaeological Society* 15, no. 1 (1971): 38–49; idem, "Notes on the Volunteers, Militia, Yeomanry, Orangemen and Fencibles in County Limerick," *Irish Sword*, no. 10 (1971): 125–40; Allan Blackstock, *An Ascendancy Army: The Irish Yeomanry, 1796–1834* (Dublin: Four Courts Press, 1998).

47. Michael A. McDonnell, *The Politics of War: Race, Class, and Conflict in Revolutionary Virginia* (Chapel Hill: University of North Carolina Press for the Omohundro Institute of Early American History and Culture, Williamsburg, Virginia, 2007); idem, "Popular Mobilization and Political Culture in Revolutionary Virginia: The Failure of the Minutemen and the Revolution from Below," *Journal of American History* 85, no. 3 (Dec. 1998): 946–81; Dale L. Clifford, "Can the Uniform Make the Citizen? Paris, 1789–1791," *Eighteenth-Century Studies* 34, no. 3 (Spring 2001): 363–82; Wayne P. Te Brake, "Violence in the Dutch Patriot Revolution," *Comparative Studies in Society and History* 30, no. 1 (Jan. 1988): 143–63; Linda Colley, *Britons: Forging the Nation, 1707–1837* (New Haven, CT: Yale University Press, 1992), 316.

48. David W. Miller, "Non-professional Soldiery, c. 1600–1800," in *A Military History of Ireland*, ed. Thomas Bartlett and Keith Jeffery (Cambridge: Cambridge University Press, 1996), 315–34; idem, "Politicization in Revolutionary Ireland: The Case of the Armagh Troubles," *Irish Economic and Social History* 23 (1996): 1–17.

49. David W. Miller, "Radicalism and Ritual in East Ulster," in *1798: A Bicentenary Perspective,* ed. Thomas Bartlett, David Dickson, Daire Keogh, and Kevin Whelan (Dublin: Four Courts Press, 2003), 196.

50. Bartlett et al., *1798,* 10.

51. Morley, *Irish Opinion.* See also Éamonn Ó Ciardha, *Ireland and the Jacobite Cause, 1685–1766: A Fatal Attachment* (Dublin: Four Courts Press, 2002). In his study of the myriad ways the War of Independence affected Great Britain and Ireland, Stephen Conway also emphasizes the British and imperial aspects of Irish politics and society. Stephen Conway, *The British Isles and the War of American Independence* (Oxford: Oxford University Press, 2000).

52. Ian R. McBride, *Scripture Politics: Ulster Presbyterians and Irish Radicalism in the Late Eighteenth Century* (Oxford: Oxford University Press, 1998), 123–33.

53. Breandán Mac Suibhne, "Whiskey, Potatoes and True-Born Patriot Paddies: Volunteering and the Construction of the Irish Nation in Northwest Ulster, 1770–1789," in Jupp and Magennis, *Crowds in Ireland,* 48.

54. Breandán Mac Suibhne, "Politicization and Paramilitarism": North-West and South-West Ulster, c. 1772–98," in Bartlett et al., *1798,* 246.

55. McBride, *Scripture Politics,* 161.

56. D. Dickson, *Old World Colony,* 443–47. On volunteering in Dublin, see Jacqueline Hill, *From Patriots to Unionists: Dublin Civic Politics and Irish Protestant Patriotism, 1660–1840* (Oxford: Clarendon Press, 1997), 146–53.

57. Jean Agnew, ed., *The Drennan–McTier Letters,* vol. 1, *1776–1793* (Dublin: Women's History Project / Irish Manuscripts Commission, 1998), 1:138. While Drennan's letters have long been an important source for historians of Presbyterian radicalism and the United Irishmen, McTier's side of this extraordinary correspondence from 1776 to 1819 has not been similarly utilized. This situation is likely to change however, with the publication of the first complete edition of the letters. See Catriona Kennedy, "'Womanish Epistles?' Martha McTier, Female Epistolarity and Late Eighteenth-Century Irish Radicalism," *Women's History Review* 13, no. 4 (Dec. 2004): 649–67.

58. Agnew, *Drennan–McTier Letters,* 1:2.

59. McTier was a fervent reader of political pamphlets, not only on Irish issues, but also by such authors as Richard Price (she hoped his work would "awaken the people of England" to the folly of the war with the colonies) and Edmund Burke on imperial and British politics. Ibid., 1:7, 14, 73.

60. This neglect has begun to be addressed. See Mary O'Dowd, *A History of Women in Ireland, 1500–1800* (London: Pearson Education, 2005); Catriona Kennedy, "'A Gallant Nation': Chivalric Masculinity and Irish Nationalism in the 1790s," in *Public Men: Masculinity and Politics in Modern Britain,* ed. Matthew McCormack (New York: Palgrave Macmillan, 2007), 73–92. For women and the United Irish movement, see Nancy Curtin, "Women and Eighteenth-Century Republicanism," in *Women in Early Modern Ireland,* ed. Margaret MacCurtain and Mary O'Dowd (Edinburgh: Edinburgh University Press, 1991); idem, "'A Nation of Abortive Men': Gendered Citizenship and Early Irish Republicanism," in

Reclaiming Gender: Transgressive Identities in Modern Ireland, ed. Marilyn Cohen and Nancy J. Curtin (New York: Macmillan, 1999).

61. Karen Harvey, "The History of Masculinity, circa 1650–1800," *Journal of British Studies* 44, no. 2 (April 2005): 296–311. On social and cultural aspects of masculinity, see Susan Dwyer Amussen, "'The Part of a Christian Man': The Cultural Politics of Manhood in Early Modern England," in *Political Culture and Cultural Politics in Early Modern England: Essays Presented to David Underdown*, ed. Susan Dwyer Amussen and Mark A. Kishlansky (Manchester: Manchester University Press, 1995), 213–33; Alexandra Shepard, *Meanings of Manhood in Early Modern England* (Oxford: Oxford University Press, 2003); Tim Hitchcock and Michele Cohen, eds., *English Masculinities, 1660–1800* (London: Addison Wesley, 1999).

62. Stefan Dudink and Karen Hagemann, "Masculinity in Politics and War in the Age of Democratic Revolutions, 1750–1850," in *Masculinities in Politics and War: Gendering Modern History*, ed. Stefan Dudink, Karen Hagemann, and John Tosh (Manchester: Manchester University Press, 2004), 8.

63. Stefan Dudink, "Masculinity, Effeminacy, Time: Conceptual Change in the Dutch Age of Democratic Revolutions," in Dudink, Hagemann, and Tosh, *Masculinities in Politics and War*, 77–95.

64. Ibid., 81–82.

65. Matthew McCormack, *The Independent Man: Citizenship and Gender Politics in Georgian England* (Manchester: Manchester University Press, 2005).

66. Jacqueline Hill, *From Patriots to Unionists*, 4–15; Maurizio Viroli, *For Love of Country: An Essay on Patriotism and Nationalism* (Oxford: Oxford University Press, 1997).

67. Joep T. Leersen, "Anglo-Irish Patriotism and Its European Context: Notes Towards a Reassessment," *Eighteenth-Century Ireland* 3 (1988): 7–24.

68. Stephen Small, "The Twisted Roots of Irish Patriotism: Anglo-Irish Political Thought in the Late-Eighteenth Century," *Éire-Ireland* 35, no. 3–4 (2000/2001): 187–216.

69. J. T. Leersen, *Mere Irish and Fíor-Ghael: Studies in the Idea of Irish Nationality, its Development and Literary Expression prior to the Nineteenth Century* (Cork: Cork University Press in association with Field Day, 1996), 10.

70. Small, "Twisted Roots."

71. See the pamphlet published in the wake of threats on Foster's life, defending his public record, *Observations on the Parliamentary Conduct of John Foster* (Dublin, 1784), and A. P. W. Malcomson's biography, *John Foster: The Politics of the Anglo-Irish Ascendancy* (Oxford: Oxford University Press, 1978).

72. James Kelly examines this apparent contradiction in Flood's career in *Henry Flood: Patriots and Politics in Eighteenth-Century Ireland* (Dublin: Four Courts Press, 1998).

73. James E. Bradley, *Religion, Revolution, and English Radicalism: Nonconformity in Eighteenth-Century Politics and Society* (Cambridge: Cambridge University Press, 1990), 122–24.

74. J. R. R. Adams, *The Printed Word and the Common Man: Popular Culture in Ulster, 1700–1900* (Belfast: Institute of Irish Studies, Queen's University Belfast, 1987), 43–51.

75. For this election, see McBride, *Scripture Politics,* 136–39; Peter Jupp, "County Down Elections, 1783–1831," *Irish Historical Studies* 18, no. 70 (1972): 177–206.

76. *An Historical Account of the late Election of Knights of the Shire for the County of Down . . .* (Dublin, 1784), 6.

77. Andrew Alexander, *The Advantages of a General Knowledge of the Use of Arms, a Sermon* (Strabane, 1779); James Crombie, *The Expedience and Utility of Volunteer Associations for National Security and Defence in the Present Critical Situation of Public Affairs Considered, in a Sermon, Preached before the United Companies of the Belfast Volunteers, on Sunday the first of August, 1779* (Belfast, 1779).

78. [Frederick Jebb and Robert Johnson], *Thoughts on the Discontents of the People Last Year, respecting the Sugar Duties* (Dublin, 1781), 5.

79. *Historical Account,* 5.

80. W. S. Dickson, *A Sermon on the Propriety and Advantages of Acquiring the Knowledge and Use of Arms, in Times of Public Danger, Preached before Echlinville Volunteers, on Sunday the 28th of March, 1779* (Belfast, 1779), 10.

81. James Crombie, *A Sermon on the Love of Country, Preached before the First Company of Belfast Volunteers* (Belfast, 1778).

82. Ibid.

83. Colin Kidd, "North Britishness and the Nature of Eighteenth-Century British Patriotisms," *Historical Journal* 39, no. 2 (June 1996): 364.

84. S. J. Connolly, "Varieties of Britishness: Ireland, Scotland and Wales in the Hanoverian State," in *Uniting the Kingdom? The Making of British History,* ed. Alexander Grant and Keith J. Stringer (London: Routledge, 1995), 196.

85. Ian McBride, "'The Common Name of Irishman': Protestantism and Patriotism in Eighteenth-Century Ireland," in *Protestantism and National Identity: Britain and Ireland, c. 1650–c. 1850,* ed. Tony Claydon and Ian McBride (Cambridge: Cambridge University Press, 1998), 237.

86. Rev. George Carson, *A Discourse Delivered at Croghan, 2nd January 1780 to the United Companies of Tullahunco and Ballyconnell Volunteers* (Dublin, 1780).

87. T. C. Barnard, "Uses of 23 October 1641," 911.

88. [Henry Joy, ed.], *Historical Collections Relative to the Town of Belfast: From the Earliest Period to the Union with Great Britain* (Belfast, 1817), 180–85.

89. McBride, *Scripture Politics,* 152–60.

90. Kevin Whelan, *The Tree of Liberty: Radicalism, Catholicism, and the Construction of Irish Identity, 1760–1830* (Notre Dame, IN: University of Notre Dame Press, 1996); T. P. Power and Kevin Whelan, eds., *Endurance and Emergence: Catholics in Ireland in the Eighteenth Century* (Dublin: Irish Academic Press, 1990); S. J. Connolly, *Religion, Law and Power: The Making of Protestant Ireland, 1660–1760* (Oxford: Oxford University Press, 1992), 263–313.

91. Karen J. Harvey, *The Bellews of Mount Bellew: A Catholic Gentry Family in Eighteenth-Century Ireland* (Dublin: Four Courts Press, 1998), 12–13.

92. Morley, *Irish Opinion*.

93. Louis Cullen, "Catholics under the Penal Laws," *Eighteenth-Century Ireland* 1 (1986): 23–36.

94. Jacqueline R. Hill, "Religious Toleration and the Relaxation of the Penal Laws: An Imperial Perspective," *Archivium Hibernicum* 44 (1989): 90–110.

95. McBride, "'Common Name of Irishman,'" 251–52.

96. For example, Minute Book of the First Newry Volunteers, PRONI, T/3202/1a; "Address of the Loughgall Volunteers," *BNL*, 11 June 1784.

97. John Brady, ed., *Catholics and Catholicism in the Eighteenth-Century Press* (Maynooth: Catholic Record Society, 1965), 222.

98. [Henry Grattan], *A Letter to the People of Ireland on the Expediency and Necessity of the Present Associations in Ireland in Favour of our own Manufactures* (Dublin, 1779), 53–54.

99. William Guthrie, *An Improved System of Modern Geography* (Dublin, 1789), 497.

100. Crombie, *Sermon on the Love of Country*.

101. *Hibernian Chronicle* (hereafter cited as *HC*), 10 June 1779.

Chapter 1. "Alehouse Politicians"

1. James W. Phillips, *Printing and Bookselling in Dublin, 1670–1800: A Bibliographical Enquiry* (Dublin: Irish Academic Press, 1998), 73–75; Adams, *Printed Word*, 37–38, 130–31.

2. For the vibrancy of the provincial book trade, see Gerard Long, ed., *Books beyond the Pale: Aspects of the Provincial Book Trade in Ireland before 1850* (Dublin: Library Association of Ireland, 1996); Máire Kennedy, "Spreading the Word in the Irish Midlands: Bookselling and Printing in the Late Eighteenth Century," *Long Room* 43 (1998): 29–37.

3. Robert Munter, *The History of the Irish Newspaper, 1685–1760* (Cambridge: Cambridge University Press, 1967); Brian Inglis, *The Freedom of the Press in Ireland, 1784–1841* (London: Faber, 1954). R. R. Madden's *History of Irish Periodical Literature from the End of the 17th Century to the Middle of the 19th Century*, 2 vols. (Dublin, 1867), is also an indispensable, if unwieldy, guide to the press. The most recent survey is Douglas Simes, "Ireland, 1760–1820," in *Press, Politics and the Public Sphere in Europe and North America, 1760–1820*, ed. Hannah Barker (Cambridge: Cambridge University Press, 2002), 113–39. For a general reevaluation of the role of print in early modern Ireland, see *Raymond Gillespie and Andrew Hadfield, eds., The Oxford History of the Irish Book*, vol. 3, *The Irish Book in English, 1550–1800* (Oxford: Oxford University Press, 2006).

4. K. Whelan, *Tree of Liberty*, 59–96; Nancy J. Curtin, *The United Irishmen: Popular Politics in Ulster and Dublin, 1791–1798* (Oxford: Oxford University Press, 1994), chaps. 7–8.

5. Mac Suibhne's study of politics and the press in Northwest Ulster demonstrates the value of the study of local newspapers. B. A. Mac Suibhne, "Patriot Paddies: The Volunteers and Irish Identity in Northwest Ulster, 1778–1786" (PhD diss., Carnegie Mellon University, 1999). On the regional press, see also Máire Kennedy, "Eighteenth-Century Newspaper Publishing in Munster and South Leinster," *Journal of the Cork Historical and Archaeological Society* 103 (1998): 67–88.

6. John Caldwell, "Particulars of the History of a North County Irish Family," Caldwell Papers, PRONI, T/3541/5/3, 73.

7. T. C. Barnard, "Learning, the Learned and Literacy in Ireland, c. 1660–1760," in *A Miracle of Learning: Studies in Manuscripts and Irish Learning; Essays in Honour of William O'Sullivan*, ed. Toby Christopher Barnard, Dáibhí Ó Cróinín, and Katharine Simms (Aldershot: Ashgate, 1998). Raymond Gillespie has demonstrated how the culture of print was central to everyday experience by the end of the seventeenth century; see his *Reading Ireland: Print, Reading and Social Change in Early Modern Ireland* (Manchester: Manchester University Press, 2005).

8. Niall Ó Ciosáin, *Print and Popular Culture in Ireland, 1750–1850* (London: Macmillan, 1997), 28–39.

9. Graeme Kirkham, "Literacy in North-West Ulster, 1680–1860," in *The Origins of Popular Literacy in Ireland: Language Change and Educational Development 1700–1920*, ed. Mary Daly and David Dickson (Dublin: Trinity College Dublin Department of Modern Irish History, 1990), 73–96. Jim Smyth discusses the rise of literacy and the penetration of the press in the context of "modernization" in Ireland in the 1790s, though this process can be pushed back to at least the 1760s. J. Smyth, *Men of No Property*, 23–32.

10. Ó Ciosáin, *Print and Popular Culture*, 6.

11. Morley, *Irish Opinion*.

12. M. Kennedy, "Eighteenth-Century Newspaper Publishing," 78.

13. Adams, *Printed Word*, 34–36. The cost of newspapers and other printed material is obviously more meaningful in relation to estimated incomes and relative to other prices. Wages in Ireland in the eighteenth century are difficult to estimate, but the most recent study suggests that in 1781 a skilled craftsman in Dublin might hope to earn 24d. per day, while a semiskilled laborer could earn 14d. In the town of Kilkenny in 1777, a craftsmen could earn 22d. and a general laborer 6½d. In 1776 a general laborer in Belfast might earn 13d. Liam Kennedy, "Price and Wages in Ireland, 1700–1850," *Irish Economic and Social History* 24 (1997): 62–104.

14. Madden, *History of Irish Periodical Literature*, 72.

15. *DEP*, 2 Jan. 1779.

16. Munter, *History of the Irish Newspaper*, 86–88.

17. Historians of the newspaper in London assume figures of between ten and twenty readers per paper. Helen Barker, *Newspapers, Politics and Public*

Opinion in Late Eighteenth-Century England (Oxford: Oxford University Press, 1998).

18. Munter, *History of the Irish Newspaper*, 86–88.

19. Ibid., 89.

20. Even by 1821 few provincial newspapers sold over one thousand copies, and most sold four hundred or fewer. Ibid.

21. This figure is based on an estimated readership of between four hundred and six hundred for each paper, though the leading Cork and Belfast papers probably had circulations of around two thousand. The number of provincial newspapers in print during the 1770s and 1780s is difficult to establish precisely as many papers were short lived, while even some major provincial papers are unfortunately no longer extant. My calculations, based on lists of titles compiled from the English Short Title Catalogue, the NEWSPLAN Project, and Madden, assumes around thirty provincial papers, though there may have been as many as forty. I have assumed a readership of between four and six for each copy.

22. Barker, *Newspapers*, chap. 4.

23. D. Dickson, "Centres of Motion," 102. With the exception of Carrick, all of these towns supported one or more newspapers during this period.

24. M. Kennedy, "Eighteenth-Century Newspaper Publishing," 81–83.

25. *Finn's Leinster Journal* (hereafter cited as *FLJ*), 10 March 1779.

26. Vincent Kinane, "The Early Book Trades in Galway," in Gerard, *Books Beyond the Pale*, 59; K. Whelan, *Tree of Liberty*, 65–71.

27. David Broderick, *The First Toll Roads: Ireland's Turnpike Roads, 1729–1858* (Cork: Collins Press, 2002).

28. Arthur Young, *A Tour in Ireland: With General Observations on the Present State of That Kingdom, Made in the Years 1776, 1777, and 1778* (Dublin, 1780), 2:56; D. Dickson, *Old World Colony*, 427–33.

29. Munter, *History of the Irish Newspaper*, 74. For the importance of infrastructure and communications in one provincial town, see Brian O' Dalaigh, *Ennis in the Eighteenth Century: Portrait of an Urban Community* (Dublin: Irish Academic Press, 1995), 24–27.

30. J. T. Gilbert, *A History of the City of Dublin*, 3 vols. (Dublin, 1854–59), 2:267.

31. The best account of the wide variety of taverns and pubs in Restoration and eighteenth-century Dublin and their connections with club life and the print industry is still Gilbert's *History of the City of Dublin*.

32. John Anketell, "Description of a Sunday Evening spent in a Coffee-House in the City of Dublin," *Poems on Several Occasions* (Dublin, 1793). Anketell was the curate of Donaghendry, Co. Tyrone.

33. *HC*, 28 Oct. 1779. There is no internal evidence to suggest that this piece was written by a local poet, and it may simply have been plagiarized from the English press, though its publication here assumes that the Cork reader could identity with the various events and persons in this description

of British imperial fortunes. The poem refers to Britain's embarrassing loss of the islands of Dominica in September 1778, Saint Vincent in June 1779, and Grenada a few days later. D'Estaing was the French admiral who besieged the British in the West Indies during these years. Sir Charles is probably Sir Charles Hardy, admiral of the fleet in 1779. Purl was a mixture of warm beer and gin and considered a morning draught.

34. John Brewer, *Party Ideology and Popular Politics at the Accession of George III* (Cambridge: Cambridge University Press, 1976), 140.

35. Benedict Anderson, *Imagined Communities: Reflections on the Origins and Spread of Nationalism* (London: Verso, 1983).

36. Munter suggests that, largely thanks to the press, the breakdown of "parochialism and provincialism" in all parts of Ireland was well under way by the 1730s. Munter, *History of the Irish Newspaper*, 168.

37. For an important account of the role of the provincial press in England to which my own approach is indebted, see K. Wilson, *Sense of the People*, 37–54, quote at 40.

38. Joad Raymond, *The Invention of the Newspaper: English Newsbooks, 1641–1649* (Oxford: Clarendon Press, 1996), 20; Daniel Woolf, "News, History and the Construction of the Present in Early Modern England," in *The Politics of Information in Early Modern Europe*, ed. Brendan Dooley and Sabrina A. Baron (London: Routledge, 2001), 80–118.

39. For a more detailed discussion of the politics of this opera, which relates such theatrical performances to the creation of a more inclusive public sphere, see Helen Burke, "The Revolutionary Prelude: The Dublin Stage in the Late 1770s and Early 1780s," *Eighteenth-Century Life* 22, no. 3 (Nov. 1998): 7–18.

40. "The Miller's Letters to the Common People," from "John Allan," were published in the *BNL*, 7 Jan., 8 Feb., and 14 March 1780. "The Miller" was possibly the Reverend William Bruce, a Presbyterian minister; see Morley, *Irish Opinion*, 242.

41. *BNL*, 7 Jan. 1780.

42. *BNL*, 18 Jan. 1780.

43. Barker, *Newspapers*, 38.

44. Brady cites six instances of the reporting of such renunciations in 1776 alone. Brady, *Catholics and Catholicism*, 180–82.

45. *HJ*, 31 July 1778.

46. *HJ*, 20 Dec. 1779.

47. Catherine Cox, "Women and Business in Eighteenth-Century Dublin: A Case Study," in *Women and Paid Work in Ireland, 1500–1930*, ed. Bernadette Whelan (Dublin: Four Courts Press, 2000).

48. Mary Pollard, *A Dictionary of Members of the Dublin Book Trade, 1550–1800* (London: Bibliographical Society, 2000), 279–80.

49. Agnew, *Drennan–McTier Letters*, vol. 1.

50. These letters were later collected as *The Modern Monitor, or Flyn's Speculations* (Cork, 1771[?]). Madden, *History of Irish Periodical Literature*, 1:174.

51. *Modern Monitor*, 180.

52. Ibid., 253–54.

53. [Frederick Jebb], *The Letters of Guatimozin on the Affairs of Ireland as First published in the Freeman's Journal* . . . (Dublin, 1779), 20.

54. [Peter Burrowes], *Plain Arguments in Defence of the People's Absolute Dominion over the Constitution* (Dublin, 1784), 36–37.

55. Gilbert, *History of Dublin*, 1:294, 2:155; J. Kelly, *Henry Flood*, 122–25.

56. J. Kelly, *Sir Edward Newenham*.

57. Ibid., 81–82.

58. Frederic M. Litto, "Addison's Cato in the Colonies," *William and Mary Quarterly*, 3rd ser., 23, no. 3 (July 1966): 431.

59. [Jebb], *Letters of Guatimozin*, 1.

60. See *HJ*, 4 June 1779. Sarsfield had also been portrayed heroically in Robert Ashton's popular play *The Battle of Aughrim*.

61. Agnew, *Drennan–McTier Letters*, 1:100–101, 126, 164.

62. *HJ*, 21 Aug. 1778.

63. *Volunteer Evening Post* (hereafter cited as *VEP*), 13 Nov. 1783.

64. *Independent Chronicle, of Universal Advertiser*, 25 April 1778.

65. *BNL*, 27 Jan. 1778.

66. *FJ*, 20 July 1780.

67. *Volunteer Journal* (Cork), 18 Nov. 1782.

68. *Volunteer's Journal, or Irish Herald* (Dublin), 13 Oct. 1783.

69. *DEP*, 18 Jan. 1780.

70. Simes, "Ireland."

71. For an account of Faulkner's career and his connections with the literary and social elite of mid-eighteenth-century Dublin, see Robert E. Ward, ed., *Prince of Dublin Printers: The Letters of George Faulkner* (Lexington: University Press of Kentucky, 1972).

72. Mathew Carey, *Autobiography* (New York, 1937); *Town and Country Magazine* (Dublin), June–July 1784.

73. PRO, State Papers (hereafter citied as SP), 63/464, fol. 361.

74. William Beresford, ed., *The Correspondence of the Right Hon. John Beresford*, 2 vols. (London, 1854), 1:171.

75. C. F. Sheridan to Lord Northington, Aug. 1784; Bolton Papers, NLI, MS 16,350 (4).

76. For a detailed account of this conflict, see Inglis, *Freedom of the Press*, 21–48.

77. PRO, HO, 100/14, fol. 239.

78. The government largely financed papers through the publication of proclamations and government advertisements in their pages. More work is needed on the government press, but see Inglis, *Freedom of the Press*, 34–38.

79. Pamphlet literature has also been central to the study of the American Revolution. For a discussion of pamphlets as a source in that context, see in particular Bernard Bailyn, *The Ideological Origins of the American Revolution* (Cambridge, MA: Harvard University Press, 1967), 1–21. For an argument that

pamphlet literature, and indeed most forms of politics, were unimportant in eighteenth-century Ireland, see Gerard O'Brien, "The Unimportance of Public Opinion in Eighteenth-Century Britain and Ireland," *Eighteenth-Century Ireland* 8 (1993): 115–27.

80. B. Harris, *Politics and the Nation*, 192–235.

81. Lucas was a chief exponent of the possibilities of the press, not only producing pamphlets but also establishing the newspaper the *Censor* to promote his views and playing a large role in the opposition *FJ* in the 1760s. His opponents in turn created an anti-Lucas newspaper, the *Tickler*. For an effort to rehabilitate Lucas's political ideas, see Jim Smyth, "Republicanism before the United Irishmen: The Case of Dr. Charles Lucas," in *Political Discourse in Seventeenth- and Eighteenth-Century Ireland*, ed. D. George Boyce et al. (Basingstoke: Palgrave, 2001), 240–55.

82. Munter, *History of the Irish Newspaper*, 86.

83. Morley suggests that the number doubled from the previous year; *Irish Opinion*, 208.

84. David Dickson, "Paine and Ireland," in *The United Irishmen: Republicanism, Radicalism, and Rebellion*, ed. David Dickson, Daire Keogh, and Kevin Whelan (Dublin: Lilliput Press, 1993), 135–50.

85. Small, *Political Thought in Ireland*, 11. This is the most recent study of the pamphlet literature, though it has little to say on distribution or reception of this material.

86. Munter, *History of the Irish Newspaper*, 88.

87. Beresford, *Correspondence*, 1:221–22.

88. Adams, *Printed Word*, 85–86.

89. D. Dickson, "Centres of Motion," 119.

90. *Baratariana: A Select Collection of Fugitive Political Pieces* (Dublin, 1772); *The Political Monitor: Exhibiting the Present State of Affairs in Ireland . . . in a Series of Letters First Published in the Freeman's Journal . . .* (Dublin, 1772); Robert Houlton, *A Selection of Political Letters which Appeared during the Administration of the Earls of Buckinghamshire and Carlisle . . .* (Dublin 1782).

91. [Jebb], *Letters of Guatimozin*.

92. Agnew, *Drennan–McTier Letters*, 1:198.

93. Ibid., 1:184, 187. McTier also seems to have been involved in helping her brother have some of his anonymous writing printed and distributed. Ibid., 1:93.

94. Brendan Clifford, ed., *William Drennan: Selected Writings*, vol. 1, *The Irish Volunteers: 1775–1790* (Belfast: Belfast Historical and Educational Society, 1998), 81–82.

95. Phillips, *Printing and Bookselling in Dublin*, 87–89; Pollard, *Dictionary*.

96. Adams, *Printed Word*, 37–38. One Belfast library in 1775 charged 13s. a year or 1s. 7½d. a month. Adams notes that many of these reading societies were regarded with suspicion by the authorities as sites of political subversion.

The emergence of circulating libraries in many towns, such as Cork, Drogheda, and Galway, seems to have occurred in the 1790s. Gerard, *Books beyond the Pale,* 24, 26, 41–42, 61.

97. Phillips, *Printing and Bookselling in Dublin,* 37–40.

98. Munter, *History of the Irish Newspaper,* 79–80; Phillips, *Printing and Bookselling in Dublin,* 54–56.

99. *Historical Account,* 115–27.

100. These epithets refer to the radical minister Thomas Ledlie Birch of Saintfield, Co. Down. For the attribution to Drennan, see Agnew, *Drennan–McTier Letters,* 1:137.

101. These songs are contained in the chapbook *Ireland's Glory.* For more examples of chapbook verses and remarks on their significance, see Andrew Carpenter, *Verse in English in Eighteenth-Century Ireland* (Cork: Cork University Press, 1998), 19–20, 387–404.

102. Georges-Denis Zimmerman, *Songs of Irish Rebellion: Political Street Ballads and Rebel Songs, 1780–1900* (Hataboro, PA: Folklore Associates, 1967), 12; K. Wilson, *Sense of the People,* 33.

103. Adele M. Dalsimer, ed., *Visualizing Ireland: National Identity and the Pictorial Tradition* (London: Faber, 1993). For a pioneering study that does pay some attention to prints, see Fintan Cullen, *Visual Politics: The Representation of Ireland, 1750–1930* (Cork: Cork University Press, 1997). See also Toby Barnard, *Making the Grand Figure: Lives and Possessions in Ireland, 1641–1770* (New Haven, CT: Yale University Press, 2004), 180–87.

104. Nicholas Robinson, "Caricature and the Regency Crisis: An Irish perspective," *Eighteenth-Century Ireland* 1 (1986): 157–76. See also Powell, *Politics of Consumption,* 132–37. For a skeptical approach to prints as historical evidence, see Eirwen Nicholson, "Consumers and Spectators: The Public of the Political Print in Eighteenth-Century England," *History* 81, no. 261 (Jan. 1996): 5–21.

105. For references to the market for prints in eighteenth-century Dublin, see Sarah Foster, "Going Shopping in Eighteenth-Century Dublin," *Things* 4 (Summer 1996): 47–48; T. C. Barnard, "Art, Architecture, Artefacts and Ascendancy," *Bullán: An Irish Studies Review* 1, no. 2 (1994): 17–34.

106. Although more interested in texts, Pollard's *Dictionary* provides a wealth of information on the print-selling and engraving businesses in Dublin.

107. *BNL,* 25 March 1785.

108. Joseph Wright of Grafton Street was responsible for many of the locally produced engravings in *Exshaw's Magazine* from 1783 to 1784. *BNL,* 4 July 1780.

109. *FJ,* 9 Nov. 1784.

110. *BNL,* 11 Jan. 1780; *DEP,* 5 Feb. 1780.

111. Lewis Walpole Library, Yale University, New Haven, CT.

112. *DEP,* 5 Oct. 1780.

113. Many of these prints were purchased from London and depict London scenes and figures, though Irish subject matter is also included.

114. Barnard, *Making the Grand Figure,* 185.

115. Agnew, *Drennan–McTier Letters,* 1:209.

116. Roy Porter, "Seeing the Past," *Past and Present* 118 (Feb. 1988): 190; Nicholson, "Consumers and Spectators," 8.

117. *HJ,* 22 Nov. 1779. For a later reference to this print, see "The Upright Statesman, or the D———L turned Politician," *Exshaw's Magazine,* 1783. Prints satirizing Richard Twiss, an English travel writer regarded as overly critical of Irish culture, were also available from hawkers.

118. *BNL,* 16 July 1784.

119. *Dublin Journal,* 1 Jan. 1754, quoted in Pollard, *Dictionary,* 374.

120. Nicholson, "Consumers and Spectators," 17.

121. For example, "Miss Kitty in Dispute, or a new Mode of Fighting a Duel with weapons of Female Invention," Lewis Walpole Library, Yale University, New Haven, CT.

122. *London Evening Post,* 25–27 Feb. 1755, quoted in Tim Clayton, *The English Print, 1688–1802* (New Haven, CT: Yale University Press, 1997), 148; *HJ,* 17–19 Jan. 1780. The print in question was "The Engagement between D'Orvilliers and Keppel." F. G. Stephens and M. D. George, eds., *Catalogue of Political and Personal Satires Preserved in the Department of Prints and Drawings in the British Museum* (London: British Museum, 1873–1954), 5:5626.

Chapter 2. "Paddy Shall Rise"

1. Pádraig Ó Snodaigh, "Notes on the Volunteers, Militia, Yeomanry and Orangemen of County Louth," *Journal of the Louth Archeological and Historical Society* 18, no. 4 (1976): 284.

2. *DEP,* 20 July 1780.

3. John Hempton, ed., *The Siege and History of Londonderry* (Dublin, 1861), 423.

4. *DEP,* 13 July 1780.

5. Guy Beiner, "Between Trauma and Triumphalism: The Easter Rising, the Somme, and the Crux of Deep Memory in Modern Ireland," *Journal of British Studies* 46, no. 2 (April 2007): 366–89; Ian McBride, "Introduction: Memory and National Identity in Modern Ireland," in *History and Memory in Modern Ireland,* ed. Ian McBride (Cambridge: Cambridge University Press, 2001), 1–43; Breandán Mac Suibhne, "Three Drunken Nights and a Hangover: The Siege, the Apprentice Boys and Irish National Identity, 1779–80," in *The Sieges of Derry,* ed. William Kelly (Dublin: Four Courts Press, 2001), 85–95. As Mac Suibhne notes, the relief of the siege had been celebrated only sporadically before the 1780s.

6. McBride, "Memory and National Identity," 18–19.

7. Guy Beiner, *Remembering the Year of the French: Irish Folk History and Social Memory* (Madison: University of Wisconsin Press, 2006).

8. N. Rogers, *Crowds,* 246. Transparencies were pictures made "with translucent paints on materials like calico, linen, [and] oiled paper and lighted from

behind in the manner of stained glass." Richard D. Alrick, *The Shows of London* (Cambridge: Cambridge University Press, 1978), 95.

9. These free-trade celebrations took place following North's initial announcement of free trade in December 1779 and after the passage of the bill in March 1780.

10. N. Rogers, *Crowds*, 23.

11. This identification was not simply a cognitive but also an emotional experience. As Kertzer argues, following Victor Turner, public ritual was experienced between the two poles of the cognitive and the emotional, so that "the emotions aroused in ritual infuse the cognitive view fostered by the rite, rendering it compelling." See Kertzer, *Ritual, Politics, and Power* (New Haven, CT: Yale University Press, 1990), 100. For a historical account of this interaction, see Vernon, *Politics and the People*, chap. 3.

12. Jacqueline R. Hill, "National Festivals"; J. Kelly, "Glorious and Immortal Memory"; Barnard, "Uses of 23 October 1641"; Judith Hill, *Irish Public Sculpture: A History* (Dublin: Four Courts Press, 1998); Yvonne Whelan, *Reinventing Modern Dublin: Streetscape, Iconography, and the Politics of Identity* (Dublin: University College Dublin Press, 2003). For a recent example of such an approach applied to nineteenth-century Ireland, see Gary Owens, "Nationalism without Words: Symbolism and Ritual Behaviour in the Repeal 'Monster Meetings' of 1843-5," in Donnelly and Miller, *Irish Popular Culture*, 242-69.

13. Vernon, *Politics and the People*, 107–10.

14. *DEP*, 18 March 1780. The same report appeared in the *BNL*, 21 March 1780.

15. Ibid.

16. On the rhetoric of print and the generic qualities of reportage in America, see David Waldstreicher, *In the Midst of Perpetual Fetes: The Making of American Nationalism, 1776–1820* (Chapel Hill: University of North Carolina Press, 1997), 10-11, 32-35. On the relationship between newspapers and the nation, see also K. Wilson, *Sense of the People*.

17. J. Kelly, "Glorious and Immortal Memory," 42–43.

18. James Kelly, "Introduction: The Emergence of Political Parading, 1660–1800," in *The Irish Parading Tradition: Following the Drum*, ed. T. G. Fraser (London: Macmillan, 2000), 17.

19. See also Powell, *Politics of Consumption*, 17–28.

20. Jonah Barrington, *Recollections of Jonah Barrington* (Dublin, n.d.), 45. For Orange toasting in the 1790s, see 156–57.

21. B. Harris, *Politics and the Nation*, 201, 214-15. Kelly discusses the political toasts of the 1760s and 1770s in "Glorious and Immortal Memory," 44-45. Toasting was also central to the politics of the American Revolution. See Richard J. Hooker, "The American Revolution Seen through a Wine Glass," *William and Mary Quarterly*, 3rd ser., 11, no. 1 (Jan. 1954): 52-77; David Waldstreicher, "Rites of Rebellion, Rites of Assent: Celebrations, Print Culture, and the Origins of American Nationalism," *Journal of American History* 82, no. 1 (June 1995): 44.

22. On speech acts and the culture and social rules of drinking, see Charles O. Frake, "How to Ask for a Drink in Subanun," *American Anthropologist* 66, no. 6, pt. 2 (Dec. 1964): 127–32.

23. Agnew, *Drennan–McTier Letters,* 1:31.

24. *Dartmouth MSS* (London, 1887–96), 3:239–40. The act of toasting generated considerable controversy in the early eighteenth century. See J. Kelly, "Glorious and Immortal Memory," 33–34, 40.

25. *BNL,* 30 July 1779; *BNL,* 13 Aug. 1779.

26. At the Royal George Inn in Omagh, Co. Tyrone, for example, the local Volunteer company toasted the Glorious Revolution of 1688; King William III; 1 July 1690; 1 Aug. 1689; 12 July 1691; and 16 April 1746 (*DEP,* 9 Oct. 1779).

27. *BNL,* 7 Jan. 1780.

28. *BNL,* 30 July 1779.

29. *BNL,* 25 June 1779.

30. *BNL,* 13 Aug. 1779.

31. N. Rogers, *Crowds,* chap. 4.

32. *BNL,* 23 March 1779.

33. *Proceedings at Large of the Court-Martial on the Trial of the Honourable Augustus Keppel, Admiral of the Blue* (Dublin, 1779); *BNL,* 13 April 1779.

34. English celebrations, including the use of transparencies and effigies, were described in detail in the Irish press. See *FJ,* 20 Feb. 1779; N. Rogers, *Crowds,* 131–32.

35. *FJ,* 20 Feb. 1779.

36. This account is based on the descriptions of the celebrations in the following newspapers: *HJ,* 24 Feb. 1779; *FJ,* 20 Feb. 1779; *BNL,* 23 Feb. 1779; *DEP,* 20 Feb. 1779; *DEP* 25 Feb. 1779.

37. The emotional aspects of patriotism have received little attention from historians. On celebrations, see Stephen Conway, "'A Joy Unknown for Years Past': The American War, Britishness, and the Celebration of Rodney's Victory at the Saints," *History* 86, no. 282 (April 2001): 180–99.

38. As David Kertzer notes, "The power of ritual lies in the ability of its component symbols to synthesize complex ideas and to give them social expression"; see his "Role of Ritual in Political Change," in *Cultural and Political Change,* ed. Myron J. Aronoff (New Brunswick, NJ: Transaction, 1983), 54.

39. [Joy], *Historical Collections,* 142.

40. *BNL,* 23 Feb. 1779; *HJ,* 26 Feb. 1779.

41. *DEP,* 25 Feb. 1779.

42. *BNL,* 23 Feb. 1779.

43. *FJ,* 25 Feb. 1779.

44. *HJ,* 24 Feb. 1779; *BNL,* 26 Feb. 1779.

45. Mac Suibhne, "Patriot Paddies," 96–98.

46. *HC,* 1 March 1779.

47. *FLJ,* 3 March 1779.

48. *FJ*, 23 Feb. 1779; J. T. Gilbert, *Calendar of Ancient Records of Dublin*, 19 vols. (Dublin, 1889–1944), 13:51.

49. *HJ*, 26 April 1779. A Keppel club was still meeting in Dublin as late as 1784. See Jacqueline Hill, *From Patriots to Unionists*, 144.

50. K. Wilson, *Sense of the People*, 140–65, 253–68; Gerald Jordan and Nicholas Rogers, "Admirals as Heroes: Patriotism and Liberty in Hanoverian England," *Journal of British Studies* 28, no. 3 (July 1989): 201–24.

51. *HJ*, 24 Feb. 1779.

52. *DEP*, 20 Feb. 1779.

53. *BNL*, 23 Feb. 1779.

54. *FJ*, 20 Feb. 1779.

55. *BNL*, 23 Feb. 1779.

56. *DEP*, 9 Oct. 1779.

57. *An Irregular Pindaric Ode* (Dublin, 1757); *BNL*, 20 July 1756; Judith Hill, *Irish Public Sculpture*, 51. The statue did not last long, however, and was removed in 1763. For a recent account of the politics of the Minorca crisis, see K. Wilson, *Sense of the People*, 179–85. A print, to be found in the Lewis Walpole Library and titled "The Three Renowned Hibernian Heroes," dating from around 1756, even attempts to create a pantheon of Irish imperial heroes. The three figures shown in the print—William Blakeney, Peter Warren, and William Johnson—were all Irish born and had achieved some fame for their imperial exploits.

58. *BNL*, 23 Feb. 1779.

59. See the poem on the corrupt ministry with an elegy to Palliser from "Lucifer," *FJ*, 23 Feb. 1779.

60. Robert Blair St. George, *Conversing by Signs: Poetics of Implication in Colonial New England Culture* (Chapel Hill: University of North Carolina Press, 1998), 251.

61. *HJ*, 24 Feb. 1779.

62. Estimates of the number of Volunteers vary. One report suggests that the number present was closer to two thousand (Perceval Papers, PRONI, D/906/168/166).

63. These placards were described in the press, with some minor differences, but this account is taken from Beresford, *Correspondence*, 1:73. The first placard was on the north, facing the House of Commons, with the others on the west, south, and east, respectively.

64. *DEP*, 6 Nov. 1779.

65. PRO, SP, 63/467, fol. 95.

66. Gilbert, *History*, 3:42–52; J. Kelly, "Glorious and Immortal Memory," 29–33.

67. *BNL*, 9 Nov. 1779; Henry Grattan Jr., ed., *Memoirs of the Life and Times of the Rt. Hon. Henry Grattan*, 5 vols. (London, 1839–46), 1:400.

68. *Walker's Hibernian Magazine* (hereafter cited as *WHM*) (1779), 654–55.

69. Perceval Papers, PRONI, D/906/168/166.

70. PRO, SP, 63/467, fol. 95.

71. *FLJ*, 10 Nov. 1779.

72. *BNL*, 9 Nov. 1779.

73. There were two main features of these concessions: the laws prohibiting the export of woolen manufactures were repealed, and Ireland was given access to colonial markets. See W. E. H. Lecky, *History of Ireland in the Eighteenth Century*, 5 vols. (London: Longmans Green, 1913), 2:242–43.

74. *HJ*, 3 Jan. 1780.

75. *DEP*, 18 Jan. 1780.

76. Ibid.

77. *DEP*, 1 Jan. 1780.

78. Conway, *British Isles*, 214–15.

79. *HC*, 23 Dec. 1779.

80. Martyn J. Powell, *Britain and Ireland in the Eighteenth-Century Crisis of Empire* (Basingstoke: Palgrave, 2003), 184.

81. *HJ*, 31 Dec. 1779.

82. *BNL*, 31 Dec. 1779. This issue of the paper also provides an interpretation of these transparencies.

83. It is not known who painted these transparencies, though one on a very similar theme of the unity between Hibernia and Britannia, based on a drawing by Francis Wheatley, was displayed in the Theatre Royal a few months later. See *HJ*, 16 Feb. 1780. A final symbol on Ryder's house, suggesting his motives in supporting the government, declared: "The theatre of Dublin free while the public please and mine be the lot to please the public." This referred to an attempt by the government in 1779 to regulate the Dublin stage. Ryder had opposed this bill; he claimed that it would create a monopoly. The bill was consequently abandoned. See Gilbert, *History*, 2:201–2.

84. *DEP*, 8 Feb. 1780.

85. *HJ*, 5 Jan. 1780.

86. For Limerick, see *BNL*, 7 Jan. 1780. Celebrations were not confined to large towns. For celebrations in Coleraine and Tanderagee, see *BNL*, 11 Jan. 1780.

87. *HC*, 3 Jan. 1780.

88. Francis Dobbs, *A History of Irish Affairs, from the 12th of October, 1779, to the 15th September, 1782, the Day of Lord Temple's Arrival* (Dublin, 1782), 13. Dobbs outlined this argument more fully in his pamphlet *A Letter to the Right Honourable Lord North on His Propositions in Favour of Ireland* (Dublin, 1780).

89. John Beresford to John Robinson, 13 Dec. 1779, in Beresford, *Correspondence*, 1:114.

90. Earl of Buckinghamshire to Lord George Germain, 21 Dec. 1779, in *Stopford-Sackville MSS* (London, 1904–10), 3:264–65.

91. *HC*, 23 Dec. 1779. For the fierce passions that the issue of illuminations could provoke, see Curtin, *United Irishmen*, 233–34, which recounts the "illumination riots" of 1793–94. E. P. Thompson describes how an "Irish mob" armed

with shillelaghs protected the home of Thomas Hardy against a loyalist crowd in 1797, when he refused to illuminate it on the occasion of a naval victory. E. P. Thompson, *The Making of the English Working Class* (New York: Vintage, 1964), 76.

92. *HC*, 23 Dec. 1779.

93. *BNL*, 31 Dec. 1779.

94. *FLJ*, 15 Dec. 1779.

95. The cited item in the newspaper recounts an anecdote of "Paddy in London" in which again such stereotypes are used for comic effect and to the advantage of the Irishman. For English representations of Irish national character, see David Hayton, "Anglo-Irish Attitudes: Changing Perceptions of National Identity among the Protestant Ascendancy in Ireland, ca. 1690–1750," *Studies in Eighteenth-Century Culture* 17 (1987): 145–57.

96. Mac Suibhne, "Whiskey, Potatoes."

97. *HJ*, 13 Dec. 1779.

98. *DEP*, 18 March 1780.

99. *HC*, 13 March 1780.

100. *BNL*, 10 March 1780; *FLJ*, 8 March 1780.

101. PRO, SP, 63/468, fol. 40.

102. *FJ*, 22 June 1780.

103. See Conway, *British Isles*.

Chapter 3. Shopping for Ireland

1. *HC*, 27 May 1779. According to the *Encyclopædia Britannica*, a device was "any emblem used to represent a certain family, person, action or quality; with a suitable motto, applied in a figurative sense," noting that "the essence of a device consists in a metaphorical similitude between the things representing and represented." *Encyclopædia Britannica; or, a Dictionary of Arts, Sciences, &c.* (Edinburgh, 1778–83), 4:2435. The advertised devices seem to be no longer extant.

2. *DEP*, 31 July 1779.

3. Small, *Political Thought in Ireland*; Morley, *Irish Opinion*. For a study of this political culture that suggests the importance of the material culture of patriotism, see McBride, *Scripture Politics*, 123–33.

4. In particular see Barnard, *Making the Grand Figure*.

5. Powell, *Politics of Consumption*.

6. Of course, this is not to ignore the fact that pamphlets were themselves part of this commercialized political culture, with some selling in large numbers. By the 1770s parliamentary debates had also become commercialized, with many newspapers printing reports of these debates, often to the exclusion of any other news.

7. For the use of newspaper advertisements to show the range of opportunities for sociability and consumption for the Dublin gentry, see Tighearnan Mooney and Fiona White, "The Gentry's Winter Season," in *The Gorgeous Mask:*

Dublin, 1700–1850, ed. David Dickson (Dublin: Trinity History Workshop, 1987), 1–16. See also Foster, "Going Shopping."

8. For example, Eileen Black, "Volunteer Portraits in the Ulster Museum," *Irish Sword* 13 (1978–9): 181–84; F. Glenn Thompson, "The Flags and Uniforms of the Irish Volunteers and Yeomanry," *Bulletin of the Irish Georgian Society* 33 (1990): 3–30; Catriona MacLeod, "Irish Volunteer Glass," *Irish Sword* 7 (1965–6): 241–60.

9. For a pioneering account of the "commercialization of politics," see McKendrick, Brewer, and Plumb, *Birth of Consumer Society.* For examples of work that connects politics and consumption, see Martin Daunton and Matthew Hilton, eds., *The Politics of Consumption: Material Culture and Citizenship in Europe and America* (Oxford: Berg, 2001); Victoria de Grazia, ed., *The Sex of Things: Gender and Consumption in Historical Perspective* (Berkeley: University of California Press, 1996).

10. T. H. Breen, "An Empire of Goods: The Anglicization of Colonial America, 1690–1776," *Journal of British Studies* 25, no. 4 (Oct. 1986): 467–99; idem, "'Baubles of Britain': The American and Consumer Revolutions of the Eighteenth Century," *Past and Present* 69 (May 1988): 73–104; Clare Midgley, "Slave Sugar Boycotts, Female Activism and the Domestic Base of British Anti-Slavery Culture," *Slavery and Abolition* 17, no. 3 (Dec. 1996): 137–62; Charlotte Sussman, *Consuming Anxieties: Consumer Protest, Gender, and British Slavery, 1713–1833* (Stanford, CA: Stanford University Press, 2000); C. A. Bayly, "The Origins of Swadeshi (Home Industry): Cloth and Indian Society, 1700–1930," in *The Social Life of Things: Commodities in Cultural Perspective,* ed. Arjun Appadurai (Cambridge: Cambridge University Press, 1988), 285–322.

11. Breen has provocatively recast popular mobilization in the American Revolution in terms of the politics of material culture. Breen, *Marketplace of Revolution.*

12. T. C. Barnard, "Integration or Separation? Hospitality and Display in Protestant Ireland, 1660–1800," in *A Union of Multiple Identities: The British Isles, 1750–1850,* ed. Laurence Brockliss and David Eastwood (Manchester: Manchester University Press, 1997), 141.

13. T. C. Barnard, "The World of Goods and County Offaly in the Early Eighteenth Century," in *Offaly: History and Society; Interdisciplinary Essays on the History of an Irish County,* ed. William Nolan and Timothy P. O'Neill (Dublin: Geography Publications, 1998), 380; Foster, "Going Shopping."

14. Harvey, *Bellews of Mount Bellew.*

15. For evidence that Catholic poor did participate in a consumer culture, see D. Dickson, *Old World Colony.*

16. K. Whelan, *Tree of Liberty,* 27–31.

17. Maureen Wall, *Catholic Ireland in the Eighteenth Century: Collected Essays of Maureen Wall* (Dublin: Geography Publications, 1989); David Dickson, "Catholics and Trade in Eighteenth-Century Ireland: An Old Debate Revisited," in Power and Whelan, *Endurance and Emergence,* 57–84.

18. David Dickson, "The Place of Dublin in the Eighteenth-Century Irish Economy," in *Ireland and Scotland, 1600–1850: Parallels and Contrasts in Economic and Social Development,* ed. Martin Thomas Devine and David Dickson (Edinburgh: John Donald, 1983), 177–92, at 182; Mooney and White, "Gentry's Winter Season"; Foster, "Going Shopping"; Peter Clark and Raymond Gillespie, eds., *Two Capitals: London and Dublin 1500–1840* (Oxford: Oxford University Press, 2001), 265–95. For urban life outside Dublin, see Borsay and Proudfoot, *Provincial Towns,* especially the chapters by Crawford, Simms, and Barnard.

19. Young, *Tour of Ireland,* 2:333.

20. D. Dickson, *Old World Colony;* Crawford, "Evolution of Ulster Towns," 140–56.

21. Barnard, "World of Goods," 372.

22. Crawford, "Evolution of Ulster Towns," 142; L. A. Clarkson, "An Anatomy of an Irish town: The Economy of Armagh, 1770," *Irish Economic and Social History* 5 (1978): 27–45.

23. Barnard, "World of Goods."

24. Jonathan Swift, *Irish Tracts 1728–1733,* ed. Herbert Davis, vol. 12 of *Prose Writings of Jonathan Swift* (Oxford: Oxford University Press, 1939–1968), xix, 126–27.

25. Barnard, *New Anatomy of Ireland,* 284–85; *Dublin Intelligencer,* 16 June 1731, quoted in Munter, *History of the Irish Newspaper,* 154; Sarah Foster, "Consumer Nationalism in 18th-Century Ireland," *History Today* 47, no. 6 (1997): 45–46; Helen Burke, "Putting on Irish 'Stuff': The Politics of Anglo-Irish Cross-Dressing," in *The Clothes That Wear Us: Essays on Dressing and Transgressing in Eighteenth-Century Culture,* ed. Jessica Munns and Penny Richards (Delaware: University of Delaware Press, 2000), 236–37.

26. Jacqueline Hill, *From Patriots to Unionists,* 145.

27. Thomas Bartlett, "'This famous island set in a Virginian sea': Ireland in the British Empire, 1690–1801," in *The Oxford History of the British Empire: The Eighteenth Century,* ed. P. J. Marshall (Oxford: Oxford University Press, 1998), 255; David Lammey, "The Free Trade Crisis: A Reappraisal," in *Parliament, Politics, and People: Essays in Eighteenth-Century Irish History,* ed. Gerard O'Brien (Dublin: Irish Academic Press, 1989), 77–78.

28. Lammey has examined the absence of interest in Smith's ideas by most proponents of free trade; see his "Free Trade Crisis."

29. *BNL,* 14 March 1780.

30. For an account of restrictions on trade, see Lammey, "Free Trade Crisis," 69–72.

31. [Grattan], *Letter,* 7.

32. *HJ,* 30 Nov. 1778.

33. Barnard, "Languages of Politeness," 196.

34. For example, "Mercator," *HC,* 26 April 1779.

35. *DEP,* 21 Aug. 1779.

36. *HJ*, 5 June 1778; for similar appeals to elite women, see *HJ*, 6 Sept. 1778.

37. Patrick Kelly, "The Politics of Political Economy in Mid-Eighteenth-Century Ireland," in *Political Ideas in Eighteenth Century Ireland*, ed. S. J. Connolly (Dublin: Four Courts Press, 2000), 118–19.

38. For such a critique of the Irish elite, see, for example, *HJ*, 14 Sept. 1778. For a similar crisis of authority in India related to consumption, see Bayly, "Origins of Swadeshi," 297–302.

39. *Dublin Evening Journal*, 19 May 1778.

40. *HJ*, 9 May 1779.

41. *DEP*, 14 April 1781.

42. For similar appeals to female consumers based on sentiment in the context of the abolitionist campaign in the 1790s, see Sussman, *Consuming Anxieties*, 122–29.

43. *DEP*, 21 Aug. 1779; *DEP*, 4 Sept. 1779.

44. *HJ*, 30 April 1779. This fashion for simplicity in dress appears not to be unique to Ireland in the final decades of the eighteenth century, but rather a trend across Europe. See Aileen Ribeiro, *The Art of Dress: Fashion in England and France, 1750–1820* (New Haven, CT: Yale University Press, 1995), 70–71.

45. *HJ*, 24 May 1779.

46. An extensive literature exists on the concept of luxury; see, for example, J. G. A. Pocock, *The Machiavellian Moment: Florentine Political Thought and the Atlantic Republican Tradition* (Princeton, NJ: Princeton University Press, 1975); Christopher J. Berry, *The Idea of Luxury: A Conceptual and Historical Investigation* (Cambridge: Cambridge University Press, 1994). For further examples in an Irish context, see W. S. Dickson, *Sermon on the Propriety*, 15; *HJ*, 20 May 20 1778; John Edwards, *The Patriot Soldier: A Poem* (Dublin, 1784), 23–24; *WHM* (1780), 22–23.

47. *The Times, Addressed to the Virtuous and Spirited Free Men of Ireland* (Dublin, 1780).

48. Similar fears over consumption of foreign goods by men were voiced in colonial New England in the 1760s and 1770s. See Anne S. Lombard, *Making Manhood: Growing Up Male in Colonial New England* (Cambridge: Cambridge University Press, 2003), 162–65.

49. Some correspondents to newspapers, however, did claim that the free-trade campaign was promoted by "interested" parties hoping to profit from patriotism and the consumption of Irish goods.

50. For a study of newspaper advertising in eighteenth-century England, see Neil McKendrick, "George Packwood and the Commercialization of Shaving: The Art of Eighteenth-Century Advertising," in McKendrick, Brewer, and Plumb, *Birth of Consumer Society*, 146–94.

51. "The Connaughtman's Visit to Dublin," a satirical poem depicting a Volunteer review in the Phoenix Park, described the opportunities for consumption

at these occasions. The awestruck provincial noted that "such standing of Whiskey and Sheeben vas there, I thought on my shoul it vas sweet Leitrim whair." See Carpenter, *Verse in English,* 388–92.

52. For the similar creation of a market of patriotic ephemera in England, see McKendrick, Brewer, and Plumb, *Birth of Consumer Society,* 238–41.

53. *DEP,* 18 Jan. 1780.

54. *DEP,* 17 April 1781; *BNL,* 14 Jan. 1780.

55. *DEP,* 20 Nov. 1779.

56. *DEP,* 12 July 1781.

57. *DEP,* 2 March 1780.

58. See also *The Exercise of a Company of Foot, Compiled Chiefly from the Practice of the Volunteers of Belfast* (Belfast, 1778).

59. Other examples include *Plan of Review for the Regiment of Dublin Volunteers, Commanded by . . . the Duke of Leinster; for the 12th of October, 1783: . . . to Commemorate the Address of Parliament to His Majesty. Presented the 12th Day of October, M DCC LXXIX, in Order to Obtain a Free Trade for Ireland* (Dublin[?], 1783); Corps of Independent Dublin Volunteers, *Plan of a Field Day for the Dublin Volunteers* (Dublin, 1780).

60. Barnard, *Making the Grand Figure,* 176–87; Foster, "Going Shopping," 47–48; Pollard's *Dictionary* is an important source of information on the print-selling and engraving businesses in Dublin.

61. *HJ,* 24 Nov. 1779. This print, the title of which anticipates a United Irishmen anthology of ballads and poems, is probably the one of the same name included in *Exshaw's Magazine.* See Stephens and George, *Catalogue,* 5:5572.

62. *HJ,* 3 Jan. 1780.

63. *DEP,* 5 Feb. 1780; *DEP,* 2 March 1780.

64. *Volunteer's Journal* (Dublin), 31 Oct. 1783.

65. Stana Nenadic, "Print Collecting and Popular Culture in Eighteenth-Century Scotland," *History* 82, no. 266 (April 1997): 210, 216.

66. *DEP,* 9 Sept. 1780.

67. *BNL,* 3 Sept. 1779. For other examples of merchants in Belfast and the surrounding towns, see the advertisements in *BNL,* 29 Jan. 1779, 5 March 1779, 22 June 1779, 14 Jan. 1780, and 25 Feb. 1780.

68. Minutes of the Snug Club of Newry, 31 Jan. 1780, PRONI, T/3202/3a.

69. Gilbert, *History,* 1:43–44.

70. Ibid., 2:112.

71. Ibid., 2:313.

72. Ibid., 2:167.

73. Drinking and tavern culture have received little attention, but on the social uses of alcohol, see Barnard, "Integration or Separation?" 137–39; Powell, *Politics of Consumption.*

74. *HJ,* 30 July 1779.

75. *HJ,* 28 April 1779.

76. PRO, SP, 63/464, fol. 315. For the resolutions of the Aggregate Body, see *HJ*, 28 April 1779.

77. On male patterns of consumption, see Margot Finn, "Men's Things: Masculine Possession in the Consumer Revolution," *Social History* 25, no. 2 (May 2000): 133–55.

78. McKendrick, Brewer, and Plumb, *Birth of Consumer Society*, 252.

79. *A Guide to the Irish Volunteer, Yeomanry and Militia Relics* (Belfast, 1938), 40. The revived Volunteers in the 1790s purchased similar jugs celebrating the French Revolution and the destruction of the Bastille (ibid., 41). Both the National Museum of Ireland and the Belfast Museum hold a range of jugs, teapots, and bowls celebrating the Volunteers.

80. National Museum of Ireland (hereafter cited as NMI), Art and Industrial Division, Leramic Collection, 1971–233.

81. *HJ*, 27 July 1778.

82. *HJ*, 23 Aug. 1779.

83. Ibid.

84. Just as women were not wholly absent from taverns, however, men were not excluded from the rituals of tea drinking. See Barnard, *Making the Grand Figure*, 129.

85. *A Catalogue of a Collection of Pottery and Porcelain illustrating Popular British History Lent by Henry Willett of Brighton* (London, 1899), 43.

86. Mairead Reynolds, "Wedgwood in Dublin, 1772–1777," *Irish Arts Review* 1, no. 2 (1984): 36–38; Sarah Richards, *Eighteenth-Century Ceramics: Products of a Civilized Society* (Manchester: Manchester University Press, 1999). On Wedgwood's marketing abilities and the recycling of patriotic goods, see McKendrick, Brewer, and Plumb, *Birth of Consumer Society*.

87. NMI, 3–1934; *Guide*, 39–40.

88. This Volunteer fabric was used variously for curtains, quilts, and perhaps later, as a wall hanging.

89. *DEP*, 3 July 1779.

90. *DEP*, 1 July 1779.

91. As Helen Burke has shown, the figure of the suffering weaver as representing the plight of Ireland was firmly established by Swift in the disputes of the 1720s. Burke, "Putting on Irish 'Stuff.'"

92. Paddy Churchill, *The Association; or, the Prospect of Wealth and Liberty; a Satyrical, Political, and Panegyrical Poem, Addressed to the Patriotic Sons and Daughters of Ireland* (Dublin, 1779), 10.

93. [William Drennan], *A Letter to Edmund Burke* (Dublin, 1780), 18.

Chapter 4. The New Magna Carta

1. Maurice R. O'Connell, *Irish Politics and Social Conflict in the Age of the American Revolution* (Philadelphia: University of Pennsylvania Press, 1965), 134–43, 176–83; Lammey, "Free Trade Crisis."

2. For example, Jim Smyth has provided the most detailed account of the Dublin crowd in 1779, though his account does not involve a study of the wider context of this campaign. J. Smyth, *Men of No Property*. The work of David Lammey offers the most recent study of the free trade movement, particularly with regard to its parliamentary aspects and effect on Anglo-Irish relations, though he also explores some aspects of popular mobilization. Lammey, "Free Trade Crisis."

3. Vernon, *Politics and the People*, 4–6; James A. Epstein, *In Practice: Studies in the Language and Culture of Popular Politics in Modern Britain* (Stanford, CA: Stanford University Press, 2003).

4. For a critique of an "episodic" approach to the history of popular politics, see T. Harris, "Introduction," 10–11.

5. *HJ*, 27 May 1778. Tabinet is a fabric similar to poplin.

6. *HJ*, 29 May 1778.

7. *HJ*, 8 June 1778; *HJ*, 21 Sept. 1778.

8. *HJ*, 29 May 1778.

9. Clark, *British Societies and Clubs*.

10. James Livesey, "The Dublin Society in Eighteenth-Century Irish Political Thought," *Historical Journal* 47, no. 3 (Sept. 2004): 615–40.

11. T. Harris, *London Crowds*, 168, 170.

12. B. Harris, *Politics and the Nation*, 232–33.

13. *Wexford Journal*, 15 Feb. 1776. A similar association organized to suppress the Rightboys in Cork raised £2000 for its campaign. J. S. Donnelly, Jr., "The Rightboy Movement 1785–8," *Studia Hibernica*, nos. 17–18 (1977–78): 187.

14. *Clonmell Gazette*, 12 Jan. 1778.

15. *HC*, 29 March 1779.

16. Eugene Black, *The Association: British Extraparliamentary Political Organization, 1769–1793* (Cambridge, MA: Harvard University Press, 1963).

17. Nancy Curtin, "Symbols and Rituals of United Irish Mobilisation," in Gough and Dickson, *Ireland and the French Revolution*, 74. On oaths and swearing in general, see Petri Mirala, "Lawful and Unlawful Oaths in Ireland, 1760–1835," in *Politics and Political Culture in Britain and Ireland, 1750–1850: Essays in Tribute to Peter Jupp*, ed. Allan Blackstock and Eoin Magennis (Belfast: Ulster Historical Foundation, 2007), 209–22; Miller, "Radicalism and Ritual," 206–9. The question of oaths was central to Protestant criticisms of Catholic loyalty throughout the century. By 1796 swearing oaths related to secret societies had been outlawed.

18. B. Harris, *Politics and the Nation*, 210–25. For the theory and development of the association movement in Britain and Ireland, see T. H. Parssinen, "Association, Convention and Anti-parliament in British Radical Politics, 1771–1848," *English Historical Review* 88, no. 348 (July 1973): 504–33. Parssinen mentions the emergence of associations for parliamentary reform in Ireland, but not those for free trade, which predated the Wyvill's associational movement.

19. Churchill, *Association*, vi.

20. *A Scheme for a Constitutional Association with some Obvious Reasons for Adopting such a Measure* (Dublin, 1780), 5.

21. *HJ*, 29 May 1778.

22. *HJ*, 8 Sept. 1779.

23. *HJ*, 11 June 1779.

24. *HJ*, 23 June 1779.

25. [Grattan], *Letter*, 44–45. Kelly attributes this pamphlet to Henry Flood (J. Kelly, *Henry Flood*, 258), though as Morley argues, the positive depiction of Catholics suggests Grattan as the more likely author. Morley, *Irish Opinion*, 209.

26. [Grattan], *Letter*, 41–42.

27. *HJ*, 11 June 1779.

28. [Pollock], *Owen Roe O'Nial*, 40.

29. *HC*, 24 June 1779.

30. *HJ*, 25 Aug. 1779.

31. *HJ*, 11 June 1779.

32. *Magee's Weekly Packet*, 6 Nov. 1779.

33. *HJ*, 23 July 1779.

34. Rhetoric suggesting the presence of hidden enemies and conspiracies to undermine the aims of patriots would also hardly have seemed outrageous to patriots schooled in a "paranoid style" of thought. For the centrality of conspiracy theories to Irish Protestants, see Jim Smyth, "Anti-Catholicism, Conservatism, and Conspiracy: Sir Richard Musgrave's *Memoirs of the Different Rebellions in Ireland*," *Eighteenth-Century Life* 22, no. 3 (Nov. 1998): 62–73.

35. *HJ*, 14 April 1779.

36. As Livesey suggests, proponents of earlier forms of association in Ireland also argued that associating would have a similar effect, particularly in helping overcome sectarian divisions and allowing Catholics a form of participation in civic life. Livesey, "Dublin Society."

37. [Grattan], *Letter*, 53–54.

38. [Jebb], *Letters of Guatimozin*, 16.

39. *HJ*, 23 July 1779.

40. *HJ*, 28 April 1779.

41. For the resolutions of the Aggregate Body, see *HJ*, 28 April 1779.

42. *HJ*, 30 July 1779.

43. *BNL*, 30 June 1778.

44. Churchill, *Association*, vi.

45. *Association Hibernia's Palladium . . .* (Sligo, 1781), 20.

46. *HJ*, 30 April 1779.

47. *BNL*, 23 April 1779.

48. For the debate in the Northwest, see Mac Suibhne, "Patriot Paddies," 98–107.

49. *HJ*, 23 July 1779.

50. It is likely, however, that Catholics were better represented in the non-consumption associations than in the Volunteers due to Protestant opposition to the (illegal) arming of Catholics.

51. *HJ*, 30 July 1779.

52. Neal Garnham, "Local Elite Creation in Early Hanoverian Ireland: The Case of the County Grand Jury," *Historical Journal* 42, no. 3 (Sept. 1999): 623–42. For the politicization of the grand jury, see ibid., 628, 638.

53. Ibid., 629.

54. PRO, HO, 100/8, fol. 150; For similar apprehensions, see Stowe MS, Huntington Library, San Marino, CA, ST 17/ 2/31–32; PRO, HO, 100/12, fol. 201.

55. *BNL*, 9 April 1779.

56. *FLJ*, 14 April 1779.

57. *HJ*, 14 April 1779.

58. *BNL*, 20 April 1779; *HJ*, 26 April 1779; *FLJ*, 28 April 1779; *HJ*, 30 June 1779; *HJ*, 16 Aug. 1779.

59. *HC*, 8 April 1779; *BNL*, 13 April 1779.

60. David Lammey, "A Study of Anglo-Irish Relations between 1772 and 1782 with Particular Reference to the 'Free Trade' Movement" (PhD diss., Queens University Belfast, 1984), 200.

61. PRO, SP, 63/467, fol. 45.

62. *BNL*, 5 Nov. 1779.

63. *HC*, 18 Nov. 1779.

64. *BNL*, 26 Nov. 1779.

65. B. Harris, *Politics and the Nation*, 220.

66. On the theory of representation, see Paul Langford, "Property and 'Virtual Representation' in Eighteenth-Century England," *Historical Journal* 31, no. 1 (March 1988): 83–115.

67. *BNL*, 16 Nov. 1779.

68. J. Kelly, *Sir Edward Newenham*, 154.

69. *HC*, 18 Nov. 1779. For instructions, see, for example *DEP*, March–April 1780.

70. Conservative political ideas in eighteenth-century Ireland have only recently begun to receive the attention they merit, with historians previously focusing on forms of oppositional politics, particularly those movements and ideas that seem to point in the direction of the United Irishmen or, in an older tradition, in the direction of full-blown Irish nationalism. See James Kelly, "Conservative Protestant Political Thought in Late Eighteenth-Century Ireland," in *Political Ideas in Eighteenth-Century Ireland*, ed. Sean J. Connolly (Dublin: Four Courts Press, 2000), 185–220.

71. [Jebb], *Letters of Guatimozin*, 62.

72. *BNL*, 19 Feb. 1779.

73. This pamphlet was reprinted in several newspapers: *HJ*, 30 Aug. 1779; *HC*, 6 Sept. 1779.

74. *HJ*, 3 Sept. 1779; *HC*, 9 Sept. 1779.

75. PRO, SP, 63/461, fol. 29.

76. PRO, SP, 63/460, fol. 328.

77. *HC*, 13 Sept. 1779.

78. *HC*, 23 Sept. 1779; *HJ*, 13 Sept. 1779; *HJ*, 25 Oct. 1779.

79. The literature on the crowd is obviously vast, but for the Irish context see the collection inspired by the work of Mark Harrison on English crowds: Jupp and Magennis, *Crowds in Ireland*.

80. Seamus Cummins, "Extra-Parliamentary Agitation in Dublin in the 1760s," in *Religion, Conflict and Coexistence in Ireland: Essays Presented to Monsignor Patrick Corish*, ed. Richard Vincent Comerford, M. Cullen, Jacqueline R. Hill, and C. Lennon (Dublin: Gill & Macmillan, 1990), 118–34.

81. For an example of this practice by the Aggregate Body, see *HJ*, 7 June 1779.

82. PRO, SP, 63/465, fol. 32.

83. PRO, SP, 63/467, fol. 109; Jim Smyth observes that "popular political literacy" could also have played a role in motivating the crowd. J. Smyth, *Men of No Property*, 133.

84. Powell, *Politics of Consumption*, 7–28.

85. For a similar point on the place of trade in popular politics, see Jacqueline Hill, *From Patriots to Unionists*, 148.

86. *HJ*, 26 June 1778.

87. *Stopford-Sackville MSS*, 3:255.

88. *FJ*, 21 July 1778.

89. *HJ*, 22 July 1778; *DEP*, 13 Aug. 1778.

90. *FJ*, 30 July 1778.

91. *BNL*, 9 June 1779; *HJ*, 4 June 1779; *HJ*, 7 June 1779.

92. It was later claimed that he was attacked in error. *BNL*, 16 July 1779.

93. For criticisms of press attempts to provoke the crowd, see *HJ*, 4 June 1779; *HJ*, 6 Sept. 1779; *DEP*, 25 Nov. 1779.

94. *FJ*, 10 June 1779.

95. *HJ*, 23 June 1779.

96. *DEP*, 20 July 1779. The sanbenito was the robe in which the Inquisition dressed penitents.

97. *HJ*, 27 Dec. 1779.

98. Beresford, *Correspondence*, 1:67.

99. PRO, SP, 63/467, fol. 106.

100. *HC*, 18 Nov. 1779. The *DEP* estimated five to six thousand, while the *HJ* put the figure at eight thousand. *HJ*, 19 Nov. 1779.

101. PRO, SP, 63/467, fol. 109.

102. Beresford, *Correspondence*, 1:75–76.

103. *HJ*, 19 Nov. 1779.

104. *Stopford-Sackville MSS*, 3:255.

105. Patrick Fagan, "The Dublin Catholic Mob (1700–1750)," *Eighteenth-Century Ireland* 4 (1989): 133–42.

106. Brady, *Catholics and Catholicism*, 204–5. This notice was printed in most newspapers. *DEP*, 25 Nov. 1779.

107. St. George, *Conversing by Signs*, 293.

108. Beresford, *Correspondence*, 1:77.

109. Harris observes that the parliament had begun to serve as "cynosure" of liberty in Ireland by the 1750s. B. Harris, *Politics and the Nation*, 202.

110. *BNL*, 5 Nov. 1779.

111. *HJ*, 4 June 1779.

112. Oath-bound societies were also a central part of agrarian protest movements, such as the Whiteboys.

113. Beresford, *Correspondence*, 1:88.

Chapter 5. A Rage *Militaire*

1. John Moore, County Down, to Arthur Annesley, London, 14 Aug. 1780, Annesley Papers, PRONI, D/2309/4/3.

2. Danny Mansergh, *Grattan's Failure: Parliamentary Opposition and the People of Ireland, 1779–1800* (Dublin: Irish Academic Press, 2005), 55–56; 70.

3. James Kelly, "Select Documents XLIII: A Secret Return of the Volunteers of Ireland in 1784," *Irish Historical Studies* 26, no. 103 (1989): 268–92.

4. Ó Snodaigh, "Notes on the Volunteers . . . of County Roscommon"; idem, "Notes on the Volunteers . . . of County Waterford"; idem, "Volunteers . . . of Co. Kildare"; idem, "Notes on the Volunteers . . . in County Limerick"; P. D. H. Smyth, "The Volunteer Movement in Ulster: Background and Development, 1745–85" (PhD diss., Queen's University, Belfast, 1974), 66.

5. Colley, *Britons*. See also John E. Cookson, *The British Armed Nation, 1793–1815* (Oxford: Oxford University Press, 1997).

6. Clark, *British Societies and Clubs*. On the forms of association in Ireland, see Powell, *Politics of Consumption*, 80–89; Barnard, "Languages of Politeness"; D. Dickson, "'Centres of Motion.'"

7. Crossle and Lepper, *History*, 247.

8. D. Dickson, *Old World Colony*, 445.

9. Alexander, *Advantages*; Crombie, *Experience and Utility*.

10. Joy MSS, Linen Hall Library, Belfast, TD 2777, 5, 45.

11. Kathleen Wilson, "Urban Culture and Political Activism in Hanoverian England: The Example of Voluntary Hospitals," in *The Transformation of Political Culture: England and Germany in the Late Eighteenth Century*, ed. Eckhart Hellmuth (Oxford: Oxford University Press, 1990), 165–84.

12. Miller, "Non-Professional Soldiery," 315–34.

13. Connolly, *Religion, Law and Power*, 201–4.

14. NLI, MS 5785, 27–28, quoted in Jim O'Donovan, "The Militia in Munster, 1715–78," in O'Brien, *Parliament, Politics, and People*, 32.

15. Connolly, *Religion, Law and Power*, 136.

16. Neal Garnham, "Ireland's Protestant Militia 1715–1776: A Military Assessment," *Irish Sword* 20, no. 80 (1996): 131–36. Garnham does conclude, however, that the militias, despite their inadequacies, can be seen as part of an "unacknowledged military tradition in Ireland" (136).

17. [Joy], *Historical Collections*, 90; P. D. H. Smyth, "Volunteer Movement," 28. The main difference seems to have been that many independent companies were unregimented, and their status implied a degree of voluntary service under a local notable.

18. Eliga Gould, *The Persistence of Empire: British Political Culture in the Age of the American Revolution* (Chapel Hill: University of North Carolina Press, 2000).

19. Cummins, "Extra-Parliamentary Agitation."

20. P. D. H. Smyth, "Volunteer Movement," 41.

21. Charles Lucas, *An Address to the Right Honourable the Lord Mayor, the Worshipful the Board of Aldermen, the Sheriffs, Commons, Citizens and Freeholders of Dublin, Relating to the Intended Augmentation of the Military Force in the Kingdom of Ireland* (Dublin, 1768). Lucas also devoted considerable attention to "outrages" committed by the army in Ireland (13, 20–30). Several pamphlets were published on this issue: *Hibernia to Her Favorite Sons: A Letter on a Very Interesting and Important Occasion, the Increase of the Military Establishments of this Kingdom . . .* (Dublin, 1768); *Considerations on the Present State of the Military Establishment of this Kingdom, Addressed to the Knights, Citizens and Burgesses of Ireland, in Parliament Assembled . . .* (Dublin, 1768).

22. Alexander Haliday to A. Stewart, 20 Nov. 1771, Stewart of Ards Papers, PRONI, D/4137/a/1/7.

23. Pádraig Ó Snodaigh has drawn attention to the British context of volunteering in his "The Volunteers of '82: A Citizen Army or Armed Citizens—A Bicentennial Retrospect," *Irish Sword* 15, no. 60 (1983): 178.

24. Conway, *British Isles*, 124–25.

25. Miller, "Non-professional soldiery," 326–27; Peter Smyth, "'Our Cloud-Cap't Grenadiers': The Volunteers as a Military Force," *Irish Sword* 13 (1778–79): 185–207.

26. Conway, *British Isles*, 162–63.

27. John Cartwright to Francis Dobbs, 12 Jan. 1780, Dobbs Papers, NLI, MS 2251, fol. 27. Dobbs also corresponded with other English radicals such as John Jebb, seeking advice on, among other issues, how to proceed with the Catholic question.

28. T. Harris, *London Crowds*, 25–26.

29. J. Smyth, *Men of No Property*, 35.

30. On the martial aspect of this movement, see Eoin F. Magennis., "A 'Presbyterian Insurrection'? Reconsidering the Hearts of Oak Disturbances of July 1763," *Irish Historical Studies* 31 (1998): 178–79. On the Hearts of Steel, see J. S. Donnelly, Jr., "Hearts of Oak, Hearts of Steel," *Studia Hibernica* 21 (1981): 49.

31. Because minute books were the records of local independent forces, their survival was obviously a haphazard affair. Although many companies probably kept minute books, only a tiny proportion has survived, with a bias toward companies in the North, with some from Munster also surviving.

32. Minute Book of the First Newry Volunteers, PRONI, T/3202/1a.

33. *Charlemont MSS* (London, 1891), 1:52.

34. Joy MSS, Linen Hall Library, Belfast, TD 2777. This protocol was also followed by other companies in the North, such as the Armagh Volunteers; see P. Smyth, "Our Cloud Cap't Grenadiers," 192–93.

35. Minute Book of the First Newry Volunteers, PRONI, T/3202/1a.

36. James Hamilton to Earl of Abercorn, 19 July 1778, Abercorn Papers, PRONI, T/2541/IA2/2/41.

37. Minutes of the Free and Independent Company of Rathfriland, Ulster Museum, Belfast (hereafter cited as UM), Acc. 571, 603–1914.

38. Minutes of the Free and Independent Company of Rathfriland, UM.

39. Minutes of the Doneraile Rangers, NLI, MS 12,155.

40. T. G. F. Paterson, "The County of Armagh Volunteers of 1778–1793," *Ulster Journal of Archaeology*, 3rd ser., 5 (1942): 40. For similar resolutions, see Boyne Society, *Rules, Orders, and Regulations of the Military Corps of the Cork Boyne Society* (Cork, 1780), 4.

41. Minute Book of the First Newry Volunteers, PRONI, T/3202/1a.

42. For the distribution of these arms, see *Charlemont MSS*, 1:352–58.

43. Ibid., 1:52.

44. Ibid., 1:352. These were probably arms distributed to local militias in 1759–60 when a French invasion was feared.

45. 14 May 1780, Charlemont MS, Royal Irish Academy (hereafter cited as RIA), MS 12/R/11/52.

46. 28 Aug. 1780, Charlemont MS, RIA, MS 12/R/11/62.

47. James O'Donovan, "The Anatomy of the Volunteers in Cork, 1775–1782: Part I," *Cork Historical and Archaeological Society* 87 (1982): 34.

48. *BNL*, 6 Aug. 1779.

49. *Charlemont MSS*, 1:360.

50. Hamilton to Abercorn, 2 April 1780, Abercorn Papers, PRONI, T/2541/IA1/13/22.

51. *DEP*, 11 Feb. 1780.

52. While referred to as "the Royal Society" of Wexford Independent Volunteers, this is likely the same company, as many companies were relatively inconsistent in how they referred to themselves. *DEP*, 2 March 1780. Colclough seems to have been particularly generous in his support of the Volunteers, with

the *HJ* reporting in August 1779 that he had clothed the Enniscorthy corps for the second time. *HJ,* 16 August 1779.

53. Barrington, *Recollections,* 58.

54. Hamilton to Abercorn, 19 July 1778.

55. Abercorn Papers, PRONI, T/2541/IA1/13/10.

56. Frederick Augustus Hervey, Earl of Bristol, to John Thomas Foster, 21 May 1780, J. L. Foster Papers, RIA, MS 23/G/39.

57. *BNL,* 14 Sept. 1779; Ennis Volunteers Records and Accounts, NLI, MS 838.

58. Ennis Volunteers Records and Accounts, NLI, MS 838.

59. Miller, "Radicalism and Ritual," 196.

60. *DEP,* 14 March 1780. For similar criticisms of "aristocratic"' control over the Volunteers, see [Drennan], *Address,* 25–27.

61. *Charlemont MSS,* 1:365. Again, it seems that accepting government arms without a government commission or any form of official control was compatible with the maintenance of "independence."

62. Minute Book of the Men of Mourne [transcript], UM, Acc. 19-1914, 11.

63. Some of their expenses were met by the Earl of Inchiquin; in February 1780 they also thanked the inhabitants of Ennis for their subscription. The Newry Volunteers opened a "general subscription . . . for the purpose of laying in a stock of Powder and Ball," while most companies initiated similar systems to offset general expenses.

64. Ennis Volunteers Records and Accounts, NLI, MS 838.

65. Minute Book of the Portaferry Volunteers, Nugent Papers, PRONI, D 552/A/4/3/5.

66. *HJ,* 3–6 Sept. 1779.

67. Dorothea Herbert, *Retrospections of Dorothea Herbert* (Dublin: Town House, 1988), 57.

68. Minutes of the Free and Independent Company of Rathfriland, UM.

69. G. A. Hayes-McCoy, *A History of Irish Flags from Earliest Times* (Dublin: Irish Academic Press, 1979), 110.

70. Scott Hughes Myerly, *British Military Spectacle: From the Napoleonic Wars through the Crimea* (Cambridge, MA: Harvard University Press, 1996), 18–19, 88–89.

71. Minute Book of the Men of Mourne, UM, 1, 3, 14; Minutes of the Doneraile Rangers, NLI, MS 12,155, fol. 1.

72. P. D. H. Smyth, "Volunteer Movement," 74–75.

73. Minute Book of the Men of Mourne, UM, 8.

74. Lord Pembroke, quoted in Conway, *British Isles,* 42.

75. Minute Book of the Men of Mourne, UM, 13.

76. Ibid., 8.

77. Charlemont MS, RIA, MS 12/R/11.

78. Stephen Wood, "Gorgets of the 'Gorgeous Infantry,'" *Irish Arts Review* 3, no. 4 (1986): 49–52.

79. *DEP,* 9 Sept. 1779. In October 1779 the Second Company of Newry Volunteers was presented with colors "richly embroidered and remarkably elegant" by Isaac Corry, the local MP, followed by a ceremony to consecrate the colors, presided over by Rev. Boyle Moody. *HJ,* 25 Oct. 1779. The text of this consecration ceremony was published but the only extant copy, in the NLI, has been misplaced. Boyle Moody, *The Ceremony of Consecrating the Colours of a Regiment, as Performed by the Second Company of Newry Volunteers on . . . 16th October, 1779* (Newry, 1779).

80. *DEP,* 24 Aug. 1780.

81. For the role of women in these ceremonies and the use of female symbols on these colors, see chap. 7. In October 1779 James Spruson, painter of Hercules Lane, announced in the *BNL* that he "painted drums and colours for Volunteers in the neatest way." Quoted in Paterson, "County of Armagh Volunteers," 104–6.

82. Few of the hundreds of colors produced are extant, but some are preserved in the National Museum of Ireland, the Ulster Museum, and in local museums and churches. See F. G. Thompson, "Flags and Uniforms"; Hayes-McCoy, *History of Irish Flags,* 76–102.

83. *DEP,* 4 Sept. 1780.

84. *DEP,* 19 Oct. 1780.

85. James Hamilton to the Earl of Abercorn, 28 Dec. 1779, Abercorn Papers, PRONI, T/2541/IA2/2/118.

86. James Hamilton to the Earl of Abercorn, 5 Dec.1779, Abercorn Papers, PRONI, T/2541/IA2/2/115.

87. *Lothian MSS,* 357–58.

88. The main objections to the nomination of Hamilton (he seems to have been no relation to his proposer) was his lack of military experience and his residence in England. Stewart, on the other hand, had extensive military experience. Hamilton to Abercorn, 5 Dec. 1779.

89. *Charlemont MSS,* 1:51.

90. Abercorn Papers, PRONI, T/2541/IA/13/22.

91. William Steel Dickson, *A Narrative of the Confinement and Exile of William Steel Dickson, D.D.* (Dublin, 1812), 12. For evidence that Thomas Connolly, the Duke of Leinster, and the Earl of Shannon joined for these reasons, see their correspondence in *Lothian MSS* (London, 1905), 356–58.

92. For the Tandy-Leinster dispute, see *DEP,* March–April 1780.

93. *Lothian MSS,* 356.

94. Sir Richard Musgrave, *Memoirs of the Different Rebellions in Ireland* (Fort Wayne, IN: Round Tower Books, 1995), 43.

95. [Drennan], *Letter to Edmund Burke,* 15–16.

96. Patrick Rogers, *The Irish Volunteers and Catholic Emancipation (1778–1793): A Neglected Phase of Ireland's History* (London: Burns, Oates & Washbourne, 1934), is the most detailed study of this question.

97. *DEP,* 8 Aug. 1780.

98. Ó Snodaigh, "Class and the Irish Volunteers," *Irish Sword* 16, no. 64 (Summer 1986): 169.

99. Brendan Clifford, ed., *Scripture Politics: Selections from the Writings of William Steel Dickson* (Belfast: Belfast Historical and Educational Society, 1991), 16.

100. O'Hara Papers, NLI, MS 36,396 (1).

101. Kevin Whelan, "Politicization in County Wexford and the Origins of the 1798 Rebellion," in Gough and Dickson, *Ireland and the French Revolution,* 157–59.

102. For an account of religious tensions in County Meath, see Martyn J. Powell, "Popular Disturbances in Late Eighteenth-Century Ireland: The Origins of the Peep of Day Boys," *Irish Historical Studies* 34, no. 135 (2005): 249–65.

103. *DEP,* 10 July 1781. For another example of opposition to the arming of Catholics or the relaxation of the law, see "Manlius," *HJ,* 20 Dec. 1779.

104. *HJ,* 21 July 1779.

105. Pádraig Ó Snodaigh, "Notes on the Volunteers, Militia, Yeomanry and Orangemen of Co. Meath," *Riocht na Midhe* 6 (1978–79): 10–15.

106. *DEP,* 17 July 1781.

107. *DEP,* 7 June 1781.

108. *DEP,* 31 May 1781. By 1781 only the Volunteers of Meath and Wexford were refusing to associate with Catholics in arms. Ó Snodaigh, "Class and the Irish Volunteers," 169, 173.

109. Ó Snodaigh, "Notes on the Volunteers . . . of County Louth."

110. Robert E. Ward, John F. Wrynn, and Catherine Coogan Ward, eds., *Letters of Charles O'Conor of Belanagare: A Catholic Voice in Eighteenth-Century Ireland* (Washington, DC: Catholic University of America Press, 1988), 410.

111. Ibid., 386–87.

112. PRO, SP, 63/465, fol. 30.

113. John Caldwell, "Particulars of the History of North County Family," Caldwell Papers, PRONI, T/3541/5/3, 8.

114. Brady, *Catholics and Catholicism,* 121, 181.

115. For examples of opposition to the arming of Catholics or the relaxation of the law, see *HJ,* 20 Dec. 1779; *HJ,* 25 Aug. 1779. For criticism of the Meath Volunteers, see "Despiser of Narrow Minds," *DEP,* 14 June 1781; "Philo Patriae," *DEP,* 30 March 1780; *DEP,* 13 July 1780.

116. Guthrie, *An Improved System of Modern Geography,* 495.

Chapter 6. "Playing the Man"

1. The classic account of this period in terms of the rise of the middle class is O'Connell, *Irish Politics.*

2. Shannon Papers, PRONI, D 2707/A/2/2/49; see also Conolly Papers, NLI, MS 41,341/6.

3. Conway, *British Isles*, 199.

4. *Munster Journal*, 23 Aug. 1779, in PRO, SP, 63/466, fol. 128. The *BNL* published a prologue to the play in November 1778, but it is unclear if the play was actually performed in that town; see *BNL*, 17 Nov. 1778.

5. It was performed in Belfast during the 1775–76 season and again (as an interlude) in 1778–79 and 1779–80. John C. Greene, *Theatre in Belfast, 1736–1800* (Bethlehem, PA: Lehigh University Press, 2000), 157, 178.

6. "The Camp," in *The Dramatic Works of Richard Brinsley Sheridan*, ed. Cecil Price (Oxford: Oxford University Press, 1973), 749. Camps were established in Ireland, with a large camp at Clonmel, another at Kinsale, while other smaller camps were set up at Kilworth, Aghada, and Ardfinnan in 1779. J. A. Houlding, *Fit for Service: The Training of the British Army, 1715–1795* (Oxford: Oxford University Press, 1981), 332n19. Volunteer reviews, however, served as the main focus of militarized sociability and press interest in Ireland, with accounts of the Coxheath camp meriting more mentions in the press than Ireland's own camps.

7. *HJ*, 22 Oct. 1779. For other songs, see *WHM*, May 1783, 272.

8. *HJ*, 10 June 1779.

9. Agnew, *Drennan–McTier Letters*, 1:51.

10. This role is discussed in more detail in the next chapter.

11. *HC*, 7 June 1779. The report also described the cross-class dimensions of mobilization, suggesting that the "lower class of people" had provided support and hospitality for the regular troops who had also been celebrating the king's birthday and were on their way to Bantry Bay.

12. *HC*, 7 June 1779.

13. *HJ*, 11 June 1779; *HJ*, 23 July 1779; *BNL*, 18 June 1779.

14. *DEP*, 22 Aug. 1778.

15. James Crombie, *The Propriety of Setting Apart a Portion of the Sabbath for the Purpose of Acquiring the Knowledge and Use of Arms, in Times of Public Danger, Illustrated. A Sermon, Preached before the Belfast Volunteer Company, 4 March 1781* (Belfast, 1781), 19–20. For similar fears, see William Nevin, *The Nature and Evidence of an Over-Ruling Providence Considered. A Sermon Preached before the Downe Volunteers . . . on the 5th of September 1779* (Belfast, 1779), 28.

16. John Rogers, *A Sermon Preached at Lisnavein, Otherwise Ballybay New Erection, on Saturday, June 10. 1780 to the Lisnavein Independent Rangers, Trough Volunteers . . .* (Edinburgh, 1780), 15–16.

17. Ibid., 33.

18. Nevin, *Nature*, 28–29.

19. PRO, SP, 63/460, fol. 82.

20. PRO, SP, 63/460, fol. 328. It has recently been argued that such fears were far from groundless. See Morley, *Irish Opinion*.

21. For expressions of loyalty by the Catholic Committee in 1779, see R. D. Edwards, ed., "Minute Book of the Catholic Committee, 1773–92," *Archivium Hibernicum* 9 (1942): 40–41.

22. Ward, Wrynn, and Ward, *Letters of Charles O'Conor*, 384. For the text of the Roscommon address, see ibid., 387–88.

23. PRO, SP, 63/460, fol. 56. This address was signed by twenty-four Catholics.

24. PRO, SP, 63/460, fol. 139.

25. PRO, SP, 63/462, fol. 24.

26. *BNL*, 6 Aug. 1779.

27. PRO, SP, 63/463, fol. 9. See also PRO, SP, 63/462, fol. 20, for an address in April 1778 from the "Roman Catholics of Ireland" with over three hundred signatures, which was also published in the *London Gazette*.

28. For an account of O'Leary's colorful career, see James Kelly, "'A Wild Capuchin of Cork': Arthur O'Leary (1729–1802)," in *Radical Irish Priests, 1660–1970*, ed. Gerard Moran (Dublin: Four Courts Press, 1998), 39–61.

29. *BNL*, 7 Sept. 1779. O' Leary's pamphlet on this subject was titled *An Address to the Common People of the Roman Catholic Religion, Concerning the Apprehended French Invasion* (Cork, 1779). This address went through two editions in 1779 and was reprinted again in 1781.

30. For accounts of lavish hospitality, see Robert Bell, *A Description of the Condition and Manners, as well as of the Moral and Political Character of the Peasantry of Ireland such as they were between the Years 1780 and 1790* (London, 1804), 35; Thomas Campbell, *Philosophical Survey of the South of Ireland in a Series of Letters to John Wilkinson* (London, 1777), 42; Barnard, "Languages of Politeness and Sociability," 203–10.

31. Young, *Tour of Ireland*, 2:155.

32. Powell, *Politics of Consumption*, 12–13.

33. On dueling and concepts of honor, see James Kelly, *'That Damn'd Thing Called Honour': Duelling in Ireland, 1570–1860* (Cork: Cork University Press, 1995). Little attention has been paid to masculinity in an Irish context. For changing notions of masculinity in England, see Hitchcock and Cohen, *English Masculinities*; R. Shoemaker, "Male Honour and the Decline of Public Violence in Eighteenth-Century London," *Social History* 26, no. 2 (May 2001): 190–208.

34. *DEP*, 27 May 1780.

35. J. Kelly, *Duelling in Ireland*, 158–67. Patrick Guinness, "'Man being in his natural state the most naked and helpless of all creatures': The Meeting Book of the Kildare Knot of the Friendly Brothers of St Patrick, 1758–1791," *Journal of the County Kildare Archaeological Society* 19 (2000–2001): 116–50.

36. J. Kelly, *Duelling in Ireland*, 127–28.

37. Ann Blair to James Blair, Blair Papers, PRONI, D/717/11; Barrington, *Personal Sketches*; J. Kelly, *Duelling in Ireland*, 139–47.

38. *Volunteer's Journal* (Dublin), 29 Oct. 1783; J. Kelly, *Duelling in Ireland*, 134–37.

39. For Volunteer involvement in antidueling societies, see Guinness, "Meeting Book of the Kildare Knot," 122. In June 1783, for example, a duel was

fought between Volunteers at Killala over a slight that occurred during the election of officers, and many such incidences occurred among Volunteers; see Notes on the Irish Volunteers and the Irish Military Returns ca. 1769–1783, PRONI, T/963.

40. Preston, *Contrast*; Edwards, *Patriot Soldier*.

41. Alexander, *Advantages*, 24–25.

42. *HJ*, 8 Sept. 1779.

43. Agnew, *Drennan–McTier Letters*, 1:2, 87.

44. [William Drennan], *An Address to the Volunteers of Ireland by the Author of a Letter to Edmund Burke Esq., Containing Reflections on Patriotism, Party Spirit, and the Unity of Free Nations* (Dublin, 1781), 33.

45. William Todd Jones, MP for the Borough of Lisburn, "letter to the Irish Volunteers Reviewed at Belfast on the 12th of July 1784," NLI, MS 10,539.

46. J. Rogers, *Sermon Preached at Lisnavein*; Carson, *Discourse*. Both sermons also share a concern with the dangers of popery, with Rogers citing Carson's sermon in support of his own virulent anti-Catholicism. J. Rogers, *Sermon Preached at Lisnavein*, 24. Rogers and Carson were both prominent seceders. Rogers also opposed the relaxation of the penal laws against Catholics at Dungannon. On the importance of Volunteer sermons, see McBride, *Scripture Politics*, 127–29.

47. Alexander Maclaine, *A Sermon Preached at Antrim, December 18, 1745 Being the National Fast* (Dublin, 1746); Gabriel Stokes, *Love of Our Country, Distinguished From False Pretences; a Sermon, Preached in the Cathedral of Waterford, January 15th, 1797* (Dublin, 1797). This passage from Samuel was also quoted by Alexander, *Advantages*, 28. Men in colonial New England were also frequently exhorted to "play the men" by ministers, particularly during the American Revolution. Lombard, *Making Manhood*, 9, 166; William Linn, *A Military Discourse, Delivered in Carlisle, March the 17th, 1776, to Colonel Irvine's Battalion of Regulars, and a Very Respectable Number of the Inhabitants* (Philadelphia, 1776).

48. Crombie used a similar passage describing the same incident from 2 Chron. 14:13, in *Propriety*, 7.

49. Carson, *Discourse*, 13.

50. Ibid., 6–7.

51. Ibid., 9.

52. Ibid., 13–14.

53. Ibid., 15.

54. Ibid., 22.

55. Ibid., 19.

56. Ibid., 20.

57. Ibid., 22.

58. Alexander, *Advantages*, 12.

59. For the important and contested place of the siege of Derry in Protestant memory, see Jim Smyth, "Siege, Myth and History: Derry, 1688–1998," in *The*

Sieges of Derry, ed. William Kelly (Dublin: Four Courts Press, 2001), 18–30; Ian R. McBride, *The Siege of Derry in Ulster Protestant Mythology* (Dublin: Four Courts Press, 1997).

60. Alexander, *Advantages*, 20.

61. J. Rogers, *Sermon Preached at Lisnavein*, 28.

62. Ibid., 25–26.

63. Alexander, *Advantages*, 13.

64. Ibid., 6.

65. Ibid., 7–8.

66. Rev. Francis Turner, *A Constitutional Sermon: Preached on Sunday, the 7th of November, 1779, in the Parish Church of Killrush, before the Enniscorthy Buffs* (Wexford, 1779); idem, *A Sermon Preached by the Rev. Francis Turner, A.B. on Sunday, the 8th of August, 1784, in the Cathedral of Ferns, before the Enniscorthy Buffs, Commanded by Colonel Phaire* (Dublin, 1784), 5–6, 22. For a conservative sermon on free trade, see Robert Law, *The Moral Duties Necessary to Secure the Advantages of a Free Trade with a Caution Against Some Abuses to Which the Beginnings of Manufactures and Commerce are Peculiarly Exposed* (Dublin, 1780).

67. *DEP*, 11 March 1780.

68. *The Volunteer*, 12 June 1781. Fintan Cullen has noted the influence of images of the heroes of the American War of Independence disseminated in Ireland on the portrayal of the Volunteers. F. Cullen, *Visual Politics*, 63.

69. Grattan, *Memoirs*, 2:124.

70. For the importance of clothing in portraiture, see T. H. Breen, "The Meaning of 'Likeness': American Portrait Painting in an Eighteenth-Century Consumer Society," *Word & Image* 6 (Oct.–Dec. 1990): 325–50.

71. David Kuchta, *The Three-Piece Suit And Modern Masculinity: England, 1550–1850* (Berkeley: University of California Press, 2002), 7.

72. Eileen Black, "Volunteer Portraits."

73. *DEP*, 4 Aug. 1778; Brady, *Catholics and Catholicism*, 190.

74. Dobbs, *History of Irish Affairs*, 37.

75. *Volunteer's Journal* (Dublin), 21 July 1784. The paper also suggested that no Volunteer "ought to have a British crown over an Irish harp on breastplates, buttons, drums or colours." On the relationship between the Volunteers and "cultural nationalism," see Mary Helen Thuente, *The Harp Re-strung: The United Irishmen and the Rise of Irish Literary Nationalism* (Syracuse, NY: Syracuse University Press, 1994). On the use of the color green as a nationalist symbol in the 1790s, see Curtin, *United Irishmen*, 249–50.

76. *DEP*, 13 July 1780.

77. For this earlier tradition and connections with the Volunteers, see *BNL*, 20 April 1778; Joy MSS, Linen Hall Library, Belfast, TD 2777, 4, 101.

78. *BNL*, 30 July 1779.

79. *DEP*, 16 March 1780; *DEP*, 23 March 1780.

80. Herbert, *Retrospections*, 59.

81. Leadbetter Diary, NLI, MS 9305.

82. *FLJ*, 5 Feb. 1780. Volunteers turned out not only for funerals of fellow soldiers. In 1781 large numbers attended the funeral of Mrs. Matthews, who may have been the wife of one of their number. *DEP*, 3 July 1781.

83. Scrope Bernard Papers, PRONI, T/2627/6/1/21. For more descriptions of funerals, see T. G. F. Paterson, "The Volunteer Companies of Ulster," *Irish Sword*, no. 7 (1965–66): 96, 101, 103, 109, 113; no. 8 (1967–68): 216–17.

84. *DEP*, 26 June 1779. See also *DEP*, 27 July 1779.

85. *DEP*, 3 July 1779.

86. Rev. Samuel Butler, *A Sermon Preached in the Parish Church of St. Michan, Dublin, on Sunday the 17th day of October 1779* (Dublin, 1779), 8.

87. *DEP*, 27 Aug. 1778. The author also suggested that religious divisions were a central aspect of the dispute, claiming the reverend was a "friend of the papists."

88. *A Defence of the Armed Societies of Ireland with Respect to their Legality* (Cork, 1779), 7

89. [Jebb and Johnson], *Thoughts on the Discontents*, 6–7.

90. *A Volunteer's Queries, in Spring, 1780; humbly offered to the consideration of all descriptions of men in Ireland* (Dublin, 1780), 14.

91. *HJ*, 22 Oct. 1779.

92. *FJ*, 27 March 1779.

93. Francis Dobbs, *Thoughts on Volunteers* (Dublin, 1781), 11–12.

94. Joy MSS, Linen Hall Library, TD 2777, 4, 46–47.

95. Alexander, *Advantages*, 22. For similar claims, see Crombie, *Propriety*, 33–34.

96. *BNL*, 9 Nov. 1779. This debate over the reforming power of the Volunteers can be seen as part of a more general concern with the reform of popular culture in late eighteenth-century Europe. Peter Burke, *Popular Culture in Early Modern Europe* (New York: New York University Press, 1978), chap. 8.

Chapter 7. Petticoat Government

1. For a similar account of these paintings, see Mary O'Dowd, "The Women in the Gallery: Women and Politics in Eighteenth-Century Ireland," in *From the United Irishmen to Twentieth-Century Unionism: Essays in Honour of A. T. Q. Stewart*, ed. Sabine Wichert (Dublin: Four Courts Press, 2004), 35–47.

2. Kathleen Wilson, *The Island Race: Englishness, Empire, and Gender in the Eighteenth Century* (New York: Routledge, 2002), 93. Wilson is reacting to studies examining the role of women in Georgian Britain that have attacked the idea of a division between public and private spheres as a mere ideological construction belied by the actual experience of women. For an influential statement of

this argument, see Amanda Vickery, "Golden Age to Separate Spheres? A Review of the Categories and Chronology of English Women's History," *Historical Journal* 36, no. 2 (June 1993): 383–414.

3. Anthony John Fletcher, *Gender, Sex and Subordination in England, 1500–1800* (New Haven, CT: Yale University Press, 1995).

4. Daire Keogh and Nicholas Furlong, eds., *The Women of 1798* (Dublin: Four Courts Press, 1998); C. Kennedy, "Womanish Epistles."

5. Jacqueline Hill, "Convergence and Conflict in Eighteenth-Century Ireland," *Historical Journal* 44, no. 4 (Dec. 2001): 1046; O'Dowd, *History of Women in Ireland*, 43–61. The social and economic history of women in eighteenth-century Ireland has received attention in recent years, particularly in the work of James Kelly. Rosemary Raughter has examined the role of Protestant and Catholic women in charitable activities. See MacCurtain and O'Dowd, *Women in Early Modern Ireland*.

6. Kathleen Wilson, "Citizenship, Empire, and Modernity in the English Provinces, c. 1720–1790," *Eighteenth-Century Studies* 29, no. 1 (Fall 1996): 78.

7. Linda K. Kerber, *Women of the Republic: Intellect and Ideology in Revolutionary America* (Chapel Hill: University of North Carolina Press, 1980), 54.

8. Conway, *British Isles*, 86–93.

9. K. Wilson, "Citizenship, Empire, and Modernity," 78–79.

10. Joan Scott, "Experience," in *Feminists Theorize the Political*, ed. Judith Butler and Joan W. Scott (London: Routledge, 1992), 22–40; Epstein, *In Practice*.

11. For an overview of attitudes to women's involvement in politics, see Kerber, *Women of the Republic*, chap. 1.

12. William Crawford, *The Connection Between Courage and the Moral Virtues Considered in a Sermon Preached Before the Volunteer Company of Strabane Rangers, Sunday 12th Sept 1779* (Strabane, 1779), 16–17.

13. Agnew, *Drennan–McTier Letters*, 1:87, emphasis in original.

14. Nancy Curtin, "Women"; idem, "Nation of Abortive Men."

15. Preston, *Contrast*, 22. For a similar account of women's patriotism, inspired by classical examples, see Edwards, *Patriot Soldier*, 25–27.

16. [Joy], *Historical Collections*, 289.

17. *The Triumph of Prudence over Passion: Or the History of Miss Mortimer and Miss Fitzgerald by the Authoress of Emeline* (Dublin, 1781), 16–17.

18. Ibid., 5.

19. For the role of elite women in electoral politics, see Gearoid Ó Tuathaigh, "The Role of Women in Ireland under the New English Order," in *Women in Irish Society*, ed. Margaret MacCurtain and Donnch Ó Corrain (Westport, CT: Greenwood Press, 1979); Peter J. Jupp, "The Role of Royal and Aristocratic Women in British Politics, c. 1782–1832," in *Chattel, Servant or Citizen: Women's Status in Church, State and Society*, ed. Mary O'Dowd and Sabine Wichert (Belfast: Queen's University Press, 1995), 103–13. For work on women and politics in Britain, see Hannah Barker and Elaine Chalus, eds., *Gender in Eighteenth-Century*

England (London: Longman, 1997); Kathryn Gleadle and Sarah Richardson, eds., *Women in British Politics, 1760–1860: The Power of the Petticoat* (London: Macmillan, 2000).

20. Agnew, *Drennan–McTier Letters*, 1:127.

21. [Joy], *Historical Collections*, 251.

22. T. C. Barnard, "Considering the Inconsiderable: Elections, Patrons and Irish Elections, 1659–1761," in *The Irish Parliament in the Eighteenth Century: The Long Apprenticeship*, ed. D. W. Hayton (Edinburgh: Edinburgh University Press, 2001), 115.

23. *VEP*, 4 Dec. 1783.

24. O'Dowd, *History of Women in Ireland*, 48–9; Elaine Chalus, "Elite Women, Social Politics, and the Political World of Late Eighteenth-Century England," *Historical Journal* 43, no. 3 (Sept. 2000): 669–97.

25. *Petticoat Government, Exemplified in a Late Case in Ireland* (London, 1780), 1. For further details of this dispute, see PRONI, MIC/639/2, which includes a manuscript version of the pamphlet; PRONI, T/3075/4/84. Robert Day is suggested as the author by the calendar of the Fitzgerald Papers in the PRONI.

26. *Petticoat Government*, 2.

27. Ibid., 15, 11, 25.

28. Ann Blair to James Blair, 1774, Blair Papers, PRONI, D/717/4.

29. [Joy], *Historical Collections*, 133–36.

30. Ibid., 135.

31. McBride, *Scripture Politics*, 134–44; Jacqueline Hill, *From Patriots to Unionists*, 153–56.

32. Agnew, *Drennan–McTier Letters*, 1:79–81.

33. For a general account of women's bodies as symbols, see Marina Warner, *Monuments and Maidens: The Allegory of the Female Form* (New York: Atheneum, 1985).

34. Belinda Loftus, *Mirrors: William III & Mother Ireland* (Dundrum: Picture Press, 1990), 52–58.

35. Mary Helen Thuente, "The Origin and Significance of the Angel Harp," in *Back to the Present, Forward to the Past: Irish Writing and History since 1798*, ed. Patricia A. Lynch, Joachim Fischer, and Brian Coates (Amsterdam: Rodopi, 2006), 230–57.

36. This flag is held at the County Museum, Armagh, Northern Ireland.

37. Joan Landes, *Visualizing the Nation: Gender, Representation, and Revolution in Eighteenth-Century France* (Ithaca, NY: Cornell University Press, 2001), 79.

38. *DEP*, 1 July 1779.

39. *FJ*, 1 June 1780.

40. Stephens and George, *Catalogue*, 5:6002.

41. Lewis Perry Curtis, "The Four Erins: Feminine Images of Ireland, 1780–1900," *Éire-Ireland* 33, no. 3/4–34, no. 1 (1998): 70–102. See, for example, "Hibernia in Distress," which depicts Hibernia, her harp broken, being trampled on by

Lord North and other English politicians as they drain the Irish exchequer. Stephens and George, *Catalogue*, 5:4942.

42. Stephens and George, *Catalogue*, 5:5653. The female personifications of nations in the eighteenth century were frequently sexualized; see, for example, K. Wilson, *Sense of the People*, 223–24.

43. *DEP*, 11 May 1780.

44. The image of a dignified and proud Hibernia emerges during the 1750s, which paralleled the development of the female personifications of Britain and America. Loftus, *Mirrors*, 52–54.

45. Landes, *Visualizing the Nation*, 9.

46. Mary Helen Thuente has also observed that the Volunteers used both heroic and pathetic images of Hibernia. Thuente, "Liberty, Hibernia, and Mary Le More," in Keogh and Furlong, *Women of 1798*, 14. See also Loftus, *Mirrors*, 52.

47. Quotation from Joy MSS, Linen Hall Library, TD 2777, 4, 178. Agnew, *Drennan–McTier Letters*, 1:51.

48. Edwards, *Patriot Soldier*, 25.

49. Grattan, *Memoirs*, 2:124.

50. *DEP*, 5 April 1781.

51. *DEP*, 24 Aug. 1780.

52. Burke, "Revolutionary Prelude."

53. *Saunder's Newsletter*, 24 April 1780.

54. *DEP*, 4 Nov. 1779; *Magee's Weekly Packet*, 6 Nov. 1779.

55. "The Camp," 705-50.

56. Mary Webster, *Francis Wheatley* (London: Routledge, 1970), 40–41. For a more detailed discussion of this painting, see O'Dowd, "Women in the Gallery," 44–45. Wheatley's career in Ireland is discussed in James Kelly, "Francis Wheatley: His Irish paintings, 1779–83," in Dalsimer, *Visualizing Ireland*; F. Cullen, *Visual Politics*.

57. For this fashion, see Ribeiro, *Art of Dress*.

58. *BNL*, 7 Aug. 1778.

59. "Frolic, or the Female Volunteers," advertisement in *HJ*, 19 Jan. 1780. It is not evident if this print was produced locally or imported from London, though there is no print of this title in Stephens and George, *Catalogue*.

60. Dror Wahrman, "Percy's Prologue: From Gender Play to Gender Panic in Eighteenth-Century England," *Past and Present* 159 (May 1998): 113–60; Dianne Dugaw, *Warrior Women and Popular Balladry, 1650–1850* (Cambridge: Cambridge University Press, 1989), 143–62. See also William Preston, *The Female Congress; or, the Temple of Cotytto: A Mock Heroic Poem* (Dublin, 1779).

61. *WHM*, June 1780, 338.

62. Song on the Volunteers, printed for *Exshaw's Magazine*.

63. Gillian Russell, *The Theatres of War: Performance, Politics, and Society, 1793–1815* (Oxford: Clarendon Press, 1995), 39–41.

64. [William Drennan], "Notes on Volunteers," Drennan Papers, PRONI, T/965/6b.

65. Dobbs, *History of Irish Affairs*, 37.

66. For a similar argument about such conventional descriptions of cross-dressing on the English stage, see Wahrman, "Percy's Prologue," 122–23.

67. *FDJ*, 5 June 1781, quoted in O'Connell, *Irish Politics*, 94.

68. *The Manual Exercise* (Monaghan, n.d.).

69. *VEP*, 4 Dec. 1783. For another satire on political association of women, caused by the emergency of the war, see "Plan to set up Belle Assemble," *DEP*, 23 Feb. 1781; and "The Female Parliament," *WHM*, 1782, 191–92.

70. *VEP*, 24 Feb. 1784.

71. For an account of a similar change in attitudes in England in the early 1780s, see Wahrman, "Percy's Prologue."

72. For a critique of this narrative, see Vickery, "Golden Age to Separate Spheres?"

73. Clare Midgley makes some reference to the Irish context in her "Slave Sugar Boycotts." See also Nini Rodgers, "Two Quakers and a Utilitarian: The Reaction of Three Irish Women Writers to the Problem of Slavery, 1789–1807, *Proceedings of the Royal Irish Academy* 100, no. 4, C (2000): 137–57; and Kevin O'Neill, "Mary Shackleton Leadbetter: Peaceful Rebel," in Keogh and Furlong, *Women of 1798*, 137–62.

74. Thomas Bartlett, "Bearing Witness: Female Evidences in Court Martials Convened to Suppress the 1798 Rebellion," in Keogh and Furlong, *Women of 1798*, 64–68; John Beatty, ed., *Protestant Women's Narratives of the Irish Rebellion of 1798* (Dublin: Four Courts Press, 2001). For women and loyalism in Britain in the 1790s, see Colley, *Britons*.

Chapter 8. "A Democratical Spirit"

1. Auckland Papers, British Library (hereafter cited as BL), Add. MSS 34,4119, fols. 396–97, 402–3. Cooke was secretary to the chief secretary and also held the office of clerk of the stationery stores under the Duke of Rutland. He went on to become an influential undersecretary.

2. Dobbs, *History of Irish Affairs*, 46–48.

3. It has been estimated that the 143 corps represented were just less than half of the total number of corps active in Ulster at this time, though this meeting was still the largest representative body assembled in the country; see James Kelly, "The Politics of Volunteering, 1778–93," *Irish Sword* 22, no. 88 (2000): 147–48.

4. C. H. Wilson, *A Compleat Collection of the Resolutions of the Volunteers, Grand Juries &c. of Ireland* (Dublin, 1782), 1–3.

5. These resolutions were not spontaneous but rather drawn up in advance by Francis Dobbs and Joseph Pollock, with the blessing of Lord Charlemont,

while leading parliamentary patriots Flood and Grattan also had a hand in determining the agenda. Dobbs, *History of Irish Affairs*, 51–53.

6. Many of these resolutions were collected and published by C. H. Wilson the same year. The similarity in the language of many of the resolutions suggests a coordinated campaign to gather support for the Dungannon resolutions. See, for example, C. H. Wilson, *Compleat Collection*, 10, 26, 33.

7. See, for example, ibid., 85–86, 10, 59–60, 90

8. PRO, HO, 100/1, fol. 19.

9. For conflict in Waterford, see C. H. Wilson, *Compleat Collection*, 72–73, 135–36; PRO, HO, 100/1, fol. 3.

10. PRO, HO, 100/1, fol. 3.

11. Ibid.

12. The resolutions are collected in C. H. Wilson, *Compleat Collection*, 144–47. For the structure of politics in Tipperary, see Thomas P. Power, *Land, Politics, and Society in Eighteenth-Century Tipperary* (Oxford: Oxford University Press, 1993), chap. 7.

13. Powell, *Britain and Ireland*, 208–15.

14. McBride, *Scripture Politics*, 131–32.

15. Dobbs, *History of Irish Affairs*, 84.

16. Clifford, *William Drennan*, 2:35.

17. Ibid., 2:42–43.

18. Dobbs, *History of Irish Affairs*, 138.

19. Ibid., 152–9.

20. Ibid., 83.

21. [Joy], *Historical Collections*, 209–12.

22. Beresford, *Correspondence*, 1:221–22.

23. Morley, *Irish Opinion*, 307.

24. G. A. Hayes-McCoy, "Fencible Corps in Ireland, 1782–1803," *Irish Sword*, no. 2 (1955): 140–43.

25. *Charlemont MSS*, 1:76.

26. [Joy], *Historical Collections*, 216. The Belfast Volunteers lent their support to the Galway resolutions.

27. Ibid., 221.

28. Ennis Volunteers Records and Accounts, NLI, MS 838. The Ennis Volunteers had supported the Dungannon resolutions in 1782 though in relatively moderate language. C. H. Wilson, *Compleat Collection*, 55.

29. Paterson, "County of Armagh Volunteers," 105. See also Minutes of the Doneraile Rangers, NLI, MS 12,155.

30. *FJ*, 24 Sept. 1782; *FJ*, 29 Oct. 1782.

31. P. D. H. Smyth, "The Volunteers and Parliament, 1779–1784," in *Penal Era and Golden Age: Essays in Irish History, 1690–1800*, ed. T. Bartlett and D. W. Hayton (Belfast: Ulster Historical Foundation, 1979), 128n62.

32. [Joy], *Historical Collections*, 231.

33. Clifford, *William Drennan*, 2:51. Drennan was abroad for much of the dispute and adopted a neutral position in public, though his letters show he opposed the scheme.

34. For a sympathetic but humorous account of Dobbs's trials over the renunciation issue, see Clifford, *William Drennan*, 2:35–45.

35. *Charlemont MSS*, 1:77. For more personal reasons for joining, see the case of Sam McTier, related in Agnew, *Drennan–McTier Letters*, 1:65

36. Clifford, *William Drennan*, 2:51.

37. Recent accounts of this bill suggest that it was actually a "recognition" of the status quo at the time of the repeal of the Declaratory Act. Powell, *Britain and Ireland*, 226.

38. On the concept of the antiparliament, see Parssinen, "Association."

39. Reform, in the broadest sense, has received renewed attention. See Arthur Burns and Joanna Innes, eds., *Rethinking the Age of Reform* (Cambridge: Cambridge University Press, 2003). For reform in an Irish context, see T. C. Barnard, "Reforming Irish Manners: The Religious Societies in Dublin during the 1690s," *Historical Journal* 35, no. 4 (Dec. 1992): 805–38.

40. J. Smyth, *Men of No Property*, 81.

41. Ibid., 96.

42. James Kelly, "Parliamentary Reform in Irish Politics: 1760–90," in Dickson, Keogh, and Whelan, *United Irishmen*, 74–78.

43. NLI, MS 2251.

44. P. D. H. Smyth, "Volunteer Movement," chap. 8; McBride, *Scripture Politics*, 134–39.

45. [Joy], *Historical Collections*, 250–51.

46. *Historical Account*.

47. McBride, *Scripture Politics*, 138–39.

48. [Drennan], *Letter to Edmund Burke*, 15–16.

49. On the necessary personal qualities, see Agnew, *Drennan–McTier Letters*, 1:82.

50. On these provincial meetings, see *Proceedings Relative to Ulster Assembly of Volunteer Delegates* (Belfast, 1783); *The History of the Proceedings and Debates of the Volunteer Delegates of Ireland on the Subject of Parliamentary Reform* (Dublin, 1784).

51. *Volunteer's Journal* (Dublin), 5 Nov. 1783.

52. PRO, HO, 100/12, fol. 152, 4 March 1784.

53. Other petitions were presented by corporations, and though the petition from Newry mentioned that the "inhabitants" of the town were present, the rest clearly identify their legitimate right to petition parliament on reform. *Journals of the House of Commons of the Kingdom of Ireland*, 19 vols. (Dublin, 1796–1800), 21:447–84 (hereafter cited as *JHC*). *JHC* records the receipt of petitions and their subject, but not the actual language of the documents.

54. PRO, HO, 100/12, fol. 190. For a similar petition from County Down freeholders, see *Volunteer's Journal* (Dublin), 9 Jan. 1784.

55. *JHC,* 21:459. Counterpetitions were received from Kilkenny, Cork, and Down.

56. Earl of Hillsborough, 11 Feb. 1784, Pelham Papers, BL, Add. MSS 33,101, fol. 50.

57. P. D. H. Smyth, "Volunteer Movement," 186–87.

58. PRO, HO, 100/13, fol. 44.

59. PRO, HO, 100/13, fol. 180.

60. Jacqueline Hill, *From Patriots to Unionists.*

61. Similar developments were under way in London around the same time. See Barker, *Newspapers,* chap. 3.

62. PRO, HO, 100/13, fol. 187.

63. PRO, HO, 100/14, fols. 58, 66. Though the petition was rejected, a copy was forwarded to the king and to Pitt. Other petitions were sent to the king from Tipperary, Sligo, and Dublin County. PRO, HO, 100/14, fols. 108–9, 131–32, 139. In September the government circulated its own petitions at county meetings. See PRO, HO, 100/14, fols. 123, 127. On the Belfast petition, see [Joy], *Historical Collections,* 315.

64. PRO, HO, 100/14, fol. 102.

65. PRO, HO, 100/14, fol. 105.

66. J. Smyth, *Men of No Property,* 138; PRO, HO, 100/14, fols. 147–48; Jacqueline Hill, *From Patriots to Unionists,* 179.

67. *A Reform of the Irish House of Commons Considered* (Dublin, 1783), 22–23. English antireform literature was republished in Dublin to buttress local output. *Thoughts on a Parliamentary Reform* (London and Dublin, 1784).

68. Barker, *Newspapers,* 176.

69. *Reform of the Irish House,* 23.

70. *VEP,* 5 Feb. 1784.

71. For these gendered attacks on reform, see chapter 7.

72. *VEP,* 7 Nov. 1783.

73. *VEP,* 29 Nov. 1783. The letters of the "Dungannon Delegate" were published along with replies from a "Munster Delegate" as *Letters of a Dungannon and Munster Delegate, which appeared shortly after the plan of Parliamentary reform, proposed by the Grand National Convention* (Dublin, 1784). Stephen Small has examined this pamphlet as an example of the "inherent tensions in radicalism," but it seems the pamphlet is actually opposed to any sort of radical reform. The writer attacks the resolutions of the convention in order to discredit reform, and much of the tone is mocking rather than laudatory. The publication of these letters in the *VEP* also supports the notion that they are hardly examples of radical reformism. Small, *Political Thought in Ireland,* 123, 131.

74. *VEP,* 1 Jan. 1784.

75. *VEP,* 5 Feb. 1784.

76. *Reform of the Irish House of Commons Considered,* 28.

77. The key role played by northern Presbyterians in this conspiracy and their republican tendency was central to much antireform writing. See, for example, *Reform of the Irish House of Commons Considered*. For the importance of Presbyterians to the reform movement, see McBride, *Scripture Politics*, chap. 6.

78. *The Alarm; or, an Address to the Nobility, Gentry, and Clergy of the Church of Ireland as by Law Established* (Dublin, 1783), 3–10.

79. *Volunteer's Journal* (Dublin), 6 Aug. 1784.

80. *Volunteer's Journal* (Dublin), 13 Aug. 1784; *Volunteer's Journal* (Dublin), 20 Aug. 1784.

81. *Voice of the People*, 33.

82. [Burrowes], *Plain Arguments*, 41, 44.

83. Ibid., 55.

84. Ibid., 57.

85. William Todd Jones, "letter to the Irish Volunteers," NLI, MS 10,539.

86. William Todd Jones, *Letter to the Electors of the Borough of Lisburn* (Dublin, 1784), 19.

87. "Memmius" also argued for a tradition of Catholic liberty through an appeal to history, such as the "continental democracies" as well as the records of Aragon and Castile. *Voice of the People*, 33.

88. Jones, *Letter to the Electors*, 33.

89. Ibid., 41. Jones also argues that under James II, it was Irish Catholics who had first demanded an Irish bill of rights, and a repeal of Poyning's Law, again anticipating modern patriot concerns. Ibid., 47.

90. Ibid., 25.

91. P. Rogers, *Irish Volunteers and Catholic Emancipation*.

92. McBride, *Scripture Politics*, 152–60.

93. *Thoughts on the Conduct and Continuation of the Volunteers of Ireland* (Dublin, 1783), 20.

94. *Alarm*, 23.

95. PRO, HO, 100/13, fol. 79; *Rutland MSS.*, 4 vols. (London, 1888–1905), 3:93.

96. McBride makes a similar point; see his *Scripture Politics*, 157.

97. Minute Book of the First Newry Volunteers, PRONI, T/3202/1a.

98. PRO, HO, 100/14, fol. 195.

99. Dean of Armagh to George Hamilton, 20 Oct. 1784, Bolton Papers, NLI, MS 16,350, fol. 47. Blackhall was an agent for the Cope estate at Portnorris. Miller, "Politicization in Revolutionary Ireland," 1–17.

100. "Methodized Abridgement of the Conduct of the Several Counties of Ireland in regard to Requisitions, Meetings, Delegates, Volunteers etc," Bolton Papers, NLI, MS 15,958 (1).

101. The report is not consistent in mentioning whether Catholics have been recruited in a county. Of those mentioned, Donegal, Derry, Tyrone, Louth, Down, Roscommon, Leitrim, Galway, Kings County, Dublin, Queens County,

Carlow, Kilkenny, Limerick, and Cork, were said to have sizable numbers of Catholic Volunteers. Antrim was said to have few, and Armagh none at all. No mention is made of the denominational makeup of companies in Cavan, Longford, Westmeath, Meath, Kildare, Wicklow, Wexford, Waterford, Tipperary, Clare, or Kerry. According to Ó Snodaigh, in "Notes on the Volunteers, Militia, Yeomanry, and Orangemen of County Cavan," *Breifne* 3, no. 11 (1968): 320–39, Catholics were being admitted in both Meath and Cavan at this stage, and even earlier in Kerry and Longford. No returns were made in the report for Mayo, Fermanagh, or Monaghan.

102. *Volunteer's Journal* (Dublin), 20 Aug. 1784.

103. *The Parliamentary Register; or, History of the Proceedings and Debates of the House of Commons of Ireland* (Dublin, 1784–95), 4:41.

104. *VEP,* May 1784; J. Kelly, "Select Documents XLIII," 272.

105. *Observations on the Parliamentary Conduct of John Foster,* 34–35.

106. *Fortescue MSS* (London, 1892), 1:239.

107. *Rutland MSS,* 3:124.

108. PRO, SP, 63/469, fol. 120; *WHM* (1784), 553–56.

109. Robert Day, August 1784, Talbot-Crosbie Papers, NLI, MS 2054.

110. Bolton Papers, NLI, MS 16,350, fol. 66.

111. James Kelly, "The Irish Parliamentary Reform Movement: The Administration and Popular Politics, 1783–85" (MA thesis, University College Dublin, 1981), 209–10; Jacqueline Hill, *From Patriots to Unionists,* 177.

112. PRO, HO, 100/14, fol. 87.

113. PRO, HO, 100/9, fol. 58. Reports suggest that such problems were not confined to the capital. The price of oats and oatmeal increased drastically in the North, while food riots occurred in Clonmel. PRO, HO, 100/12, fols. 71–74.

114. Jacqueline Hill, *From Patriots to Unionists,* 172–73.

115. *An Essay on the Necessity of Protecting Duties* (Dublin, 1783), 11.

116. *Volunteer's Journal* (Dublin), 20 Aug. 1784.

117. PRO, HO, 100/10, fol. 284. This crowd had apparently been called out by the beadle of St. Catherine's parish by the ringing of a bell; see PRO, HO, 100/10, fol. 291.

118. John Beresford to Eden, Dublin, 15 April 1784, Auckland Papers, BL, Add. MSS 34,419, fols. 387–88. Beresford noted that rumors were circulating of a plan to kill John Foster, the chancellor of the exchequer, and several other leading politicians.

119. PRO, HO, 100/12, fol. 268.

120. *Rutland MSS,* vol. 3, 14, I, 86–87; Beresford, *Correspondence,* 1:255; PRO, HO, 100/12, fol. 268.

121. Thomas Bernard, bishop of Killaloe, 8 May 1784, Heron Papers, NLI, MS 13,047 (3). Many members of the administration held similar views about conspiracies in 1784.

122. Only John Beresford seems to have raised doubts about the existence of

a wide-ranging conspiracy supported by America and France. Auckland Papers, BL, Add. MSS 34,419, fols. 411–12.

123. The use of political cartoons was itself a relatively novel feature in Irish newspapers. Carey was obviously proud of this particular publication. In his new career in Philadelphia, he published the pamphlet *The Plagi-Scurriliad* with a frontispiece depicting the author holding this notorious edition of the paper.

124. *JHC*, 21:548–49.

125. PRO, HO, 100/12, fol. 268.

126. PRO, HO, 100/12, fol. 287. On the uncovering of what seems to have been an actual conspiracy that hints at a determined and violent political underworld among Dublin artisans, located in the largely Catholic weaving districts, see PRO, HO, 100/12, fol. 291; PRO, HO, 100/12, fols. 309–13.

127. *Volunteer's Journal* (Dublin), 29 Dec. 1783.

128. *Volunteer's Journal* (Dublin), 5 April 1784; *Volunteer's Journal* (Dublin), 16 July 1784; *Volunteer's Journal* (Dublin), 19 July 1784; *Volunteer's Journal* (Dublin), 13 Aug. 1784; PRO, HO, 100/13, fol. 180.

129. *Cork Evening Post* (hereafter cited as *CEP*), 15 April 1784.

130. *CEP*, 31 May 1784.

131. [Joy], *Historical Collections*, 286–87.

132. *HC*, 15 April 1784.

133. *CEP*, 31 May 1784.

134. *CEP*, 10 May 1784.

135. PRO, HO, 100/13, fols. 159, 161. For similar violence in Cork by sail-cloth weavers against Thomas Wilson, see *CEP*, 21 June 1784.

136. PRO, HO, 100/13, fol. 194; *Volunteer's Journal* (Dublin), 16 July 1784. Kirkpatrick was probably a mistaken target of the crowd's wrath. Only a few days earlier, he had signed a strongly worded petition from the freeholders and inhabitants of Dublin, in support of parliamentary reform and protective duties. This probably explains the reaction by many Volunteers to the attack. For the petition, see PRO, HO, 100/13, fol. 180.

137. *Volunteer's Journal* (Dublin), 21 July 1784.

138. *Rutland MSS*, 3:109.

139. For the breaking of oaths and crowd violence, see PRO, HO, 100/14, fol. 34; *Volunteer's Journal* (Dublin), 13 Aug. 1784. For the seriousness with which oaths could be taken and how their taking or breaking could legitimate violent action, see Walter, *Understanding Popular Violence*, 292–94; Knights, *Representation and Misrepresentation*.

140. PRO, HO, 100/13, fols. 167–68.

141. PRO, HO, 100/14, fols. 80–81.

142. *Volunteer's Journal* (Dublin), 6 Aug. 1784.

143. PRO, HO, 100/14, fol. 85. Rutland claimed that the soldiers had been fired on first from a window.

144. *Volunteer's Journal* (Dublin), 6 Aug. 1784.

145. *HJ*, 19 July 1784, quoted in Pollard, *Dictionary*, 183.

146. Zimmerman, *Songs of Irish Rebellion*, 122.

147. The parishes of St. Nicholas, St. Ann's, and St. Audeon's all issued such resolutions. *Volunteer's Journal* (Dublin), 20 Aug. 1784; *Volunteer's Journal* (Dublin), 8 Sept. 1784. These parishes had earlier passed resolutions in favor of non-consumption and protective duties. For the role of vestries in the expression of "public opinion," see Jacqueline Hill, *From Patriots to Unionists*, 174–75.

148. [William Drennan], *Letters of Orellana, an Irish Helot, to the Seven Northern Counties not Represented in the National Assembly of Delegates* (Dublin, 1785), 5–6.

149. David Dickson, *New Foundations: Ireland, 1660–1800*, 2nd ed., rev. and enlarged (Dublin: Irish Academic Press, 2000), 165.

Conclusion

1. For these exceptions, see McBride, *Scripture Politics*; Mac Suibhne, "Whiskey."

2. Agnew, *Drennan–McTier Letters*, 1:177.

3. McBride, *Scripture Politics*, 143–44.

4. *Lothian MSS*, 428.

5. *Rutland MSS*, 3:99.

6. Ibid., 124.

7. James Kelly, *Prelude to Union: Anglo-Irish Politics in the 1780s* (Cork: Cork University Press, 1992).

8. James Kelly, "Inter-Denominational Relations and Religious Toleration in Late Eighteenth-Century Ireland: The 'Paper War' of 1786–88," *Eighteenth-Century Ireland* 3 (1988): 39–60.

9. James Kelly, "The Genesis of 'Protestant Ascendancy': The Rightboy Disturbances of the 1780s and Their Impact upon Protestant Opinion," in O'Brien, *Parliament, Politics and People*, 93–127.

10. Cullen, "Catholics under the Penal Laws," 25. For disputes in Armagh, see David Miller, "Politicization in Revolutionary Ireland"; idem, "The Armagh Troubles, 1784-95," in *Irish Peasants: Violence and Political Unrest, 1780–1914*, ed. Samuel Clark and James S. Donnelly, Jr. (Madison: University of Wisconsin Press, 1983), 155–91.

11. On the state in the 1790s, see J. Smyth, *Revolution, Counter-Revolution*.

12. Dickson, *New Foundations*, 183–86.

13. Inglis, *Freedom of the Press*, 25–48.

14. Helen Burke, *Riotous Performances: The Struggle for Hegemony in the Irish Theater, 1712–1784* (Notre Dame, IN: University of Notre Dame Press, 2003), 281–90.

15. On the legacy of Volunteer politics in America, see Maurice Bric, *Ireland, Philadelphia and the Re-invention of America, 1760–1800* (Dublin: Four Courts

Press, 2008). After 1785, Dublin radicals, under the leadership of the enormously popular Napper Tandy, seemed to have concentrated more on local municipal issues than on national politics. For these campaigns, see Jacqueline Hill, *From Patriots to Unionists*, 170–90.

16. J. Smyth, *Revolution, Counterrevolution*, 6.

17. Bartlett, *Fall and Rise*, 317. On funerals, potato digging, and race meetings as forms of spectacle and a means of occupying public space, see Curtin, *United Irishmen*, 241–43.

18. On O'Connell and consumption, see Paul A. Pickering, "'Irish First': Daniel O'Connell, the Native Manufacture Campaign, and Economic Nationalism, 1840–44," *Albion* 32, no. 4 (2000): 598–616.

19. C. Kennedy, "'Gallant Nation'"; idem, "'Womanish Epistles?'"; Mary O'Dowd, "O'Connell and the Lady Patriots: Women and O'Connellite Politics, 1823–45," in Blackstock and Magennis, *Politics and Political Culture*, 283–303. For a provocative account of the neglected gendered politics of the money bill dispute, see Chris Mounsey, "Searching in the Dark: Towards a Historiography of Queer Early Modern and Enlightenment (Anglo) Ireland," in *Queer Masculinities, 1550–1800: Situating Same-Sex Desire in the Early Modern World*, ed. Katherine O'Donnell and Michael O'Rourke (New York: Palgrave, 2006), 1–16.

20. Samuel McSkimin, *Annals of Ulster from 1790 to 1798* (Belfast: J. Cleeland, 1906), 9; [Henry Joy and William Bruce, eds.], *Belfast Politics; Or, a Collection of the Debates, Resolutions, and Other Proceedings of that Town, in the Years 1792 and 1793* (Belfast, 1794), 52–54.

21. [Joy], *Historical Collections*, 385. See also the mix of toasts to the Volunteers, the French Revolution, and abolition given by Waddell Cunningham at a dinner in Belfast in May 1792 to celebrate the Polish Revolution. [Joy and Bruce], *Belfast Politics*, 47–48.

22. D. Dickson, *Old World Colony*, 465. William Drennan, a founding member of the United Irishmen, was still identifying volunteering as a formative political experience in 1795. See William Drennan, *A Philosophical Essay on the Moral and Political State of Ireland in a Letter to his Excellency Earl Fitzwilliam* (Dublin, 1795), 10–11.

23. Printed Ephemera Issued by the Eighty-Two Club, 1845–1846, NLI, MS 35,142. I owe this reference to Mary Broderick, Department of Prints and Drawings, NLI.

24. The memory of 1782 and the Volunteers requires further research. See *The First Annual Meeting of the Eighty-Two Club* (Dublin, 1846); *History and Proceedings of the Eighty-Two Club* (Dublin, 1845); Gary Owens, "Visualizing the Liberator: Self-Fashioning, Dramaturgy, and the Construction of Daniel O'Connell," *Éire-Ireland* 33, no. 3/4–34, no. 1 (1998): 109; idem, "Nationalism without Words," 253.

25. [Drennan], *Letter to Edmund Burke*, 18.

26. This prognosis of British political culture by Irish commentators was

also widely adopted by patriot and oppositionist writers in England in the 1770s and 1780s. See K. Wilson, *Sense of the People.*

27. Miller, "Non-professional Soldiery," 315–34; Ó Snodaigh, "Notes on the Volunteers . . . of County Roscommon."

28. [Drennan], *Address,* 25–27.

29. McBride, *Scripture Politics,* 161.

30. Bolton Papers, NLI, 16,350 (4).

Bibliography

Primary Sources

MANUSCRIPTS

British Library, London
    Auckland Papers (Add. MSS 34,418–19)
    Pelham Papers (Add. MSS 33,100–101)
Linen Hall Library, Belfast
    Joy MSS (TD 2777)
National Library of Ireland, Dublin
    Bolton Papers (MS 15,800–980; MS 16,350–70)
    Bellew Papers (MS 27,126)
    Conolly Papers (MS 40,242; MS 41,341/6)
    Dobbs Papers (MS 2251)
    Ennis Volunteers Records and Accounts, 1778–1792 (MS 838)
    Heron Papers (MS 13,047–50)
    John Barter Bennet MS (MS 4161)
    Leadbetter Diary (MS 9305)
    Minutes of the Doneraile Rangers, 1779–1792 (MS 12,155)
    O'Hara Papers (MS 20,282; MS 20,398; MS 36,396)
    Talbot-Crosbie Papers (MS 2054)
    William Todd Jones, "letter to the Irish Volunteers" (MS 10,539)
Public Record Office, London (now the National Archives)
    HO 55/11–12 (Home Office Papers, Miscellaneous Addresses)
    HO 100/1–14 (Home Office Papers, Ireland, 1782–84)
    SP 63/445–80 (State Papers, Ireland, 1775–82)
Public Record Office of Northern Ireland, Belfast
    Abercorn Papers (T/2541)
    Additional Drennan Papers (D/456)
    Annesley Papers (D/2309/4/3)

Blair Papers (D/717)
Caldwell Papers (T/3541)
Drennan Notebooks (D/531)
Drennan Papers (T/965)
Fitzgerald Papers (T/3075)
Hervey/Bruce Papers (D/1514)
Holham Papers (T/3429)
Minute Book of the First Newry Volunteers (T/3202/1a)
Minute Book of the Portaferry Volunteers, Nugent Papers (D/552/A/4/3/5)
Minutes of the Snug Club of Newry (T/3202/3a)
Notes on the Irish Volunteers and the Irish Military Returns ca. 1769-1783 (T/963)
Pelham Papers (T/755/2)
Perceval Papers (D/906)
Scrope Bernard Papers (T/2627)
Shannon Papers (D 2707/A/2/2)
Stewart of Ards Papers (D/4137)
Royal Irish Academy, Dublin
   Charlemont MS (MS 12/R/1-30)
   J. L. Foster Papers (MS 23/G/39)
Ulster Museum, Belfast
   Minute Book of the Men of Mourne (Acc. 19-1914)
   Minutes of the Free and Independent Company of Rathfriland (Acc. 571, 603-1914)
   Rev. Samuel Barber Papers (Acc. 570, 588, 591, 602-1914)

PUBLICATIONS OF THE HISTORICAL MANUSCRIPTS COMMISSION

Carlisle MSS. London, 1897.
Charlemont MSS. London, 1891.
Dartmouth MSS. London, 1887-96.
Donoughmore MSS. 1891.
Emly MSS. 1895.
Fortescue MSS. London, 1892.
Knox MSS. Various Collections, VI. 1909.
Lothian MSS. London, 1905.
Rutland MSS. 4 vols. London, 1888-1905.
Stopford-Sackville MSS. London, 1904-10.

PARLIAMENTARY PAPERS

Journals of the House of Commons of the Kingdom of Ireland. 19 vols. Dublin, 1796-1800.

NEWSPAPERS AND PERIODICALS

Belfast News-Letter
Clonmell Gazette
Cork Evening Post
Dublin Evening Journal
Dublin Evening Post
Exshaw's Magazine (Dublin)
Finn's Leinster Journal (Kilkenny)
Freeman's Journal (Dublin)
Gentleman's Magazine (Dublin)
Hibernian Chronicle (Cork)
Hibernian Journal (Dublin)
Independent Chronicle, of Universal Advertiser
Magee's Weekly Packet
The Parliamentary Register (Dublin)
Saunders' News-Letter (Dublin)
Town and Country Magazine (Dublin)
The Volunteer (Dublin)
Volunteer Evening Post (Dublin)
Volunteer Journal (Cork)
Volunteer's Journal (Dublin)
Walker's Hibernian Magazine (Dublin)
Wexford Journal

PRINTED COLLECTIONS OF DOCUMENTS

Agnew, Jean, ed. *The Drennan-McTier Letters*. Vol. 1, *1776–1793*. Dublin: Women's History Project/Irish Manuscripts Commission, 1998.
Barrington, Jonah. *Recollections of Jonah Barrington*. Dublin, n.d.
Beresford, William, ed. *The Correspondence of the Right Hon. John Beresford*. 2 vols. London, 1854.
Brady, John, ed. *Catholics and Catholicism in the Eighteenth-Century Press*. Maynooth: Catholic Record Society, 1965.
Carey, Mathew. *Autobiography*. New York, 1937.
Carpenter, Andrew, ed. *Verse in English in Eighteenth-Century Ireland*. Cork: Cork University Press, 1998.
Clifford, Brendan, ed. *Scripture Politics: Selections from the Writings of William Steel Dickson*. Belfast: Belfast Historical and Educational Society, 1991.
———, ed. *William Drennan: Selected Writings*. Vol. 1, *The Irish Volunteers: 1775–1790*. Belfast: Belfast Historical and Educational Society, 1998.
Edwards, R. D., ed. "Minute Book of the Catholic Committee, 1773–92." *Archivium Hibernicum* 9 (1942): 1–172.

Gilbert, J. T. *Calendar of Ancient Records of Dublin*. 19 vols. Dublin, 1889–1944.

Grattan, Henry, Jr., ed. *Memoirs of the Life and Times of the Rt. Hon. Henry Grattan*. 5 vols. London, 1839–46.

Guinness, Patrick. "'Man being in his natural state the most naked and helpless of all creatures': The Meeting Book of the Kildare Knot of the Friendly Brothers of St Patrick, 1758–1791." *Journal of the County Kildare Archaeological Society* 19 (2000–2001): 116–50.

Herbert, Dorothea. *Retrospections of Dorothea Herbert*. Dublin: Town House, 1988.

[Joy, Henry, ed.]. *Historical Collections Relative to the Town of Belfast: From the Earliest Period to the Union with Great Britain*. Belfast, 1817.

[Joy, Henry, and William Bruce, eds.]. *Belfast Politics; Or, a Collection of the Debates, Resolutions, and Other Proceedings of that Town, in the Years 1792 and 1793*. Belfast, 1794.

Kelly, James. "Select Documents XLIII: A Secret Return of the Volunteers of Ireland in 1784." *Irish Historical Studies* 26, no. 103 (1989): 268–92.

Musgrave, Sir Richard. *Memoirs of the Different Rebellions in Ireland*. Fort Wayne, IN: Round Tower Books, 1995.

Price, Cecil, ed. *The Dramatic Works of Richard Brinsley Sheridan*. Oxford: Oxford University Press, 1973.

Stephens, F. G., and M. D. George, eds. *Catalogue of Political and Personal Satires Preserved in the Department of Prints and Drawings in the British Museum*. London: British Museum, 1873–1954.

Swift, Jonathan. *Irish Tracts 1728–1733*. Edited by Herbert Davis. Vol. 12 of *Prose Writings of Jonathan Swift*. Oxford: Oxford University Press, 1939–68.

Ward, Robert E., ed. *Prince of Dublin Printers: The Letters of George Faulkner*. Lexington: University Press of Kentucky, 1972.

Ward, Robert E., John F. Wrynn, and Catherine Coogan Ward, eds. *Letters of Charles O'Conor of Belanagare: A Catholic Voice in Eighteenth-Century Ireland*. Washington, DC: Catholic University of America Press, 1988.

Zimmerman, Georges-Denis. *Songs of Irish Rebellion: Political Street Ballads and Rebel Songs, 1780–1900*. Hataboro, PA: Folklore Associates, 1967.

PAMPHLETS AND BOOKS

An Address to the Dungannon and Leinster Volunteer Delegates on the Matter of Parliamentary Reform. Dublin, 1783.

An Address to the Right Honourable Henry Grattan, Esq. by the Independent Dublin Volunteers . . . London, 1782.

An Address to the Right Honourable the Lord Mayor, the Worshipful the Board of Aldermen, the Sheriffs, Commons, Citizens and Freeholders of Dublin, Relating to the Intended Augmentation of the Military Force in the Kingdom of Ireland. Dublin, 1768.

The Alarm; or, an Address to the Nobility, Gentry, and Clergy of the Church of Ireland as by Law Established. Dublin, 1783.

Alexander, Andrew. *The Advantages of a General Knowledge of the Use of Arms, a Sermon.* Strabane, 1779.

Anketell, John. *Poems on Several Occasions.* Dublin 1793.

Association Hibernia's Palladium . . . Sligo, 1781.

Baratariana: A Select Collection of Fugitive Political Pieces. Dublin, 1772.

Barber, Samuel. *A Sermon Delivered in the Meeting-House of Rathfriland, October 24, 1779, to the Castlewellan Rangers and Rathfriland Volunteers.* Newry, 1779.

Bell, Robert. *A Description of the Condition and Manners, as well as of the Moral and Political Character of the Peasantry of Ireland such as they were between the Years 1780 and 1790.* London, 1804.

Booker, John. *A Sermon Preached at Edgworthstown, March 19, 1780 Before the Edgworthstown Division of County of Longford Volunteers.* Dublin, 1780.

Boyne Society. *Rules, Orders, and Regulations of the Military Corps of the Cork Boyne Society.* Cork, 1780.

———. *Rules and Orders, to be Observed and Kept by Every Member of the Boyne Society, of the City of Cork, as Agreed to by Said Society, on the first day of July, 1776.* Dublin, 1776.

[Burrowes, Peter]. *Plain Arguments in Defence of the People's Absolute Dominion over the Constitution.* Dublin, 1784.

Butler, Rev. Samuel. *A Sermon Preached in the Parish Church of St. Michan, Dublin, on Sunday the 17th day of October 1779.* Dublin, 1779.

Campbell, Thomas. *Philosophical Survey of the South of Ireland in a Series of Letters to John Wilkinson.* London, 1777.

Carson, Rev. George. *A Discourse Delivered at Croghan, 2nd January 1780 to the United Companies of Tullahunco and Ballyconnell Volunteers.* Dublin, 1780.

Churchill, Paddy. *The Association; or, the Prospect of Wealth and Liberty; a Satyrical, Political, and Panegyrical Poem, Addressed to the Patriotic Sons and Daughters of Ireland.* Dublin, 1779.

A Collection of the Letters which have been Addressed to the Volunteers of Ireland, on the Subject of a Parliamentary Reform, by the Earl of Effingham, Doctor Price, Major Cartwright, Doctor Jebb, and the Rev. Mr. Wyvill . . . London, 1783.

A Concise Compendium of Military Manoeuvres, Represented by Accurate Engravings . . . Particularly Addressed to the Irish Volunteers. Dublin, 1781.

Considerations on the Present State of the Military Establishment of this Kingdom, Addressed to the Knights, Citizens and Burgesses of Ireland, in Parliament Assembled. Dublin, 1768.

Corps of Independent Dublin Volunteers. *An Address to the Right Honourable Henry Grattan, Esq. by the Independent Dublin Volunteers, . . . with Mr. Grattan's Answer . . . To which is Annexed, the Resolutions of the Lawyers Committee and Corps . . .* London, 1782.

———. *Plan of a Field Day for the Dublin Volunteers*. Dublin, 1780.

———. *The Report of the Committee of Independent Dublin Volunteers, Appointed to draw up an address to Colonel Grattan*. Dublin, 1782.

Crawford, William. *The Connection Between Courage and the Moral Virtues Considered in a Sermon Preached Before the Volunteer Company of Strabane Rangers, Sunday 12th Sept 1779*. Strabane, 1779.

Crombie, James. *The Expedience and Utility of Volunteer Associations for National Defence and Security in the Present Critical Situation of Public Affairs Considered, in a Sermon, Preached before the United Companies of the Belfast Volunteers, on Sunday the first of August, 1779*. Belfast, 1779.

———. *The Propriety of Setting Apart a Portion of the Sabbath for the Purpose of Acquiring the Knowledge and Use of Arms, in Times of Public Danger, Illustrated. A Sermon, Preached before the Belfast Volunteer Company, 4 March 1781*. Belfast, 1781.

———. *A Sermon on the Love of Country, Preached before the First Company of Belfast Volunteers, on Sunday, the 19th of July, 1778*. Belfast 1778.

The Dangers of Popery, a Dream Verified by Recent Facts and Authentic Documents in a Letter to a Friend. Dublin, 1782.

A Defence of Great Britain Against a Charge of Tyranny in the Government of Ireland. By an Irishman. Dublin, 1779.

A Defence of the Armed Societies of Ireland with Respect to their Legality. Cork, 1779.

Delap, Hugh. *A Sermon, Preached in the Old-Bridge Meeting-House near Omagh, the 14th of November 1779: before the Omagh and Cappagh Volunteers*. Strabane, 1779.

Dickson, William Steel. *A Narrative of the Confinement and Exile of William Steel Dickson, D.D.* Dublin, 1812.

———. *A Sermon on the Propriety and Advantages of Acquiring the Knowledge and Use of Arms, in Times of Public Danger, Preached before Echlinville Volunteers, on Sunday the 28th of March, 1779*. Belfast, 1779.

Dobbs, Francis. *A History of Irish Affairs, from the 12th of October, 1779, to the 15th September, 1782, the Day of Lord Temple's Arrival*. Dublin, 1782.

———. *A Letter to the Right Honourable Lord North on His Propositions in Favour of Ireland*. Dublin, 1780.

———. *Thoughts on Volunteers*. Dublin, 1781.

The Dreamer Awakened . . . By Solon. Dublin, 1782.

[Drennan, William]. *An Address to the Volunteers of Ireland, by the Author of a Letter to Edmund Burke Esq., Containing Reflections on Patriotism, Party Spirit, and the Unity of Free Nations*. Dublin, 1781.

———. *A Letter to Edmund Burke*. Dublin, 1780.

———. *Letters of Orellana, an Irish Helot, to the Seven Northern Counties not Represented in the National Assembly of Delegates*. Dublin, 1785.

Drennan, William. *A Philosophical Essay on the Moral and Political State of Ireland in a Letter to his Excellency Earl Fitzwilliam*. Dublin, 1795.

Drought, Thomas. *Letters on Subjects Interesting to Ireland and Addressed to the Irish Volunteers.* Dublin, 1783.

Edwards, John. *The Patriot Soldier: A Poem.* Dublin, 1784.

An Essay on the Necessity of Protecting Duties. Dublin, 1783.

The Exercise of a Company of Foot, Compiled Chiefly from the Practice of the Volunteers of Belfast. Belfast, 1778.

The First Annual Meeting of the Eighty-Two Club. Dublin, 1846.

Flood, Henry. *The Two Speeches of Henry Flood, Esq. on the Repeal of the Declaratory Act of the Sixth of George I.* Dublin, 1782.

[Grattan, Henry]. *A Letter to the People of Ireland on the Expediency and Necessity of the Present Associations in Ireland in Favour of our own Manufactures.* Dublin, 1779.

————. *Observations on the Mutiny Bill; with some Strictures on Lord Buckinghamshire's Administration in Ireland.* Dublin, 1781.

Guthrie, William. *An Improved System of Modern Geography.* Dublin, 1789.

Hibernia to Her Favorite Sons: A Letter on a Very Interesting and Important Occasion, the Increase of the Military Establishments of this Kingdom . . . Dublin, 1768.

An Historical Account of the late Election of Knights of the Shire for the County of Down . . . Dublin, 1784.

History and Proceedings of the Eighty-Two Club. Dublin, 1845.

The History of the Proceedings and Debates of the Volunteer Delegates of Ireland on the Subject of Parliamentary Reform. Dublin, 1784.

[Hely-Hutchinson, John]. *The Commercial Restraints of Ireland Considered.* Dublin, 1779.

Houlton, Robert. *A Selection of Political Letters which Appeared during the Administration of the Earls of Buckinghamshire and Carlisle* . . . Dublin 1782.

Ireland's Glory; or, a Comparative View of Ireland in the Years 1776 and 1783. Dublin, 1783.

An Irregular Pindaric Ode. Dublin, 1757.

[Jebb, Frederick]. *The Letters of Guatimozin on the Affairs of Ireland as First published in the Freeman's Journal* . . . Dublin, 1779.

[Jebb, Frederick, and Robert Johnson]. *Thoughts on the Discontents of the People Last Year, respecting the Sugar Duties.* Dublin, 1781.

Jones, William Todd. *Letter to the Electors of the Borough of Lisburn.* Dublin, 1784.

Law, Robert. *The Moral Duties Necessary to Secure the Advantages of a Free Trade with a Caution Against Some Abuses to Which the Beginnings of Manufactures and Commerce are Peculiarly Exposed.* Dublin, 1780.

A Letter to the Volunteers Upon the Subject of Parliamentary Reform. Dublin, 1784.

Letters of a Dungannon and Munster Delegate, which appeared shortly after the plan of Parliamentary reform, proposed by the Grand National Convention. Dublin, 1784.

Levingston, Samuel. *The Obligation Men are Under to Exert Themselves for the Defence of their Country, &c. A Sermon, Preached before the Clare Volunteers, on the 9th of January, 1780.* Newry, 1780.

Linn, William. *A Military Discourse, Delivered in Carlisle, March the 17th, 1776, to Colonel Irvine's Battalion of Regulars, and a Very Respectable Number of the Inhabitants.* Philadelphia, 1776.

A List of the Grenadier Company of the Dublin Volunteers, with the Dates of their Admissions into the Corps. Dublin, 1783.

Lucas, Charles. *An Address to the Right Honourable the Lord Mayor, the Worshipful the Board of Aldermen, the Sheriffs, Commons, Citizens and Freeholders of Dublin, Relating to the Intended Augmentation of the Military Force in the Kingdom of Ireland.* Dublin, 1768.

Maclaine, Alexander. *A Sermon Preached at Antrim, December 18, 1745 Being the National Fast.* Dublin, 1746.

The Manual Exercise. Monaghan, n.d.

Maurice, Thomas. *Ierne Rediviva: an Ode. Inscribed to the Volunteers of* Ireland. Dublin, 1782.

The Modern Monitor, or Flyn's Speculations. Cork, 1771.

Moody, Boyle. *The Ceremony of Consecrating the Colours of a Regiment, as Performed by the Second Company of Newry Volunteers on . . . 16th October, 1779.* Newry, 1779.

Nevin, William. *The Nature and Evidence of an Over-Ruling Providence Considered. A Sermon Preached before the Downe Volunteers . . . on the 5th of September 1779.* Belfast, 1779.

O' Leary, Arthur. *An Address to the Common People of the Roman Catholic Religion, Concerning the Apprehended French Invasion.* Cork, 1779.

Observations on the Parliamentary Conduct of John Foster. Dublin, 1784.

The Patriot Soldier; or, Irish Volunteer, A Poem; By a Member of the Belfast First Volunteer Company. Belfast, 1789.

Petticoat Government, Exemplified in a Late Case in Ireland. London, 1780.

Plan of Review for the Regiment of Dublin Volunteers, Commanded by . . . the Duke of Leinster; for the 12th of October, 1783: . . . to Commemorate the Address of Parliament to His Majesty. Presented the 12th Day of October, M DCC LXXIX, in Order to Obtain a Free Trade for Ireland. Dublin[?], 1783.

Plan of Review for the Volunteer Corps, which are to Assemble at Belfast, in July, 1781. Belfast[?], 1781?

The Political Monitor: Exhibiting the Present State of Affairs in Ireland . . . in a Series of Letters First Published in the Freeman's Journal . . . Dublin, 1772.

[Pollock, Joseph]. *The Letters of Owen Roe O'Nial.* Dublin, 1779.

Preston, William. *The Contrast; or, a Comparison between the Characters of the English and the Irish in the year 1780.* Dublin, 1780.

———. *The Female Congress; or, the Temple of Cotytto: A Mock Heroic Poem.* Dublin, 1779.

Proceedings at Large of the Court-Martial, on the Trial of the Honourable Augustus Keppel, Admiral of the Blue. Dublin, 1779.

Proceedings Relative to Ulster Assembly of Volunteer Delegates. Belfast, 1783.

A Reform of the Irish House of Commons Considered. Dublin, 1783.

The Revival: an Ode for St. Patrick's Day. Inscribed to the Volunteers of Ireland. Dublin, 1780.

Rogers, John. *A Sermon Preached at Lisnavein, Otherwise Ballybay New Erection, on Saturday, June 10. 1780 to the Lisnavein Independent Rangers, Trough Volunteers . . .* Edinburgh, 1780.

A Scheme for a Constitutional Association with some Obvious Reasons for Adopting such a Measure. Dublin, 1780.

Seymour-Conway, Francis, 1st Marquis of Hertford. *A Letter to the Belfast Company of Volunteers, in the Province of Ulster.* Dublin, 1782.

Sinclair, Robert. *Fortitude Explained and Recommended. A Sermon, Delivered before the Larne Volunteers, the first of August, 1779.* Belfast, 1779.

The Songs, Duets, Trios, Choruses, and Finales in the new Comic Opera of the Contract, as Performed at the Theatre Royal, Smock Alley. Dublin, 1783.

Stokes, Gabriel. *Love of Our Country, Distinguished From False Pretences; a Sermon, Preached in the Cathedral of Waterford, January 15th, 1797.* Dublin, 1797.

Thoughts on a Parliamentary Reform. London and Dublin, 1784.

Thoughts on the Conduct and Continuation of the Volunteers of Ireland. Dublin, 1783.

Thoughts Upon the Present Situation of Ireland in a Letter from the north to a friend in Dublin . . . Dublin, 1782.

The Times, Addressed to the Virtuous and Spirited Free Men of Ireland. Dublin, 1780.

The Triumph of Prudence over Passion: Or the History of Miss Mortimer and Miss Fitzgerald by the Authoress of Emeline. Dublin, 1781.

Turner, Rev. Francis. *A Constitutional Sermon: Preached on Sunday, the 7th of November, 1779, in the Parish Church of Killrush, before the Enniscorthy Buffs.* Wexford, 1779.

———. *A Sermon Preached by the Rev. Francis Turner, A.B. on Sunday, the 8th of August, 1784, in the Cathedral of Ferns, before the Enniscorthy Buffs, Commanded by Colonel Phaire.* Dublin, 1784.

The Usurpations of England the Chief Source of the Miseries of Ireland . . . by a Native of Ireland and a lover of the British Empire. Dublin, 1780.

The Voice of the People in a Letter to the Secretary of his Grace the Duke of Rutland. By a Private Volunteer. Dublin, 1784.

A Volunteer's Queries, in Spring, 1780; humbly offered to the consideration of all descriptions of men in Ireland. Dublin, 1780.

Walker, Joseph C. *An Historical Essay on the Dress of the Ancient and Modern Irish.* Dublin, 1788.

Wilson C. H. *A Compleat Collection of the Resolutions of the Volunteers, Grand Juries &c. of Ireland.* Dublin, 1782.

Young, Arthur. *A Tour of Ireland: With General Observations on the Present State of That Kingdom, Made in the Years 1776, 1777, and 1778*. London, 1780.

Secondary Sources

Adams, J. R. R. *The Printed Word and the Common Man: Popular Culture in Ulster, 1700–1900*. Belfast: Institute of Irish Studies, Queen's University Belfast, 1987.

Altick, Richard Daniel. *The Shows of London*. Cambridge: Cambridge University Press, 1978.

Anderson, Benedict. *Imagined Communities: Reflections on the Origins and Spread of Nationalism*. London: Verso, 1983.

Appadurai, Arjun, ed. *The Social Life of Things: Commodities in Cultural Perspective*. Cambridge: Cambridge University Press, 1986.

Bailyn, Bernard. *The Ideological Origins of the American Revolution*. Cambridge, MA: Harvard University Press, 1967.

Barker, Hannah, and Elaine Chalus, eds. *Gender in Eighteenth-Century England*. London: Longman, 1997.

Barker, Helen. *Newspapers, Politics and Public Opinion in Late Eighteenth-Century England*. Oxford: Oxford University Press, 1998.

Barnard, T. C. "Art, Architecture, Artefacts and Ascendancy." *Bullán: An Irish Studies Review* 1, no. 2 (1994): 17–34.

———. "Considering the Inconsiderable: Elections, Patrons and Irish Elections, 1659–1761." In *The Irish Parliament in the Eighteenth Century: The Long Apprenticeship*, edited by D. W. Hayton, 107–27. Edinburgh: Edinburgh University Press, 2001.

———. "Integration or Separation? Hospitality and Display in Protestant Ireland, 1660–1800." In *A Union of Multiple Identities: The British Isles, 1750–1850*, edited by Laurence Brockliss and David Eastwood, 127–46. Manchester: Manchester University Press, 1997.

———. "The Languages of Politeness and Sociability in Eighteenth-Century Ireland." In *Political Discourse in Seventeenth- and Eighteenth-Century Ireland*, edited by G. Boyce et al., 193–221. Basingstoke: Palgrave, 2001.

———. "Learning, the Learned and Literacy in Ireland, c. 1660–1760." In *A Miracle of Learning: Studies in Manuscripts and Irish Learning; Essays in Honour of William O'Sullivan*, edited by Toby Christopher Barnard, Dáibhí Ó Cróinín, and Katharine Simms, 209–35. Aldershot: Ashgate, 1998.

———. *Making the Grand Figure: Lives and Possessions in Ireland, 1641–1770*. New Haven, CT: Yale University Press, 2004.

———. *A New Anatomy of Ireland: The Irish Protestants, 1649–1770*. New Haven, CT: Yale University Press, 2003.

———. "Reforming Irish Manners: The Religious Societies in Dublin during the 1690s." *Historical Journal* 35, no. 4 (Dec. 1992): 805–38.

———. "The Uses of 23 October 1641 and Irish Protestant Celebrations." *English Historical Review* 106, no. 421 (Oct. 1991): 889–920.

———. "The World of Goods and County Offaly in the Early Eighteenth Century." In *Offaly: History and Society; Interdisciplinary Essays on the History of an Irish County,* edited by William Nolan and Timothy P. O'Neill, 371–92. Dublin: Geography Publications, 1998.

Bartlett, Thomas. *The Fall and Rise of the Irish Nation: The Catholic Question, 1690–1830.* New York: Barnes & Noble, 1992.

———. "Militarization and Politicization in Ireland (1780–1820)." In *Culture et pratiques politiques en France et en Irlande, XVIe–XVIIIe siècle,* edited by Louis Bergeron and L. M. Cullen, 125–36. Paris: Centre de Recherches Historiques, 1991.

———. "'This famous island set in a Virginian sea': Ireland in the British Empire, 1690–1801." In *The Oxford History of the British Empire: The Eighteenth Century,* edited by P. J. Marshall, 253–75. Oxford: Oxford University Press, 1998.

Beatty, John, ed. *Protestant Women's Narratives of the Irish Rebellion of 1798.* Dublin: Four Courts Press, 2001.

Beiner, Guy. "Between Trauma and Triumphalism: The Easter Rising, the Somme, and the Crux of Deep Memory in Modern Ireland." *Journal of British Studies* 46, no. 2 (April 2007): 366–389.

———. *Remembering the Year of the French: Irish Folk History and Social Memory.* Madison: University of Wisconsin Press, 2006.

Berry, Christopher J. *The Idea of Luxury: A Conceptual and Historical Investigation.* Cambridge: Cambridge University Press, 1994.

Black, Eileen. "Volunteer Portraits in the Ulster Museum." *Irish Sword* 13 (1978): 181–84.

Black, Eugene. *The Association: British Extraparliamentary Political Organization, 1769–1793.* Cambridge, MA: Harvard University Press, 1963.

Blackstock, Allan. *An Ascendancy Army: The Irish Yeomanry, 1796–1834.* Dublin: Four Courts Press, 1998.

Blackstock, Allan, and Eoin Magennis, eds. *Politics and Political Culture in Britain and Ireland, 1750–1850: Essays in Tribute to Peter Jupp.* Belfast: Ulster Historical Foundation, 2007.

Borsay, Peter, and Lindsay Proudfoot, eds. *Provincial Towns in Early Modern England and Ireland: Change, Convergence and Divergence.* Oxford: Oxford University Press, 2002.

Bradley, James E. *Religion, Revolution, and English Radicalism: Nonconformity in Eighteenth-Century Politics and Society.* Cambridge: Cambridge University Press, 1990.

Breen, T. H. "'Baubles of Britain': The American and Consumer Revolutions of the Eighteenth Century." *Past and Present* 69 (May 1988): 73–104.

———. "An Empire of Goods: The Anglicization of Colonial America, 1690–1776." *Journal of British Studies* 25, no. 4 (Oct. 1986): 467–99.

———. *The Marketplace of Revolution: How Consumer Politics Shaped American Independence.* Oxford: Oxford University Press, 2004.

———. "The Meaning of 'Likeness': American Portrait Painting in an Eighteenth-Century Consumer Society." *Word & Image* 6 (Oct.–Dec. 1990): 325–50.

Brewer, John. *Party Ideology and Popular Politics at the Accession of George III.* Cambridge: Cambridge University Press, 1976.

Bric, Maurice. *Ireland, Philadelphia and the Re-invention of America, 1760–1800.* Dublin: Four Courts Press, 2008.

———. "Priests, Parsons, and Politics: The Rightboy Protest in County Cork, 1785–1788." *Past and Present* 100 (Aug. 1983): 100–123.

Broderick, David. *The First Toll Roads: Ireland's Turnpike Roads, 1729–1858.* Cork: Collins Press, 2002.

Burke, Helen M. "Putting on Irish 'Stuff': The Politics of Anglo-Irish Cross-Dressing." In *The Clothes That Wear Us: Essays on Dressing and Transgressing in Eighteenth-Century Culture,* edited by Jessica Munns and Penny Richards, 233–49. Delaware: University of Delaware Press, 2000.

———. "The Revolutionary Prelude: The Dublin Stage in the Late 1770s and Early 1780s." *Eighteenth Century Life* 22, no. 3 (Nov. 1998): 7–18.

———. *Riotous Performances: The Struggle for Hegemony in the Irish Theater, 1712–1784.* Notre Dame, IN: University of Notre Dame Press, 2003.

Burke, Peter. *Popular Culture in Early Modern Europe.* New York: New York University Press, 1978.

Burns, Arthur, and Joanna Innes, eds. *Rethinking the Age of Reform.* Cambridge: Cambridge University Press, 2003.

Butler, Judith, and Joan Scott, eds. *Feminists Theorize the Political.* London: Routledge, 1992.

A Catalogue of a Collection of Pottery and Porcelain Illustrating Popular British History Lent by Henry Willett of Brighton. London, 1899.

Chalus, Elaine. "Elite Women, Social Politics, and the Political World of Late Eighteenth-Century England." *Historical Journal* 43, no. 3 (Sept. 2000): 669–97.

Clark, Peter. *British Societies and Clubs, 1580–1800: The Origins of an Associational World.* Oxford: Clarendon Press, 2000.

Clark, Peter, and Raymond Gillespie, eds. *Two Capitals: London and Dublin, 1500–1840.* Oxford: Oxford University Press, 2001.

Clarkson, L. A. "An Anatomy of an Irish Town: The Economy of Armagh, 1770." *Irish Economic and Social History* 5 (1978): 27–45.

Claydon, Tony. "The Sermon, the 'Public Sphere' and the Political Culture of Late Seventeenth-Century England." In *The English Sermon Revised: Religion, Literature and History, 1600–1750,* edited by Lori Anne Ferrell and Peter McCullough, 208–34. Manchester: Manchester University Press, 2001.

Claydon, Tony, and Ian McBride, eds. *Protestantism and National Identity: Britain and Ireland, c. 1650–c. 1850.* Cambridge: Cambridge University Press, 1998.

Clayton, Tim. *The English Print, 1688–1802.* New Haven, CT: Yale University Press, 1997.

Clifford, Dale L. "Can the Uniform Make the Citizen? Paris, 1789-1791." *Eighteenth-Century Studies* 34, no. 3 (Spring 2001): 363-82.

Colley, Linda. *Britons: Forging the Nation, 1707-1837*. New Haven, CT: Yale University Press, 1992.

Connolly, S. J. "'Ag Deanamh Commanding': Elite Responses to Popular Culture, 1660-1850." In *Irish Popular Culture, 1650-1850*, edited by James S. Donnelly, Jr., and Kerby A. Miller, 173-200. Dublin: Irish Academic Press, 1998.

———. "Eighteenth-Century Ireland: Colony or Ancien Regime?" In *The Making of Modern Irish History: Revisionism and the Revisionist Controversy*, edited by D. George Boyce and Alan O'Day, 15-33. London: Routledge, 1996.

———. *Religion, Law, and Power: The Making of Protestant Ireland, 1660-1760*. Oxford: Oxford University Press, 1992.

———. "Varieties of Britishness: Ireland, Scotland and Wales in the Hanoverian State." In *Uniting the Kingdom? The Making of British History*, edited by Alexander Grant and Keith J. Stringer, 193-207. London: Routledge, 1995.

Conway, Stephen. *The British Isles and the War of American Independence*. Oxford: Oxford University Press, 2000.

———. "'A Joy Unknown for Years Past': The American War, Britishness, and the Celebration of Rodney's Victory at the Saints." *History* 86, no. 282 (April 2001): 180-99.

———. "'Like the Irish'? Volunteer Corps and Volunteering in Britain during the American War." In *Britain and America Go to War: The Impact of War and Warfare, 1754-1815*, edited by Julie Flavell and Stephen Conway, 143-69. Gainesville: University Press of Florida, 2004.

———. *War, State, and Society in Mid-Eighteenth-Century Britain and Ireland*. Oxford: Oxford University Press, 2006.

Cookson, John E. *The British Armed Nation, 1793-1815*. Oxford: Oxford University Press, 1997.

Cox, Catherine. "Women and Business in Eighteenth-Century Dublin: A Case Study." In *Women and Paid Work in Ireland, 1500-1930*, edited by Bernadette Whelan, 30-43. Dublin: Four Courts Press, 2000.

Crawford, W. H. "The Evolution of Ulster Towns, 1750-1850." In *Plantation to Partition: Essays in Ulster History in Honour of J. L. McCracken*, edited by P. Roebuck, 140-56. Belfast: Blackstaff Press, 1981.

Cressy, David. *Bonfires and Bells: National Memory and the Protestant Calendar in Elizabethan and Stuart England*. Berkeley: University of California Press, 1989.

Crossle, Philip, and John Heron Lepper. *History of the Grand Lodge of Free and Accepted Masons of Ireland*. Dublin, 1925.

Cullen, Fintan. *Visual Politics: The Representation of Ireland, 1750-1930*. Cork: Cork University Press, 1997.

Cullen, L. M. "Catholics under the Penal Laws." *Eighteenth-Century Ireland* 1 (1986): 23-36.

———. "Late Eighteenth-Century Politicization in Ireland: Problems in Its

Study and Its French Links." In *Culture et pratiques politiques en France et en Irlande, XVIe–XVIIIe siècle,* edited by Louis Bergeron and L. M. Cullen, 137–57. Paris: Centre de Recherches Historiques, 1991.

———. "The Political Structures of the Defenders." In *Ireland and the French Revolution,* edited by Hugh Gough and David Dickson, 117–38. Dublin: Irish Academic Press, 1990.

Cummins, Seamus. "Extra-Parliamentary Agitation in Dublin in the 1760s." In *Religion, Conflict and Coexistence in Ireland: Essays Presented to Monsignor Patrick Corish,* edited by Richard Vincent Comerford, M. Cullen, Jacqueline R. Hill, and C. Lennon, 118–34. Dublin: Gill & Macmillan, 1990.

Curtin, Nancy J. "'A Nation of Abortive Men': Gendered Citizenship and Early Irish Republicanism." In *Reclaiming Gender: Transgressive Identities in Modern Ireland,* edited by Marilyn Cohen and Nancy J. Curtin, 33–52. New York: Macmillan, 1999.

———. *The United Irishmen: Popular Politics in Ulster and Dublin, 1791–1798.* Oxford: Oxford University Press, 1994.

———. "Women and Eighteenth-Century Republicanism." In *Women in Early Modern Ireland,* edited by Margaret MacCurtain and Mary O'Dowd, 133–44. Edinburgh: Edinburgh University Press, 1991.

Curtis, Lewis Perry. "The Four Erins: Feminine Images of Ireland, 1780–1900." *Éire-Ireland* 33, no. 3/4–34, no. 1 (1998): 70–102.

Dalsimer, Adele M., ed. *Visualizing Ireland: National Identity and the Pictorial Tradition.* London: Faber, 1993.

Daunton, Martin, and Matthew Hilton, eds. *The Politics of Consumption: Material Culture and Citizenship in Europe and America.* London: Berg, 2001.

de Grazia, Victoria, ed. *The Sex of Things: Gender and Consumption in Historical Perspective.* Berkeley: University of California Press, 1996.

Dickson, David. "'Centres of Motion': Irish Cities and the Origins of Popular Politics." In *Culture et pratiques politiques en France et en Irelande XVIe–XVIIIe siècle,* edited by Louis Bergeron and L. M. Cullen, 101–22. Paris: Centre de Recherches Historiques, 1991.

———, ed. *The Gorgeous Mask: Dublin, 1700–1850.* Dublin: Trinity History Workshop, 1987.

———. *New Foundations: Ireland, 1660–1800.* 2nd ed., rev. and enlarged. Dublin: Irish Academic Press, 2000.

———. *Old World Colony: Cork and South Munster 1630–1830.* Madison: University of Wisconsin Press, 2005.

———. "Paine and Ireland." In *The United Irishmen: Republicanism, Radicalism, and Rebellion,* edited by David Dickson, Daire Keogh, and Kevin Whelan, 135–50. Dublin: Lilliput Press, 1993.

———. "The Place of Dublin in the Eighteenth-Century Irish Economy." In *Ireland and Scotland, 1600–1850: Parallels and Contrast in Economic and Social Development,* edited by Martin Thomas Devine and David Dickson, 177–92. Edinburgh: John Donald, 1983.

Donnelly, James S., Jr. "Hearts of Oak, Hearts of Steel." *Studia Hibernica* 21 (1981): 7–73.

———. "Propagating the Cause of the United Irishmen." *Studies* 69 (1980): 5–23.

———. "The Rightboy Movement 1785–8." *Studia Hibernica* 17–18 (1977–78): 120–202.

Donnelly, James S., Jr., and Kerby A. Miller, eds. *Irish Popular Culture, 1650–1850*. Dublin: Irish Academic Press, 1998.

Dudink, Stefan, Karen Hagemann, and John Tosh, eds. *Masculinities in Politics and War: Gendering Modern History*. Manchester: Manchester University Press, 2004.

Dugaw, Dianne. *Warrior Women and Popular Balladry, 1650–1850*. Cambridge: Cambridge University Press, 1989.

Dwyer Amussen, Susan. "'The Part of a Christian Man': The Cultural Politics of Manhood in Early Modern England." In *Political Culture and Cultural Politics in Early Modern England: Essays Presented to David Underdown*, edited by Susan Dwyer Amussen and Mark A. Kishlansky, 213–33. Manchester: Manchester University Press, 1995.

Epstein, James A. *In Practice: Studies in the Language and Culture of Popular Politics in Modern Britain*. Stanford, CA: Stanford University Press, 2003.

Fagan, Patrick. "The Dublin Catholic Mob (1700–1750)." *Eighteenth-Century Ireland* 4 (1989): 133–42.

Finn, Margot. "Men's Things: Masculine Possession in the Consumer Revolution." *Social History* 25, no. 2 (May 2000): 133–55.

Fletcher, Anthony John. *Gender, Sex and Subordination in England, 1500–1800*. New Haven, CT: Yale University Press, 1995.

Foster, Sarah. "Consumer Nationalism in 18th-Century Ireland." *History Today* 47, no. 6 (1997): 44–51.

———. "Going Shopping in Eighteenth-Century Dublin." *Things* 4 (Summer 1996): 32–61.

Frake, Charles O. "How to Ask for a Drink in Subanun." *American Anthropologist* 66, no. 6, pt. 2 (Dec. 1964): 127–32.

Fraser, T. G., ed. *The Irish Parading Tradition: Following the Drum*. London: Macmillan, 2000.

Garnham, Neal. "Ireland's Protestant Militia 1715–1776: A Military Assessment." *Irish Sword* 20, no. 80 (1996): 131–36.

———. "Local Elite Creation in Early Hanoverian Ireland: The Case of the County Grand Jury." *Historical Journal* 42, no. 3 (Sept. 1999): 623–42.

Gilbert, J. T. *A History of the City of Dublin*. 3 vols. Dublin, 1854–59.

Gillespie, Raymond. "Political Ideas and Their Social Contexts in Seventeenth-Century Ireland." In *Political Thought in Seventeenth-Century Ireland: Kingdom or Colony*, edited by Jane H. Ohlmeyer, 107–27. Cambridge: Cambridge University Press, 2000.

———. *Reading Ireland: Print, Reading and Social Change in Early Modern Ireland*. Manchester: Manchester University Press, 2005.

——. *Seventeenth-Century Ireland: Making Ireland Modern*. Dublin: Gill and Macmillan, 2006.

Gillespie, Raymond, and Andrew Hadfield, eds. *The Oxford History of the Irish Book*. Vol. 3, *The Irish Book in English, 1550–1800*. Oxford: Oxford University Press, 2006.

Gleadle, Kathryn, and Sarah Richardson, eds. *Women in British Politics, 1760–1860: The Power of the Petticoat*. London: Macmillan, 2000.

Gough, Hugh, and David Dickson, eds. *Ireland and the French Revolution*. Dublin: Irish Academic Press, 1990.

Gould, Eliga. *The Persistence of Empire: British Political Culture in the Age of the American Revolution*. Chapel Hill: University of North Carolina Press, 2000.

Greene, John C. *Theatre in Belfast, 1736–1800*. Bethlehem, PA: Lehigh University Press, 2000.

A Guide to the Irish Volunteer, Yeomanry and Militia Relics. Belfast, 1938.

Habermas, Jürgen. *The Structural Transformation of the Public Sphere: An Inquiry into a Category of Bourgeois Society*. Cambridge, MA: MIT Press, 1991.

Harris, Bob. *Politics and the Nation: Britain in the Mid-Eighteenth Century*. Oxford: Oxford University Press, 2002.

Harris, Tim. *London Crowds in the Reign of Charles II: Propaganda and Politics from the Restoration until the Exclusion Crisis*. Cambridge: Cambridge University Press, 1987.

——, ed. *The Politics of the Excluded, c. 1500–1850*. New York: Palgrave, 2001.

Harvey, Karen. "The History of Masculinity, circa 1650–1800." *Journal of British Studies* 44, no. 2 (April 2005): 296–311.

Harvey, Karen J. *The Bellews of Mount Bellew: A Catholic Gentry Family in Eighteenth-Century Ireland*. Dublin: Four Courts Press, 1998.

Hayes-McCoy, G. A. "Fencible Corps in Ireland, 1782–1803." *Irish Sword*, no. 2 (1955): 140–45.

——. *A History of Irish Flags from Earliest Times*. Dublin: Irish Academic Press, 1979.

Hayton, David. "Anglo-Irish Attitudes: Changing Perceptions of National Identity among the Protestant Ascendancy in Ireland, ca. 1690–1750." *Studies in Eighteenth-Century Culture* 17 (1987): 145–57.

Hempton, John, ed. *The Siege and History of Londonderry*. Dublin, 1861.

Hill, Jacqueline R. "Convergence and Conflict in Eighteenth-Century Ireland." *Historical Journal* 44, no. 4 (Dec. 2001): 1039–63.

——. *From Patriots to Unionists: Dublin Civic Politics and Irish Protestant Patriotism, 1660–1840*. Oxford: Clarendon Press, 1997.

——. "National Festivals, the State, and 'Protestant Ascendancy' in Ireland, 1790–1829." *Irish Historical Studies* 24, no. 93 (May 1984): 30–51.

——. "Religious Toleration and the Relaxation of the Penal Laws: An Imperial Perspective." *Archivium Hibernicum* 44 (1989): 90–110.

Hill, Judith. *Irish Public Sculpture: A History*. Dublin: Four Courts Press, 1998.

Hitchcock, Tim, and Michele Cohen, eds. *English Masculinities, 1660–1800*. London: Addison Wesley, 1999.

Hooker, Richard J. "The American Revolution Seen through a Wine Glass." *William and Mary Quarterly*, 3rd ser., 11, no. 1 (Jan. 1954): 52–77.

Houlding, J. A. *Fit for Service: The Training of the British Army, 1715–1795*. Oxford: Oxford University Press, 1981.

Hunt, Lynn. *Politics, Culture, and Class in the French Revolution*. Berkeley: University of California Press, 1984.

Inglis, Brian. *Freedom of the Press in Ireland, 1784–1841*. London: Faber, 1954.

Jacob, Margaret C. *Living the Enlightenment: Freemasonry and Politics in Eighteenth-Century Europe*. Oxford: Oxford University Press, 1991.

Jordan, Gerald, and Nicholas Rogers. "Admirals as Heroes: Patriotism and Liberty in Hanoverian England." *Journal of British Studies* 28, no. 3 (July 1989): 201–24.

Jupp, Peter. "County Down Elections, 1783–1831." *Irish Historical Studies* 18, no. 70 (1972): 177–206.

——. "The Role of Royal and Aristocratic Women in British Politics, c. 1782–1832." In *Chattel, Servant or Citizen: Women's Status in Church, State and Society*, edited by Mary O'Dowd and Sabine Wichert, 103–13. Belfast: Queen's University Press, 1995.

Jupp, Peter, and Eoin Magennis, eds. *Crowds in Ireland, c. 1720–1920*. New York: St. Martin's Press, 2000.

Kelly, James. "Conservative Protestant Political Thought in Late Eighteenth-Century Ireland." In *Political Ideas in Eighteenth-Century Ireland*, edited by Sean J. Connolly, 185–220. Dublin: Four Courts Press, 2000.

——. "'The Genesis of 'Protestant Ascendancy': The Rightboy Disturbances of the 1780s and Their Impact upon Protestant Opinion." In *Parliament, Politics and People: Essays in Eighteenth-Century Irish History*, edited by Gerard O'Brien, 93–127. Dublin: Irish Academic Press, 1989.

——. "'The Glorious and Immortal Memory': Commemoration and Protestant Identity in Ireland, 1660–1800." *Proceedings of the Royal Irish Academy* 94, C (1994): 25–52.

——. *Henry Flood: Patriots and Politics in Eighteenth-Century Ireland*. Dublin: Four Courts Press, 1998.

——. "Inter-Denominational Relations and Religious Toleration in Late Eighteenth-Century Ireland: The 'Paper War' of 1786–88." *Eighteenth-Century Ireland* 3 (1988): 39–60.

——. "The Irish Parliamentary Reform Movement: The Administration and Popular Politics, 1783–85." MA thesis, University College Dublin, 1981.

——. "Parliamentary Reform in Irish Politics: 1760–90." In *The United Irishmen: Republicanism, Radicalism, and Rebellion*, edited by David Dickson, Daire Keogh, and Kevin Whelan, 74–87. Dublin: Lilliput Press, 1993.

———. "The Politics of Volunteering, 1778-93." *Irish Sword* 22, no. 88 (2000): 139-57.

———. *Prelude to Union: Anglo-Irish Politics in the 1780s.* Cork: Cork University Press, 1992.

———. *Sir Edward Newenham, MP, 1734-1814: Defender of the Protestant Constitution.* Dublin: Four Courts Press, 2004.

———. *That Damn'd Thing Called Honour: Duelling in Ireland, 1570-1860.* Cork: Cork University Press, 1995.

———. "'A Wild Capuchin of Cork': Arthur O'Leary (1729-1802)." In *Radical Irish Priests, 1660-1970,* edited by Gerard Moran, 39-61. Dublin: Four Courts Press, 1998.

Kelly, Patrick. "The Politics of Political Economy in Mid-Eighteenth-Century Ireland." In *Political Ideas in Eighteenth Century Ireland,* edited by S. J. Connolly, 105-29. Dublin: Four Courts Press, 2000.

Kelly, William, ed. *The Sieges of Derry.* Dublin: Four Courts Press, 2001.

Kennedy, Catriona. "'A Gallant Nation': Chivalric Masculinity and Irish Nationalism in the 1790s." In *Public Men: Masculinity and Politics in Modern Britain,* edited by Matthew McCormack, 73-92. New York: Palgrave Macmillan 2007.

———. "'Womanish Epistles?' Martha McTier, Female Epistolarity and Late Eighteenth-Century Irish Radicalism." *Women's History Review* 13, no. 4 (Dec. 2004): 649-67.

Kennedy, Liam. "Price and Wages in Ireland, 1700-1850." *Irish Economic and Social History* 24 (1997): 62-104.

Kennedy Máire. "Eighteenth-Century Newspaper Publishing in Munster and South Leinster." *Journal of the Cork Historical and Archaeological Society* 103 (1998): 67-88.

———. "Spreading the Word in the Irish Midlands: Bookselling and Printing in the Late Eighteenth Century." *Long Room* 43 (1998): 29-37.

Keogh, Daire, and Nicholas Furlong, eds. *The Women of 1798.* Dublin: Four Courts Press, 1998.

Kerber, Linda K. *Women of the Republic: Intellect and Ideology in Revolutionary America.* Chapel Hill: University of North Carolina Press, 1980.

Kertzer, David I. *Ritual, Politics, and Power.* New Haven, CT: Yale University Press, 1990.

———. "The Role of Ritual in Political Change." In *Cultural and Political Change,* edited by Myron J. Aronoff, 53-74. New Brunswick, NJ: Transaction, 1983.

Kidd, Colin. *British Identities before Nationalism: Ethnicity and Nationhood in the Atlantic World, 1600-1800.* Cambridge: Cambridge University Press, 1999.

———. "North Britishness and the Nature of Eighteenth-Century British Patriotisms." *Historical Journal* 39, no. 2 (June 1996): 361-82.

Kirkham, Graeme. "Literacy in North-West Ulster, 1680-1860." In *The Origins of Popular Literacy in Ireland: Language Change and Educational Development,*

1700–1920, edited by Mary Daly and David Dickson, 73–96. Dublin: Trinity College Dublin Department of Modern Irish History, 1990.

Knights, Mark. *Representation and Misrepresentation in Later Stuart Britain: Partisanship and Political Culture.* Oxford: Oxford University Press, 2006.

Kuchta, David. *The Three-Piece Suit and Modern Masculinity: England, 1550–1850.* Berkeley: University of California Press, 2002.

Lammey, David. "The Free Trade Crisis: A Reappraisal." In *Parliament, Politics, and People: Essays in Eighteenth-Century Irish History*, edited by Gerard O'Brien, 69–92. Dublin: Irish Academic Press, 1989.

———. "A Study of Anglo-Irish Relations between 1772 and 1782 with Particular Reference to the 'Free Trade' Movement." PhD diss., Queens University, Belfast, 1984.

Landes, Joan. *Visualizing the Nation: Gender, Representation, and Revolution in Eighteenth-Century France.* Ithaca, NY: Cornell University Press, 2001.

Langford Paul. "Property and 'Virtual Representation' in Eighteenth-Century England." *Historical Journal* 31, no. 1 (March 1988): 83–115.

Lecky, W. E. H. *History of Ireland in the Eighteenth Century.* 5 vols. London: Longmans, Green, 1913.

Leersen, J. T. "Anglo-Irish Patriotism and Its European Context: Notes Towards a Reassessment." *Eighteenth-Century Ireland* 3 (1988): 7–24.

———. *Mere Irish and Fíor-Ghael: Studies in the Idea of Irish Nationality, Its Development and Literary Expression prior to the Nineteenth Century.* Cork: Cork University Press, 1996.

Litto, Frederic M. "Addison's Cato in the Colonies." *William and Mary Quarterly*, 3rd ser., 23, no. 3 (July 1966): 431–49.

Livesey, James. "The Dublin Society in Eighteenth-Century Irish Political Thought." *Historical Journal* 47, no. 3 (Sept. 2004): 615–40.

Loftus, Belinda. *Mirrors: William III & Mother Ireland.* Dundrum: Picture Press, 1990.

Lombard, Anne S. *Making Manhood: Growing Up Male in Colonial New England.* Cambridge, MA: Harvard University Press, 2003.

Long, Gerard, ed. *Books beyond the Pale: Aspects of the Provincial Book Trade in Ireland before 1850.* Dublin: Library Association of Ireland, 1996.

MacLeod, Catriona. "Irish Volunteer Glass." *Irish Sword* 7 (1965–6): 241–60.

Mac Suibhne, Breandán. "Patriot Paddies: The Volunteers and Irish Identity in Northwest Ulster, 1778–1786." PhD diss., Carnegie Mellon University, 1999.

———. "Politicization and Paramilitarism: North-West and South-West Ulster, c. 1772–98." In *1798: A Bicentenary Perspective*, edited by Thomas Bartlett, David Dickson, Daire Keogh, and Kevin Whelan, 243–78. Dublin: Four Courts Press, 2003.

———. "Whiskey, Potatoes and True-Born Patriot Paddies: Volunteering and the Construction of the Irish Nation in Northwest Ulster, 1770–1789." In

Crowds in Ireland, c. 1720–1920, edited by Peter Jupp and Eoin Magennis, 45–82. New York: St. Martin's Press, 2000.

Madden, R. R. *The History of Irish Periodical Literature from the End of the 17th Century to the Middle of the 19th Century.* 2 vols. Dublin, 1867.

Magennis, Eoin F. "A 'Presbyterian Insurrection'? Reconsidering the Hearts of Oak Disturbances of July 1763." *Irish Historical Studies* 31 (1998): 165–87.

Malcomson, A. P. W. *John Foster: The Politics of the Anglo-Irish Ascendancy.* Oxford: Oxford University Press, 1978.

Mansergh, Danny. *Grattan's Failure: Parliamentary Opposition and the People of Ireland, 1779–1800.* Dublin: Irish Academic Press, 2005.

Maxwell, Constantia. *Country and Town in Ireland under the Georges.* Dundalk: Dundalgan Press, 1949.

McBride, Ian. "'The Common Name of Irishman': Protestantism and Patriotism in Eighteenth-Century Ireland." In *Protestantism and National Identity: Britain and Ireland, c. 1650–c. 1850*, edited by Tony Claydon and Ian McBride, 236–64. Cambridge: Cambridge University Press, 1998.

———, ed. *History and Memory in Modern Ireland.* Cambridge: Cambridge University Press, 2001.

———. *Scripture Politics: Ulster Presbyterians and Irish Radicalism in the Late Eighteenth Century.* Oxford: Oxford University Press, 1998.

———. *The Siege of Derry in Ulster Protestant Mythology.* Dublin: Four Courts Press, 1997.

McCormack, Matthew. *The Independent Man: Citizenship and Gender Politics in Georgian England.* Manchester: Manchester University Press, 2005.

McCormack, W. J. *The Dublin Paper War, 1786–88: A Bibliographical and Critical Enquiry.* Dublin: Irish Academic Press, 1993.

McDonnell, Michael A. *The Politics of War: Race, Class, and Conflict in Revolutionary Virginia.* Chapel Hill: University of North Carolina Press for the Omohundro Institute of Early American History and Culture, Williamsburg, VA, 2007.

———. "Popular Mobilization and Political Culture in Revolutionary Virginia: The Failure of the Minutemen and the Revolution from Below." *Journal of American History* 85, no. 3 (Dec. 1998): 946–81.

McDowell, R. B. *Ireland in the Age of Imperialism and Revolution, 1760–1801.* Oxford: Oxford University Press, 1979.

McKendrick, Neil, John Brewer, and J. H. Plumb. *The Birth of Consumer Society: The Commercialization of Eighteenth-Century England.* Bloomington: Indiana University Press, 1982.

McSkimin, Samuel. *Annals of Ulster from 1790 to 1798.* Belfast: J. Cleeland, 1906.

Midgley, Clare. "Slave Sugar Boycotts, Female Activism and the Domestic Base of British Anti-slavery Culture." *Slavery and Abolition* 17, no. 3 (Dec. 1996): 137–62.

Miller, David W. "The Armagh Troubles, 1784–95." In *Irish Peasants: Violence and Political Unrest, 1780–1914*, edited by Samuel Clark and James S. Donnelly, Jr., 155–91. Madison: University of Wisconsin Press, 1983.

———. "Non-professional Soldiery, c. 1600–1800." In *A Military History of Ireland*, edited by Thomas Bartlett and Keith Jeffery, 315–34. Cambridge: Cambridge University Press, 1996.

———. "Politicization in Revolutionary Ireland: The Case of the Armagh Troubles." *Irish Economic and Social History* 23 (1996): 1–17.

———. "Radicalism and Ritual in East Ulster." In *1798: A Bicentenary Perspective*, edited by Thomas Bartlett, David Dickson, Daire Keogh, and Kevin Whelan, 195–211. Dublin: Four Courts Press, 2003.

Mirala, Petri. "Freemasonry in Ulster, 1733–1813." PhD diss., University of Dublin, Trinity College, 1999.

———. *Freemasonry in Ulster, 1733–1813: A Social and Political History of the Masonic Brotherhood in the North of Ireland.* Dublin: Four Courts Press, 2007.

Moody, T. W., and W. E. Vaughan, eds. *A New History of Ireland.* Vol. 4, *Eighteenth-Century Ireland, 1691–1800.* Oxford: Oxford University Press, 1986.

Moore, Sally F., and Barbara G. Myerhoff, eds. *Secular Rituals.* Amsterdam: Van Gorcum, 1977.

Morley, Vincent. *Irish Opinion and the American Revolution, 1760–1783.* Cambridge: Cambridge University Press, 2002.

Mounsey, Chris. "Searching in the Dark: Towards a Historiography of Queer Early Modern and Enlightenment (Anglo) Ireland." In *Queer Masculinities, 1550–1800: Situating Same-Sex Desire in the Early Modern World,* edited by Katherine O'Donnell and Michael O'Rourke, 1–16. New York: Palgrave, 2006.

Munter, Robert. *The History of the Irish Newspaper, 1685–1760.* Cambridge: Cambridge University Press, 1967.

Myerly, Scott Hughes. *British Military Spectacle: From the Napoleonic Wars through the Crimea.* Cambridge, MA: Harvard University Press, 1996.

Nenadic, Stena. "Middle-Rank Consumers and Domestic Culture in Edinburgh and Glasgow, 1720–1840." *Past and Present* 145 (1994): 122–56.

———. "Print Collecting and Popular Culture in Eighteenth-Century Scotland." *History* 82, no. 266 (April 1997): 203–22.

Nicholson, Eirwen. "Consumers and Spectators: The Public of the Political Print in Eighteenth-Century England." *History* 81, no. 261 (Jan. 1996): 5–21.

O'Brien, Gerard. "The Unimportance of Public Opinion in Eighteenth-Century Britain and Ireland." *Eighteenth-Century Ireland* 8 (1993): 115–27.

Ó Ciardha, Éamonn. *Ireland and the Jacobite Cause, 1685–1766: A Fatal Attachment.* Dublin: Four Courts Press, 2002.

Ó Ciosáin, Niall. *Print and Popular Culture in Ireland, 1750–1800.* London: Macmillan, 1997.

O'Connell, Maurice R. *Irish Politics and Social Conflict in the Age of the American Revolution.* Philadelphia: University of Pennsylvania Press, 1965.

Ó Dalaigh, Brian. *Ennis in the Eighteenth Century: Portrait of an Urban Community.* Dublin: Irish Academic Press, 1995.

O'Donovan, James. "The Anatomy of the Volunteers in Cork, 1775–1782: Parts 1–2." *Cork Historical and Archaeological Society* 87 (1982): 27–42, 118–27.

O'Dowd, Mary. *A History of Women in Ireland, 1500–1800*. London: Pearson Education, 2005.

———. "The Women in the Gallery: Women and Politics in Eighteenth-Century Ireland." In *From the United Irishmen to Twentieth-Century Unionism: Essays in Honour of A. T. Q. Stewart*, edited by Sabine Wichert, 35–47. Dublin: Four Courts Press, 2004.

Ó Snodaigh, Pádraig. "Class and the Irish Volunteers." *Irish Sword* 16, no. 64 (Summer 1986): 165–84.

———. "Notes on the Volunteers, Militia, Orangemen and Yeomanry of County Roscommon." *Irish Sword*, no. 12 (1975–76): 15–35.

———. "Notes on the Volunteers, Militia, Yeomanry, and Orangemen of County Cavan." *Breifne* 3, no. 11 (1968): 320–39.

———. "Notes on the Volunteers, Militia, Yeomanry and Orangemen of County Louth." *Journal of the Louth Archeological and Historical Society* 18, no. 4 (1976): 279–93.

———. "Notes on the Volunteers, Militia, Yeomanry and Orangemen of Co. Meath." *Riocht na Midhe* 6 (1978–79): 3–32.

———. "Notes on the Volunteers, Militia, Yeomanry and Orangemen of County Monaghan." *Clogher Record* 9, no. 2 (1977): 142–66.

———. "Notes on the Volunteers, Militia, Yeomanry and Orangemen of County Waterford." *An Cosantóir* 35 (1975): 319–22, 341–47.

———. "Notes on the Volunteers, Militia, Yeomanry, Orangemen and Fencibles in County Limerick." *Irish Sword*, no. 10 (1971): 125–40.

———. "Some Police and Military Aspects of the Irish Volunteers." *Irish Sword* 13, no. 52 (1978–79): 217–29.

———. "The Volunteers, Militia, Yeomanry and Orangemen of Co. Kildare in the Eighteenth Century." *Journal of the County Kildare Archaeological Society* 15, no. 1 (1971): 38–49.

———. "The Volunteers of '82: A Citizen Army or Armed Citizens—A Bicentennial Retrospect." *Irish Sword* 15, no. 60 (Summer 1983): 177–88.

Ó Tuathaigh, Gearoid. "The Role of Women in Ireland under the New English Order." In *Women in Irish Society*, edited by Margaret MacCurtain and Donncha Ó Corrain, 26–36. Westport, CT: Greenwood Press, 1979.

Owens, Gary. "Nationalism without Words: Symbolism and Ritual Behavior in the Repeal 'Monster Meetings' of 1843–5." In *Irish Popular Culture, 1650–1850*, edited by James S. Donnelly, Jr., and Kerby A. Miller, 242–69. Dublin: Irish Academic Press, 1998.

———. "Visualizing the Liberator: Self-Fashioning, Dramaturgy, and the Construction of Daniel O'Connell." *Éire-Ireland* 33, no. 3/4–34, no. 1 (1998): 103–29.

Ozouf, Mona. *Festivals and the French Revolution*. Cambridge, MA: Harvard University Press, 1976.

Parssinen, T. H. "Association, Convention and Anti-parliament in British

Radical Politics, 1771-1848." *English Historical Review* 88, no. 348 (July 1973): 504-33.

Paterson, T. G. F. "The County of Armagh Volunteers of 1778-1793." *Ulster Journal of Archaeology*, 3rd ser., 4 (1941): 101-27; 5 (1942): 31-61; 7 (1944): 76-95.

———. "The Volunteer Companies of Ulster." *Irish Sword* 7 (1965-66): 90-116, 204-30, 308-12; 8 (1967-68): 23-32, 92-97, 210-17.

Phillips, James W. *Printing and Bookselling in Dublin, 1670-1800: A Bibliographical Enquiry*. Dublin: Irish Academic Press, 1998.

Pickering, Paul A. "'Irish First': Daniel O'Connell, the Native Manufacture Campaign, and Economic Nationalism, 1840-44." *Albion* 32, no. 4 (2000): 598-616.

Pocock, J. G. A. *The Machiavellian Moment: Florentine Political Thought and the Atlantic Republican Tradition*. Princeton, NJ: Princeton University Press, 1975.

Pollard, Mary. *A Dictionary of Members of the Dublin Book Trade, 1550-1800*. London: Bibliographical Society, 2000.

Porter, Roy. "Seeing the Past." *Past and Present* 118 (Feb. 1988): 186-205.

Powell, Martyn J. *Britain and Ireland in the Eighteenth-Century Crisis of Empire*. Basingstoke: Palgrave, 2003.

———. *The Politics of Consumption in Eighteenth-Century Ireland*. New York: Palgrave Macmillan, 2005.

———. "Popular Disturbances in Late Eighteenth-Century Ireland: The Origins of the Peep of Day Boys." *Irish Historical Studies* 34, no. 135 (2005): 249-65.

Power, Thomas P. *Land, Politics, and Society in Eighteenth-Century Tipperary*. Oxford: Oxford University Press, 1993.

Power, T. P., and Kevin Whelan, eds. *Endurance and Emergence: Catholics in Ireland in the Eighteenth Century*. Dublin: Irish Academic Press, 1990.

Raymond, Joad. *The Invention of the Newspaper: English Newsbooks, 1641-1649*. Oxford: Clarendon Press 1996.

Reynolds, Mairead. "Wedgwood in Dublin, 1772-1777." *Irish Arts Review* 1, no. 2 (1984): 36-38.

Ribeiro, Aileen. *The Art of Dress: Fashion in England and France, 1750-1820*. New Haven, CT: Yale University Press, 1995.

Richards, Sarah. *Eighteenth-Century Ceramics: Products of a Civilized Society*. Manchester: Manchester University Press, 1999.

Robb, C. J. "The Ulster Volunteers of '82 : Their Medals, Badges, etc." *Ulster Journal of Archaeology* 1 (1938): 118.

Robinson, Nicholas. "Caricature and the Regency Crisis: An Irish Perspective." *Eighteenth-Century Ireland* 1 (1986): 157-76.

Rodgers, Nini. "Equiano in Belfast: A Study of the Anti-slavery Ethos in a Northern Town." *Slavery and Abolition* 18, no. 2 (Aug. 1997): 73-89.

———. "Ireland and the Black Atlantic in the Eighteenth Century." *Irish Historical Studies* 33, no. 126 (Nov. 2000): 174-92.

———. *Ireland, Slavery and Anti-slavery: 1612-1865*. New York: Palgrave Macmillan, 2007.

——. "Two Quakers and a Utilitarian: The Reaction of Three Irish Women Writers to the Problem of Slavery, 1789-1807." *Proceedings of the Royal Irish Academy* 100, no. 4, C (2000): 137-57.

Rogers, Alisdair, and Steven Vertovec, eds. *The Urban Context: Ethnicity, Social Networks, and Situational Analysis.* Oxford: Oxford University Press, 1995.

Rogers, Nicholas. *Crowds, Culture, and Politics in Georgian England.* Oxford: Oxford University Press, 1998.

Rogers, Patrick. *The Irish Volunteers and Catholic Emancipation (1778-1793): A Neglected Phase of Ireland's History.* London: Burns, Oates & Washbourne, 1934.

Russell, Gillian. *The Theatres of War: Performance, Politics, and Society, 1793-1815.* Oxford: Clarendon Press, 1995.

Scott, Joan. "Experience." In *Feminists Theorize the Political,* edited by Judith Butler and Joan W. Scott, 22-40. London: Routledge, 1992.

Shepard, Alexandra. *Meanings of Manhood in Early Modern England.* Oxford: Oxford University Press, 2003.

Shoemaker, R. "Male Honour and the Decline of Public Violence in Eighteenth-Century London." *Social History* 26, no. 2 (May 2001): 190-208.

Simes, Douglas. "Ireland, 1760-1820." In *Press, Politics and the Public Sphere in Europe and North America, 1760-1820,* edited by Hannah Barker, 113-39. Cambridge: Cambridge University Press, 2002.

Small, Stephen. *Political Thought in Ireland, 1776-1798.* Oxford: Oxford University Press, 2002.

——. "The Twisted Roots of Irish Patriotism: Anglo-Irish Political Thought in the Late-Eighteenth Century." *Éire-Ireland* 35, no. 3-4 (2000-2001): 187-216.

Smyth, Jim. "Anti-Catholicism, Conservatism, and Conspiracy: Sir Richard Musgrave's *Memoirs of the Different Rebellions in Ireland.*" *Eighteenth-Century Life* 22, no. 3 (Nov. 1998): 62-73.

——. *The Men of No Property: Irish Radicals and Popular Politics in the Late Eighteenth Century.* New York: St. Martin's Press, 1992.

——. "Popular Politicization, Defenderism and the Catholic Question." In *Ireland and the French Revolution,* edited by Hugh Gough and David Dickson, 109-16. Dublin: Irish Academic Press, 1990.

——. "Republicanism before the United Irishmen: The Case of Dr. Charles Lucas." In *Political Discourse in Seventeenth- and Eighteenth-Century Ireland,* edited by D. George Boyce et al., 240-56. Basingstoke: Palgrave, 2001.

——, ed. *Revolution, Counter-Revolution and Union.* Cambridge: Cambridge University Press, 2003.

——. "Siege, Myth and History: Derry, 1688-1998." In *The Sieges of Derry,* edited by William Kelly, 18-30. Dublin: Four Courts Press, 2001.

Smyth, Peter. "'Our Cloud-Cap't Grenadiers': The Volunteers as a Military Force." *Irish Sword* 13 (1979): 185-207.

———. "The Volunteer Movement in Ulster: Background and Development, 1745–85." PhD diss., Queens University, Belfast, 1974.

———. "The Volunteers and Parliament, 1779–1784." In *Penal Era and Golden Age: Essays in Irish History, 1690–1800*, edited by T. Bartlett and D. W. Hayton, 113–36. Belfast: Ulster Historical Foundation, 1979.

Stewart, A. T. Q. *A Deeper Silence: The Hidden Origins of the United Irishmen*. Belfast: Blackstaff Press, 1998.

St. George, Robert Blair. *Conversing by Signs: Poetics of Implication in Colonial New England Culture*. Chapel Hill: University of North Carolina Press, 1998.

Sussman, Charlotte. *Consuming Anxieties: Consumer Protest, Gender, and British Slavery, 1713–1833*. Stanford, CA: Stanford University Press, 2000.

Te Brake, Wayne P. "Violence in the Dutch Patriot Revolution." *Comparative Studies in Society and History* 30, no. 1 (1988): 143–63.

Thompson, E. P. *The Making of the English Working Class*. New York: Vintage, 1964.

Thompson, F. Glenn. "The Flags and Uniforms of the Irish Volunteers and Yeomanry." *Bulletin of the Irish Georgian Society* 33 (1990): 3–30.

Thuente, Mary Helen. *The Harp Re-strung: The United Irishmen and the Rise of Irish Literary Nationalism*. Syracuse, NY: Syracuse University Press, 1994.

———. "The Origin and Significance of the Angel Harp." In *Back to the Present, Forward to the Past: Irish Writing and History since 1798*, edited by Patricia A. Lynch, Joachim Fischer, and Brian Coates, 230–57. Amsterdam: Rodopi, 2006.

Vernon, James. *Politics and the People: A Study in English Political Culture, c. 1815–1867*. Cambridge: Cambridge University Press, 1993.

Vickery, Amanda. "Golden Age to Separate Spheres? A Review of the Categories and Chronology of English Women's History." *Historical Journal* 36, no. 2 (June 1993): 383–414.

Viroli, Maurizio. *For Love of Country: An Essay on Patriotism and Nationalism*. Oxford: Oxford University Press, 1997.

Wahrman, Dror. "Percy's Prologue: From Gender Play to Gender Panic in Eighteenth-Century England." *Past and Present* 159 (May 1998): 113–60.

Waldstreicher David. *In the Midst of Perpetual Fetes: The Making of American Nationalism, 1776–1820*. Chapel Hill: University of North Carolina Press, 1997.

———. "Rites of Rebellion, Rites of Assent: Celebrations, Print Culture, and the Origins of American Nationalism." *Journal of American History* 82, no. 1 (June 1995): 37–61.

Wall, Maureen. *Catholic Ireland in the Eighteenth Century: Collected Essays of Maureen Wall*. Dublin: Geography Publications, 1989.

Walter, John. *Understanding Popular Violence in the English Revolution: The Colchester Plunderers*. Cambridge: Cambridge University Press, 1999.

Warner, Marina. *Monuments and Maidens: The Allegory of the Female Form*. New York: Atheneum, 1985.

Webster, Mary. *Francis Wheatley*. London: Routledge, 1970.

Whelan, Kevin. "Politicization in County Wexford and the Origins of the 1798 Rebellion." In *Ireland and the French Revolution*, edited by Hugh Gough and David Dickson, 156–78. Dublin: Irish Academic Press, 1990.

———. *The Tree of Liberty: Radicalism, Catholicism, and the Construction of Irish Identity, 1760–1830*. Notre Dame, IN: University of Notre Dame Press, 1996.

Whelan, Yvonne. *Reinventing Modern Dublin: Streetscape, Iconography, and the Politics of Identity*. Dublin: University College Dublin Press, 2003.

Wilentz, Sean, ed. *Rites of Power: Symbolism, Ritual, and Power since the Middle Ages*. Philadelphia: University of Pennsylvania Press, 1985.

Wilson, Kathleen. "Citizenship, Empire, and Modernity in the English Provinces, c. 1720–1790." *Eighteenth-Century Studies* 29, no. 1 (Fall 1996): 69–96.

———. *The Island Race: Englishness, Empire, and Gender in the Eighteenth Century*. New York: Routledge 2002.

———. *Sense of the People: Politics, Culture and Imperialism in England, 1715–1785*. Cambridge: Cambridge University Press, 1995.

———. "Urban Culture and Political Activism in Hanoverian England: The Example of Voluntary Hospitals." In *The Transformation of Political Culture: England and Germany in the Late Eighteenth Century*, edited by Eckhart Hellmuth, 165–84. Oxford: Oxford University Press, 1990.

Wood, Stephen. "Gorgets of the 'Gorgeous Infantry.'" *Irish Arts Review* 3, no. 4 (1986): 49–52.

Woolf, Daniel. "News, History and the Construction of the Present in Early Modern England." In *The Politics of Information in Early Modern Europe*, edited by Brendan Dooley and Sabrina A. Baron, 80–118. London: Routledge, 2001.

Zaret, David. "Petitions and the 'Invention' of Public Opinion and the English Revolution." *American Journal of Sociology* 101, no. 6 (May 1996): 1497–1555.

Index

HISTORY *of* IRELAND
and the IRISH DIASPORA

CPSIA information can be obtained
at www.ICGtesting.com
Printed in the USA
BVHW041626080222
628185BV00014B/250